Enough

What Coercive Control Steals
What Recovery Makes Possible

GEOFFREY CLOW WITH GEORGIE BAILEY

Foreword by Becki Koon

First published in 2025 by Twinkling of the Soul,
a registered business name of Heart Centred Support Pty Ltd
22a Larakia Street, Waramanga, ACT 2611, Australia
twinklingofthesoul.com

ISBN: 978-1-7642451-4-2

Visit **twinklingofthesoul.com** for coercive control recovery tools grounded
in lived experience. You'll find author insights, upcoming guided courses, and
can join our e-newsletter to be first to hear about new releases, survivor-led resources, and the
launch of the Enough companion app.

Contents

1   Dismantled

Slowly, piece by piece, until you barely recognise yourself

2 Hollowed

You didn't feel like you anymore

3 Stolen

Not lost. Taken

4 Disappeared

The dull ache of parts of you vanishing

5 Inheritance

What was passed down, and carried forward

6 Reveal

When the damage finally makes sense, and so does your pain

7 Knowing

The story doesn't hold like it used to. And neither do you

8   Aftermath

This is what the damage looks like. And it makes perfect sense

9   Release

You stop holding what was never yours to carry

10 Indisputable

This is the part where you stop doubting yourself

11 Return

You return, not to them, but to you

12   Recovery

This is recovery. Raw, slow, and yours

13   Reveal

This isn't a comeback. It's a becoming

14 Never Too Late

By Georgie Bailey

Introduction

This book is for you if you lived under someone else's rules—invisible ones that changed by the hour, until fear became routine and peace felt suspicious.

If you tracked their moods like weather patterns, knew the sound of their car pulling up meant scanning the house for anything that might set them off, and learned to gauge their emotional temperature before they'd even spoken. The way their jaw clenched meant silence for days. The way they set down their keys meant you'd done something wrong.

It's for you if you stopped asking for what you needed because asking became dangerous. If you learned to shrink before anyone asked you to—making yourself smaller at parties, quieter at dinner, invisible in your own home.

You became an expert at reading micro-expressions: the narrowing of eyes that meant an explosion was coming, the silence that preceded punishment, the shift in breathing that warned you to brace. You could feel the air pressure change before the storm, like animals sense earthquakes.

You apologised for existing too loudly. For laughing at the wrong time. For feeling what they didn't approve of. You learned to ration your own light, dim yourself down to match their darkness.

You perfected the art of being invisible in plain sight. Present but not present. Speaking without being heard. Existing without taking up space. A ghost in your own life, haunting the edges of rooms you paid rent for.

You swallowed your words until your throat ached. Your wants until you forgot what wanting felt like. Your rage until it turned inward and became something else— depression, anxiety, mysterious illnesses no doctor could explain.

You smiled when you meant to scream. Said "it's fine" when nothing was. Became a translator of silences, a master at playing a game no one should ever have to play.

All just to stay safe. All just to survive another day in a house that felt like a courtroom where you were always on trial.

It's for you if you were told you were crazy so many times you started keeping screenshots, recordings, evidence—not for court, but for yourself. To prove you weren't imagining it. That your memory wasn't lying.

You were dismantled slowly. Not with fists, but with words that cut deeper than bruises. With kindness that came with conditions. With charm that fooled everyone else while you lived with the monster behind it.

This book doesn't just name the abuse. It names the training that taught you to doubt yourself, the conditioning that made you accept the unacceptable, the slow erosion that made you forget who you were before them.

It names the silence that surrounded you: how friends disappeared, how family told you to try harder, how therapists suggested you communicate better, how everyone had opinions except the one that mattered—that you were being systematically destroyed.

It names the roles you never auditioned for but played perfectly: peacekeeper, mind reader, emotional regulator, shock absorber. The one who held it all together while falling apart in private.

It names how systems failed you. How police said it was a civil matter. How courts said there was no evidence. How child services said the kids seemed fine. How everyone needed proof of what doesn't leave marks.

How people told you it wasn't that bad because they never hit you. Because you had a nice house. Because they seemed so charming. Because you were still functioning—smiling in photos, raising kids, going to work—while quietly dying inside.

It's for you if you were misdiagnosed with anxiety when it was actually hypervigilance.

Depression when it was learned helplessness. Borderline when it was trauma. Paranoid when you were right all along.

It's for you if you were disbelieved by the very people meant to help. Or worse—if you were never asked. Never given the words. Never shown that what you lived through had a name.

Enough pretending it was complicated when it was abuse. Enough minimising because others had it worse. Enough carrying the truth alone, as if it was yours to protect.

There's a reason this book is called Enough.

Because that's what every survivor of coercive control eventually has to say. To them. To the world. To themselves.

Enough.

What You'll Find Here

Written in Survivor Language

This book isn't written at you. It's written *for* you. Not in therapist-speak that makes you feel studied. Not in theory that keeps you at arm's length. But in the same words you've typed into Google at 3 a.m. with shaking hands: am I crazy? is it abuse if they never hit me? why do I feel scared when nothing's wrong? can emotional abuse cause memory problems? why do I apologise for everything?

We're not researchers watching through one-way glass. We're survivors who know what it's like when your partner's car pulls into the driveway and your whole body goes rigid. When you rehearse a simple request seventeen times and it still comes out wrong. When you explain why you need permission to buy coffee and watch your friends' faces go carefully blank.

That's what makes this book different: it's written in the language of hypervigilance, of walking on eggshells, of being fluent in someone else's moods while forgetting your own needs existed.

What Happened to You Has a Name

Maybe you can't name it yet. You just know you became "the problem." Conversations you didn't even start somehow became your fault. You were losing your mind in a relationship everyone else envied. You sat in couples therapy and left with homework to "communicate better" while they sat there looking reasonable. You tried explaining to your brother and heard yourself sounding paranoid. You Googled symptoms and found everything from anxiety to ADHD, but nothing captured the specific hell of being systematically erased.

This book does what no one else did: it names coercive control exactly as you lived it. Not sanitised for comfort. Not balanced for fairness. Just the truth, raw as a wound, the way survivors tell it when we finally stop pretending we're fine.

Tactics Exposed. Tools That Actually Work

Each chapter takes one tactic apart—not in theory, but in the exact ways it played out. How they made you the villain of every story while they posed as the long-suffering partner. How they turned your normal reactions into "evidence" you were unstable. How they convinced everyone you were difficult while dismantling you behind closed doors.

And then—this is crucial—each chapter offers something you can actually do. Not breathing exercises when you can barely breathe. Not homework you'll never finish. But small, specific acts that land in real life. What to write on your bathroom mirror when shame hits. How to steady yourself when your body reacts like it's under attack in the middle of a normal day. What to say to yourself when you hear "sorry" tumble out of your mouth for simply existing.

These aren't abstractions. They're survival tools—things you can use when you're still shaking, still doubting, still hearing their voice in your head.

What Recovery Actually Looks Like

Recovery isn't Instagram quotes over sunrise photos. It's excavation work—digging yourself out from under what they buried you beneath.

It looks like sitting in a supermarket car park, sobbing because you just bought shampoo without asking permission. It looks like rage so pure it scares you, followed by grief so heavy you can't get out of bed. It looks like recognising yourself in these pages and having to close the book because your hands are shaking.

That's not setback. That's your nervous system recognising truth after being fed lies. That's your body remembering what happened, even when they convinced you it didn't.

Reading someone else's survival story in words that could be your own diary entries changes everything. It's evidence you're not crazy—you were being driven toward breakdown. Proof it really happened—even without witnesses or bruises. Proof someone else survived—scarred and changed, but free.

A Survivor's Voice — Georgie Bailey

This book grew from conversations with Georgie Bailey, a survivor who lived through forty years of abuse and wanted others to know what she wished she'd known sooner. Her insights thread through every chapter—not as inspiration, not as theory, but as the raw truth of someone who endured and still found her way back.

In Part 14, Never Too Late, you'll hear Georgie in her own words. How she was systematically erased and still came back. How she found real love after believing she was unlovable. How she rebuilt after losing almost everything.

She wanted you to know: you are not unworthy. You are not too late. Even when your body carries the cost, even when recovery is messy and imperfect, freedom is possible. What you've been told about yourself isn't truth—it's training.

Her life is proof of that—proof that even after years of devastation, she reclaimed love, joy, and self-trust. Her illness didn't erase that. It made it all the more remarkable.

Content Note

Before you begin, know what you may encounter here.

This book addresses coercive control — not conflict, not "relationship problems," but a deliberate system of domination designed to erode freedom, identity, and safety. It works through surveillance, restriction, gaslighting, humiliation, and the steady dismantling of autonomy.

You'll also encounter its many faces: financial abuse, sexual coercion, spiritual manipulation, domestic violence, medical gaslighting, and the grief that follows. And alongside them, the fight to reclaim your life.

Some chapters may feel confronting. If something feels too close, pause, skip, or return later.

How This Book Can Help You

This book is big because coercive control is layered. To see it clearly, you sometimes need to circle back or revisit an old wound from a new angle. That's not repetition — it's clarity.

And you don't have to read in order. Start where you need. Skip what feels too close. This isn't a sequence to finish — it's a companion to lean on.

Throughout, you'll find Practical Steps: small, concrete actions to help you put down what was never yours, rebuild trust in yourself, and reclaim pieces of your life. Use them when you're ready.

Not All Hurt Comes From The Same Place

Some people hurt you because they're unequipped. They avoid difficult conversations. They shut down when you cry. They don't know how to sit with pain—yours or their own. They get defensive. They make everything about them. They leave you lonely in a room full of their fears.

It still hurts. But it's not the same as what came next.

Some people don't just hurt you. They hunt you.

They study you first. Watch what makes you smile, what makes you trust, what makes you doubt yourself. They mirror your kindness back to you until you see yourself in them. They learn your wounds and weaknesses like a burglar cases a house.

Then they use what they've learned. Your childhood trauma becomes their weapon. Your fears become their leverage. Your love becomes their trap. They know exactly which buttons to push, which words will destroy you, which silences will make you beg.

They don't stumble into hurting you. They orchestrate it.

They wear their mask so perfectly that the world applauds their performance. Your friends think they're charming. Your family thinks you're lucky. Therapists suggest you communicate better. Meanwhile, you're dying behind closed doors, and no one sees it because they've made sure no one's looking.

That fog you lived in? Where you couldn't think straight, couldn't trust your memory, couldn't explain why you were terrified of someone everyone else loved? That wasn't "complicated." That wasn't "toxic." That wasn't "just a bad relationship."

That was psychological violence. Deliberate. Methodical. Designed to break you without leaving marks anyone else could see.

This book exists to name it clearly. Because you don't recover from systematic psychological torture with breathing exercises and positive thinking. You don't heal from coercive control/narcissistic abuse by "focusing on the good times." You don't rebuild from intentional destruction with a podcast and some yoga.

You recover by calling it what it was: abuse. Calculated, deliberate abuse.

You recover by understanding the difference between human limitation and predatory behaviour.

You recover by never again mistaking malice for mistake, strategy for stumbling, abuse for ordinary human messiness.

Some people hurt you because they're human.
Some people hurt you because they're dangerous.

Learning the difference can save your life.

For Beautiful, Courageous Georgie

Without her,
I wouldn't have known what love really was,
the kind that cracks you open
and calls you home at the same time.

Through what we built together,
the magic, the mischief, the quiet evenings,
I saw what long-term coercive control had done to a person.

Not just to their voice.
But to the bright thing inside that makes someone themselves.
The thing that makes them laugh too loud,
dance in kitchens,
believe in tomorrow.

I watched that bright thing trying to come back.
Watched her remember who she was
before someone tried to erase her.

With paint on her hands.
With songs sung in the shower.
With a defiance that looked like joy
but was really survival.

Even when her body started failing,
the delayed tax of years of living in fear,
she kept reaching for beautiful things.

Kept teaching me that recovery
isn't about getting better. It's about getting free.
Loving her changed me.

xx

Showed me the terrible, beautiful weight
of witnessing someone's becoming.

Of holding someone while they remember they were worthy
long before anyone tried to tell them otherwise.

This book exists because she existed.
And because existence alone was never all she gave.

She gave courage, truth, love—
and she found a way to name what was done to her,
even when it felt impossible, even when it hurt.

Because she chose joy as rebellion.
Because she proved that love after abuse
isn't just possible, it's revolutionary.

She was the love I never saw coming.
The one who found me anyway.
And she's the reason this book doesn't look away.

The reason it tells the truth about what coercive control does,
not just to the person living through it,
but to everyone who loves them,
everyone who watches them disappear,
everyone who celebrates when they come back.

Georgie, this is for you my love.
This is for every survivor still finding their way back.
This is for everyone who loves them while they do.

"It took me many years
to unlearn the patterns that had
been instilled in me from childhood.

But writing has been
a powerful tool in my healing journey.

Through writing,
I've been able to process my
traumas, to think out loud, and to
gain a deeper understandingof myself.

I've learned to listen to my instincts,
to trust myself, and to take charge
of my own life."

~ Georgie Bailey

Foreword
by Becki Koon

There are moments when the culmination of all life experiences collapses into a singularity of purpose, an intervention designed by a creative life force that reaches beyond mere personal gain into a collective field for the benefit of humanity as a whole, a oneness by divine design.

This book and everything birthed from its pages is one of purpose guided by love, the love story of two souls who shape the world the rest of us get to experience.

It is driven by a desire to expand that compassionate love,
to expose us to the nature of coming together in vulnerability,
raw and exposed in our human wounding and healing,
showing all who read… we are ENOUGH!

I met Geoff shortly after Georgie left the earth's dimensional field.
Buried in grief, Geoff reached out to me from the other side of the planet. He found me through a series of serendipitous events
that led him to my best-selling book, 20 Days Changed Everything.

You see, we shared an undeniable reality: loss of a love so great that the next step to breathe was almost unbearable. And yet, we found our way to life through a deep-seated knowing our journeys had something more the world needed to glean from us, spurred on by our beloveds, Georgie and Jack, from the other side.

The love we experienced never leaves us but only expands and evolves into a new expression of divine awareness and wisdom.
The four of us became a team in the discovery of the human heart,
and the capacity we had for feeling the depths of all forms of emotions.

The healing we created was exactly what earthbound Geoff and Becki needed.

When I wrote my second bestselling book, Breathe The Deep Waters Of Love, about my journey through a life-threatening diagnosis twenty months after my beloved Jack passed, I asked Geoff if he would write the foreward.

By this time, we had developed a beautiful working relationship
that not only supported us as friends but amplified the internal calling to offer the world our lives, the lives of our beloveds.

We began dreaming about possibilities.
The ability to be emotionally raw,
to open up to vulnerability and share publicly,
is an act that opens hearts.

When we allow for authenticity, we realize as humans we are far more connected and alike than we have known or understood.

The healing journey thus becomes not only Becki and Geoff's road to wholeness, but the lives we have lived have the potential to impact others at the heart level, supporting all who engage with us to feel safe in the discovery of what self-discovery and self-love mean.

Enough is unlike any other book out there—
a book that navigates the depths of trauma
from a survivor who also happens to be a trauma-informed counselor, offering attainable support, concrete ideas, and love.

You don't have to hide from how you feel.

Geoff gently takes your hand while walking with you
because he can,
because he knows,
because he is pure of heart.

His dedication to your healing is evident.
His purpose in sharing his beloved Georgie's life story,
her writing, and her self-discovery comes from a sacred love,
a calling forth of honoring so great that it crosses dimensions and radiates divine intent.

I found myself while reading, contemplating my own experiences of trauma and
coercive control.

Early on in my life,
I found myself on a healing journey from sexual abuse.
I am not new to walking with and through the wreckage of early childhood trauma.

And yet, it is as if Geoff opened a window into my soul,
and a gentle breeze of awareness blew into my heart,
allowing an even deeper layer to be illuminated and transformed.

Thank you, Geoff.
Thank you, Georgie.
Thank you, my beloved Jack.

For it is in the expansion of love that we can share hope,
to help you trust you can find your voice [as Geoff and I found ours], to see the truth
behind the control, and to honor the fact that YOU ARE ENOUGH!

No matter how you arrived at reading these pages.

Preface

"I was looked at, but I wasn't seen."
~ Albert Camus

Her name was Georgie Bailey (née Booker). For decades, she was invisible. She survived forty years of abuse—childhood neglect, a violent first marriage, and then twenty-two years of coercive control that almost finished what the others started.

Georgie called those years her frog pot period. You know the story: drop a frog in boiling water, it jumps out. Drop it in lukewarm water and heat it slowly, it dies without noticing. That's coercive control. It doesn't kick down the door screaming. It brings you flowers. It says, "I'm just trying to take care of you." And before you know it, the flowers are wilted, the door is locked from the outside, and you can't remember the last time you made a choice that wasn't pre-approved.

That's the brilliance—and the horror—of coercive control. It isn't a rough patch or two strong personalities clashing. It's a system—a deliberate pattern with one aim: to dismantle the other person. It is psychological torture carried out by someone claiming to love you. That's the magic trick. Everyone else sees devotion. Inside, it's demolition.

By the time I met Georgie, she was forty-five and technically "free." She was still startled at sounds, still asking permission to order food, still learning she was allowed to pick the colour of the bloody towels.

She wrote, too. Poetry. Fragments. Then the whole story: Never Too Late. Complete. Neglect. Violence. Erasure. Escape. Recovery. Joy. She never told me she'd finished it. Maybe after decades of being told her words meant nothing, she couldn't believe they mattered. But there it was.

Proof that someone can disappear and still return. Proof that forty years of abuse doesn't have to be the ending.

This book begins with Georgie. And it ends with her, too. The first thirteen parts are what we unpacked together: how coercive control works, what it steals, and how you claw your way back. The final part is Georgie's gift—her story, in her own words.

Who's it for? First, survivors. Because they deserve more than hashtags and hollow sympathy. Their reality deserves to be named. It's also for the people who orbit them: parents asking why she stayed, new partners baffled by the aftermath.

And yes, it's for the suits in courtrooms and uniforms on the beat. Judges, lawyers, police. The ones who still confuse psychological torture with "a difficult marriage." If you want to know what this crime actually looks like—the patterns, the damage, the way it erases a person—this book will save you the trouble of pretending you don't.

And Georgie didn't just survive. She learned to live again. To travel, to paint, to cook, to love without apology. Even when illness came for her, even when she had to fight one more battle she didn't choose, she carried the same courage, humour, and refusal to be erased into that fight too. She wanted you to know: even after everything, joy is still possible.

This book tells the truth, plain. Coercive control is psychological torture. It starts off as care, but its aim is your destruction. Recovery is brutal. And possible.

Even when you think you're gone.
Even after decades.
Even when you can't remember who you were before.

Especially then. Because at some point, you stop excusing. You stop minimising. You stop accepting the wilted apology flowers and believing the lies. You finally say the word that should have ended it the first time someone tried to erase you.

Enough.

*"One way we raise awareness
is by having the courage
to share our stories,
so others begin to understand
the challenges we face,
and why change is needed."*

~ Georgie Bailey

Part 1
Dismantled

Slowly, piece by piece,
until you barely recognise yourself

1.1
You Shouldn't Have Had to Survive This

Author's Note:

If you're here, you've probably lived through something you didn't think you'd survive. Not all at once. But piece by piece. Over years. Maybe decades. Not everyone gets it. Not everyone understands what it does to you to be slowly erased, until even your breath feels too loud.

But I do. So let me say this: I'm sorry. I'm sorry you had to hold it all together for that long. I'm sorry for the birthdays that didn't feel like yours. For the friends you drifted from because you couldn't explain. For the time that disappeared. For the way your body braced every time a door closed too hard. I'm sorry for the silence after you spoke up and weren't believed. I'm sorry for the things you can't get back. And I'm sorry the people who should've known better made you feel like it was your fault.

The Damage Hides in the Everyday

You're standing in your kitchen, staring at the coffee maker, and you can't remember if you're allowed to buy the good coffee this week. Not because of money—there's money. But because last time you did, the silence lasted three days. The sighing. The slamming. The "must be nice" comments.

Now you're frozen, running calculations that have nothing to do with your bank balance and everything to do with their mood. This is what people don't see. It's not always bruises. It's the slow removal of your ability to make simple choices. To trust your own judgment. To live without permission.

A woman told me she sold her photography business—ten years of work—because he said it was "too much stress for the family." What he meant was: too much independence. Too many people who knew her without him. She cancelled a master's degree two weeks before it started. He hadn't said no—just went cold. Stopped talking. Stopped touching. Made every dinner feel like a funeral until she "chose" to withdraw.

By thirty-nine, she had no business, no degree, no passport (he'd hidden it "for safekeeping"), and no money of her own. "I thought I was compromising, like good partners do," she said. Then she paused. "Except compromise means both people give something up. I was the only one getting smaller."

No One Saw What It Took to Keep Going

Most people don't know what it takes to survive coercive control. They don't know you rehearse simple sentences in the shower: "Can I visit my mum this weekend?" Neutral tone. Not too eager. The right time, the right mood. They don't know you keep a mental spreadsheet of their emotions. Tuesday: lighter. Wednesday: jaw tight, avoid requests. Thursday: work stress, stay invisible. Friday: good day, might be safe to mention groceries.

You stopped reacting because reactions were "drama." You stopped needing because needs were "selfish." You monitored your own voice like a sound engineer, adjusting constantly to keep the peace. Until one day you catch your reflection and don't recognise the careful, quiet person staring back. When did your voice get so soft? When did you start making yourself so small?

Your body kept the score even when your mind made excuses. Stomach pain. Migraines. Autoimmune issues no doctor could explain. Your body didn't shut down because something was wrong with you. It shut down because it couldn't sustain that level of vigilance forever. That dissociation wasn't weakness. It was your nervous system's emergency response to prolonged psychological danger.

Practical Step

Write a letter to yourself that begins: "I'm sorry you had to…" Write it to the part of you that survived—who stayed when leaving felt impossible, who left when it was the only way, who lost things that can't be replaced. You don't have to forgive anyone or make meaning of it. Just witness what you carried. Honour what it cost. Let someone—even if it's you—finally say: "This shouldn't have happened to you."

Why It Matters

Because when you put those words on paper, you're giving yourself something you were denied: recognition. Not an excuse. Not a lesson. Just the truth. And truth is the ground recovery stands on.

If You Remember One Thing

You survived systematic psychological dismantling most people can't even imagine.

You shrank yourself to manage their rage while your own fear ate you alive. You disappeared from your life—quit the job, stopped seeing friends, cancelled plans—until you were isolated.

I'm sorry no one saw it for what it was. I'm sorry they called it "marital problems" when someone was deliberately breaking you down. I'm sorry you screamed in silence for years and the damage was invisible enough that no one believed you.

You don't have to soften what happened. You don't have to present "both sides." You don't have to make it palatable. You survived psychological torture designed to leave no evidence—and you survived even when it cost everything.

None of it should have happened. Not the monitoring disguised as care. Not the isolation disguised as love. Not the control disguised as protection.

Even if no one else names it, you can. Even if no one witnessed the silent treatments, the interrogations, the small cruelties— you lived through them. Even if no one validates your reality, it was real.

You were never the problem. The problem was someone who needed to destroy you to feel powerful.

1.2
It Didn't Happen All at Once
That's What Made It Dangerous

Author's Note:

This chapter is about the kind of harm you often can't see until you're trapped inside it. If you've ever been asked "Why didn't you leave?" instead of "How did they keep you trapped?"—this is for you. If you've struggled to explain why you stayed, why you didn't recognise it sooner, or why you still wonder if it "counts" as abuse, you're not alone.

Because coercive control isn't a single moment. It's a deliberate system created by someone who claimed they loved you, while quietly dismantling your sense of self, your friendships, your reality, your hope—until you barely recognised the person staring back at you in the mirror.

And that's exactly how it's designed to work.

It Started Small. So You Didn't Call It Abuse

You're at dinner with friends, telling a story about work, animated and engaged. He catches your eye across the table. That specific look—not quite a frown, but enough. "You're being a bit loud, babe." Said with a smile. Everyone laughs. You laugh too. But you lower your voice for the rest of the night.

Next time you're out, you monitor your volume before he has to. You catch yourself mid-sentence, dial it back. Better to self-correct than see that look again.

He mentions your best friend "seems a bit toxic." Not directly. Just observations. "She's always complaining about something." "Does she ever ask about you?" "I just think you deserve better friends." You start noticing these things too. When she cancels plans, you don't reschedule.

He gives you a look when you order dessert. Doesn't say anything. Just raises an eyebrow, glances at your stomach. So next time, you say you're full. The time after that, you don't even look at the dessert menu.

"Why do you always have to make everything such a big deal?" when you asked why he was three hours late. "You're so sensitive" when his joke hurt your feelings. "I was just trying to help" when his criticism made you cry.

It wasn't violence. It wasn't yelling. Just tiny corrections that felt like care. Cold silences that felt like your fault. Mild guilt that felt like growth. Each adjustment so small you could explain it away.

Until one day you're sitting at dinner, and you realise you haven't said what you really think in months. You've been editing yourself so long, you've forgotten your original voice.

They Didn't Break You. They Bent You Slowly

They didn't ban you from seeing family. They just made visits complicated. Picked fights the morning you were meant to leave. Sulked when you got back. Called constantly while you were there. "I just missed you." "Your mum always makes you stressed." "We barely get time together as it is."

Eventually, it was easier not to go.

They didn't forbid friendships. They just made them exhausting. Interrogations after every coffee date. "What did you talk about?" "Did you mention our argument?" "She's probably jealous of what we have." The post-mortem lasted longer than the actual visit.

Eventually, you stopped making plans.

They didn't take your bank cards. They just suggested joint accounts. "It's easier for bills." Then questioned every purchase. "Another coffee?" "Do you really need new trainers?" "We should be saving." But their purchases were never questioned. Their needs were never excessive.

Eventually, you stopped buying things without permission.

They didn't tell you to shut up. They just interrupted. Corrected. Rolled their eyes. Started scrolling their phone mid-sentence. "You already told me this." "That's not how it happened." "Are you nearly done?"

Eventually, you stopped talking.

You Didn't See It Coming. That's the Point

It wasn't a cliff edge you could spot and avoid. It was a gradient so gentle you didn't notice the elevation change until you looked back and couldn't see where you started.

A woman told me she didn't realise she'd stopped laughing until a colleague made her laugh at work and she had to hide in the bathroom because she was sobbing. "I'd forgotten what my own laugh sounded like," she said. "I'd been performing acceptable emotions for so long, actual joy felt foreign."

She tried to map the progression later, to find the moment it went wrong. But there wasn't one. "It was like gaining weight," she said. "You don't notice day to day. Then suddenly your clothes don't fit and you can't pinpoint when it happened."

The dinner conversations that slowly became monologues you weren't part of. The weekend plans that somehow always became their plans. The opinions you used to have that gradually got replaced with "I don't mind" and "Whatever you think."

They weren't reckless. They were architects. Every criticism came wrapped in concern: "I just want you to be your best self." Every restriction came disguised as protection: "I just worry about you." Every act of control looked like love: "I just want us to be close." The kindness—the flowers after fights, the compliments after criticism, the affection after withdrawal—that wasn't separate from the abuse. It was part of it. The sugar that made the poison go down.

Practical Step

Write down five changes you made to avoid conflict or keep them happy. How you dressed. What you watched on TV. When you showered. How you loaded the dishwasher. Foods you stopped eating. Topics you stopped discussing.

Now ask yourself: Would you have made those changes if you felt safe? Would you have made them for anyone else? Do they make sense to you now?

This isn't about blame. It's about pattern recognition—seeing how many pieces of yourself you traded for the peace that never came.

Why It Matters

Because when you can name the pattern, you stop blaming yourself for not seeing it sooner. When you understand it was designed to be invisible, you stop calling yourself stupid for missing it. When you recognise it as strategy—not accident—you stop trying to figure out what you did wrong.

If You Remember One Thing

You didn't miss red flags. You were living inside a thousand beige ones. Tiny compromises that looked reasonable. Small adjustments that seemed like growth. Minor sacrifices that felt like love.

They didn't shove you into a cage. They built it around you slowly, bar by bar, while telling you it was a home. Each bar looked like care. The lock looked like commitment. The walls looked like intimacy.

That's not oversight. That's exactly how coercive control works.

It masquerades as love while dismantling your autonomy. It presents itself as protection while cutting off your exits. It calls itself commitment while erasing your boundaries. It demands trust while destroying your reality.

You weren't naive for believing someone who said they loved you. You were human, extending trust to someone who weaponised it. You were kind, making space for someone who took everything.

It wasn't love. Love doesn't require you to disappear. It was a control system designed to look like relationship. And whether you're still inside it, just starting to name it, or years into recovery, these truths remain:

You didn't imagine it. You didn't cause it. You didn't deserve it.

And you get to rebuild, one small reclamation at a time. One opinion reformed. One boundary restored. One laugh that's really yours.

You don't owe them understanding. You don't owe anyone a perfect explanation. You just begin, right where you are, with the truth that it happened, it was real, and it was never your fault.

1.3
You Don't Need to Call Them
a Narcissist for It to Be Abuse

Author's Note:

There's a lot of talk out there about narcissists. What they do. Why they do it. How to spot them. How to expose them. But this chapter is here to name something else: what happens when all the attention goes to who they were, and you forget to ask what it did to you.

You can get lost in definitions. You can spend years trying to figure out what label fits them best. But this book was never about putting them under a microscope. It's about putting you back in the centre of your own story.

You Can Lose Years Chasing the Right Word

You're three hours deep in a forum at 2 a.m., cross-referencing symptoms. Covert narcissist? Vulnerable narcissist? Maybe borderline? The tabs multiply. The checklist grows. You've bookmarked seventeen articles and none of them quite fit.

You bring printouts to therapy. "Look, he does this but not that. He fits six criteria but needs seven. What does that mean?" Your therapist suggests focusing on your feelings. You nod, then go home and Google "narcissistic personality disorder vs antisocial."

A woman told me she spent eighteen months trying to diagnose her ex. Read every book. Listened to every podcast. Filled notebooks with evidence, patterns, theories. "I became an expert on personality disorders," she said. "I could debate the DSM criteria in my sleep."

But when I asked what the relationship had done to her, she went quiet. "I couldn't answer. I'd spent so long studying him, I'd forgotten to look at myself. I knew his patterns but not my own damage. I could list his traits but not my losses."

She looked at her hands. "He could be anything—narcissist, sociopath, or just an arsehole. But I became nothing. I disappeared while trying to solve him."

That's when she realised: the diagnosis didn't matter. The damage did.

Some Narcissists Control. Some Controllers Aren't Narcissists

Not all coercive controllers are narcissists. Some are insecure. Some are entitled. Some learned it from their parents. Some just like power. Not all narcissists are coercive controllers. Some are just self-absorbed. Some hurt people through neglect, not design. Some damage without intent.

But here's what matters:
If someone cut you off from friends or family.
If they gaslit you until you doubted your own memory.
If they tracked where you went or who you spoke to.
If they controlled your money, your food, your sleep.
If they made you ask permission for ordinary things.
If they left you afraid in your own home—they were abusive.
Not confused. Not overwhelmed. Not "going through something." Abusive.

The label on their behaviour doesn't change what it did to you.

Forget What They Are. Remember What You Lost

You don't need a diagnosis to name what happened. You don't need nine DSM criteria, a therapist's confirmation, or a personality assessment.

You need what you already have: the truth of what it felt like. The way your stomach dropped when their car pulled up. The rehearsals in your head before asking for anything. The way you started agreeing with things you didn't believe just to avoid the fight. The friends who faded. The hobbies that died. The opinions that went underground. Because coercive control isn't about what they were. It's about what they took from you.

We Use the Word 'Narcissist' Because Survivors Recognise It

You'll see the word narcissist in this book. Not because we're diagnosing anyone, but because when survivors hear it, they exhale. Finally. A word that captures something.

You know what it means. The charm that turns to contempt behind closed doors. The way they could twist any situation until you were apologising. The rage over tiny imperfections. The cold silence that lasted days. The way your pain became their inconvenience, your success became their threat, your needs became attacks.

You know the Jekyll and Hyde switch. Charismatic at dinner parties, cruel in the car home. Generous in public, withholding in private. Concerned parent at school meetings, contemptuous partner at breakfast.

You know what it's like to apologise for things you didn't do, just to make it stop. To take blame for their affairs. To comfort them after they hurt you. To manage their emotions while yours went underground.

If you've lived it, the word 'narcissist' isn't clinical. It's shorthand for a specific kind of hell. It's validation that others have been there too. It's permission to stop trying to fix someone who was never broken—just harmful.

Practical Step

Stop asking "What were they—narcissist, sociopath, addict?" Start asking "What did I lose?"

Write three specific changes. Something you stopped doing—seeing certain friends, wearing bright colours, singing in the shower. Something you started doing to keep peace—checking their mood before speaking, rehearsing simple requests, hiding receipts. Something about yourself you forgot—what made you laugh, what you were good at, what brought you joy. This isn't about them anymore. It's about naming what's missing—so you know what to rebuild.

Why It Matters

When you stop trying to solve them, you can start recovering you. Their diagnosis won't heal your hypervigilance. Their label won't restore your confidence. Understanding their psychology won't return your lost years. But naming your losses? That's where recovery begins.

If You Remember One Thing

This book isn't about diagnosing them. It's about believing you.

Whether they were narcissistic, sociopathic, or just systematically cruel, the label doesn't change what you survived. It doesn't minimise the nights you couldn't breathe. It doesn't undo the ways you had to reshape yourself to stay safe.

You don't need a clinical term to trust what your body remembers—the tension, the scanning, the bracing. You don't need their diagnosis to validate your diagnosis: that you were being harmed.

You don't need their admission to call it what it was. You don't need a judge's ruling to know you were imprisoned. You don't need a therapist's permission to say: "This destroyed me."

You just need the pattern: control, isolation, manipulation, fear. Your truth: it happened. Your story: you survived it.

And you've always had that. Even when they tried to rewrite it. Even when others doubted it. Even when you doubted yourself.

The evidence isn't in their diagnosis. It's in your damage. And that's enough proof for anyone who matters—starting with you.

1.4
There Were Two Sides
Only One of Them Was Abuse

Author's Note:

This chapter is about naming the truth: coercive control has one driver, not two. It shows up inside relationships of every kind—intimate, family, workplace, church, community. The setting changes. The pattern doesn't. If you've ever been told "it takes two to tango" when you described being silenced, gaslit, or made afraid—you know how cruel that line lands. It's not just wrong. It's complicit. It hands half the blame to someone already carrying all the damage.

But coercive control isn't a dance. It's not two people "bringing out the worst in each other." It's one person tightening the leash while the other learns to shrink. It's one person setting traps while the other tries to survive the minefield. Not mutual. Not miscommunication. Not "just a bad patch." One person chose control. One person endured it.

Survival Is Never Complicity

A woman told me she wanted to scream when her friend said "it takes two to tango" after she'd finally shared what was happening at home. "Which part was my tango?" she asked. "When I stopped seeing friends to keep him calm? When I agreed with things I didn't believe to avoid three-day silences? When I became someone I didn't recognise just to survive another week?"

She was shaking as she said it. Not from anger. From the effort of holding back years of being told she was half the problem. "Was it my tango when I rehearsed simple sentences in the shower? 'Can we visit my sister?' Practising the right tone, waiting for the right mood. Was that me dancing?"

Her friend had never woken up apologising for things they didn't do. Never stood in their kitchen, voice trembling, saying "I never said that" while someone insisted they had. Never watched their own memories become unreliable. That isn't two people clashing. That's one person systematically erasing another. You weren't giving as good as you got. You were trying to survive. And survival is never complicity.

They Created Waves, Then Blamed You for Drowning

You're in the kitchen. "Please stop turning everything into a fight," you say, exhausted. He smirks. "Maybe stop being so dramatic then."

Just like that, the conversation flips. It's not about what he did anymore. It's about how you responded. You're defending your tone instead of addressing his behaviour. You're explaining your emotions instead of discussing his provocations. The real issue—his constant criticism, his deliberate baiting—vanishes. Now you're the problem for reacting to the problem.

Everyone else sees two people "arguing." They don't see the setup. The way he pushes every button he's mapped for years, then acts shocked when you finally respond. They see your raised voice. They don't see the thousand paper cuts that caused it. This wasn't a fight. This was calculated destruction dressed as disagreement.

You Became a Detective in Your Own Life

Tuesday, he says you never told him about dinner plans. You pull out your phone— there's your message from Sunday. Time-stamped. Clear. He glances at it, shrugs. "I don't remember that."

Wednesday, you mention Tuesday's conversation. "What conversation?" he asks, performing perfect confusion. By Thursday, you're screenshotting everything. Your phone fills with evidence of conversations that supposedly never happened. Proof you're not losing your mind, even though you feel like you are.

A survivor told me she had thirty-seven folders of screenshots. "Text messages. Emails.

Photos of handwritten notes. I needed proof I existed. That my words were real. That I wasn't inventing everything like he said I was." She paused. "You know what's fucked up? I still have them. Three years later. Still can't delete them. Like I might need to prove reality again."

That's not mutual dysfunction. That's one person deliberately destabilising another's reality.

When Therapists Miss It Too

You're in couples therapy. The therapist turns to you: "What's your contribution to the dynamic?" Your stomach drops. You've just explained the silent treatments, the gaslighting, the way you can't make simple decisions without calculating his mood. But now you're being asked to find your fault in being systematically broken down.

He sits there, calm, reasonable. "I just want us both to take responsibility," he says, and the therapist nods. You try to explain that "taking responsibility" has become code for accepting blame for his behaviour. That you've been trained to apologise for his moods, his reactions, his choices. "That sounds like you're not willing to look at your part," the therapist says gently.

A woman told me she spent two years in couples therapy that nearly killed her. "Every session became more ammunition for him. I'd share something vulnerable, and that night he'd use it against me. The therapist kept talking about 'communication styles' while I was being psychologically tortured."

When abuse is happening, couples therapy isn't neutral. It's dangerous.

When You Broke, They Pointed at the Pieces

Three weeks of silent treatment. Three weeks of existing in the same house with someone who won't acknowledge you're alive. You've begged. You've apologised for things you didn't do. You've written letters explaining your perspective. Nothing.

Today, you're in the kitchen. "Can you please just listen to what I'm saying?" He's already walking away. "Here we go again," he mutters, loud enough to hear, quiet enough to deny. Something breaks. You throw the dish towel down. Not at him. Just down. Just something to make the frustration visible.

Later, he tells everyone you "completely lost it." He mentions the dish towel. He doesn't mention the three weeks that led to it. He doesn't mention his calculated indifference, his strategic dismissals. When you finally shatter under systematic pressure, they point at the pieces and say, "See? This is what I've been dealing with."

Neutrality Is Complicity

"I don't want to take sides." A woman told me her best friend said this after months of her partner systematically cutting her off from support. "She thought she was being fair," she said. "But he didn't need people to take his side. He just needed them to stay neutral. Their neutrality meant no one would help me. That was his victory."

When someone says they "don't want to get involved" in abuse, they're already involved. They've chosen the side of the person doing harm. There are two sides to every story. Yes. One side used silent treatment as punishment. One side begged for communication. One side rewrote history. One side kept receipts just to remember what was real. One side isolated and controlled. One side tried to maintain connection and autonomy. Both sides are not the same.

Your Hope Wasn't Weakness

They say you must have played a part. And yes, you did. You stayed when he apologised with flowers. You believed the promises to change. You made excuses to your sister when she noticed you seemed different. You covered his cruelty with your kindness.

But hope isn't complicity. You didn't lie about conversations. You didn't pretend events never happened. You didn't systematically dismantle someone's sense of reality. You didn't isolate someone from their support system. You tried to love someone who saw love as ownership. You tried to build trust with someone who weaponised vulnerability.

You tried to compromise with someone who saw flexibility as weakness.

That's not playing a part in abuse. That's being abused by someone who exploited your humanity.

Practical Step

Make two lists. Call the first "What I Did to Survive"—stayed quiet to avoid fights, agreed just to keep peace, stopped seeing certain people, apologised for their moods, made myself smaller.

Call the second "What They Did to Control"—silent treatment, gaslighting, isolation tactics, financial control, twisting facts until I doubted myself.

Look at these lists. One shows survival strategies. The other shows abuse tactics. These aren't two people hurting each other. This is one person hurting, one person enduring.

Why It Matters

Because the world wants abuse to be mutual. It's more comfortable that way. If it's "both people," no one has to take a stand. No one has to help. No one has to face their complicity in staying silent.

Naming it clearly—this was abuse, not conflict—breaks that comfortable lie. It puts responsibility where it belongs—not on you for surviving abuse, but on them for perpetrating it.

If You Remember One Thing

They'll keep calling it mutual. They'll say every relationship has problems. They'll insist you gave as good as you got. But you know the truth.

You remember your voice getting smaller, not louder. You remember editing yourself in real-time, not speaking freely. You remember the relief when they left and the dread when they returned. That's not mutual conflict. That's fear.

You didn't argue your way into abuse. You didn't overreact your way into being gaslit.

You didn't provoke your way into being controlled. Whatever they want to call it—complicated, toxic, difficult—you know what it was: Systematic dismantling disguised as love. Deliberate destruction disguised as relationship.

You survived coercive control. Not a bad relationship. Not mutual dysfunction. Abuse.

And recognising that difference is where recovery begins.

1.5
It's Not Abuse. I Never Touched You

Author's Note:

This chapter is for anyone who was told, "It's not abuse. I never touched you." For anyone who looked in the mirror and wondered why they felt broken when there were no bruises to point to. Abuse isn't measured in broken bones. It's measured in the way your body learns to brace for impact even when no hand is raised. Your nervous system doesn't wait for fists—it just asks one question, over and over: Am I safe?

They Didn't Need to Hit You for It to Hurt Like Hell

You walk into the kitchen and automatically scan: coffee cup on counter (dirty), phone cord tangled, his keys missing from the hook. Your shoulders are already up around your ears before you've even seen him. That wasn't fragility. That was your nervous system doing exactly what it was trained to do—assess for threat, prepare for impact, brace for what might come.

A woman told me she could predict his mood by the sound of his footsteps on the stairs. "Heavy meant angry. Quick meant impatient. Slow meant he was planning something." Her body had become a seismograph, registering tremors others couldn't feel.

The Seventeen Versions of "Fine"

2 a.m., staring at the ceiling, replaying the way he said "fine" when you asked about dinner plans. Was it actually fine? The sarcastic fine? The we'll-talk-about-this-later fine? The you'll-pay-for-this-tomorrow fine?

You'd learned to decode seventeen different versions of "fine," and tomorrow's peace depended on guessing right. Sleep became impossible because your nervous system was still working—still calculating, still preparing, still trying to keep you safe from a danger that lived in tone, not touch.

The Sound of Keys in the Door

You hear his car in the driveway and your stomach drops. Not because anything bad has happened—nothing has happened yet. But your body remembers yesterday's silent treatment, last week's explosion over the grocery bill, the way conversations become minefields without warning.

You mute the TV. Straighten the cushions. Check your appearance in the hallway mirror. Mentally rehearse "normal." By the time he walks in, you've already edited yourself three times.

Your friend later says, "But he never actually hurt you, right?" Right. He never actually hurt you. He just made your own home feel like enemy territory.

When Your Body Speaks First

The therapist asks what you're feeling. You say, "Fine." She points to your hands— you're gripping the chair arms like you're about to fall off a cliff. White knuckles. Rigid forearms. "That," she says gently, "is not fine."

You look down, surprised. There's a band of pain across your upper back from holding yourself so tight. Your breathing is shallow. Your leg has been bouncing for ten minutes straight. This is what trauma looks like without bruises—it lives in muscles that never fully relax, in breath that never quite deepens.

This Is What Survival Looked Like

You stopped wearing your favourite red shirt because he once said it looked "desperate." Now it hangs in your wardrobe like evidence of someone you used to be.

You rehearse conversations before having them, editing out anything that might be "too much." You've become your own censor, cutting yourself down before he has the chance. You learned to read micro-expressions like your safety depended on it— because it did. The slight squint that meant irritation. The jaw clench that preceded coldness. The particular silence that meant you'd done something wrong but wouldn't find out what until later.

Your sister says, "You seem jumpy lately." You laugh it off. But she's right—you flinch at sudden movements, startle at raised voices, freeze when anyone seems upset.

There Was No Proof but Your Body Knew

Sarah collapsed at work on a Tuesday. Not from hunger or illness—but from the weight of pretending everything was normal while her nervous system screamed emergency. The paramedic taking her blood pressure asked quietly, "When did you last feel safe?" She couldn't remember. That answer revealed more than any test ever could.

The Morning After Nothing Happened

You wake up exhausted after eight hours of sleep—except it wasn't really sleep. It was eight hours of your body staying partially alert, ready to respond to danger. Your jaw aches from clenching. Your neck is stiff from sleeping curled and defensive. Your stomach is in knots over a conversation that might happen. Or might not. The uncertainty is almost worse. Nothing happened to you. But also, everything happened to you. The threat of threat. The violence of walking on eggshells.

Your Body Testified Before You Could

"Any history of domestic abuse?" the doctor asks, scanning your symptoms: chronic headaches, insomnia, digestive issues, muscle tension that never releases. "No," you say automatically. "He never hit me." She looks up from her clipboard. "I didn't ask if he hit you. I asked about domestic abuse." The words lodge in your throat. Later, sitting in your car in the surgery car park, you replay that distinction for twenty minutes. The way she separated violence from abuse. The way she seemed to know what you couldn't say.

Your body had been testifying all along—in symptoms, in stress responses, in the way you held yourself constantly bracing. The evidence was written in your muscles, your nervous system, your inability to ever fully exhale.

Practical Step

Right now, notice your body. Don't change anything—just notice. Are your shoulders up? Jaw tight? Holding your breath? Stomach clenched? This isn't weakness. This is your body speaking—a message it's been carrying for months, maybe years. Start there. With believing what your body knows.

Why It Matters

You can't think your way out of a nervous system trained by fear.

But you can begin listening to what your body has been trying to tell you. That's where recovery starts—not with understanding why, but with believing what is.

If You Remember One Thing

They didn't need to hit you for your body to register danger. The way your stomach dropped at the sound of keys—that was real. The way your jaw ached through dinner—that was evidence. The way you rehearsed every word before speaking—that was survival.

There were no photos. No bruises. No police reports. But the proof was in the headaches that started in year two, the insomnia that became normal, the way you stopped trusting your own ease.

"He never hit me" doesn't mean "He never hurt me." Your body knew the truth long before you could name it. Long before anyone else would. That truth still lives in you.

And it's waiting for you to believe it.

1.6
The Scans Showed Nothing
Your Body Showed Everything

Author's Note:

This chapter is for anyone who left the doctor's office with a prescription and no answers. For anyone who kept showing up sick, tired, aching, anxious, and was told it was "just stress." If you've ever wondered why your body keeps breaking down even though the tests say you're fine, this is for you. Even when the abuse was quiet, your body heard every bit of it.

Your Body Kept the Score in Ways No Test Could Measure

You're in the waiting room for your fourth specialist this year. Gastroenterologist. Before this it was the neurologist for migraines. Before that, rheumatologist for joint pain. Before that, cardiologist for chest pains that feel like heart attacks but aren't.

The intake form asks: "When did symptoms begin?"

You write a date. Then stare at it. That was two months after you moved in together. Three months after he convinced you to stop therapy because "talking to strangers about our relationship is betrayal."

For the first time, you see what your body's been trying to tell you all along.

They Didn't Need to Hit You for Your Body to Break Down

Your stress hormones didn't check whether the threat was a scream or silence, a glare or a fist. They just flooded your system. Heart pounding. Digestion stalling. Muscles bracing. Night after night. Year after year.

A woman told me her chronic pain started the same month she married him. "I thought it was coincidence for ten years," she said. "Then I left him. Within six months, the pain was gone."

Your body doesn't need bruises to register danger. It just needs threat. And threat was your daily bread.

The Doctor Asked the Wrong Questions

"Any history of domestic violence?" the nurse asks at your check-up, ticking boxes on her screen.

You pause too long. She looks up.

"He never hit me," you say automatically.

"I didn't ask if he hit you."

That pause stretches between you like a bridge you're not ready to cross. Your heart rate spikes. Your shoulders lock. Your body is answering the question your words can't.

Later, the gastroenterologist says stress can cause stomach issues. He prescribes antacids, suggests yoga. You want to tell him: My stomach knots when I hear his key in the door. I can't eat breakfast because mornings are when he lists everything I did wrong yesterday. I throw up before family dinners because I know he'll humiliate me with a smile.

But you take the pills and pretend they help.

What Your Symptoms Were Really Saying

Maybe it's chronic fatigue that doctors can't explain. You sleep ten hours and wake exhausted. They run tests. Everything's "normal." But your body's been in fight-or-flight for three years—of course it's exhausted.

Maybe it's migraines that started when he began critiquing every meal you cooked, every outfit you wore, every word you said. The neurologist gives you pills that don't touch them. Because the trigger isn't in your brain chemistry—it's in your kitchen.

Maybe it's the jaw pain requiring a night guard because your body won't stop clenching, even in sleep. Your dentist says it's stress. You want to laugh. Or cry. Stress doesn't cover it.

Maybe it's autoimmune flare-ups—your system attacking itself because it can't tell the difference between actual threats and Tuesday dinner conversations anymore.

A survivor told me she mapped her medical records against her relationship timeline. "Every mystery illness, every unexplained symptom, every emergency room visit—they all lined up with escalations in his control. My body was documenting the abuse the whole time."

What the Scans Couldn't See

MRI: normal. Blood work: fine. X-rays: clear. Hormone levels: within range.

But they couldn't scan for hypervigilance—the way you monitor his breathing patterns to gauge safety. They couldn't test for the exhaustion of tracking someone's moods twenty-four hours a day. They couldn't image shoulders locked in permanent defence, even during sleep.

They couldn't measure the cost of never fully exhaling in your own home.

The emergency doctor says you're having panic attacks, not heart attacks. He says it like that should be reassuring. But your body knows: a heart can break in more ways than one.

Your Timeline Tells the Truth

The fibromyalgia diagnosis came six months after the wedding. The thyroid problems started the year he isolated you from your sister. The chronic migraines began when he started working from home. The IBS flares tracked perfectly with his moods.

Your body wasn't mysteriously breaking down. It was precisely documenting what was happening to you.

Practical Step

Draw a timeline. On top, write your symptoms and when they started—not when they got bad enough to see a doctor, but when you first noticed them. On the bottom, write what was happening in your relationship at that time: New rules. Lost friendships. Increased monitoring. First silent treatment.

Look at how they line up. Your body has been telling the truth all along.

Why It Matters

Your body isn't broken. It's been doing exactly what bodies do in threatening environments—trying to keep you alive. Understanding this isn't just validation. It's the beginning of teaching your body that it's finally safe to stop bracing, stop scanning, stop preparing for impact that isn't coming anymore.

If You Remember One Thing

The scans showed nothing. But your body showed everything.

Every headache was real. Every sleepless night counted. Every wave of unexplained fatigue was your nervous system saying: I can't keep doing this. The irritable bowel that flared during conflict. The chronic pain that started when you lost your voice. The autoimmune condition that emerged when your body couldn't tell friend from foe anymore—because in your home, love and danger wore the same face.

Your symptoms weren't mysterious. They weren't "all in your head." They were your body testifying in the only language it knows: inflammation, exhaustion, pain. They were evidence of what you survived, written in the alphabet of symptoms no scan could read.

Your body fought for you all along, even when no one believed the battle was real. And now? Now you can thank it for surviving. Now you can slowly, carefully, teach it that the war is over. That it can finally rest.

What the Experts Have Said

"After a traumatic experience, the human system of self-preservation seems to go onto permanent alert, as if the danger might return at any moment."
— Judith Herman, *Trauma and Recovery*

"Traumatized people chronically feel unsafe inside their bodies… They learn to hide from their selves."
— Bessel A. van der Kolk, *The Body Keeps the Score*

"Although humans rarely die from trauma, if we do not resolve it, our lives can be severely diminished by its effects. Some people have even described this situation as a 'living death.'"
— Peter A. Levine, *Healing Trauma*

"Trauma is not what happens to you but what happens inside you."
— Gabor Maté, *The Myth of Normal*

"How safe we feel is crucial to our physical and mental health and happiness."
— Stephen W. Porges, *Our Polyvagal World*

1.7
They Are Charming in Public But Cruel in Private

Author's Note:

This chapter is about the kind of abuse that hides behind charm. If you ever felt like you were living with two different people—one everyone adored, and one only you knew—this will help you trust what happened behind closed doors.

You Were the Stagehand. He Was the Star

He makes everyone laugh at parties. Tells stories with perfect timing, perfect gestures, perfect pauses for effect. Calls you "babe" with such warmth that people smile. Pulls out your chair. Touches your shoulder. Wraps his arm around you for photos. "He's a keeper," your friend whispers. "You're so lucky."

But you know what's coming. The shift happens before you've even reached the car. His hand drops from your back. His smile vanishes like it was never there. The voice that charmed everyone goes flat, cold.

"You barely spoke all night. People probably think you're brain-dead." Or: "Did you have to laugh so loud at Tom's jokes? Desperate much?"

You were the stagehand, invisible, making sure nothing went wrong. He was the star, and everyone loved the show. The only audience that ever saw both acts was you.

Everyone Thought He Was Wonderful, So You Thought It Was You

At the grocery store, the cashier gushes about how lovely he is. He beams, touches your shoulder like you're precious. In the car: "That woman never shuts up. And why do you stand there like a corpse?"

He volunteers at the food bank. Helps neighbours. Remembers birthdays. He praises you publicly: "She's brilliant, this one." Then punishes you privately: "You made yourself look stupid tonight. Embarrassing."

How could someone so universally adored be abusive? It must be you.

A woman told me she kept a journal trying to figure out what she was doing wrong. "I documented everything—what I wore, what I said, how I stood. I thought if I could crack the code, I could get the public version at home too."

There was no code. The cruelty wasn't triggered by anything she did. It was triggered by privacy.

The Wedding Speech That Broke You

At your sister's wedding, he gives a toast about marriage. How relationships take work. How you have to choose love every day. How blessed he feels to have found his person—he looks at you—his best friend, his partner, his everything.

Your mother tears up. Squeezes your hand. "You found a good one," she whispers.

In the hotel room, he loosens his tie. "Did you see everyone watching me? That's how you give a speech. Maybe you should take notes instead of stuttering through your maid of honour disaster."

You stare at the ceiling until morning, replaying his public declaration of love, trying to reconcile it with the contempt in his voice now.

They Don't Just Hide Who They Are. They Hide What They're Doing

He tells people you're "going through something." That you've been "stressed" and "withdrawn." He expresses concern with just the right amount of worry. "I'm trying to support her, but she won't let me in."

So when you finally crack—when you cry at dinner or snap at a gathering—everyone already has context. He looks confused. Hurt. Like a man doing his best with a difficult woman.

A survivor told me: "He spent two years telling everyone I was depressed. So when I finally told my friend what was happening, she said, 'He mentioned you've been struggling. Maybe you should see someone.' She thought my abuse was depression. He'd made sure of it."

The Charm Was Never Love. It Was Camouflage

At dinner with his colleagues, he tells a "funny" story about your quirks. "She's adorably neurotic," he says, kissing your temple. Later, when you say it hurt: "It's called banter. This is why people think you're uptight."

A woman told me her ex gave a speech at her fortieth birthday. Called her his queen, his rock, his reason for living. Two hours later, in the car, he called her pathetic for "lapping up attention like a desperate dog."

"I stopped celebrating anything after that," she said.

The version everyone knows? Rehearsed. Calculated. Strategic. The version you live with? That's who he really is. He doesn't need to charm you anymore—he has you. The charm is for reputation management. For alibis. For ensuring that when you finally speak up, no one believes you.

Practical Step

Draw a line down the middle of a page.

Left side: How They Act in Public
—Tells the server I'm "the boss" at home
—Brags about my promotion
—Holds my hand during dinner

Right side: How They Act in Private
—Calls me a controlling bitch
—Says I'm nothing special
—Won't touch me for days

Don't edit. Don't explain. Just document the difference. This isn't inconsistency—it's evidence.

Why It Matters

When their charm is camouflage, your clarity is survival. Seeing the pattern written down stops you from gaslighting yourself into believing it's all in your head.

If You Remember One Thing

They treated you differently on purpose.

They gave everyone else warmth, humour, patience, interest. You got the coldness. The criticism. The contempt. You got just enough glimpses of the public version to keep you hoping it might come home.

You kept trying to earn what everyone else got for free. You thought if you could just be funnier, quieter, prettier, less sensitive, you'd unlock the person everyone else knew.

But there was no formula. The cruelty wasn't a response to your flaws. It was a choice. They could control it—that's why it only happened in private. They knew exactly what they were doing—that's why the mask never slipped in public.

The fact you still remember how good they could be? That's proof of how hard you fought to believe in something that was never real.

Now you get to stop chasing it. Because it was never love. It was performance. And you were never the problem. You were the only witness.

1.8
I Never Said That (Yes, They Did)

Author's Note:

This chapter is about gaslighting in its most familiar form: the denial of something they absolutely said. The term comes from a 1944 film where a husband manipulates gas lights to make his wife think she's losing her mind. But gaslighting isn't about gas or lights—it's about someone deliberately making you question your own reality. If you've ever walked away from a conversation questioning your own memory, this will help you stop second-guessing what you know you lived through.

What Gaslighting Feels Like

You're standing in the doorway, car keys in hand. You repeat his words back to him. Almost verbatim. Not yelling. Not accusing. Just clarifying. "You said if I left dinner early you'd be furious."

He blinks. The corner of his mouth twitches into a smirk. He tilts his head like you've just told him the moon is made of cheese. "I never said that."

Your stomach drops. The keys feel heavy in your hand. You know you heard it. Twenty minutes ago, in this exact spot. You remember the tone—low, threatening. The timing—right after you mentioned your sister needed you. The way he didn't look at you when he said it, just kept scrolling his phone. But now you're not sure. Maybe you misheard. Maybe you misunderstood. Maybe you're remembering it wrong. Maybe you're too sensitive. Maybe—

That's what gaslighting feels like. Not the moment they lie, but the moment after. The moment you stop trusting what you know you heard.

It Wasn't About the Words

You're sitting on your bed, phone in hand, reading your text again. Then again. It's short, civil, clear. You checked it four times before sending: "Can't make lunch tomorrow. Have that work deadline."

Their response makes your chest tight: "Wow. That's really aggressive. No wonder people think you're intense."

You scroll back to your message. Read it again. Where's the aggression? You were calm. You know you were calm. The words are right there on the screen, neutral and careful. But they say you weren't, so maybe... you weren't?

Twenty minutes later, you're typing an apology. "Sorry if that came across wrong. I didn't mean to sound harsh." Your fingers hesitate over send. You weren't harsh. But here you are, apologising for a tone that existed only in their rewriting of it.

A woman told me she started recording conversations on her phone. "Not to use against him. Just to listen back later and check if I really was as 'hostile' as he said." She paused, looked down at her hands. "I never was. Not once."

They Rewrite the Past So You Can't Stand on It

It's Thursday night. You're washing dishes. He walks up behind you, leans against the counter. "You're lucky I put up with you."

The words land like stones in your chest. You keep washing the same plate, water too hot, hands turning red. A week later, you bring it up. You've practised how to say it without sounding accusatory. "When you said I was lucky you put up with me—"

He looks genuinely confused. His eyebrows furrow. "Why would I say something like that? That doesn't even sound like me."

You feel your certainty wavering. "You did, though. Last Thursday. In the kitchen."

He laughs. Actually laughs. "Babe, I think you might have dreamt that."

You find yourself nodding. Laughing nervously. "Maybe. Sorry. I must have misunderstood something else." The worst part isn't the lie. It's how quickly you abandon your own truth.

They Hate Your Clarity Because It Threatens Their System

You've gotten specific this time. No room for confusion. "We were in the car. Tuesday. After I turned off the radio. You said I was being dramatic about my mother's illness."

They pause. Just long enough to make you question yourself. Then they sigh, that particular sigh that means you're being difficult. "God, you really hold onto things, don't you? Most people would have moved on by now."

They don't argue the facts. They argue your right to remember them.

They Want You to Doubt Yourself

You're at a party. You just told a story about your promotion. Later, in the car: "You told that all wrong," they say.

"What do you mean?"

"You said you got promoted in March. It was April."

"No, it was definitely March. I remember because—"

"And you said your boss called you. But you told me last week that you went to his office."

Your mind races. Did you say that? You don't think you did, but now you're not sure. They seem so certain. They're always so certain.

"Did I?" you ask.

They pat your hand. Smile. "A little. But don't worry, I knew what you meant. I covered for you."

Just like that, your voice is no longer yours. You need them to interpret your own words. To tell you what you really meant. What you really said. What really happened.

A survivor told me she started writing everything down immediately after it happened. Times, dates, exact phrases. "Not because I didn't trust him," she said. "Because I'd stopped trusting myself." Her journal became her anchor. When he said she was making things up, she didn't argue. She just reread her own words. Proof that she wasn't crazy. That it really happened. That her mind was still hers.

Practical Steps

Start protecting your reality before it slips away. When they say something that matters—especially something hurtful or confusing—make a quick note in your phone. Just the basics: date, time, what was said. Not paragraphs, just enough to anchor yourself later. "Tuesday 8pm: Said I embarrass him in front of friends." That's all. These breadcrumbs lead you back to your truth when they try to steal it.

If it's safe and legal where you are, screenshot messages that twist your words. Not to build a case—just to remind yourself that you're not imagining things. Hide them in a folder if you need to. Call it something boring like "Receipts" or "Old Photos."

In the moment when they deny saying something, practise these responses without getting pulled into debate. Say "I remember it differently" and then stop talking. Let the silence sit. Or try "I'm not going to argue about this" and physically step away. Go to another room. Take a walk. Or simply say "Okay" with zero emotion and change the subject completely.

These aren't about winning. They're about not handing over your reality for them to edit.

Why It Matters

Every time you doubt your memory, you hand over a piece of your reality to someone else to manage. Getting your life back starts with trusting yourself again—even when, especially when, someone tells you you're wrong. Those notes you keep aren't just words on a screen. They're proof that your mind works fine, that what happened actually happened.

If You Remember One Thing

When you hear "I never said that," remember this: Yes, they did. You heard it right the first time.

They called you forgetful. Dramatic. Too sensitive. Unreliable. They said you make things up, twist words, remember wrong. They tried to make your memory the problem. But you were right all along.

You heard what you heard. You know what you know. Your clarity isn't confusion—their lies are. You don't need to convince them of your truth. You don't need them to admit what they said. You don't need their validation to know what you experienced.

Just hold onto this: Your memory is yours. Your truth is yours. Your reality is yours. And no amount of "I never said that" can steal what you know you lived through.

1.9
Silence is Violence. Just a Quieter Kind

Author's Note:

If you ever found yourself walking on eggshells around someone who rarely raised their voice, but still left you anxious, erased, or ashamed, this is for you. It was violence. Just a quieter kind.

Silence That Controls

He doesn't scream. He doesn't hit. He doesn't slam doors. He just goes quiet. Cold. Heavy. That kind of moody silence that fills every corner of the house like toxic gas. If you ask what's wrong, he says, "Nothing." If you push, you're "starting drama." If you leave him alone, you're "emotionally unavailable." Just silence that makes your chest tight and your hands shake. Silence that soaks the room in shame and dread.

A woman told me she could feel his mood shift from three rooms away. "The quality of quiet changed. Happy quiet felt light. Angry quiet felt like drowning."

Silence that controls, isolates, and makes your body brace? That's violence. Just harder to prove.

It Didn't Look Like Control, but You Stopped Speaking Freely

You started rehearsing before you spoke. Running through different versions in your head. Will this trigger him? Is this worth the risk? You softened your tone. Chose smaller words. Let them interrupt. Let them correct you. Let them finish your sentences with their version of what you meant. Eventually, you only spoke when it felt safe. And then, gradually, you stopped speaking at all. That's not maturity. That's not "picking your battles." That's survival.

A survivor told me she realised she'd become silent at her own dinner table. "My kids were talking, he was talking, and I was just... there. Like furniture with opinions I'd forgotten how to voice."

You Called It 'Help' Because They Said It Was

"I'm just trying to help." That's what they say while dismantling your confidence, piece by piece. Your outfit? "Not flattering." Your friend? "Toxic." Your idea? "Unrealistic." Until one day you can't choose a meal without their opinion. Can't trust your own taste. Can't remember the last decision you made alone.

A woman told me her ex picked out every outfit "for her own good." She hadn't worn purple—her favourite colour—in two years. "He said it made me look sallow. Now I wear purple every day." That wasn't help. That was erosion.

Silence Isn't Peace When It's Used as Punishment

He'd go silent for hours. Sometimes days. You'd wake to him moving through the house like you didn't exist. No explanation. No warning. Just ice. At first you begged him to talk. Then you begged him to yell. Anything was better than the silence that made you invisible in your own home.

It wasn't a cooling-off period. It was psychological warfare. That kind of silence makes your body lock up. Your shoulders rise. Your breathing goes shallow. It's not calm—it's freeze. And when it happens repeatedly, your body learns to live like the war never ends.

You Felt Trapped but Didn't Know Why

Technically, you had freedom. No locked doors. No shouting. No visible chains. But you couldn't breathe. Couldn't plan anything without calculating their mood. Couldn't laugh too loud or cry too long without being "too much." You stopped being a person. You became a performance of someone who wouldn't upset them. And still, you told yourself: "It's not abuse. They never even raise their voice."

A survivor said: "He never stopped me going anywhere. He just made coming home so miserable that I stopped going out." That's not freedom. That's captivity that looks like choice.

Practical Steps

If it feels safe, jot down when you edit yourself. When you pause, reword, or soften to avoid their reaction—even tiny moments. Then write what you actually wanted to say. The real words. The full volume. Ask yourself: Does this silence feel safe or strategic? Peace feels spacious. Punishment feels suffocating. Start speaking one true sentence a day—to yourself if nowhere else. "I don't like this." "I disagree." "I want something different." Your voice needs practice being real again.

Why It Matters

You're not just tracking fear. You're recovering the voice that went underground. Every time you notice the editing, you're closer to speaking without permission. Naming strategic silence as violence stops you from confusing control with calm.

If You Remember One Thing

Abuse isn't always loud. It doesn't always bruise. Sometimes it sounds like silence that stretches for days. Sometimes it looks like "helpful" criticism that shrinks your world. Sometimes it hides behind concern that controls every choice.

If it made you small, it was abuse. If it made you invisible in your own life, it was abuse. If your body learned to brace for nothing and everything, it was abuse.

You don't need their permission to call it what it was. You don't need witnesses to validate what only you lived through. You just need your own recognition. And now you have it.

Violence doesn't always roar. Sometimes it whispers. Sometimes it starves you with silence. But your body knew. And it was right.

1.10
They Don't Just Lie to You
They Make You Lie to Yourself

Author's Note:

This chapter names the wreckage left behind by gaslighting. If you've ever felt like you couldn't trust your memory, your instincts, or even your own voice, this is why. You weren't the problem. They needed you to question yourself. They denied what happened. Twisted your words. Dismissed your reactions. And called it communication, care, honesty—anything but what it really was. But it wasn't love. It was control. And now, you start believing yourself again.

By the Time I Agreed, I Didn't Trust Myself Either

You're standing in the bedroom doorway, hands shaking. The conversation happened twenty minutes ago. He called you "just like your mother—cold and selfish." You heard it. You felt it land in your chest like ice.

Now he's tilting his head, voice patient, like he's explaining something to a child. "I said you seemed stressed, like your mother gets sometimes. You always do this. You twist everything into an attack."

You open your mouth to argue, then close it. Maybe you did mishear. You have been stressed. Maybe you are being dramatic. He seems so certain, so calm. You're the one shaking.

"Maybe you're right," you hear yourself say. And just like that, another piece of your truth slips away. Not because he convinced you. Because you convinced yourself.

That's what gaslighting does. It recruits you as an accomplice in your own confusion. You become the one editing your memories, questioning your reactions, minimising your experiences—doing their work for them.

When You Doubt Yourself, Their Power Grows

It started small. A raised eyebrow when you stated a fact. "The restaurant closed at nine." His eyebrow lifts. "Are you sure about that?" Now you're not sure. Maybe it was ten.

A smirk when you expressed a feeling. "That hurt my feelings." The corner of her mouth twitches. Suddenly you feel childish, oversensitive. You add quickly, "But I'm probably overreacting."

Your words get rephrased until they're unrecognisable. "I need some space tonight" becomes "You're threatening to leave me." You try to correct the record, but the conversation has already moved on. You're defending yourself against words you never said.

Over time, the doubt moves in permanently. You stop trusting your gut—it must be wrong. Your memory—it must be faulty. Your own eyes—they must have missed something. The person who taught you to doubt yourself becomes your only compass. And they keep spinning you in circles.

You Start Outsourcing Your Sanity

You're at dinner with friends. Normal conversation. Nothing controversial. But as you walk to the car, you turn to him: "Was I rude just then? I feel like maybe I talked too much."

He considers, then nods slowly. "A little. But don't worry, I don't think anyone noticed."

Your stomach drops. You replay every word you said, looking for the rudeness you can't find but must be there. You apologise to him. Promise to do better. The next dinner, you barely speak.

You text your sister after every argument: "Am I being unreasonable?" You poll friends: "Is it weird that this upset me?" You google "signs you're toxic" at 2 AM, taking quiz after quiz. You've stopped checking in with yourself entirely. Their opinion has become more real than your experience.

A woman told me she kept a secret notebook rating her own behaviour each day. "Good day—didn't upset him." "Bad day—cried when he yelled." She was grading herself on how well she absorbed his abuse. She'd become her own prison guard.

They Make You Doubt Whether You're the Liar

The fight always goes the same way. You bring up something real—a broken promise, a cruel comment, a boundary crossed. They flip it immediately: "You're the manipulative one. You're twisting things. You're trying to make me the bad guy."

You start to wonder. Are you manipulative? You do get upset. You do bring up problems. Maybe you are the difficult one. You find yourself at 3 AM googling "Am I the gaslighter?" taking online quizzes, reading articles, terrified you might be the problem.

But here's what those 3 AM searches won't tell you: The person frantically questioning their own reality usually isn't the one distorting it. The one who has you questioning everything? They're never questioning anything.

A survivor told me: "I'd get so frustrated when he'd deny obvious things that I'd eventually raise my voice. Then he'd go completely calm and say, 'See? You're out of control. You're the abusive one.' I spent years thinking my frustration was proof I was toxic. But frustration is what happens when someone keeps lying to your face. It's not abuse. It's human."

You Don't Just Lose Clarity. You Lose Yourself

By the end, you don't recognise your own thoughts. Every opinion feels borrowed. Every feeling needs verification. Every memory requires a witness.

You edit yourself mid-sentence: "I think—well, maybe not—actually, never mind." You rehearse conversations in your head, then rehearse the rehearsal. You apologise reflexively: "Sorry, this is probably stupid, but..." You ask permission for preferences: "Is it okay if I like this song?"

You've become a ghost haunting your own life, so quiet even you can't hear yourself anymore. You walk on eggshells around your own thoughts. Second-guess your own feelings. Fact-check your own experiences. You're so used to shrinking your truth to fit theirs, you've forgotten what your voice sounds like without apology wrapped around it.

This isn't just confusion. It's identity theft done with a smile.

Practical Steps

Create a daily practice of stating one small truth without apology or explanation. Stand in front of the mirror each morning and say something only you can know: "I feel tired." "I like this shirt." "That made me sad." Don't justify it. Don't take it back. Just let it exist.

At night, add three simple observations from your day: "Lunch was at noon." "It rained." "I felt peaceful during that song." You're retraining your brain to trust its own observations without external confirmation.

When you catch yourself asking "Was I wrong?" stop and ask instead "What did I experience?" The first question gives your power away. The second brings it back. You felt what you felt. That's not debatable.

Why It Matters

These small acts of self-belief are how you stop cooperating with your own confusion. Every time you state a truth without apology, you take back territory they stole. Every time you trust your own experience without verification, you rebuild the bridge between you and yourself.

If You Remember One Thing

They didn't just lie to you. They trained you to lie to yourself. You learned to do their job for them—doubting your thoughts before they even had to.

That wasn't sensitivity. That was survival. Your mind was trying to make sense of senseless cruelty by assuming you must be wrong. It's what minds do when reality keeps shifting—they blame themselves for not keeping up.

But your instincts were never wrong. They were inconvenient.

Start with the smallest truth you can hold without apology: I felt what I felt. Then build from there. Your clarity is what they feared. Your clarity is what frees you.

The antidote is as small as one truth said without apology.

Part 2
Hollowed

You didn't feel like you anymore

2.1
They Pretend Not to Get It
So You Keep Explaining

Author's Note:

This is for anyone who explained themselves until their voice trembled—not from anger, but from exhaustion. When someone keeps saying, "I don't understand," what they often mean is, "I don't want to." That's not miscommunication. It's a tactic to spin confusion into a trap. This chapter helps you see the trap and step out.

The More You Explain, the More You Doubt Yourself

You said it once. Clear. Simple. "Please stop calling me names." He tilts his head, squints, and says, "I don't know what you mean. When was I angry?" Your throat tightens. You list examples. You soften your voice. By the time you finish, you're apologising for asking to be treated with decency.

That's the trick: they act confused so you keep talking—until you sound uncertain, even to yourself. They weren't confused. They knew exhaustion was more effective than argument.

They Use Misunderstanding as a Weapon, Not a Mistake

They don't ask for clarity. They ask loaded questions:
"So you think it's all my fault?"
"Are you calling me a bad person?"
They interrupt, perform wounded confusion, repeat your words out of context. You wear yourself out trying to explain. That was the goal.

A woman told me she once spent three hours trying to explain why she needed him to tell her when he'd be home late. "By the end, he had me apologising for being controlling. I just wanted to know whether to cook dinner."

Your Fear of Being Misunderstood Is the Hook They Use

You don't want to seem angry. Or cold. Or unreasonable. So you rephrase. You find gentler words. You cushion your truth with qualifiers. "I feel like maybe sometimes you might not hear what I'm trying to say." Instead of: "You ignore me."

And they still say, "I don't know what you mean. You're being vague. Can you give me specifics?" So you do. You list dates, times, exact words. They shake their head. "That's not how I remember it."

As long as you're trying to clarify, you're still engaged. Still in the room. Still under their influence. Still hoping that if you just find the right words, they'll finally understand. But they understood from the beginning. They just preferred to watch you struggle.

They Don't Want to Understand. They Want to Control the Narrative

You're not being misunderstood. You're being rewritten. They twist your "I'm hurt" into "You're saying I'm abusive." They turn your "Please listen" into "You never let me speak."

They transform your tears into manipulation, your silence into sulking, your attempts at clarity into attacks. Then they tell others their version: you're impossible to please, always upset about something, they can never do anything right. They're just trying to love you, but you make it so hard.

They don't misunderstand you. They misrepresent you. On purpose. With precision.

Exhaustion Keeps You Quiet. That's the Point

By the time you realise they've twisted everything, you're too tired to untangle it. You stop talking. Not because you've moved on, but because they've worn down your will to be heard.

A woman told me she used to send paragraphs of text trying to explain. Her partner would reply: "Wow. You're spiraling." "My words weren't clarifying anything," she said. "They were just giving her ammunition."

Practical Step

Say it once. Clearly. "I need this to stop." "That hurt me." Then stop explaining. If they claim confusion, say: "I've been clear." Or: "I don't have to explain this again."

Walk away. Don't trade your breath for their performance. Save your energy for your next true moment. If you need proof for yourself, write it down and timestamp it—not to argue, but to anchor your memory.

For many survivors, the first time they say "I've been clear" and walk away, their heart races—then slows. That's often the first moment they hear themselves again.

Why It Matters

When you stop explaining, they lose the script. Your clarity doesn't need their comprehension to be true. Their refusal to understand is what makes them unsafe—not you.

If You Remember One Thing

You weren't wrong for wanting to be heard.
They trained you to explain until your own truth felt fragile.

Silence doesn't make you cold — it makes you free.
You don't need their agreement to know what happened.

You don't need their permission to believe yourself.
Your voice is still yours, even when you choose not to spend it on them.

2.2
You Were Taught
Your Feelings Were Wrong

Author's Note:

This chapter is about what happens when you're trained to believe your feelings are wrong. If you've ever apologised for being hurt, or swallowed emotion to keep the peace, this is for you.

Shame doesn't arrive loud. It grows quietly, every time your needs were punished, dismissed, or called too much. Eventually, you stop showing your feelings at all. You stay quiet. You say sorry. And you tell yourself it's just easier that way.

This Is How They Train You to Doubt Yourself

You're crying on the stairs. He stands above you, arms folded. Silent. You've just said you felt hurt. That you didn't like how he spoke to you in front of his friends. You didn't yell. You didn't accuse. You just said it.

He exhales like you're exhausting him. Says nothing. Just that long, disappointed breath. Five minutes later, you're apologising. Not for hurting him—you didn't. For ruining his mood. For being "too sensitive." For having feelings at all.

That's what coercive control does. It bends reality so subtly, you start saying sorry for reacting like a normal human being.

They Twist Your Feelings into Proof You're the Problem

You cry, they roll their eyes. "Here we go again." You get quiet, they accuse you of sulking. "Now you're punishing me with silence." You raise your voice, they act scared. "I can't talk to you when you're like this."

Suddenly you're the one backpedalling. "Sorry. I didn't mean to overreact." But you didn't overreact. You reacted to being hurt. And instead of care, you got a performance. A staged withdrawal. An icy silence. A mirror showing you someone unrecognisable— someone difficult, dramatic, impossible to love.

A woman told me she once cried after her partner forgot their anniversary. He said, "This is why I can't do nice things for you. You always find something to be upset about." She ended up apologising for crying. On their anniversary. That he forgot.

They Frame Your Human Reaction as a Flaw

They sigh when you express need. Shake their head when you show hurt. Speak in low, careful tones like you're a child having a tantrum. Meanwhile, your voice rises—not because you're unstable, but because you're desperate to be heard.

When the conversation ends, you're the one left ashamed. They weaponise your reaction and walk away calm, like they didn't just spend an hour pushing every button they installed.

A woman told me: "I didn't even remember what I was upset about. I just knew I felt cornered." Later that night, he said, "See? You're unstable." She apologised. Not because she believed it. Because she couldn't stand the look in his eyes when she didn't.

Apologising Becomes a Survival Strategy

You say sorry because it buys peace. Because it softens their mood. Because you've learned that admitting fault—even when you've done nothing wrong—is faster than enduring another passive-aggressive interrogation.

"I'm sorry I got emotional."
"I'm sorry I ruined dinner."
"I'm sorry I'm so difficult."

It's not about truth anymore. It's about containment. About making yourself smaller so they'll stop making you feel smaller.

They Hurt You, Then Demand You Apologise

They snap at you. Dismiss you. Disrespect you. And when you show pain—real, raw, human pain—they say, "There you go again. Always playing the victim."

They create the wound, then blame you for bleeding. Make you feel guilty for having a normal response to abnormal treatment. So you doubt yourself. Twist into an apology just to restore peace.

A woman told me she apologised for "making things tense" after her partner ignored her birthday. She brought him breakfast in bed the next morning.
"That's when I realised," she said, "I was nurturing the person who kept erasing me."

Practical Steps

Notice when you apologise. Write it down. Ask yourself: Was I apologising for feeling, or for causing actual harm?

If it's for feeling, stop. Breathe. Replace "I'm sorry" with: "I'm allowed to feel this way." Or try: "This matters to me."

When you feel the reflex to apologise for having emotions, try: "I see we're both upset." It's neutral. It doesn't hand over power.

Practice one day without apologising for your feelings. Just one. See what happens.

Why It Matters

You're retraining your nervous system to stop treating emotions as crimes. Every time you resist the false apology, you reclaim the right to feel without permission.

If You Remember One Thing

You didn't apologise because you were wrong. You apologised because you were trained to believe your feelings were too loud, too messy, too much.

Your tears weren't dramatic. Your anger wasn't intense. Your hurt wasn't oversensitive. It was all just inconvenient to someone who needed you quiet.

Your response was always human. It just didn't suit the story they were selling.

And now that you see it? You don't owe them another sorry. Not for crying. Not for speaking. Not for bleeding from wounds they kept pretending didn't exist.

Your feelings were never wrong. They were evidence. Evidence that you were being harmed. And they trained you to apologise for the proof.

2.3
They Knew What They Were Doing
They Did It Anyway

Author's Note:

This chapter is about a truth most of us resist: sometimes they knew exactly what they were doing, and they did it anyway. It's easier to call it a mistake, a misunderstanding, a bad day. The alternative feels like accusing someone you loved of deliberate cruelty. But some people hurt on purpose. They see the damage. They hear the pain. And they keep going.

If you've held onto the hope that it was all confusion, that's human. This chapter is for when that hope begins to crack — when you glimpse the possibility that the harm was chosen, not accidental. You don't have to rage at this truth. You just need to know you're allowed to see it.

He Tested the Same Spot. On Purpose

You're at his mother's house for Sunday dinner. You've told him three times: "Please don't bring up my job situation in front of your family." His mum asks how work is going. He grins. "Oh, she's still figuring things out. Aren't you, love? Still looking for something that... fits." He emphasises "fits," pauses, smiles without his eyes—the exact cadence of the dig.

Your face burns. Not from embarrassment. From recognition. He knows exactly what he's doing. Same topic. Same tone. Same wound. You don't keep hitting the same nerve by accident.

A woman told me her partner would "accidentally" mention her weight at every family gathering, despite her begging him not to. "He'd say, 'Oh, did I say that out loud?' But the smirk gave him away. He enjoyed watching me shrink."

They Didn't Forget. They Wanted to Hurt You Again

You told them what mattered. What hurt. What boundaries you needed.
"Please don't joke about my past."
"Please don't share that story."
"Please don't bring that up in public."

And they did it anyway. Then acted surprised. "Oh, I forgot you were sensitive about that." But they didn't forget. Forgetting doesn't come with a grin. Forgetting doesn't target the same wound repeatedly. They remembered. They just gave themselves permission to ignore what you'd asked.

Because respecting your request would mean changing their behaviour. And change was never the plan.

They Reframed. On Purpose

You say, "That really hurt me." They reply, "You're always twisting things." Suddenly you're not expressing pain—you're defending your sanity. The conversation flips from your hurt to their victimhood. That's not confusion. That's strategy. They understood you perfectly. Clear communication threatened their control, so they had to dismantle your clarity.

A woman told me her ex would beg for honesty, then explode when she provided it. After enough explosions, she started lying to keep peace. Then he called her dishonest. "He didn't misunderstand me," she said. "He trained me to be afraid of the truth."

They Meant to Keep You Off Balance

You said no. They pushed. You set a boundary. They called it cruel. You explained your needs. They called you needy. Then said, "I was just trying to help." But their help always came with a cost. A dig. A reminder of your failures. A subtle message that you couldn't manage without them. You paid for their "help" with your confidence. Your autonomy. Your sense of self. Until even your boundaries came with apologies attached.

They Did It on Purpose Because It Worked

Every time you forgave without consequence, they did it again.
Every time you explained instead of enforcing, they pushed further.
Every time you softened your boundary, they took more.

This wasn't trial and error. It was calculated escalation—they tested, learned, and pushed until you bowed. You learned to tolerate it because tolerating kept you safer in the moment. Not because you were weak, but because they made resistance exhausting.

A survivor told me: "I kept thinking if I just explained it better, he'd understand. It took me years to realise—he understood perfectly. My explanations were just showing him how much I'd endure." Another said: "He watched me shrink, smiled, and kept doing it—and I kept apologising for even noticing."

Practical Step

Start tracking what "help" actually feels like in your body. Notice the signals—your chest tightening, your stomach dropping, your shoulders curling in.

Ask yourself: Did I feel supported, or shamed? Safe, or small? Did my body relax, or brace?

Write a single word beside each instance—"safe" or "small." Over time, you'll see the pattern.

Why It Matters

Because abusers and coercive controllers use "good intent" as cover for control. They'll insist they were helping while your body was screaming otherwise.

You're allowed to measure actions by their impact—not their excuses.
And if the impact is repeated harm, that's the truth that counts.

If You Remember One Thing

They timed their jabs to see you unravel—small comments that made your cheeks burn, questions meant to trip you up in front of friends. They watched the colour drain from your face and smiled at how it made you move slower, smaller.

They pushed boundaries to see how far you'd go to keep the peace—and took pleasure when you gave in.

They engineered the stress. They measured your collapse. They treated you like a game piece.

Here's what changes when you finally see it: you stop trying to decode kindness from cruelty.

You stop searching for the magic words that would have made them care. You stop replaying every conversation to find the version of yourself that would have been "enough."

Because there was never a right way to ask. Never a misunderstanding to clear up. Never a version of you they intended to love.

It wasn't your failure to explain. It wasn't your reactions. It wasn't you.

They understood perfectly—and they chose to hurt you. That knowing is relief. Not instant, but real. The certainty that what happened was deliberate gives you ground to stop fixing what they broke.

It was never about what you did wrong. It was always about what they chose to do.

2.4
They Pushed You Until You Snapped Then Called You Crazy

Author's Note:

This chapter is about how abusers deliberately provoke you into breaking, then use your reaction as evidence you're the problem. If you've ever walked away wondering how you became the villain in your own story, this will help you recognise what really happened: you were set up.

They Keep Their Cool So They Can Frame Your Fire

You're at the kitchen counter, knuckles white from gripping the worktop. The tears come—hot, angry, years of held-back words finally spilling out. You try to explain why something hurt. Why it matters. Why you need him to see you.

He leans in the doorway, arms crossed, watching you unravel like it's light entertainment. No flinch. No apology. That slight tilt of the head—he's waiting for the moment you break.

When you finally sob and lose your footing, he says, calm as anything, "See? This is exactly what I mean. You're completely irrational."

And then it clicks—this wasn't an argument. It was a trap. He wasn't trying to understand. He was timing the moment you'd crack.

They Engineer Your Explosion

The drumroll isn't loud. It's patient and surgical—a whisper, a casual erase, a repeated small cut. He denies a conversation you clearly had. He reframes a cutting remark as "banter." He interrupts until you stop finishing sentences. Alone, each move looks minor—but together they add up.

When the glass finally tips and you break, he switches to stage mode: measured voice, concerned face, lines that sound reasonable to anyone listening—"I'm trying to have a conversation," "Why are you getting so upset?" That performance is his alibi. It hides the slow work that pushed you there.

Later he comforts in public, recommends "getting help," and tells family you're volatile—never mentioning the years of small, intentional provocation that led to that moment.

They Stay Calm to Look Like the Victim

Watch the performance: rational tone, quiet disappointment, the small shake of the head that says, "I'm trying so hard." They make themselves the reasonable one while your distress reads as instability.

A man told me his wife used to whisper barbs under her breath at dinners—"You're pathetic, look at them"—and when he left the table upset she turned to the family with concern: "He's been so volatile lately." No one saw the whisper. Everyone saw the outburst.

The Aftermath Is Part of the Plan

After you snap, the script flips. Sudden calm. "It's okay, come here." Or concern turned tactic: "I think you need help. This isn't normal." They'll tell others they tried to help, that you keep exploding, that you're unpredictable.

What they'll omit is the slow, methodical erosion—the deliberate pushing until you had nowhere left to go but through.

Practical Step

Build an exit sentence. Something calm, short, and repeatable, designed to pause or end the conversation without fuelling the fire.

Try:
"This isn't productive."
"I'm stepping away for now."
"We can talk later—or not."

Why It Matters

This isn't about retreat. It's about protection. You're not walking away to avoid the truth. You're walking away to keep hold of it.

If You Remember One Thing

You weren't unstable. You were being broken down on purpose.

They pushed until you cracked—then called the cracks your fault.
Now you see the hands that did the pushing.

Your quiet is no longer collapse—it's defiance.
Your pause is no longer weakness—it's power.

You don't owe them proof of your sanity.
You owe yourself the freedom to stop playing their game.

2.5
You Couldn't Plan Anything Without Them Changing It

Author's Note:

This chapter is for anyone who stopped making plans because they always got derailed. If you ever felt like your life was built on shifting sand—couldn't maintain a routine, couldn't anticipate joy, because they'd always interrupt, cancel, "forget," or manufacture chaos—this explains why.

It wasn't absent-mindedness. It was coercive control. And it was designed to keep you uncertain, off-balance, and dependent.

It Wasn't Just the Holidays They Ruined. It Was Your Ability to Hope

You're standing in the bedroom, wearing the dress you bought specifically for tonight. The one that made you feel like maybe, just maybe, you could still be that person who gets excited about things. Anniversary dinner. The restaurant where you had your first date. You'd booked it three weeks ago, confirmed it yesterday, even texted him a reminder this morning.

He walks in, sees you dressed up, and his face does that thing—that practiced confusion that makes your stomach drop. "Oh. That's tonight?"

The pause is staged. He wants you to feel the drop.

"Shit, babe. I told Mark I'd watch the match with him. You should've reminded me properly."

The reservation confirmation is still in his inbox. Right under the betting app notifications that ping every hour. But somehow you're the one apologising, calling the restaurant, cancelling the babysitter, ordering takeaway that sits cold on the counter while he cheers at the television.

A woman told me she stopped celebrating her birthday after her husband "forgot" three years running. "The third year," she said, "I saw him delete the calendar reminder from his phone the day before. That's when I knew—he didn't forget. He just enjoyed watching me stop expecting things."

They Created Chaos to Keep Control

Watch the pattern. It's never the small things they sabotage. It's the job interview. The family visit. The therapy appointment. The friend's wedding. The moments that matter most.

The car suddenly needs repairs the day of your interview. They're "too ill" to watch the kids during your course. They pick a fight so explosive the morning of the wedding that you're too drained to face people. And always, always, there's plausible deniability.

They're not controlling—you're just "bad at communicating." They're not sabotaging—you're "expecting too much."

A man told me he used to love cooking elaborate Sunday dinners for friends. His partner would invariably invite her family over at the last minute, or develop a migraine, or start redecorating the dining room that morning.

"After two years," he said, "I stopped buying ingredients. Stopped inviting people. She'd won without ever saying 'don't cook for your friends.'"

Every Cancellation Trained You to Stop Hoping

Think about what happens after enough derailed plans. You stop making them. Not consciously at first—you just notice you're not booking things anymore. Not scheduling that coffee with your sister. Not signing up for the gym class. Not planning the holiday.

When people ask what you're doing next weekend, next month, next year, you go blank. Because planning requires believing the future is yours to shape. And they've taught you it isn't.

They Weaponised Uncertainty

The cruelest part? Sometimes they'd follow through. Just often enough to keep you hoping. They'd show up for the dinner, be charming at the party, remember the anniversary—just when you'd stopped expecting it.

These intermittent rewards are more addictive than consistency. They keep you hooked, always wondering if this time will be different.

But notice: they decided when to show up. They controlled when you got to have joy. Your happiness became something they dispensed, not something you could create.

Practical Step

Start with one small, unannounced plan just for you. A coffee shop visit. A morning walk. A film on your phone. Don't tell them. Don't ask permission. Don't negotiate the timing.

This isn't about defiance—it's about remembering that you're allowed to decide what happens in your own life.

The first time you complete a plan without interference or guilt, notice how foreign it feels. That's how long it's been since your time was yours.

Why It Matters

Because every completed plan, no matter how small, is evidence that you can trust yourself again. That the future isn't just something that happens to you—it's something you can shape.

If You Remember One Thing

They didn't ruin your plans through carelessness. They dismantled them strategically, systematically, until you stopped believing you deserved to look forward to anything.

You weren't flaky or unreliable. You were surviving in a system designed to make certainty impossible and hope dangerous.

Every cancelled plan was a brick removed from the foundation of your autonomy.

But here's what they never counted on: you remembering that plans are just decisions about the future. And decisions can be reclaimed.

Each time you follow through on a plan of your own, you build the muscle they tried to break. Each walk, each coffee, each kept promise is proof: your future is yours again.

And this time, no one gets to move the goalposts but you.

2.6
They Didn't Misunderstand You
They Needed You Confused

Author's Note:

This chapter is about what happens when your words are twisted until you barely recognise yourself in them. If you've ever tried to express a simple feeling and ended up defending your intentions, your tone, your entire character, you're not alone. They didn't misunderstand you. They needed you confused.

Because confusion kept you explaining, apologising, shrinking. And that's how they stayed in control.

He Didn't Miss the Point. He Moved It

You're sitting on the edge of the bed, hands clasped, trying to find the simplest possible words. No accusations. No blame. Just the truth.

"I need you to hear me," you say. "That's all. Just hear me."

He stares at you like you've thrown acid in his face. His whole body recoils. "Wow. So I'm a terrible listener now? After everything I do for you?"

And just like that, the conversation pivots. You're no longer talking about feeling unheard. You're defending yourself against the crime of having needs. You're listing all the times he has listened, reassuring him he's not terrible, apologising for how your words "came across."

Twenty minutes later, you're exhausted, he's the victim, and you still haven't been heard.

A woman told me she once spent three hours trying to explain why she needed help with the housework. "By the end," she said, "I was comforting him about how hard he works, promising I appreciated him, swearing I wasn't calling him lazy. The dishes? Still in the sink. But somehow I was the one apologising."

They Don't Misunderstand You. They Rewrite You

Watch how it works. Like a magician's sleight of hand. By the time you realise the trick, your reality has already disappeared.

You say: "I felt hurt when you cancelled."
They hear: "You're a terrible person who ruins everything."

You say: "Could we talk about the budget?"
They hear: "You're financially irresponsible and I don't trust you."

You say: "I need some space tonight."
They hear: "I hate you and want a divorce."

The shift is immediate. Practised. They defend against accusations you never made. They fight phantoms while you stand there, bewildered, trying to pull the conversation back to earth.

They've turned "I felt dismissed" into "You're saying I'm an abusive monster."
They've turned "Can we discuss this?" into "You're attacking me again."

And now you're not discussing the original issue. You're not even in the same conversation anymore. You're in their maze, where every corridor leads back to their victimhood.

Confusion Is the Goal, Not the Side Effect

This isn't poor communication skills. It's weaponised bewilderment. They need you confused because confusion makes you malleable. When you don't trust your own words, you stop using them. When you can't predict how they'll be twisted, you stop speaking altogether.

A man told me his wife would literally rewrite history mid-argument. "I'd say, 'You promised to pick up the kids,' and she'd say, 'I never said that. You said you'd do it. Why are you trying to gaslight me?'" He started recording conversations on his phone, not to use against her, but to reassure himself he wasn't losing his mind.

Practical Step

Keep a reality anchor. After difficult conversations, write down three things: what you actually said, what they claimed you said, and how you felt. Don't elaborate or justify— just document. Notice how your chest eases when you see your real words on the page. That's your nervous system recognising clarity. That's your body remembering truth.

Why It Matters

Because clarity is survival. Your unshaken perception is the one thing they can't afford you to keep. Each documented truth rebuilds the foundation they're trying to erode.

Your Clarity Terrifies Them

Watch what happens when you refuse to enter the maze. When you stay simple, specific, unchanging.

"I need you to hear me."
"No, I didn't say that. I said I need you to hear me."
"That's not what we're discussing. We're discussing how I feel unheard."
"I'm not attacking you. I'm sharing my experience."

They'll escalate. They'll try every exit ramp—tears, rage, sulking, deflection. But when you hold your line, something shifts. The fog lifts. The game becomes visible. You see the strings they've been pulling all along.

A woman told me the day she stopped explaining herself was the day everything changed. "He said, 'You obviously think I'm a monster.' And instead of defending myself, I just said, 'I think I deserve to be heard.' He had nowhere to go with that. The whole manipulation just... collapsed."

If You Remember One Thing

They didn't misunderstand you. They understood perfectly. That's why they needed to scramble your signal, twist your words, make you doubt your own tongue.

Your confusion wasn't evidence of poor communication. It was evidence of sabotage. They needed you uncertain because your certainty threatened their control.

You weren't unclear. You weren't confusing. You weren't asking for too much. You were speaking your truth, and they couldn't bear to hear it. So they made sure you couldn't bear to speak it.

Your words meant what you meant. Your feelings were real. Your needs were valid. No twist can erase that.

Trust your voice. It was clear all along.

2.7
Death by a Thousand Yells

Author's Note:

This chapter is about shouting as a weapon—not once in stress, but as a pattern of control. If you've been yelled into silence, trained to flinch at nothing, or blamed for "making it a fight" when all you wanted was safety, this will help you name what really happened. They didn't yell because they lost control. They yelled to keep it.

Your Body Knew It Wasn't Safe

You're standing in the kitchen, holding a mug of tea that's gone cold because you've been frozen in place for twenty minutes. Waiting. Listening to his footsteps upstairs, trying to decode his mood from the weight of each step. Then it starts.

"Where the FUCK are my keys?"

Your whole body contracts. Heart hammering. Hands shaking so hard the tea sloshes over the rim. You know exactly where his keys are—on the hall table where he left them. But that doesn't matter. This isn't about keys.

He storms downstairs, face already twisted with rage. You point to the keys, voice barely a whisper: "They're right there."

"Don't fucking patronise me. You moved them. You always move my shit."

You didn't. You both know you didn't. But you're already apologising, already shrinking, already trying to make yourself smaller so there's less of you for the sound to hit.

A woman told me she could predict her husband's yelling by the way he closed the car door. "If it slammed, I had maybe thirty seconds before he'd find something—

anything—to explode about. The mail on the counter. My shoes by the door. The way I said hello. By year three, I was hiding in the bathroom when I heard his car pull up."

He Didn't Yell to Be Heard. He Yelled to Shut You Down

Think about what happens when someone yells at you. Your prefrontal cortex—the part that forms sentences, makes arguments, holds logic—goes offline. Your amygdala takes over. Fight, flight, freeze, fawn. You're not thinking anymore. You're surviving.

They know this. They use it.

You try to explain yourself. They get louder.
You try to reason. They drown you out.
You start crying. They mock the tears or yell harder.

Eventually, you stop trying to speak at all. Because what's the point? Your words can't compete with their volume. Your logic can't penetrate their rage. Your tears just fuel their fire.

And that's exactly what they wanted. Your silence.

The Yelling Rewired Your Body

It wasn't just the volume. It was the unpredictability. Tuesday's normal conversation becomes Wednesday's screaming match. The same question that got a laugh yesterday gets you berated today. You never knew which version you'd get.

So your body stayed ready. Always scanning. Always braced. Your shoulders lived near your ears. Your breath stayed shallow. Your startle response went haywire—you'd jump at doors closing, phones ringing, someone calling your name.

A man told me he still can't handle raised voices, even happy ones. "My kids get excited about something, start shouting with joy, and my body thinks I'm under attack. That's what ten years of being screamed at does. It doesn't just hurt you in the moment. It reprogrammes you."

You Started Changing Everything to Avoid the Yelling

You spoke softer, moved quieter, thought faster. You rehearsed conversations in your head, trying to find the combination of words that wouldn't trigger explosion.

You stopped having opinions. Stopped making requests. Stopped existing in any way that might provoke. You became a ghost in your own life, trying to float through without disturbing the air.

But it didn't work, did it? Because the yelling was never about what you did. It was about what it did to you.

Practical Step

Map your body's response. Next time you're somewhere safe and quiet, close your eyes and notice: Where does your body still hold that tension? Shoulders? Jaw? Chest? Put your hand there and say: "This is where the yelling lives in my body. I'm safe now. I can let it go."

Start with just noticing. You don't have to fix anything. Just acknowledge: this is what surviving all that shouting cost your nervous system. This is what you carried to stay safe.

Why It Matters

Because healing begins with recognition. Your body's hypervigilance isn't weakness—it's evidence of how hard you worked to survive. Naming the cost is the first step to reclaiming your nervous system.

You Were Never the Reason

They told you that you provoked it. That you were "impossible." That anyone would lose their temper with someone like you. They said if you just stopped being so difficult, so sensitive, so much, they wouldn't have to yell.

But here's what they never mentioned: plenty of people go their whole lives without screaming at someone they claim to love. Entire relationships exist where voices stay level even in conflict. Where disagreement doesn't mean demolition.

You weren't yelled at because you were hard to love. You were yelled at because they discovered it worked. It shut you down. It ended conversations they didn't want to have. It punished you for having needs. It kept you too destabilised to recognise what was happening.

A woman told me the day she realised the yelling was strategic was the day everything shifted. "I watched him scream at me for twenty minutes about a grocery receipt. Then his phone rang, and he answered it perfectly calm, laughing with his friend like nothing had happened. He could control it. He just chose not to with me."

If You Remember One Thing

The yelling wasn't about anger. It was about power. They didn't raise their voice because they lost control—they raised it to take control. Every shout was designed to make you smaller, quieter, less likely to challenge them.

You survived death by a thousand yells. Each one chipped away at your sense of safety, your right to speak, your belief that you deserved gentleness. But you're still here. Still finding your voice. Still learning that love doesn't sound like shouting.

Your body remembers the yelling. But it's also learning something new: what safety feels like. What calm sounds like. What it means to speak without bracing for impact.

This is your voice now. Their power ends where your voice begins.

2.8
He Didn't Hit You. He Hit the Wall

Author's Note:

This chapter is about violence that stops just short of touching you. If you've watched things get slammed, thrown, or destroyed while being told you're overreacting because "nothing happened to you," this explains what really happened. They didn't need to hit you. They needed you to know they could.

He Didn't Need to Hit You. Reminding You Was Enough

You're sitting at the kitchen table, trying to explain why you're hurt. Your voice is steady, careful. You've practised this conversation in your head a dozen times, chosen the gentlest possible words.

Mid-sentence, he stands up so fast his chair scrapes against the floor. Your body freezes. He walks to the counter, picks up his coffee mug, and hurls it at the wall. It explodes. Coffee drips down the paint. Ceramic shards scatter across the floor. You're shaking now. Can't speak. Can't move. He turns to you, eerily calm: "See what you made me do? You always push until this happens."

Later, when you tell him you were terrified, he scoffs. "Jesus Christ, I didn't even touch you. You're so dramatic." But that's the point, isn't it? He didn't need to touch you. The wall was a proxy. The mug was a message. Your body understood perfectly: next time, it might not be the wall.

A woman told me her husband would drive recklessly when they argued—speeding, swerving, slamming brakes. "I'd beg him to slow down, and he'd laugh. 'What's wrong? I'm not hurting you.' But my body knew. Every aggressive turn was him saying: your safety is in my hands, and I can take it away whenever I want."

It Started Small. Then It Escalated

First, it was just heavy sighs when you disagreed. Then cupboard doors slammed during discussions. Then his fist hitting the table during dinner, making the plates jump. Each escalation was a test. How much would you tolerate? How quickly would you back down? How small could he make you?

You started editing yourself. Choosing safer topics. Timing conversations for when he seemed calmer. Speaking in questions instead of statements. Making yourself smaller, quieter, less likely to trigger the storm.

That's how coercive control works. Not all at once. Just enough, bit by bit, until you're navigating your own home like a minefield.

The Geography of Fear

Think about how the space changed when he got angry. The room got smaller. The air got thicker. Every object became a potential weapon—not because he'd use it, but because he'd already shown you he could. The hole in the wall. The dent in the door. The replaced lamp. These weren't accidents or losses of control. They were monuments to his rage, left there as reminders.

You learned to read the room like a survival manual. Where the exits were. Which objects were within his reach. How many steps to the bathroom where you could lock the door.

A man told me he still can't sit with his back to a door. "She never hit me, but she threw things. Plates, books, whatever was close. Ten years later, I still need to see every exit. My body remembers even when my mind tries to forget."

It Wasn't Anger. It Was Authority

Watch how selective their rage was. They could slam doors at home but never at work. They could punch walls in private but stay composed in public. They could scream at you but answer their mother's call with perfect calm. This wasn't someone who "couldn't control their temper." This was someone who knew exactly when and where to deploy it. They weren't losing control—they were taking it.

Every slammed object was a boundary violation. Every aggressive movement was them claiming more space while you shrank into less. They were teaching you that in moments of conflict, your body didn't belong to you anymore—it belonged to their mood.

Your Body Remembered Everything

Even now, you might flinch at sudden movements. Jump at loud noises. Feel your chest tighten when someone's voice gets sharp. Your nervous system learned that anger equals danger. It still protects you from threats that aren't there.

This isn't weakness. This is what happens when someone weaponises their rage around you. Your body adapted to survive in an environment where violence was always one argument away.

Practical Step

Notice where fear still lives in your body. When you hear a door slam, what happens to your shoulders? When voices get loud, where does your breath go? Put your hand on that spot and tell yourself: "That was then. This is now. I'm safe."

This isn't about forcing yourself to be okay with loud noises. It's about recognising that your startle response is evidence of what you survived, not proof that you're broken.

Why It Matters

Because violence doesn't need to touch you to traumatise you. The threat of violence— the possibility hovering in every slammed door—rewires your nervous system just as effectively as a blow.

He Knew Exactly What He Was Doing

He didn't miss. He chose the wall by your head. Your things, not his. Reckless with you in the car, never when he was alone. These were calculated demonstrations. He wanted you to see what he was capable of without being able to call it abuse. He wanted fear without fingerprints.

A woman told me the moment she understood it was deliberate: "He punched a hole in the wall during an argument. Right next to the family photo. An inch from my face in the picture. Later, he hung a new frame over the hole, but we both knew what was underneath. Every time I walked past, I remembered. That was the point."

If You Remember One Thing

They didn't hit the wall because they lost control. They hit it instead of you to maintain plausible deniability while keeping you afraid. It was violence by proxy. Terror by demonstration.

You weren't dramatic for being scared. You were responding appropriately to threat. Your body recognised violence even when it didn't touch you, because proximity to rage is its own kind of assault.

The holes in the walls weren't evidence of passion. They were warnings. The broken objects weren't accidents. They were messages. And your fear wasn't an overreaction. It was survival instinct.

You survived living next to a volcano, never knowing when it would erupt but always feeling the rumble. That takes extraordinary strength.

Now you get to learn something new: what safety feels like. What it means to disagree without destruction. What it's like to live in spaces where walls stay whole and voices stay level.

This is your peace now. No one gets to shatter it again.

2.9
It Wasn't a Joke. It Was a Message

Author's Note:

This chapter is about cruelty disguised as humour. If you've ever laughed along with something that hurt, or been told you were "too sensitive" when you flinched, this will help you see the truth: it wasn't a misunderstanding. It was humiliation dressed as a joke. And you were never wrong for feeling the sting.

They Laughed to Humiliate, Then Blamed You for Hurting

You're at dinner with friends. The conversation flows, everyone relaxed, and for a moment you forget to guard yourself. You share something—maybe an achievement at work, maybe an idea you're excited about.

He cuts in: "Oh, here we go. The expert speaks." His tone is light, playful. Everyone chuckles. You force a smile, but your throat closes.

"What?" he says, catching your expression. "Can't you take a joke? God, you're so serious all the time."

The table shifts uncomfortably. Someone changes the subject. But the damage is done. You spend the rest of dinner silent, chest tight, replaying it. Were you bragging? Being too much? Why did it hurt so badly if it was just a joke? Because it wasn't. It was a public takedown wrapped in a laugh track.

A woman told me her husband would "joke" about her cooking whenever they had guests. "Careful with that dish—she's trying to poison us again!" Everyone would laugh nervously while she stood there, holding a casserole she'd spent hours making. "After five years," she said, "I stopped cooking for anyone. I couldn't bear another punchline at my expense."

The Jokes Had Patterns

Notice what they mocked. It was never random. They targeted the things you were proud of, the things you were insecure about, the things that made you unique, the things that gave you power.

They joked about your degree when you got promoted. Your appearance when you felt confident. Your friends when you made plans without them. Your family when you sought their support. Each "joke" was precision-targeted to hit where it would hurt most, then dismissed as harmless fun.

They Got You to Erase Yourself

The cruelest part? After enough "jokes," you started doing their work for them.

You'd make fun of yourself before they could. "I know I'm terrible at this, but..."
You'd downplay achievements. "It's not a big deal, really..."
You'd apologise pre-emptively. "Sorry, I'm probably being boring..."

You learned to shrink yourself before they could shrink you. To mock yourself before they could mock you. To stay small so there was less of you to target.

A man told me he stopped playing guitar after his partner kept "joking" about his "rock star delusions" whenever he practised. "I put it in the closet one day and never took it out again. She won, and she never even had to ask me to stop."

Humiliation in Private Was Worse

At least in public, there were witnesses. In private, the mask came off completely.

"You really think you're smart, don't you?"
"That outfit? Seriously?"
"Your friends only tolerate you."
"No one else would put up with you."

Always followed by: "Relax, I'm kidding. Why are you so sensitive?" But watch their face when they said it. The slight smirk. The cold eyes. They weren't laughing with you. They were laughing at what they were doing to you.

Your Body Knew It Wasn't Funny

Think about how you felt during their "jokes." Your stomach dropped. Your face burned. Your chest went hollow. You might have felt suddenly, inexplicably, like you wanted to disappear.

That wasn't oversensitivity. That was your nervous system recognising an attack. Because humiliation is violence to the psyche. It tears at your sense of self, your right to exist fully, your belief that you deserve respect.

Your body knew you were being harmed, even when your mind was trying to convince you to laugh along.

Practical Step

Write down three "jokes" that still sting. Then rewrite them as straight statements without the humour. "You're so ditzy" becomes "I think you're stupid." "Look who finally showed up" becomes "Your presence doesn't matter." See them for what they really were: attacks disguised as entertainment.

Why It Matters

Because once you see the cruelty beneath the laughter, you can't unsee it. You stop blaming yourself for being "too sensitive" and start recognising systematic degradation.

They Needed You Small So They Could Feel Big

Humiliation wasn't a communication style. It was a control tactic. Every joke that landed, every time you laughed along while dying inside, every moment you chose silence over confrontation—they were winning.

They needed you ashamed because shame is paralysing. It makes you question yourself instead of questioning them. It makes you work harder for their approval. It makes you grateful for moments when they're simply neutral, not cruel.

A woman told me the moment she understood: "He made a 'joke' about my promotion—how I probably 'charmed' my way up. I didn't laugh. I just stared at him and said, 'That's cruel.' He scrambled, said I couldn't take a joke. But I saw it then—the panic in his eyes. He needed me to laugh. My pain was the punchline."

If You Remember One Thing

You weren't too sensitive. You were being systematically shamed through humour. Every "joke" was designed to chip away at your confidence, your voice, your sense of self.

They hid behind laughter because it gave them cover. If you objected, you were the problem—too serious, no sense of humour, always overreacting. It was the perfect crime: hurt you, then blame you for bleeding.

But those weren't jokes. They were messages. Messages that you were less than. Messages that your feelings didn't matter. Messages that your pain was entertaining.

You don't need a better sense of humour. You need distance from people who find your humiliation funny. Because real love doesn't laugh at your expense. It doesn't find entertainment in your embarrassment. It doesn't need you small to feel secure.

Your sensitivity wasn't the problem. Their cruelty was. And now you know the difference between laughter that connects and laughter that cuts.

This is your dignity returning. No one gets to joke it away again.

2.10
You Thought Needing Less
Would Make You Safer

Author's Note:

This chapter is for the version of you that tried to disappear in order to survive. If you ever lowered your voice, shrunk your needs, or told yourself "it's fine" when it wasn't—just to keep the peace, stay out of trouble, make yourself easier to love—this will help you name what really happened. You weren't being selfless. You were trying to stay safe. And that instinct deserves respect, not shame.

Needing Became Too Dangerous

You're standing in the bathroom, looking at the empty shampoo bottle you've been adding water to for three weeks. You could ask him to pick some up. You could buy it yourself. But both options feel impossible.

If you ask, he'll sigh about money, about how you "go through things so fast," about how demanding you are. If you buy it yourself, he'll check the receipt, question why you didn't get the cheaper one, make you feel guilty for spending. So you add more water. Wash your hair with basically nothing. Tell yourself it's fine.

A woman told me she went six months without buying new underwear, even though hers were falling apart. "The thought of him seeing the charge on the bank statement, having to explain why I 'needed' something so basic—it was easier to just make do. I became an expert at needing nothing."

You Trained Yourself to Disappear

Watch what happened to your wants. First, you stopped mentioning the big things—the course you wanted to take, the trip to see your sister, the hobby that required supplies.

Too much conflict. Too much negotiation. Too much risk. Then the medium things went—new clothes, haircuts, the occasional treat. You told yourself you were being practical. Frugal. Low-maintenance.

Finally, even the small things became fraught. The brand of tea you preferred. The temperature you liked the house. The music you wanted to hear. You learned to say "I don't mind" so automatically that you forgot what you actually did mind.

You became adaptable. Flexible. "Easy." But really, you were just erasing yourself, one preference at a time.

They Didn't Say No. They Made You Feel Wrong for Wanting

They never had to actually deny you things. They just made wanting anything so exhausting, so shameful, so costly that you stopped asking.

The eye roll when you mentioned something you'd like. The heavy sigh when you expressed a preference. The "must be nice" when you shared a small dream. The "you're never satisfied" when you asked for anything at all.

Each reaction taught you that having needs was selfish. That wanting things was greedy. That you were too much and should be grateful for whatever you got.

A woman told me she stopped eating breakfast because her husband would comment on "how much food costs these days" every time she made toast. "It wasn't worth the guilt. I'd rather be hungry than feel like a burden for eating."

Your Body Started Keeping Score

You thought you were keeping the peace, but your body knew better. The chronic exhaustion from never being restored. The digestive issues from swallowing your needs along with your words. The headaches from constantly calculating what was safe to want.

You developed a kind of hypervigilance around your own desires—scanning, editing, minimising before they even fully formed. Is this worth the fight? Can I live without it? What's the cost of asking?

You became an expert at deprivation, but called it being "low-maintenance."

You Convinced Yourself You Liked It That Way

This is the cruellest part: you started believing your own cover story. You weren't sacrificing—you were "simple." You weren't deprived—you were "minimalist." You weren't disappearing—you were "easy-going."

You'd tell friends you didn't care where you ate, what you watched, what you did. You'd say things like "I'm not fussy" and "Whatever's easiest" until they became your identity.

But underneath that practiced indifference was a person who once had favourites. Who once knew exactly what she wanted. Who once believed her desires mattered.

Practical Step

Write down five things you genuinely want—not need, want. Start small: a specific coffee drink, a book, a colour of towel, a song played loud. Don't edit. Don't minimise. Just write what you actually want. Then notice the voices that immediately argue why you shouldn't have those things. Those voices aren't yours. They're theirs.

Why It Matters

Because recognising that you had to trade your desires for safety is the first step to reclaiming them. Your wants weren't too much. The price of having them was.

They Benefited from Your Shrinking

Every time you needed less, they gained more. More money to spend on themselves. More space to fill with their preferences. More power in every decision because you'd removed yourself from the equation.

They'd praise your "simplicity" while benefiting from your silence. Call you "easy to please" while making you impossible to satisfy. Your shrinking wasn't a personality trait—it was a survival strategy they depended on.

A woman told me the moment she understood: "I was apologising for asking for salt at dinner. Salt. At my own table. That's when I realised how small I'd made myself. I couldn't even season my food without feeling guilty."

If You Remember One Thing

You weren't low-maintenance. You were in survival mode.

You didn't have simple tastes. You had dangerous wants.

You weren't naturally selfless. You were systematically silenced.

Every "I don't mind" was really "I can't afford to mind." Every "whatever you want" was really "my wants aren't safe here." Every "it's fine" was really "the cost of not being fine is too high."

They didn't appreciate your flexibility. They exploited it. They didn't admire your simplicity. They engineered it. They didn't love how easy you were. They loved how easy you made their life by erasing yours.

But those wants you buried? They're still there. Waiting. And now you get to dig them up, dust them off, and honour them. One preference at a time. One desire at a time. One "actually, I do mind" at a time.

This is your wanting returning. And it's not too much. It never was.

112

Part 3
Stolen

Not lost. Taken

3.1
It Looked Like a Choice. It Was Isolation

Author's Note:

This chapter is about how coercive controllers don't always isolate you with threats. Sometimes they use guilt, coldness, or just enough tension that staying connected feels too costly. If you ever let friendships fade because defending them felt exhausting, this is for you. You didn't just grow distant. You were systematically cut off. And they called it your choice.

They Didn't Forbid It. They Made It Unbearable

You're getting ready to meet your friend for lunch. Nothing special—just the monthly catch-up you've done for years. As you grab your keys, he looks up from his phone. "Again? Didn't you just see her?" That was six weeks ago. You both know it. But now you're explaining, justifying, promising you won't be long. His face doesn't change, but the temperature does. The air gets thick with unspoken displeasure.

"Whatever. Do what you want." Your stomach drops. Your fingers hover over your phone, already composing the cancellation. You can feel the weight settling in your chest—the familiar trade-off between an hour of friendship and days of punishment. The cold shoulder when you return. The snippy comments. The sudden "emergency" next time you have plans.

Your thumb shakes slightly as you type: "Something's come up. Sorry." The relief is immediate and sickening.

A woman told me she cancelled so many coffee dates that her best friend stopped asking. "She thought I didn't care anymore. But every time I tried to leave the house, he'd start listing everything I should be doing instead. Or he'd be 'hurt' that I'd rather spend time with her than him. After a while, the guilt was unbearable. It was easier to just stay home."

They Made Everyone Else Seem Dangerous

Listen to how they talked about the people you loved:
Your sister was "toxic" and "always stirring up drama."
Your best friend was "using you" and "probably talks about you behind your back."
Your colleagues were "fake" and "would throw you under the bus in a second."
Your mother was "controlling" and "never liked me anyway."

Your chest tightened each time he said it, because you felt the choice forming in the air—them or him. Every relationship you had was reframed as suspicious, unsafe, or worthless. They positioned themselves as the only one who really understood you, really had your back, really loved you despite your flaws.

And slowly—so slowly you didn't notice—you started seeing your loved ones through their lens.

The Walls They Built Were Invisible

They didn't lock you in. They made the outside world feel hostile. They made connection feel like betrayal. You stopped calling your mum because he'd sulk for days afterward—and that knot in your stomach wasn't worth hearing her voice.

You stopped texting friends because he'd read over your shoulder, twisting every word until your hands would freeze over the keyboard, unable to type what you really wanted to say. These weren't choices you made freely. They were survival calculations, each one weighing immediate safety against long-term isolation.

A man told me his partner would plan "surprises" whenever he had plans with friends. "She'd book us a romantic dinner the same night as my mate's birthday. Buy theatre tickets for when I had football. Then she'd cry about how I was choosing them over her. After a year, I had no friends left. But it looked like I was the one who'd abandoned them."

They Became Your Whole World by Making the World Feel Small

Think about how your world shrank. First, you stopped seeing people who lived far away—too complicated. Then casual acquaintances—not worth the drama. Then close friends—too much explaining. Finally, even family became fraught.

Your world got smaller and smaller until it was just you and them. And they liked it that way. Because when they're your only source of connection, leaving feels like stepping into a void.

Your Isolation Was Their Insurance Policy

Every severed relationship was a lifeline cut, another voice that might have said "this isn't normal" silenced. They knew exactly what they were doing. Abusers isolate because isolation makes you dependent. When you have nowhere else to go, you stop thinking about going.

Practical Step

Because the lie of "choice" is hardest to shake, start here: Write down five people you've lost touch with during this relationship. Next to each name, write the real reason contact stopped. Not the surface excuse—the real reason. "She made comments about how selfish my friend was until I felt guilty seeing her." "He picked fights every Sunday before family lunch until I stopped going." See the pattern. See whose choice it really was.

Why It Matters

Because when you see how deliberately you were isolated, you can stop blaming yourself for "being a bad friend." You weren't bad at relationships. You were being strategically separated from them.

The People Who Loved You Didn't Stop

Here's what they never told you: those people you "grew apart from"? Many of them still wonder what happened. They didn't understand why you pulled away. They might have been hurt, confused, even angry. But most of them would welcome you back.

The sister who stopped calling after too many cancelled plans. The friend who stopped inviting you after too many excuses. The colleague who stopped checking in after too many brush-offs. They didn't stop caring. They just stopped trying to breach walls they couldn't see.

A woman told me that two years after leaving her abusive relationship, she sent a message to her old friend group: "I'm sorry I disappeared. I was in a relationship that made it impossible to maintain friendships. I'm out now." She said, "Every single one replied within hours. They'd been waiting for me to come back."

If You Remember One Thing

You didn't choose isolation. It was engineered around you, one cancelled plan at a time, one guilty feeling at a time, one twisted comment about your loved ones at a time.

They made connection cost more than you could afford—emotionally, psychologically, sometimes physically. Every friendship that faded, every family tie that weakened, every colleague you stopped talking to—these weren't your failures. They were their victories.

But isolation isn't permanent. Those connections you lost? Many of them are still there, waiting. The world they made small? It's actually vast and full of people who would celebrate your return.

You weren't antisocial. You were under siege. And now you get to lower the drawbridge and let people back in. One text, one call, one coffee date at a time.

This is your world expanding again. And there's no one left to make you feel guilty for inhabiting it fully.

3.2
They Stole Your Confidence
One Correction at a Time

Author's Note:

This chapter is about how coercive control often starts quietly—not with shouting, but with corrections. If you were made to feel self-conscious about how you spoke, if your memories were "wrong" just often enough that you stopped sharing them, this is for you. They didn't just silence you. They trained you to silence yourself.

You Didn't Stop Talking Because You Had Nothing to Say

You're at dinner with friends, telling the story about the time you got locked out in the rain. Everyone's laughing. You're animated, hands moving, building to the funny part. Then you catch his eye across the table. That look. The slight head shake. The almost imperceptible sigh. Your voice falters mid-sentence. "Actually, it wasn't that interesting," you say, trailing off. The table goes quiet. Someone changes the subject. You spend the rest of dinner replaying every word, wondering what you got wrong this time.

Later, in the car: "You always exaggerate. It wasn't even raining that hard. And you had your keys in your pocket the whole time, remember?" You don't remember it that way. But after enough corrections, you stop trusting what you remember at all.

A woman told me she used to love telling stories. "I was the one who'd have everyone in stitches at parties. Then he started 'helping' me tell them better. Correcting details. Jumping in to 'clarify.' After two years, I'd just say, 'You tell it' whenever someone asked about something. I couldn't bear to get it wrong again."

Death by a Thousand Cuts

It wasn't one big silencing. It was systematic erosion:

The raised eyebrow when you expressed an opinion.
The "Actually…" before every correction.
The "That's not quite right" in front of your family.
The "Let me explain what she means" to your friends.

Each correction felt small, reasonable even. They were just being helpful. Accurate. Precise. But watch the pattern: they never corrected themselves with the same vigour. Their stories could be embellished. Their memories were gospel. Only yours needed editing. By dessert, you weren't tasting the food anymore—you were scanning for the next correction.

They Didn't Have to Yell to Make You Shrink

Think about how it worked. You'd share something—an idea, a memory, a feeling—and they'd dissect it. Not with anger, but with surgical precision, as if they were dissecting you under a cold light.

"That's not what happened."
"You're remembering it wrong."
"Why do you always make things so dramatic?"
"That doesn't even make sense."

Said calmly. Reasonably. Like they were doing you a favour by setting you straight. But each correction carved away a piece of your confidence until speaking felt like walking through a minefield.

A man told me his wife would wait until he was mid-conversation with others, then say sweetly, "Oh honey, you're confused again. That's not how it was." He said, "I started prefacing everything with 'I think' or 'maybe I'm wrong, but…' Eventually, I just stopped talking at social events altogether."

Your Voice Became a Liability

Your throat would tighten before you spoke, already anticipating the correction. Your shoulders would rise, bracing for the dismissal. Even your breath got shallower, as if taking up less air might make your words less wrong. You started editing yourself before they could. Rehearsing sentences in your head. Checking facts obsessively. Every opinion came wrapped in disclaimers: "This probably isn't right, but..." "I might be remembering wrong..." "Sorry if this doesn't make sense..."

You learned to speak in questions instead of statements. To make yourself smaller before they could make you disappear. The cruellest part? They'd then mock you for being indecisive. Uncertain. Lacking confidence. As if they hadn't been the one systematically destroying it.

They Rewrote Your Reality

Every correction wasn't just about facts. It was about control. When they corrected your memories, they were teaching you not to trust your own mind. When they interrupted your stories, they were claiming your experiences as theirs to edit. When they dismissed your feelings, they were telling you your inner world wasn't valid.

You weren't just being corrected. You were being rewritten.

Practical Step

Write down three things you know are true about your experience but stopped saying because they made you doubt them. Don't edit. Don't qualify. Just write them as facts: "I was scared." "It happened the way I remember." "My feelings were valid."

Read them aloud to yourself. Notice how foreign it feels to speak without disclaimers. That's how long you've been editing yourself.

Why It Matters

Because reclaiming your voice starts with trusting your own narrative again. Your memories are yours. Your experiences are valid. Your voice deserves to exist unedited.

You Weren't Coached. You Were Controlled

Here's what they never wanted you to realise: confident people don't need to constantly correct others. Secure people don't need to dominate every narrative. Loving partners don't chip away at their person's voice until it disappears.

They corrected you not because you were wrong, but because your voice was threatening. Every story you told was a story they didn't control. Every opinion you expressed was a thought they didn't plant. Every memory you shared was a reality they couldn't rewrite. So they rewrote you instead.

A woman told me the day she understood: "I was telling my therapist a story, kept stopping to correct myself, saying 'actually, maybe it wasn't like that.' She asked who told me I remembered things wrong. That's when I realised—it was always him. For five years, I'd been seeing my own life through his edits."

If You Remember One Thing

You didn't lose your voice because you had nothing valuable to say. You went quiet because they made speaking feel dangerous—not through violence, but through systematic undermining.

Every correction was a small theft. Every interruption was a tiny erasure. Every "that's not right" was a brick in the wall sealing you off from your own truth. You weren't too much. You weren't dramatic. You weren't wrong. You were being edited out of your own life, one correction at a time.

But here's what remains: your voice, waiting beneath all those years of editing. Your stories, still true despite their revisions. Your thoughts, still valid despite their dismissals.

You get to speak now without checking for permission in someone else's eyes. Without apologising before you begin. Without editing yourself into nothing. This is your voice returning. Clear. Unedited. True.

3.3
They Stole Your Right To Learn

Author's Note:

This chapter is about the abuse that isolates your mind, not just your body. If you were blocked from studying, cut off from the internet, mocked for asking questions, or made to feel small for being curious, this is for you. You weren't unmotivated or scattered. You were being kept from learning because knowledge makes people powerful. And power was the one thing they couldn't let you have.

They Didn't Just Isolate You. They Cut Off Your Mind

You're sitting at the kitchen table with your laptop, trying to research something for work. The internet drops. Again. The router's steady hum goes silent. You look up to see him standing by it, unplugged cable in his hand.

"You've been on that thing all day," he says. You haven't. It's been twenty minutes.

"I need it for work," you explain, keeping your voice level.

"Use your phone then." But he knows your data is almost gone. He controls the plan. He gets unlimited. You get two gigs a month.

The screen goes dark with a soft click. Later, when you miss the deadline because you couldn't access what you needed, he'll shake his head at your "disorganisation." When your boss questions your reliability, he'll comfort you about your "attention issues." But you both know who pulled the plug.

A woman told me she had to ask permission to use the computer in her own home. "He'd stand behind me, watching what I searched, commenting on everything. Eventually, I stopped using it unless he was out. Then he password-protected it 'for security." I had a university degree, but I couldn't access Google in my own house."

Every Question Became a Battle

You'd mention wanting to take a course. "We can't afford that," while his sports subscriptions auto-renewed monthly.

You'd talk about going back to study. "What about the kids?" while he played games every evening.

You'd share something interesting you'd read. "You believe everything you see online," while he quoted his mates as gospel.

You'd ask about attending a workshop. "You never finish anything anyway," while your half-completed projects gathered dust because he'd sabotaged every one.

Each response taught you that learning wasn't for you. That curiosity was inconvenient. That growth was selfish.

They Made Learning Feel Like Betrayal

The worst part wasn't the obvious blocking. It was the emotional punishment that followed any attempt at growth.

You'd sign up for an online course. He'd suddenly need you constantly during study time.
You'd buy a book. He'd mock you for "trying to be smart."
You'd watch educational videos. He'd complain about you "ignoring him."
You'd join a study group. He'd have an emergency every meeting night.

A man told me his wife would start crying whenever he studied for his professional development. "She'd say I was choosing my career over our family. But when I missed out on promotions, she'd criticise me for not earning enough. I couldn't win."

They Sabotaged Every Attempt

Think about what happened to your learning attempts. The application forms that mysteriously went missing. The course fees that suddenly couldn't be afforded—though his hobbies never faced budget cuts. The study materials that got "accidentally" thrown out with yesterday's newspaper. The internet that always failed ten minutes into your online class, like clockwork.

These weren't coincidences. They were calculated blocks designed to keep you exactly where you were.

Your Brain Fog Wasn't Yours

You thought you couldn't concentrate. That you weren't smart enough. That you didn't have the discipline. But how can anyone learn when study time is constantly interrupted, resources are gatekept, efforts are mocked, successes are punished, and failures get weaponised?

That fog you felt? That wasn't your limitation. That was the climate they created—hostile to growth, allergic to your expansion.

Practical Step

Write down three things you've always wanted to learn but told yourself you couldn't. Next to each, write the real reason you stopped. Not "too expensive" but "he'd mock me for wasting money." Not "too busy" but "she'd create chaos if I took time for myself." See whose voice is really saying "you can't."

Why It Matters

Because recognising intellectual sabotage as abuse is the first step to reclaiming your mind. Your curiosity wasn't the problem. Their fear of your power was.

Knowledge Was Your Exit Door and They Knew It

Every blocked website was a door they slammed shut. Every mocked question was a path they wouldn't let you take. Every sabotaged course was an escape route they sealed. They understood what education meant: independence, confidence, options. A person who can research recognises manipulation. A person who learns grows beyond control. A person with qualifications has choices. They didn't want you to have choices.

A woman told me the day she left was the day she secretly enrolled in a course using the library computer. "It wasn't even about the subject. It was about proving to myself that my mind was still mine. That I could still learn. That course gave me the confidence to know I could survive without him."

If You Remember One Thing

You weren't too scattered to learn. You were being systematically distracted.
You weren't too stupid for education. You were being told you were.
You weren't unmotivated. You were being actively sabotaged.

Every time you tried to grow, they put obstacles in your path. Every time you reached for knowledge, they slapped your hand away. Every time your mind started to expand, they found ways to shrink it back down.

But your curiosity survived. Your hunger to learn, to know, to grow—it's still there. Maybe quieter, maybe hidden, but intact.

Now you get to feed it. Without mockery. Without sabotage. Without someone pulling the plug just as you're getting somewhere.

This is your mind returning to you. Curious. Capable. Free to learn whatever it wants. Your education begins when you decide it does. Not when someone gives permission.

Start with one search. One question. One free course. Watch how it feels to learn something just because you want to.

That feeling? That's your mind coming home.

3.4
They Called It Saving. It Was Financial Abuse

Author's Note:

This chapter is about control that hides behind the language of budgeting. If you were made to feel guilty for feeding your family, buying essentials, or creating small comforts in your own home, this is for you. Because it was never about money. It was about making you feel selfish for needing anything at all.

You Weren't Struggling. You Were Being Starved

You're standing at the checkout, mentally calculating again. The trolley has the basics—bread, milk, rice, the cheapest cuts of meat. Your hands shake slightly as you pay, carefully folding the receipt into your pocket. Evidence for the weekly audit.

At home, you unpack silently, quickly, before he gets back. Hide the good coffee you bought yourself—one tiny luxury in a week of lentils and rice. Your heart pounds like you're committing a crime. One bag of decent coffee. In your own house. With money from a dual income over $250,000 a year.

A woman told me she used to photograph prices at different shops to prove she'd bought the cheapest option. "We had investment properties, savings, his car. But I had to justify buying name-brand tissues. I'd stand in the supermarket aisle, paralysed, trying to calculate which purchase would cause the least interrogation."

The Sunday Tribunal

Every Sunday, he'd spread the receipts across the dining table like evidence in a trial. Yellow highlighter in hand, reading glasses perched, the performance of careful budgeting while his own purchases went unexamined.

"Why did you buy two bottles of shampoo?"
"The kids needed new socks again?"
"This seems high for groceries."

You'd stand there, explaining. Defending. Shrinking. The shampoo was on sale—buying two saved money. The kids' feet grew. Food costs what food costs. But each explanation felt like begging. Each justification carved away another piece of your dignity.

Meanwhile, his golf membership auto-renewed. His subscriptions continued. His "essential" purchases never faced scrutiny. Only yours did. Only the money that fed the family, clothed the children, kept the house running.

He Didn't Just Control Money. He Controlled Worth

She cooked for four people and two dogs on $130 a week. Made miracles from markdown meat and yesterday's vegetables. Stretched every dollar until it screamed.

He'd look at dinner and say, "We don't need to eat like this every night."

Like this. Like sitting together at a table with a home-cooked meal was extravagance. Like feeding your family was indulgence. Like care itself was wasteful.

But it was never about the money. It was about making her feel guilty for the audacity of nurturing. For the crime of creating comfort. For the sin of believing her family deserved to eat well.

They Weaponised Necessity

Think about what they made you feel guilty for. Tampons. Medication. School supplies. Winter coats. The basics of human existence became battlegrounds.

"Do you really need that?"
"Can't you make do with what you have?"
"Seems like a waste to me."

You learned to go without rather than ask. To make do rather than explain. To suffer in silence rather than face the humiliation of justifying your needs.

A man told me his wife controlled every penny while spending freely herself. "I had holes in my work boots for a year because she said we 'couldn't afford' new ones. The same week, she bought a $300 face cream. When I pointed out the inconsistency, she said I was being financially abusive by questioning her."

The Poverty of Plenty

This is the cruelest part: you weren't poor. The money existed. It sat in accounts, in investments, in his toys and her luxuries. His new golf clubs leaning against the wall while you rationed shampoo. Her designer bags in the closet while you calculated which day-old bread was cheapest.

You lived in artificial scarcity. Manufactured lack. Deliberate deprivation in the midst of abundance. You were trained to be grateful for crumbs while watching them feast.

Practical Step

Calculate what you actually had versus what you were allowed to spend. Write the real numbers: the income, the savings, the spending on their wants. Then write what you were given for necessities. See the gap. Notice how your chest eases or tightens when you see the real numbers on the page. That's your body recognising the truth.

Why It Matters

Because financial abuse thrives in shame and confusion. They needed you confused because confusion kept you compliant. When you see the numbers clearly, you can't unsee the control. When you name it as abuse, not frugality, you begin to reclaim your worth.

You Were Never the Problem

You weren't bad with money. You were brilliant with it—making nothing stretch into something, creating abundance from artificial scarcity. You weren't wasteful. You were resourceful beyond measure.

Every meal you managed to create. Every necessity you found a way to provide. Every comfort you snuck into that hostile economy—these weren't failures of budgeting. They were acts of resistance.

A woman told me that years after leaving, she still felt guilty buying groceries. "I'd stand in the cereal aisle, heart racing, hearing his voice: 'Generic is fine. You don't need name brands.' It took me two years to buy the good cereal without feeling like a criminal."

If You Remember One Thing

They called it budgeting. You lived it as deprivation.
They called it saving. You experienced it as starvation.
They called you irresponsible while you performed financial miracles.

The receipts they scrutinised weren't really about money. They were about monitoring your autonomy. Every purchase questioned was a piece of independence denied. Every justification demanded was dignity stripped away.

But here's what remains: your ability to create abundance even in manufactured scarcity. Your skill at nurturing despite being denied resources. Your persistence in caring even when care was called wasteful.

You don't have to justify feeding your family anymore. You don't have to hide the good coffee. You don't have to apologise for believing you deserve more than scraps.

This is your economy now. Where care isn't wasteful. Where comfort isn't criminal. Where you can buy the good tissues without photographing the price.

That's not indulgence. That's freedom.

3.5
They Took Your Pay
Then Put You on an Allowance

Author's Note:

This chapter is about what happens when financial control hides behind the language of partnership. If you worked, earned, and contributed, but still had to ask for your own money, this will help you name it. They weren't protecting the budget. They were keeping the power.

You Earned It. They Controlled It

You're standing at the checkout, card declined again. The heat crawls up your neck as you fumble for the other card—the one he "allows" you to use for groceries. Behind you, someone sighs. You worked forty hours this week. Your salary went into the joint account three days ago. But here you are, putting back your daughter's fever medicine because your "allowance" won't stretch that far.

You worked. You earned. You contributed. And still, you were handed pocket money like a child. They said it made sense. "I'm better with numbers." "It's easier if I handle it." "You don't need to worry about the finances."

But they kept the rest. You never saw your full pay. Never knew what was saved, what was spent, what was hidden.

You learned not to ask.

A woman told me she discovered her partner had been moving her salary into investment accounts she couldn't access. "For our future," he said. But when she asked to see the statements, he exploded. "Don't you trust me? After everything I do for this family?"

It went into a joint account. Then it disappeared.

You weren't shown balances. You weren't part of decisions. You were given a number to live on and taught to see anything more as selfish.

When you started asking where the rest went, the tension arrived fast. The sighs. The accusations. "Why are you suddenly so obsessed with money?" So you stopped asking.

They Gave You Just Enough to Stay. Never Enough to Go

You weren't just being controlled. You were being trapped.

A survivor told me, "He'd give me $100 a week for everything—petrol, kids' clothes, food. But he bought himself a new watch that cost thousands. When I pointed out the imbalance, he said I was being materialistic."

Another woman described sitting in her car after work, counting coins from the cupholder, trying to figure out if she had enough for petrol to get home. The cold spread through her chest as she realised: she couldn't leave him even if she wanted to. She couldn't afford a tank of petrol, let alone a deposit on a flat.

They calculated it perfectly—just enough to function, to meet their standards, to not complain too loudly. But never enough to save. Never enough for independence. Never enough for that first night somewhere safe.

Because freedom meant options. And options meant you might leave.

Practical Step

If you can safely do so, start documenting everything. Screenshot bank statements. Photo receipts. Keep a hidden record of what you earn versus what you're "allowed" to access.

Even if you can't keep records, notice how your body reacts when you have to ask for basics. That knot in your stomach when you need new work shoes. That tightness in your throat asking for petrol money. That tension isn't irresponsibility. It's evidence you're being controlled.

Why It Matters

Because financial abuse is still abuse. Because you weren't bad with money—you just weren't allowed to have any. Because recognising this pattern breaks the shame of feeling "irresponsible" when you were actually being systematically impoverished.

Being Paid Isn't the Same as Being Free

They praised your work ethic—until it gave you power. Then they diminished you. Rerouted your earnings. Reframed basic autonomy as something you hadn't earned.

This wasn't financial planning. It was a cage built from your own labour.

You worked full-time and asked permission to buy shampoo. You contributed equally and got an allowance. You built the wealth they controlled.

If You Remember One Thing

They didn't manage your money. They stole your autonomy.

You weren't irresponsible. You weren't wasteful. You were systematically denied access to resources you earned.

That gap between what you made and what you were allowed to touch? That was the price of your captivity. Calculated to keep you dependent, dressed up as care.

You worked. You earned. You contributed. That was never pocket money. That was freedom.

And now? You get to take it back.

3.6
They Said It Was Ours, Then Made It Theirs

Author's Note:

This chapter is about the progression from "partnership" to exclusion. If you were told that pooling resources was smart, that joint accounts meant building a future together, but then found yourself locked out of your own financial life, this will help you name it.

They didn't just control the money. They controlled access, information and decisions. And they counted on your trust to build a system that kept you out.

They Framed It as Partnership. It Was Ownership

You're sitting at the kitchen table, pen in hand, as he slides another form across to you. "Just sign here," he says, his finger tapping the line. "It's for our savings account. Better interest rate." You start to read, but he's already pulling it back. "Trust me, love. I've gone through it all. You don't need to worry about the details."

They sold it as common sense: joint accounts, pooled savings, a shared future.

But once your income hit that account, you never saw it again. You never saw balances. You never made the calls. You got a spreadsheet you weren't allowed to open. They managed everything and made sure you managed nothing.

You Weren't Asked. You Were Handled

A woman told me she found a stack of loan documents in her husband's desk drawer—all with her signature. "I don't remember signing these," she said. He laughed. "Of course you did. Last year, remember? For the investment property?"

But she didn't remember. Because he'd slipped them into a pile of "routine paperwork" while she was cooking dinner, rushing her through with "Just the usual stuff, nothing important."

They used your name to open accounts. Used your signature on forms you weren't allowed to read properly. And when you asked questions? They waved you off. Got irritated. Changed the subject. Made you feel stupid for not understanding "basic finance."

So you stopped asking, because it was easier than being made to feel paranoid or difficult.

The Mailbox Was Locked. So Was Your Life

You're standing at the letterbox again, that familiar knot forming in your stomach. The cold metal feels like a vault; his key is the password to your life. He carries it everywhere—to work, on trips, even to the corner shop. "I'll check it when I get home," he always says. But some days he doesn't. Some days the mail vanishes into his office, and the house feels different—heavier—with secrets you're not allowed to know.

A woman told me her partner installed a locking mailbox "for security." But she was never given a key. Everything went through him first—bank statements, tax documents, medical bills, legal notices. Even her own payslips.

"I'd ask about our finances," she said, "and he'd say everything was fine, not to worry. But I could see the stress in his jaw when he thought I wasn't looking. I knew something was wrong, but I had no way to find out what."

This wasn't about mail. It was about keeping you blind.

Practical Step

Make a list of any financial decision you were told was "for both of us." Then ask yourself:
Did I understand it fully?

Did I agree to it freely?
Did I have equal say?
Did I see the outcome?

If not, you weren't included. You were handled. Start requesting copies of everything with your name on it—even old documents. If it's not safe to do this openly, document what you can discreetly or seek help from a financial counsellor who understands abuse. Your right to know doesn't require their permission.

If you suspect documents were signed in your name without your consent, contact a solicitor or local domestic abuse service—they can advise on freezing accounts or retrieving records safely.

Why It Matters

Because financial abuse doesn't always show up in arguments. It shows up in signatures you don't remember. In accounts you can't access. In documents you've never seen. In vague answers that never quite add up.

Recognising this pattern breaks the gaslighting that you're "bad with money" or "too anxious about finances." You weren't anxious—you were deliberately kept uninformed.

When "Our Future" Means "My Assets"

They don't start with fine print. They start with dreams.

Talk of "our home." "Our investments." "Our security."

They make paperwork sound like partnership and joint accounts sound like commitment. You want to believe it. Of course you do. Because who questions the person who keeps saying "we"?

A woman told me her partner was obsessed with property investment. "It's our future," he'd say, spreading out glossy brochures. She trusted him. Signed what he asked. Didn't read the fine print—he said lawyers were expensive and unnecessary between partners who trusted each other.

After the relationship ended, she discovered she was listed as a guarantor, not a co-owner. He'd used her income for deposits, her name for loans, and made sure she had no legal claim to any of it. She realised every deposit built on her labour; every loan carried her name like a chain.

"I built wealth with him," she said, "and walked away with nothing. Not because I didn't contribute, but because I was never meant to own anything."

If You Remember One Thing

They didn't just control the money. They controlled the truth about it.

The access. The information. The paper trail. And they counted on your trust to keep you asking fewer questions, not more.

But you've done the maths now. You've seen the pattern. And the moment you started demanding transparency, you began taking your power back.

You were locked out of decisions about your own life. But now? Now you get to know everything.

No more signatures without reading. No more accounts without access. No more confusion dressed up as protection.

You weren't paranoid. You were being played.

Now you hold your own keys.

3.7
They Made You
Ask Permission for Everything

Author's Note:

This chapter is about the slow erosion of your right to decide. If you ever found yourself asking permission for things that should have been yours to choose—what to buy, where to go, who to see, what to eat—this will help you name it.

They didn't just control the big decisions. They trained you to hand over the small ones, until asking permission became automatic and your autonomy disappeared completely.

It Started with "Just Checking"

You're standing in the kitchen, mobile in hand, thumb hovering over your sister's number. "I'm just going to call Emma," you say, already bracing yourself.

"Now?" He doesn't look up from his laptop. "What for?"

"Just to catch up."

"Didn't you talk to her last week?" His tone is mild, but you recognise the undertone. The one that means this will become a thing if you push it.

"I'll keep it quick," you hear yourself bargaining.

He sighs. Just enough to let you know you're being difficult. "If you really need to."

You put the phone down. It's easier.

It started small: "Just checking" your plans, "just wondering" where you were going, "just curious" who you'd be with. It felt like caring. Like partnership. Like someone who wanted to be involved. But checking became asking. And asking became waiting. And waiting became permission. Until you couldn't buy a coffee without wondering if you should.

You Weren't Being Considerate. You Were Being Conditioned

They made it seem reasonable. "We should discuss big purchases." "I just like to know where you are." "It's only fair to check with me first." But "big purchases" became anything over $100. Then anything over $50. Then a coffee on your lunch break.

A woman told me she once stood in the beauty store for twenty minutes, holding a $8 lipstick, texting her partner to ask if she could buy it. "He said we needed to save money," she explained. "But that same week, he spent $400 on golf clubs without mentioning it."

"Checking" became reporting. Your whereabouts. Your timeline. Your receipts. You learned to run everything past them—easier than surviving the interrogation when you didn't.

They Made Independence Feel Like Betrayal

You bought new work shoes without asking. They sulked for three days. You made lunch plans without checking. They acted wounded. "I guess I don't matter." You decided to visit your mum. They called it thoughtless. "You never consider how this affects me."

Every act of independence became evidence that you didn't care about them. That you were selfish. Reckless. Cruel. So you started asking. Not because you needed guidance. But because you needed peace.

A woman told me she had to ask permission to use the car to visit her dying father. Her partner would sigh dramatically: "I suppose, if you really have to. Though it's inconvenient for me."

"I started lying about where I was going," she said. "Doctor's appointment instead of Dad's house. Because the guilt was unbearable. Then I realised—he knew exactly what he was doing. The guilt was the point."

Practical Step

Make a quick list of five things you now ask permission for that you used to decide freely—having a bath, calling a friend, buying groceries, going to bed, having a snack. Then ask: When did this change? Who taught you that these basic needs required approval?

If it isn't safe to write, just notice. Each time you type "Is it okay if I..." for something that should be yours to decide, pause. Feel what that request costs you.

Why It Matters

Because recognising where your autonomy went helps you understand it was taken, not lost. You didn't become indecisive. You were trained to doubt your right to decide.

They Wanted Control. Not Consultation

Real partnership involves discussion. Mutual input. Respect for individual choice. But this wasn't consultation. This was control dressed as consideration.

When you asked permission, they didn't just say yes or no. They made you justify. Explain. Defend. Prove you deserved it. Every choice became a negotiation where they held all the power.

A survivor told me, "I had to present a business case for why I needed new underwear. Mine were falling apart, but I had to justify the expense, show him the holes, explain why I couldn't wait another month. For knickers. In my own house. With my own salary."

You Became a Child in Your Own Life

You asked if you could: Buy milk. Ring your mum. Take a shower. Read before bed. Have a biscuit. Things adults don't ask permission for. Things you decided freely before you met them. But somewhere along the way, you handed over your right to choose and called it compromise. You weren't being respectful. You were being erased.

A woman told me the moment she knew how far it had gone: "I was standing in my own kitchen, thirsty, holding an empty glass, waiting for him to finish his phone call so I could ask if I could have some water. In my own house. From my own tap."

The glass felt cold in her hand. She didn't even pour it. Just stood there—waiting for permission to drink.

If You Remember One Thing

You didn't lose your ability to decide. It was taken from you, one "just checking" at a time.

They trained you to seek approval by making independence costly. Every unsanctioned choice triggered consequences—sulking, accusations, punishment dressed as hurt feelings.

They turned your autonomy into something you had to earn, rather than something you inherently owned.

But your choices were always yours to make. Your decisions always yours to own. Your life always yours to live.

No one—no matter how much they claim to love you—gets to turn you into a child who needs permission to exist.

You're an adult. You get to decide.
You always could. And now, you will.

3.8
It Wasn't About Waste. It Was About Control

Author's Note:

This chapter is about the way abusers turn the smallest details of daily life into arenas of control. If you were made to account for crumbs, monitored over leftovers, or treated like a criminal for wasting a teaspoon of food, this will help you see the truth.

It was never about thrift. It was about keeping you under constant surveillance, even in your own kitchen.

Every Meal Was Another Test

You're standing at the sink, dinner plate in hand. Three peas stuck to ceramic. A smear of sauce. Your shoulders tighten before you've even turned on the tap—muscle memory of being watched.

"What are you doing?" His voice cuts across the kitchen.

"Just washing up."

"There's still food on that plate."

You look down. The sauce is barely visible. The peas are cold, congealed. "It's nothing, just scraps—"

"It's waste." He's beside you now, taking the plate from your hands, scraping those three peas into a container the size of a matchbox. "We don't throw away food in this house."

The inspection ritual began. Not asking permission—demanding proof you hadn't failed today's test.

You learned to anticipate the surveillance. Never scrape too early. Never rinse before he'd examined the evidence. Because those three peas weren't food anymore. They were a verdict on your character.

This Wasn't About Leftovers. It Was About Surveillance

It's easy to laugh at years later. To call it quirky. "He was particular about food waste."

But it wasn't funny at the time. It was exhausting.

A woman told me she used to save teaspoons of food after every meal. Tiny portions in tiny containers, stacked in the fridge like evidence of her compliance. "I never ate them," she said. "They'd go mouldy and I'd throw them out secretly, terrified he'd check the bin."

Because it wasn't about food. It was about being watched. Measured. Found wanting. Your actions weren't your own. Even the kitchen bench became a courtroom, every plate evidence that could be used against you.

And every time you "failed," you weren't just wrong. You were selfish. Wasteful. Ungrateful. Not for big things. For crumbs.

Control Disguised as Frugality Is Still Control

They said it was about saving money. About not being wasteful.

But you watched them leave the car running for twenty minutes while they "just popped in somewhere." This wasn't about thrift. It was about power.

A survivor told me, "He'd rage about a tablespoon of pasta, but spent hundreds on gadgets he never used. The waste was never the point. The inspection was."

They weren't saving food. They were stockpiling control, one humiliating examination at a time.

And the more absurd it got, the more ridiculous you felt for complying—exactly how they wanted you to feel. Because shame about saving three peas is harder to explain than a bruise.

Everything had to pass through their scrutiny. Every crumb catalogued. Every spoonful judged. Not because it mattered—because watching you perform compliance mattered.

You Were Conditioned to Police Yourself

Eventually, the surveillance moved inside you. Your hands performed the ritual automatically—scraping, saving, storing. Matchbox containers of nothing. Clingfilm over a spoonful of sauce.

You became your own inspector, stricter than they ever were. Because if you caught yourself first, maybe they wouldn't need to.

That's what coercive control does. It installs the watcher inside your head. You patrol yourself so perfectly that they can sit back and watch you perform the imprisonment they designed.

A woman told me she still can't throw food away, years after leaving. "I stand at my own bin, holding a crust of bread, and I hear his voice: 'Do you think we're made of money?' I have to remind myself—this is my kitchen now. My bread. My choice."

Practical Step

Find something small and stale in your kitchen right now—a crust of bread, a wilted lettuce leaf, three grains of rice. Hold it over the bin. Feel any tension that rises.

Then throw it away. Deliberately. Without apology. Say this out loud as it falls: "That wasn't about waste. That was about control."

This is your kitchen now. Your bin. Your choice.

Why It Matters

Because recognising surveillance disguised as thrift helps you understand why you still feel watched in your own home. These weren't household rules. They were inspection rituals designed to keep you perpetually monitored.

If You Remember One Thing

This wasn't about leftovers. This was about making sure you never felt free, not even in your own kitchen.

They didn't want efficiency. They wanted submission. And they got it, not through violence, but through tiny punishments layered so quietly you didn't even realise how much you were shrinking to avoid them.

But now you get to throw things away. You get to waste things. You get to leave a plate in the sink without fearing inspection.

Your worth isn't measured in how many scraps you saved to avoid a lecture. It's measured in how you've survived someone who made you question every spoonful.

Those teaspoons of gravy you saved? They weren't proof you were frugal.

They were proof you were afraid.

And now? Now you get to stop being afraid of crumbs.

3.9
They Stole What Made You You

Author's Note:

This chapter is about the slow theft of your uniqueness. If you ever caught yourself saying, "I used to be more..." More bold. More creative. More curious. More you, but now you're not sure where that person went, this is for you.

Because coercive control doesn't just strip away your time or money. It dismantles your self—on purpose. One small edit at a time, until you hardly recognise who you've become.

They Fell in Love with What They Planned to Erase

You're getting ready for dinner with friends—the ones you still see. You pull out that red dress, the one that used to make you feel electric. Your hand hovers over it, then moves to the grey one instead. His voice is already in your head: "Bit much, don't you think?"

You weren't always grey.

At the start, they adored everything vivid about you. Your laugh that filled rooms. Your stories that went on tangents. The way you danced in the kitchen while cooking.

"You're not like other people," they said. "You're magic."

And then, slowly, they started editing you.

"Do you have to laugh so loud?" "That story went on a bit." "You're embarrassing yourself dancing like that."

They fell in love with your light, then spent years teaching you to turn it off.

Because they didn't love you. They loved having exclusive access to what they couldn't create themselves. And once they had it, they set about destroying it.

You Were Moulded to Meet Their Needs

A woman told me she used to paint. "Not professionally," she said, "just for joy." Her partner would stand behind her while she worked, commenting. "That colour's a bit strong." "The perspective's off." "Why waste time on hobbies?"

She stopped painting. Then she stopped humming while she cooked. Stopped wearing her grandmother's vintage jewellery. Stopped everything that made her particular.

"I thought I was growing up," she said. "Becoming more mature. But I was just disappearing."

You adjusted to survive. Changed how you laughed—quieter, less often. Stopped singing in the shower. Stopped wearing bright colours. Stopped speaking up in groups.

Because being yourself started getting punished. You became easier to manage by becoming harder to recognise. Even to yourself.

You Weren't Being Loved. You Were Being Tamed

They studied you like a project that needed fixing. Not to understand you—to reshape you.

Every quirk became a flaw to correct. Every passion became "obsessive." Every enthusiasm became "too much."

They watched you constantly. Monitoring which version of you appeared, rewarding compliance, punishing authenticity.

A survivor told me, "He'd say things like 'You were so bubbly when we met—it was exhausting.' But he chose me because I was bubbly. Then he spent five years making me apologise for it."

The more predictable you became, the safer they felt. The smaller you got, the bigger they looked by comparison.

Practical Step

List three things you used to do that made you feel fully yourself. That red lipstick you stopped wearing. That music you stopped playing. That hobby you "outgrew."

Then ask: When did I stop? Who made it feel wrong?

Try one of them this week. Just one. Feel how foreign it feels to be yourself again. That foreignness is proof of theft.

Why It Matters

Because you didn't "lose yourself" out of weakness. You were deliberately stripped of yourself by someone who couldn't tolerate your fullness. That's not your failure. That's their theft.

Naming what was taken is the first step in reclaiming it.

They Muted You in a World Meant for Volume

A woman told me she found a photo from before the relationship. "I didn't recognise myself," she said. "Not because I looked younger. Because I looked alive. My clothes had patterns. My face had expression. I was wearing red lipstick."

She held that photo and wept. Not for who she was. For who she'd been trained to stop being.

"I went to my wardrobe after that," she said. "Everything was beige, grey, black. Safe colours. Invisible colours. I'd dressed myself for years to avoid his comments."

That's what they do. They don't just dim your light. They convince you that brightness itself is the problem.

If You Remember One Thing

They didn't just take your freedom. They tried to take your essence.
Your style. Your spark. Your particular way of being human.

What they once praised became what they resented. Not because you changed—
because your light reminded them of their own darkness.

They wanted you muted because your colour exposed their greyness. They wanted you small because your fullness revealed their emptiness.

But here's what they never understood: You can't permanently erase someone's nature. You can suppress it, shame it, bury it. But it's still there, waiting.

You don't owe them the dimmed version they created. You don't owe anyone your smallness.

You owe yourself a return to whatever made you feel electric.

And this time? You keep it. You protect it. You wear it loud.
That red dress? That loud laugh? That "too much" personality?

That's not excessive. That's you.
And this time, no one gets to dim it.

3.10
They Took Everything and Gave Nothing Back

Author's Note:

This chapter is about the deep imbalance at the heart of coercive control. If you ever gave everything—energy, empathy, effort—and got silence, criticism, or control in return, this will help you name it. You weren't asking for too much. You were asking for something they never planned to give.

The Second You Had Needs, It Was Over

You're sitting on the edge of the bed, exhausted. You've spent three hours listening to his problems with his boss, his mother, his day. Your neck aches from nodding. Your throat is dry from reassuring.

"I need to talk about something," you say quietly. His face changes instantly. "Here we go. It's always something with you." "I just need—"

"You need, you need. What about what I need? I've had a terrible day and you're trying to start something."

He wanted control over everything. What you wore. What you said. How you looked at him. How you looked at other people. But the second you asked for anything back—respect, honesty, a moment of care—he collapsed into accusations. You were "too much." You were "never satisfied."

You watched him take your energy, your patience, your compassion—then rage when you asked for a crumb in return. Like a child hoarding toys they won't share, furious when asked to give one back.

And you were supposed to call that love.

They Want Loyalty. They Don't Offer Safety

You cancelled plans to be there when they were upset. They forgot your birthday. You showed up with soup when they were sick. They rolled their eyes when you had a migraine. You remembered every detail they shared. They couldn't recall your best friend's name.

A woman told me she once drove two hours in a storm because her partner said it was an emergency. When she arrived, he wanted her to pick up his dry cleaning. "But when my dad was in hospital," she said, "he couldn't even send a text."

You were expected to be steady, forgiving, endlessly available. While they disappeared, deflected, rewrote every story to make you the villain. You gave them your trust. They gave you conditions. And when you finally asked, "What am I getting back?" they acted like you'd just committed treason.

They Want Control But No Accountability

You try to set a boundary. "Please don't shout at me." "I'm not shouting! You're too sensitive." You say, "This isn't okay." "You're being dramatic." And when they cross a line? "You misunderstood." "You're twisting things." "That's not what happened."

They want the power of making all decisions but the freedom to never be questioned. Authority without accountability. Dominance without duty.

A woman told me her ex dictated the thermostat temperature setting, the groceries, even her work hours. But when she pointed out how controlling it was, he exploded: "Not everything's about you!"

"That was the moment I understood," she said. "He needed to be king, but the kingdom could never have rules that applied to him."

It wasn't just about what they refused to be accountable for. It was about what they dumped entirely on you.

They Make You Carry the Emotional Load, Then Punish You for It

You manage the relationship. Track the moods. Navigate the landmines. Smooth every conflict before it explodes. You're the translator, the mediator, the shock absorber. You carry both of you on your back while they lift nothing.

And when you're tired? "You're cold."
When you need space? "You're distant."
When you ask for support? "You're needy."

A survivor told me, "I was his therapist, his mother, his punching bag, and his cheerleader. But when I needed ten minutes of compassion after my mum died, he said I was being manipulative."

They gave nothing. Expected everything. Then called you weak when your knees finally gave way.

Practical Step

Make two lists side by side: "What They Demanded" | "What They Gave". Be specific. Include emotional labour, time, money, compromise, forgiveness. Look at the imbalance on paper. That gap? That's not love. That's extraction.

Why It Matters

Because seeing the imbalance breaks the gaslighting that you were "asking for too much." You were asking for basic reciprocity. They were taking everything and calling it even.

Their Power Depends on You Having Less

They couldn't handle your independence. Your clarity. Your ability to walk away. So they chipped away slowly. Mocked your ideas. Minimised your wins. Acted bored when you talked about what lit you up.

A woman told me her ex claimed to support her career until she got promoted. "Suddenly, my job was 'taking over everything.' My success was 'changing me.' He loved the idea of my potential—until it got bigger than his need to be superior."

The more powerful you became, the less control they had. And they needed control more than they ever needed connection.

They didn't want a partner. They wanted a resource they could deplete.

If You Remember One Thing

They want dominance without effort. Control without accountability. Power without reciprocity.

They take. And take. And take.
Then tell you you're ungrateful for not being happy with crumbs.

But here's what they never expected: You waking up to the imbalance. You counting the cost. You refusing to pretend it's equal.

They gave nothing. You gave everything.
And now? Now you're done giving to someone who was never going to give back.

Your energy is yours again. Your compassion is yours to protect. Your life is yours to fill with people who match what you bring.

The ledger is closed.

And you're finally free.

Part 4
Disappeared

The dull ache of parts of you vanishing

4.1
They Made Sure Even
Your Birthday Was About Them

Author's Note:

This chapter is about the slow erasure of self, under the guise of "sharing," "compromise," or "tradition." If you were made to feel guilty for wanting your birthday to be yours, or trained to accept scraps instead of celebration, this is where you begin to take your joy back. You weren't selfish. You were overwritten. And your life deserves to be yours again.

Your Birthday Came Second. His Came First

You're sitting at a restaurant you didn't choose, eating food you don't like, pretending the evening is about you. He's ordered for both of you—his favourite dishes, his preferred wine. The waiter brings out a dessert. "Happy birthday!" they say, placing it between you.

He takes the first bite. Then the second. You watch him eat your birthday cake while explaining why this place is better than the one you'd mentioned wanting to try.

Every year played out the same way. Maybe it started as a "combined celebration" because your birthdays were close. Maybe he said it just made sense—one dinner, one night out, one gift between you.

But it was never both. It was his preferences, his timeline, his spotlight.

And you? You learned to smile through it. To train yourself to tolerate the wine he liked. To say, "This is lovely," when what you felt was: I'm disappearing, and no one seems to notice.

It Was Framed as Sharing But It Was Always His

He said, "Let's do something together."
He said, "No need for two separate things."
He said it was easier. Simpler. More practical.

But your suggestions never survived the planning. Your favourite restaurant was "overpriced." Your preferred cake was "too sweet." The spa day you'd mentioned months ago? "Self-indulgent."

A woman told me her partner convinced her to combine their birthdays—his in March, hers in April. "We'll take turns choosing," he promised. But March came with theatre tickets (his choice), dinner at his favourite steakhouse, drinks with his friends. April came with... nothing. "We already celebrated," he'd say. "Don't be greedy."

It wasn't compromise. It was erasure dressed as efficiency.

You Were Taught That Wanting More Was Selfish

You didn't ask for much. A card with thought behind it. Your favourite flowers. A dinner where you chose the menu. A moment that felt like it was actually about you. But even small wants triggered his irritation. "You're so high-maintenance." "It's just a day." "Why do you need such a fuss?"

So you adapted. Shrunk your expectations to fit his comfort. Learned to appreciate whatever crumbs fell your way. Started pre-emptively saying, "We don't need to do anything special," because his sighs when you suggested otherwise felt heavier than disappointment.

You'd start the countdown in your head weeks before—not to celebration, but to the excuses. Preparing yourself for "I forgot," "Money's tight," "It's just another day." Lowering your hopes before he could crush them.

A survivor told me, "I stopped mentioning my birthday weeks in advance. Just stopped.

Because watching him act like it was a chore hurt more than being forgotten."

Celebration Was Something You Had to Earn

If you'd been good enough—agreeable enough, quiet enough, easy enough—maybe he'd remember. At least that's what you were made to believe.

Maybe there'd be a card. Maybe there'd be a gesture. But birthdays stopped feeling like milestones. They became tests you were set up to fail. Would he notice the date approaching? Would he care enough to plan? Would you be allowed to feel special, just once?

A woman told me about her fortieth birthday. "Milestone birthday," she'd said for months. The day came. He brought home a bottle of wine—his favourite red, the one that gave her headaches. No card. No cake. No acknowledgment of the significance.

"When I started crying," she said, "he told me I was being dramatic. That normal adults don't need birthday parties. I spent my fortieth crying into wine that burned my throat, wondering when I'd become someone whose feelings were always too much."

Practical Step

List the birthdays, anniversaries, or celebrations that were hijacked, forgotten, or made about them. Notice the pattern: How many of your special days actually felt special? How many were you convinced to minimise?

Write this truth: "My joy was never too much. It was just inconvenient for someone who needed all the light on them."

Why It Matters

Because the way someone honours your joy tells you everything about how they see your worth. When your celebrations become burdens, your existence has already been devalued.

If You Remember One Thing

You weren't asking for too much. You were asking to exist.

But when your joy required effort, they called it excessive. When your preferences needed considering, they called them difficult. When your day arrived, they made sure it still belonged to them.

That wasn't forgetfulness. It was deliberate diminishment.

Your birthday matters because you matter. Your preferences count because you count. Your joy deserves space because you deserve space.

Now? You get to celebrate exactly how you want. The restaurant you love. The cake you choose. The people who actually celebrate you, not just tolerate the inconvenience of your existence.

This year, when your birthday comes, it gets to be yours.

Entirely, unapologetically yours.

4.2
It Wasn't Criticism
It Was Training You to Disappear

Author's Note:

This chapter is about the kind of control that looks like help. If you ever stopped doing things you loved because they were so often met with eye rolls, corrections, or silence, this will help you name it. It wasn't guidance. It was criticism, repeated until you disappeared.

You Tried Everything But the Rules Kept Changing

You're plating dinner, hands steady, arranging everything just right. The pasta where he likes it. The salad on the side, not touching. You've learned his preferences like a survival manual.

He walks in, glances at the plate. "Why is it so hot? You know I can't eat it like this." Last week it was too cold. The week before, you'd served it too early. Before that, too late.

You stand there, oven mitts still on, trying to remember which version of him you're feeding tonight. Which rules apply. Which mistakes you're about to make despite doing everything exactly as he asked yesterday.

Eventually, you stopped cooking altogether. Ordered takeaway. Let him choose. Because nothing was ever right—not the seasoning, not the portions, not the way you held the spatula.

Not how you folded towels.
Not how you walked into a room.

Not how you breathed when he was in a mood.

It didn't feel like abuse. It just felt like you were always getting it wrong.

They Didn't Want You Better. They Wanted You Smaller

It started as helpful suggestions. "That dress would look better if..." "Your presentation was good, but..." "I'm only saying this because I care..."

But the suggestions never stopped. And they were never satisfied.

A woman told me her partner critiqued everything she wore. "The colour's off." "That style ages you." "Are you really wearing that?" She started changing three times before leaving the house, sometimes just staying home because it was easier than facing his assessment.

"I thought he was helping me look better," she said. "But then I realised—even when I wore what he suggested, he'd find something else wrong. The earrings. My posture. The way I smiled. He wasn't trying to help. He was teaching me that nothing about me was acceptable."

You were never praised without a "but." Never relaxed without a correction. Never allowed to exist without commentary.

It wasn't feedback. It was erosion.

You Started Pre-Correcting

You stopped playing your music—he'd mock your taste. Stopped calling friends—he'd dissect the conversations. Stopped laughing freely—too loud, too much, too embarrassing.

You became your own censor, editing yourself before he could. Choosing the safest option. The quietest path. The version least likely to trigger his commentary.

A survivor told me, "I used to love painting my nails bright colours. One day he said they looked 'trashy.' Just once. But I never wore colour again. Even now, years later, I reach for red polish and hear his voice. The bottle feels heavy in my hand."

They didn't demand you change. They just made being yourself so exhausting that changing felt like relief.

You Didn't Get Encouragement. You Got Worn Down

You'd accomplish something—a promotion, a new recipe, a finished project. You'd share it, hoping for once to hear something good.

"That's nice, but don't let it go to your head."
"I hope you can maintain it."
"Shame about the timing though."

They couldn't let you have even a moment of pure achievement. Every success had to be diluted, contextualised, diminished.

A woman told me her partner commented on how she stirred her coffee. Every morning. *Clockwise was wrong. Anticlockwise was "aggressive."* Too fast was anxious. Too slow was lazy.

"It sounds ridiculous," she said, "but nothing I did was neutral. Every gesture carried judgment. Eventually I stopped making coffee when he was around. Then I stopped eating breakfast. It was easier to shrink than to exist wrong."

Practical Step

List five things you stopped doing, not because you lost interest, but because their reaction made it unbearable. Your favourite music. That hobby. The way you used to laugh.

Then write: "I didn't stop because I wanted to. I stopped because they made joy feel like a mistake."

Why It Matters

Because recognising you were trained out of yourself—not improved, not helped, but systematically diminished—breaks the lie that you were "too sensitive" or "couldn't take feedback."

You could take feedback. What you couldn't take was constant erosion dressed as care.

If You Remember One Thing

They didn't want a better version of you. They wanted a smaller one.
One who didn't need praise, didn't seek joy, didn't exist beyond their control.

You weren't too much. You weren't not enough. You were just constantly measured against standards designed to fail.

But here's what they didn't expect: You remembering who you were before their red pen touched your life.

That person—the one who stirred coffee however they wanted, who wore bright colours, who laughed too loud—they're still there.

Waiting for you to realise the criticism was never about your flaws.
It was about their need to keep finding them.

Now you get to build yourself back. Not because you were broken. But because you finally know you never were.

You weren't broken. You were worn down.

4.3
They Used Your Spirituality to Shame You

Author's Note:

This chapter is about what happens when control wears a peaceful face. If you were ever told your pain was "low vibration," your anger was "unhealed trauma," or your truth just meant you "weren't evolved enough," this is for you. Because what they called spiritual was actually silence. And what they called peace was just power in disguise.

They Used Your Faith to Shut You Up

You're sitting across from him, trying to explain how his words hurt. Your voice is steady, careful. You've practised this conversation, chosen each word to be clear without attacking.

He closes his eyes, inhales like a bell. When he opens them, his calm reads like pity. "I hear your ego talking," he says softly. "This is your wound, not mine. I can't heal what you won't own."

You stop mid-sentence. The words you'd prepared dissolve. Suddenly you're not talking about what he did—you're defending your right to feel hurt by it.

They weaponised your hope. Your desire to grow. Your need to believe things could get better. They told you healing meant being quiet, being calm, being "the bigger person."

But none of it was spiritual. It was just another way to keep you small.

They Called Your Voice Ego So You'd Stop Using It

You said how you felt. They called it projection. You named their behaviour. They called it "shadow work." You showed anger. They said you weren't "aligned." You asked for accountability. They told you you were stuck in the "3D."

A woman told me he would sage the house after arguments—not to cleanse the air, but to mark her feelings as toxic. "He'd walk the rooms, waving sage—'clearing negative energy'—then do nothing to change the things that caused it."

The smoke erased her anger for everyone else, while he kept his patterns intact. It wasn't spiritual growth. It was spiritual gaslighting: the language of healing used to make you doubt your instincts. Your anger became "resistance." Your boundaries became "blocks." Your standards became "attachments."

Every feeling that inconvenienced him was rebranded as your spiritual failing.

They Weaponised Your Belief So You'd Keep Forgiving

"Focus on love and light."
"Let it go."
"Trust divine timing."
"Everything happens for a reason."

"Trust divine timing," he'd say, and the conversation folded closed. Letting go became code for "don't ask again." Divine timing meant waiting forever—on his terms.

A survivor told me, "He'd hurt me, then send me articles about forgiveness. Videos about twin flames who trigger each other's growth. Quotes about how 'hurt people hurt people.' Never an apology. Just spiritual homework that made his behaviour my problem to transcend."

It wasn't forgiveness. It was bypass. And not the kind that sets you free—the kind that makes you easier to control.

You Weren't Unhealed. You Were Being Manipulated

You're lying in bed after another circular conversation. He's in the other room, meditation music playing. You're scrolling through articles about "releasing resistance" and "raising your vibration," trying to figure out why you still feel so wrong.

Maybe you are too negative. Maybe you do need to work on yourself. Maybe if you could just let go, be more evolved, more peaceful, more—

Stop.

You weren't "stuck." You were paying attention.
You weren't "low vibe." You were naming real harm.
You weren't "resisting the lesson." You were resisting manipulation wrapped in chakra talk and sage smoke.

You sit cross-legged on the bathroom floor, phone in hand, scrolling through an article he sent: "The Mirror of Relationships: How Others Reflect Your Inner Wounds."
Your eyes blur. Maybe it is you. Maybe if you could just forgive more, release more, transcend more—

No.

Your gut knows better, even when your mind is drowning in their doctrine.

A woman told me her partner would meditate for hours after arguments. "Not to calm down," she said. "To avoid me. He'd sit there in lotus position while I cried, then tell me I was 'disrupting his practice.' Eventually I stopped trying to talk. Started thinking maybe I was just too unevolved to understand."

Practical Step

Write down three spiritual phrases used to shame your normal reactions:

- "I thought you were more conscious than this."
- "You're letting fear run your life."
- "A healed person wouldn't react this way."

Then write the truth: "My reaction was human. My pain was real. My anger was appropriate." If it isn't safe to write this at home, keep the list in your phone under a code word, or tell a trusted friend.

Why It Matters

Because calling truth "negativity" isn't wisdom. It's erasure. Using spirituality to silence someone isn't enlightened. It's abuse wearing prayer beads.

If You Remember One Thing

Spirituality that makes you disappear isn't spiritual.
Healing that requires your silence isn't healing.

Forgiveness that only benefits the person who caused harm isn't divine—it's convenient. And no amount of sage, crystals, or scripture justifies control.

You weren't too negative. You weren't unaligned. You weren't spiritually behind.
You were being manipulated with soft words and sacred language used like a leash.

Real spirituality doesn't shame your humanity. It doesn't punish your emotions. It doesn't demand you transcend abuse while you're still experiencing it.

You get to be angry. You get to demand accountability. You get to trust your gut over their gaslighting, even when they wrap it in white light.

Your truth doesn't need energetic permission.
Your voice doesn't need vibrational approval.

And your healing doesn't require their validation.

Not anymore.

4.4
Love Isn't Meant to Feel Like Survival

Author's Note:

This chapter is about unlearning everything you were taught to call love. If you've ever felt guilty for wanting peace, or confused intensity with passion, this is where you begin again. Love isn't supposed to hurt. And wanting it to feel safe doesn't make you needy— it makes you ready.

When You've Never Known Safety, Intensity Can Look Like Love

You're in the car after another fight. Your hands are shaking on the steering wheel. He's grabbed your face, forced you to look at him, his grip just shy of bruising. "This is how much I love you," he says, eyes wild. "No one will ever care about you like I do."

And for a moment, you believe him. Because the shouting, the jealousy, the constant checking—it all gets packaged as proof of his feelings.

He said he "cared too much." That's why he got angry when you took ten minutes to reply. That's why he couldn't sleep when you went out with friends. That's why he showed up at your work unannounced.

But it never felt like care. It felt like surveillance. Like property being monitored for theft.

A woman told me, "He'd accuse me of cheating, then pull me into bed like the sex proved I was his. I thought passion meant drama. I thought jealousy meant desire. No one ever showed me love could be calm."

For years, you mistake intensity for depth. Control for care. Anxiety for butterflies.

Because no one ever taught you that real love doesn't leave you exhausted.

If It Feels Like Control, It Isn't Care

You ask for space. They call you cold.
You wear something you love. They say, "That's not really you."
You talk about your dreams. They change the subject.
You see friends. They sulk for days.

It's subtle. Slippery. Always framed as love.

"I just worry about you."
"I'm only saying this because I care."
"I want what's best for us."

A survivor told me her partner would say, "I love you too much to let you make mistakes." She'd wanted to take an art class. He said it was a waste of money, that she'd embarrass herself, that he was protecting her from disappointment.

"I never took the class," she said. "But I realise now—he wasn't protecting me from failure. He was protecting himself from me growing."

Real love doesn't clip your wings to keep you close. It watches you fly and cheers.

Love Bombing Isn't Love. It's Leverage

The flowers arrive at your office. Dozens of roses, everyone staring, commenting how lucky you are. But you know what they don't—yesterday you mentioned needing space. This isn't romance. It's marking territory.

Grand gestures. Public declarations. Intense stares with whispered promises of "forever" on the second date. Playlists full of songs about obsession they call "our soundtrack."

But pull away, even slightly? The warmth vanishes. Suddenly you're "ungrateful." "Cold." "Playing games."

A woman told me, "He'd send me love letters, then ignore me for days if I didn't respond with enough enthusiasm. I'd find myself writing these gushing replies just to avoid the punishment. I thought it was romance. It was just manipulation with a good vocabulary."

The warmth was never love. It was bait. And the hook was always there, waiting for you to swallow the performance.

Love Doesn't Ask You to Shrink

You're getting ready for dinner with his friends. You put on the red dress—the one that makes you feel electric. You catch yourself in the mirror and smile. "You're wearing that?" His tone is mild, but you know this voice. You know what follows.

You change. Into something quieter. Something that won't "draw attention." Something that won't make him spend the evening watching other men look at you.

When you're used to conditional affection, safety starts to feel suspicious. Someone being consistently kind feels like a trick. Someone respecting your boundaries feels like disinterest. So you shrink. Not because you want to. But because it's the only version of love you were shown.

Practical Step

Write down what care felt like in your last relationship. Not what they said it was—what it actually felt like in your body.

Was it light or heavy?
Freeing or suffocating?
Expanding or contracting? Then write what you want love to feel like. Use your own words. No film quotes. No song lyrics. Just your truth.

Why It Matters

Because language can lie, but your body remembers. That tightness in your chest when they walked in? That knot in your stomach when they called? That wasn't love. That was your nervous system trying to protect you.

If It Hurts More Than It Heals, It's Not Love

You cried more than you laughed. Apologised more than you spoke. Doubted yourself more than you trusted them. You spent more time recovering from conversations than enjoying them. More energy managing their moods than experiencing your own life.

A woman told me she realised it wasn't love when she caught herself celebrating the days he wasn't home. "I'd breathe differently when his car wasn't in the drive," she said. "That's when I knew—this isn't passion. It's imprisonment."

Love isn't meant to feel like walking on glass barefoot just to reach someone who claims they care.

Another survivor said, "He told me we fought because we were 'too connected,' like conflict was proof of depth. But when I finally experienced actual love—calm, steady, safe—I realised I'd been calling warfare intimacy."

If You Remember One Thing

Recovery means redefining love entirely.

Not as fireworks that burn you. Not as anxiety rebranded as passion.
Love is steady. Love is safe. Love is waking up without checking what mood they're in first.

If you're craving gentleness, consistency, the freedom to be yourself without consequence—you're not asking for too much. You're not being unrealistic. You're not "boring."

You're asking for what love actually is.
And settling for anything less isn't compromise. It's just more survival.

Choose different. Choose peace. Choose the love that lets you breathe.

That's not lowering your standards.
That's finally naming what you've deserved all along.

Love: A Place to Come Back To
by Georgie Bailey

Love is a haven
A place you can come back to
A place you can carry with you
As you wander the weirdness of the world

Love is strength
A clear affirming of who you are
A powerful truth to rely on
As you choose which way to go

Love is a knowing
An unquestioned sense of ease
A beacon that lights the way
As you search for the way back home

Love is me just being me
Love is you just being you
Love is us together
As we let each other be

4.5
They Wouldn't Let You Pee
to Prove They Were In Control

Author's Note:

This chapter is about control over your body—how even basic needs, like going to the toilet, can become power plays in abusive relationships. If you ever had to plan your body around someone else's moods, or learned to suppress your needs just to keep the peace, this wasn't an inconvenience. It was bodily coercion. And it was never okay.

It Was Just a Toilet Stop But He Turned It Into a Test

You're three hours into the drive. Twenty minutes ago the pressure in your bladder shifted from uncomfortable to urgent. Now it's pain.

"I need to stop," you say, keeping your voice neutral.

"We're making good time," he says, eyes on the road.

"Please. I really need to go."

His hands tighten on the wheel. The car fills with that familiar tension. "You should have gone before we left."

"That was three hours ago—"

"Fine." He jerks the wheel toward the exit, parks crooked, sits with the engine running while you fumble with your seatbelt. His silence louder than any shout.

When you get back, he doesn't look at you. Radio off. Jaw clenched. Every kilometr eafter is punishment—proof that your bladder inconvenienced his schedule.

You stopped asking after that. Started timing your fluids. Stopped drinking coffee before trips. Joked about your "travel bladder" to friends, because the truth was harder to say out loud: He turned your body into a battleground. And you always lost.

It Wasn't About Time. It Was About Power

A toilet stop sounds tiny. Trivial. Easy to dismiss.

"He just likes to make good time."
"Some people hate stopping."
"It's only a few more miles."

But it wasn't about efficiency. It was about control.

A woman told me her partner would drive past service stations while she begged. "Just testing your willpower," he'd say, smiling. Once, she was in so much pain she cried. He told her she was being dramatic. "Normal adults can hold it."

He controlled the car. The route. The stops. And through that, he controlled her body. When you can't choose when to relieve yourself, you're not a passenger. You're a hostage.

He Treated Your Body Like It Was Inconvenient

You said you needed a toilet. He said, "We're nearly there."

Twenty minutes later: "Please, I can't wait."
"You're being dramatic."

Forty minutes later, you're desperate. Sweating. Your whole body focused on not wetting yourself in his car because you know—you know—he'd never let you forget it.

A survivor told me, "I finally couldn't hold it anymore. Ran across a field to find a public toilet. Cut my leg on wire getting over a fence. Blood running down into my shoe. When I got back to the car, bleeding, shaking, all he said was, 'Was that really necessary?'"

She needed stitches. He didn't take her to hospital; he called her clumsy. Said she created her own problems. The cut wasn't the issue. Her needs were. Her body was. She was.

You Were Trained to Shrink Your Needs

Eventually, you stopped drinking water before car journeys. Avoided tea at restaurants. Planned your liquid intake like military strategy. "I'll just hold it" became your mantra. Discomfort was safer than confrontation. A full bladder was easier than his rage.

You weren't being "low-maintenance." You were surviving someone who made basic needs feel like acts of war.

A woman told me she developed recurring UTIs from holding her urine so long. "The doctor asked why I wasn't going when I needed to. I couldn't explain that peeing had become a power struggle. That my partner sulked for hours if I made him stop. So I said, 'travel bladder' and laughed it off."

If you've developed infections, injuries, or sustained harm because you were prevented from meeting basic needs or accessing medical care, please reach out to a medical professional or confidential support line. Your health matters and you deserve care.

This is what coercive control does: it makes the most human needs feel like rebellion. And bodily coercion happens to people of all genders—anyone can be controlled through their basic human needs.

Practical Step

List five times your body was dismissed—needing the toilet, rest, food, water, medical care, space. For each, note who framed it as inconvenience and what you did instead.

Then write this sentence and keep it where you can see it: "My body wasn't the problem. Their need for control was."

If writing this at home feels unsafe, save the list under a code word in your phone or tell a trusted friend.

Why It Matters

Because recognising bodily coercion breaks the shame. You weren't weak for needing the toilet. You weren't dramatic for being in pain. You were being controlled through your most basic human needs.

If You Remember One Thing

They made you feel like your body was an inconvenience. Like needing to pee was selfish. Like having any bodily need was too much.

But bodies need things. That's not weakness. That's being alive.

You didn't deserve punishment for needing the toilet. For being hungry. For being tired. For being human.

Your bladder isn't a test of obedience. Your stomach isn't a measure of maintenance. Your exhaustion isn't an act of defiance.

Your body is not a provocation. It's not a burden. It's not theirs to control.

It's yours. And you get to honour its needs without permission, without apology, without fear.

Stop when you need to stop. Eat when you need to eat. Rest when you need to rest. That's not demanding. That's living.

And you're allowed to do that now. Whenever you need to.

4.6
They Kept Their Cool
You Carried The Shame

Author's Note:

You've already seen how they provoked your reactions, how they pushed until you snapped, then acted calm while you unravelled. This chapter is about what came next. The shame. The internalising. The belief that your emotion was the problem. If you ever walked away from a fight feeling like the monster, this is for you.

Because their calm wasn't maturity. It was manipulation. And your breaking point wasn't failure. It was evidence of what they put you through.

Their Calm Wasn't Peace. It Was Power

You're in the kitchen, sobbing so hard you can't catch your breath. You've been trying to explain for an hour why his words hurt, why his actions broke something in you. Your voice cracks, rises, breaks again.

He's leaning against the counter, arms crossed. Watching you fall apart like an experimenter observing results. No emotion on his face. No tension in his body. Just that slight tilt of his head, like he's waiting for you to finish your "performance."

"Are you done?" he asks quietly, when you pause to breathe.

And suddenly you see yourself through his eyes—red-faced, shaking, mascara streaking. While he stands there, composed. Reasonable. The adult in the room. You became the problem. Too emotional. Too sensitive. Too much.

But his calm wasn't kindness. It was choreographed. He knew exactly how this dance would end because he'd been leading you to this moment all day.

They Stay Calm Because They Know You Won't

They needle you with small digs throughout the day. "Forgetting" things that matter. Breaking promises casually. Dismissing your feelings as "overreactions." Each one designed to fray your nerves a little more, until you're holding yourself together by threads.

Then, when you finally respond to the accumulated damage, they shift into neutral. Cool. Measured. Therapeutic, even.

"I think you need help," they say softly, while you're shaking from what they've done. "This isn't normal."

They look like stability. You look like the storm. But they built that storm—gust by gust. Every "forget." Every broken promise. Every dismissal. And when it finally broke you, they stood serene in the eye, untouched, while you drowned in the flood they created.

They Planned Your Reaction Then Played the Innocent

They didn't just tolerate your breakdown. They orchestrated it.

A woman told me her ex would pick fights right before important events. Her birthday. Job interviews. Family visits. "He'd say something cruel, then go completely calm when I reacted. By the time we arrived anywhere, I was a wreck and he was collected. Everyone saw me as the difficult one."

She realised later: he needed her destabilised. Because when she was calm, his behaviour became visible. When she was centered, his chaos had nowhere to hide.

"He'd push my buttons during arguments," she said, "then lower his voice and say, 'You're scaring me.' He said it while smiling. Like it was a show he'd seen before, and he knew exactly how it ended."

That's not peace. That's performance.

You Weren't Crazy. You Were Under Psychological Attack

Your body was responding correctly to what was happening. The tears, the shouting, the shaking—that was your nervous system recognising danger and trying to protect you. Your reaction was what a human body is designed to do under sustained attack.

They called it "crazy." They called it "unstable." They called it "too much."

But it was none of those things. It was a human response to psychological ambush. And the more distressed you became, the more they got to play their favourite role: the calm one, the reasonable one, the one "dealing with" your emotions.

They didn't de-escalate. They engineered the escalation, then stepped back to watch you unravel. This pattern happens to people of all genders—anyone can be set up to look "unstable" by someone who knows exactly which buttons to push.

Practical Step

Write down what they said or did right before you "lost it." Not just the moment you broke, but the hours or days before. Track the setup, not just the explosion.

Notice the pattern: Did they pick fights before important moments? Say cruel things then act confused by your reaction? Push buttons then play victim?

When shame hits, ask: "Did I start this? Or was I responding to an attack designed to make me look unstable?"

If it isn't safe to keep written records at home, use a secure app, save notes under a code word, or tell a trusted friend what you're noticing.

Why It Matters

Because recognising the setup breaks the shame. You weren't unstable. You were set up by someone who needed you to unravel so they could maintain their image of calm control.

They Need You to Break So They Can Stay Clean

A woman told me her ex would provoke her all day—little jabs, broken promises, deliberate forgetting—then record her when she finally shouted.

"He had videos of me crying, yelling, 'acting crazy,'" she said. "What he didn't record was the six hours of psychological torture that came before. He knew exactly how to push me to the edge, then capture just enough to make me look unhinged."

If someone is recording your reactions, know that this is a form of abuse. Seek support from a domestic violence service who can advise on legal protections and safe documentation strategies.

They need you to cry. To shout. To collapse. Because if you stay calm, their mask slips.

If you hold your ground, their manipulation becomes visible. If you don't take the bait, they're left holding the hook. So they keep pushing, subtle then obvious, until you break enough for them to say, "See? This is what I deal with."

If You Remember One Thing

You weren't the storm. You were surviving one.

Your reaction wasn't proof you were unhinged. It was proof you were human, responding to sustained psychological pressure designed to break you.

That shame you carry? It belongs to them. They should be ashamed of pushing someone they claimed to love to the point of collapse, then using that collapse as evidence against you.

You weren't too emotional. You were targeted.

Their calm wasn't maturity. It was manipulation.

And now you know: when someone can watch you break without flinching, that's not strength. That's sadism wearing a peaceful face.

Let go of the shame. You were never the problem.
The problem was someone who needed you broken to feel whole.

You get to release that shame now. It was never yours to carry.
And you get to know this truth: Your reactions were human. Their calm was calculated.

Choose to trust your body's wisdom. It knew what they were doing, even when your mind was still catching up.

4.7
They Applauded Your Talent
Then Made Sure It Disappeared

Author's Note:

This chapter is about the kind of betrayal that doesn't scream, but still steals from you. It's about what happens when they praise your gifts in public, then strip them away in private.

If you ever hid your creativity, downplayed your passion, or stopped doing what you loved because it was easier than fighting for it, this is for you. Because what they envied wasn't just the art. It was the joy. The freedom. The part of you they couldn't control.

He Said You Were Talented, Creative, Gifted

You're at dinner with his colleagues. He's telling them about your painting, your voice animated with pride you rarely hear at home. "She's incredibly talented," he says, squeezing your shoulder. "An artist. Show them the photo of that landscape you did."

You pull out your phone, warmed by this unexpected support. They make appreciative noises. He beams like he painted it himself.

But later, at home, when you unpack the new brushes you bought?

"How much did those cost?" His voice is flat.

"They were on sale—"

"We talked about unnecessary spending."

When you ask for two hours on Sunday to paint, he sighs. "I thought we'd spend the day together. But fine, if your art is more important..."

When you finish something you're proud of—a piece that took weeks, that finally captured what you'd been reaching for—you carry it to him, still wet, heart racing with that rare creative satisfaction.

He glances up from his phone for half a second. "Nice."

So you learned to create in secret. To paint after he slept. To hide supplies like contraband. To work in stolen moments when he wasn't home, clearing everything away before his car pulled into the drive. Because part of you still believed he meant the praise. Still wanted to believe the man who bragged about your talent actually wanted you to have it.

He Said He Believed in You, Then He Buried What You Made

"I've arranged something," he announces one morning, excited. "That gallery I told you about? They want to show your work. Thirty pieces. Six weeks to prepare."

Your heart stops. A gallery show—everything you dreamed of but never dared pursue.

You pour yourself into it completely. Wake at dawn to paint. Stay up past midnight perfecting details. Your hands stained with oils, your back aching from hunching over canvases, but alive in a way you hadn't been in years.

He helps you load the paintings into his van. Drives you to the gallery. Watches you arrange them on the walls with something that looks like pride.

Opening night arrives. A handful sell—red dots appearing next to your name. You're euphoric. An artist. A real artist with sales.

Then... silence.

The show ends. You ask about collecting the unsold pieces.

"They'll handle it," he says. Weeks pass. Months.

"Where are my paintings?" He shrugs. "The gallery dealt with them."

"But where are they? There were twenty-three pieces—"

"I don't know. They didn't keep records."

"Galleries always keep—"

"Why are you making this into something? They're gone. Move on."

You check your messages. You call the gallery. You ask again. Nothing. They never reappeared. Twenty-three paintings. Hundreds of hours. Years of dreams. Vanished.

He Wasn't Proud of You. He Was Performing Ownership

He didn't celebrate your creativity. He commodified it.

Your talent made him look interesting. Cultured. The kind of man who had an artist for a partner. He could drop it into conversations like a business card.

But your actual process? The mess of it? The time it required? The joy it gave you that had nothing to do with him?

That threatened him.

A woman told me her husband would show her sculptures at parties, telling everyone how gifted she was. "But at home," she said, "he complained about the dust from the clay. The cost of materials. The space my work took up. He wanted me to be an artist in theory, not practice."

He wanted the label without the reality. The prestige without the person. The decoration without the life behind it.

The Disappearance Wasn't an Accident. It Was Deliberate Erasure

Those twenty-three paintings didn't just vanish. They were disappeared. This wasn't negligence. It was deliberate erasure. The quiet murder of the part of you that could create something beyond his control.

A woman told me her partner offered to submit her poetry collection to publishers. She gave him her only copy—handwritten, two years of work. It "got lost in the post." No record of sending. No proof it existed.

"I stopped writing for five years," she said. "Not because I thought I was bad. Because I thought I was cursed. But the only curse was him."

You didn't just lose art. You lost evidence of who you were without him. Evidence that beauty could come from you independently. Evidence that you had value beyond what you provided him.

And something inside you that used to feel safe enough to create? That got buried with the paintings.

Practical Step

Write down what creative work of yours was diminished, hidden, or disappeared. Then write this truth:

"They didn't destroy it because it was worthless. They destroyed it because it was powerful. Because it was mine. Because it was proof I existed beyond their control." If you still have creative urges, honour one tiny one this week. Draw on a napkin. Hum in the shower. Write one line. If it feels unsafe to create openly, start in private. Let creation begin to trust you again.

Why It Matters

Because creativity is life force. And killing your art was practice for killing your spirit.

Recognising this as deliberate destruction, not careless loss, breaks the shame of "giving up" on your talent.

If You Remember One Thing

What you created mattered.
Not because he validated it. Not because it sold. Not because it survived.

It mattered because it came from you. Because it was yours. Because for those hours of creating, you belonged to yourself completely.

He couldn't stand that. Couldn't stand that something beautiful existed because of you, not him. So he erased it. Then let you think you'd imagined its value.

But you didn't imagine it. You painted it. Sculpted it. Wrote it. Sang it into existence.

You weren't foolish for trusting him with your work. You were betrayed by someone who should have protected it.

You're still an artist. Even if you haven't created in years. Even if your hands shake thinking about it.

The part of you that creates? It's not dead. It's hiding. Waiting to trust that it's safe to come back.

And it is safe now.
Because now you know: anyone who truly loves you would never disappear your joy.

Start small. Start secret if you need to. But start.

Your art is waiting for you.

4.8
They Controlled Your Work
And Your Future

Author's Note:

This chapter is about career control—how coercive partners use work as a leash. If you were ever forced to quit a job, change a role, or pass up an opportunity because someone else decided what was "best," this will help you name what really happened.

They weren't supporting your future. They were managing your options.

They Called It Practical. It Was Possessive

You're holding the job offer, hands trembling with excitement. Better pay. The role you've worked toward for years. Twenty minutes further from home, but worth it.

"I got it," you say, looking up at him.
He doesn't smile. "That's quite a commute."

"It's only twenty minutes more—"
"In traffic, that's forty. Each way." He's using his reasonable voice, the one that makes you doubt yourself. "And the hours? You'd never be home."

"But it's the position I've been—"
"I just think you should consider what's really important. Us. Our life together. Not some job that'll burn you out in six months."

You put the offer letter down. By evening, you've convinced yourself he's right. Too far. Too much. Too soon.

You look back now and count: three jobs in two years. Each one you left or declined "for good reasons." His reasons. Never yours.

They Framed It as Support But It Was Sabotage

They offered to help. To "guide." To give feedback on your CV. To "practice" interviews with you.

"That outfit's too ambitious for your level."
"Don't oversell yourself—they'll see through it."
"Maybe aim lower. More realistic."

A woman told me her partner insisted on driving her to a crucial interview "for support." He picked a fight in the car about her ambition, her selfishness, her priorities. She walked into that interview shaking, unfocused, defeated. She didn't get the job.

"He held me afterward," she said, "told me it wasn't meant to be. But he made sure it wasn't."

They questioned your hours. Mocked your ambitions. Planted seeds of doubt dressed as concern.

"Don't burn yourself out." (You're weak.)
"Are you sure you're ready?" (You're not capable.)
"Maybe stay where it's safe." (Where I can control you.)

It wasn't about your safety. It was about keeping you small enough to manage.

They Used Exhaustion as a Weapon

Coercive control doesn't always come through prohibition. Sometimes it comes through pace.

You're promoted. He celebrates publicly, posts about how proud he is. But at home, he creates chaos that devours your energy.

Suddenly there are emergencies only you can handle. Crises that need immediate attention. Arguments the night before presentations. "Forgotten" responsibilities that fall on you.

A woman told me her partner pushed her toward "better" jobs—longer hours, brutal commutes, impossible pressures. When she started breaking down, missing deadlines, making mistakes, he'd shake his head sadly. "Maybe you're just not cut out for this level."

"I thought I was failing," she said. "Couldn't understand why I couldn't cope with success. But I wasn't failing. I was being undermined. He wanted me to have a job—for the money—but not a career. Never independence."

They keep you so tired you can't see straight. So depleted you believe you're the one who can't cope. So overwhelmed that "stepping back" seems like your idea.

You Didn't Lose Your Potential. You Were Blocked From Using It

Every networking event you missed because they "needed" you home.
Every conference you skipped because they sulked about being alone.
Every opportunity you declined because the fight wasn't worth it.

They didn't have to say no directly. They just had to make yes impossible. Create enough friction. Enough guilt. Enough exhaustion. Until you stop trying. Until you start believing their version: that you "never finish anything," "can't handle pressure," "always make things harder than they need to be."

But the truth? You were succeeding despite undermining. Working twice as hard under half the freedom. Building a career while someone actively dismantled it.

Practical Step

Make a timeline of your career: jobs taken, jobs left, promotions declined, opportunities missed. For each major decision, note:

- What you wanted
- What they said
- What you did
- What it cost you

Look at the pattern. How many times did their "concern" redirect your path? How many dreams got repackaged as "unrealistic"?

If it doesn't feel safe to keep a written record, walk through the timeline with a trusted friend, saying out loud what you wanted versus what you gave up.

Why It Matters

Because recognising career sabotage breaks the shame of "underachieving." You weren't failing. You were being systematically prevented from succeeding.

If You Remember One Thing

They didn't just influence your career. They orchestrated its limitations.

Every suggestion to quit. Every concern about hours. Every doubt about your abilities. Every crisis before a deadline.

It was a system designed to keep you dependent. To ensure your success always required their permission, and your independence never quite arrived.

You didn't lack ambition. Your ambition was treated as a threat.
You didn't lack ability. Your ability was undermined.
You weren't "too much" or "not ready." You were too capable for their comfort.

Your skills didn't disappear. They were suppressed.
Your potential didn't expire. It was postponed.
Your future wasn't lost. It was stolen.

But it's still yours to claim.

Now you get to decide what work looks like. What success means. What risks are worth taking.

Without asking permission. Without managing someone else's insecurity. Without dimming yourself to keep the peace.

Your career is yours now. Entirely yours.

And it can finally begin.

They set the stage, cut the lights, then blamed you for not shining.

4.9
They Weren't Listening
They Were Looping You

Author's Note:

This chapter is about the difference between conversation and confusion. If you've ever left a "discussion" feeling dizzy, small, and unable to remember what you were originally trying to say, this is for you.

Because they weren't trying to understand you. They were trying to exhaust you. And recognising the loop is how you step out of it.

It Didn't Feel Like Talking. It Felt Like Sinking

You're sitting at the kitchen table, trying to explain why his comment at dinner hurt you. Simple. Clear. One specific thing.

"When you said I was embarrassing in front of your friends—"

"I never said embarrassing."

"You said I was 'a bit much.'"

"That's not the same thing."

"But it felt—"

"So now I can't have an opinion?"

"That's not what I'm—"

"You always do this. You twist everything."

"I'm just trying to explain how—"

"Like last week when you said I was controlling."

"That was about something completely—"

"See? You can criticise me but I can't say anything."

Twenty minutes later, you're defending yourself against accusations you never made, apologising for things you didn't do, and you can't even remember what you originally wanted to say. Your head spins. Your chest feels hollow.

That's what these conversations feel like: emotional quicksand. The more you try to clarify, the deeper you sink.

You Want Resolution. They Want Control

You prepare for these conversations. Write notes. Practice staying calm. Think if you just explain it better, clearer, with the right tone, they'll understand.

You bring logic. Evidence. Specific examples.

"Yesterday, when you—"

"Why are you keeping score?"

"I'm not, I'm just—"

"This is why we have problems. You catalogue everything."

"Can we please just focus on—"

"I'm not doing this. You're impossible."

They storm off. You're left sitting there, notes crumpled in your hand, wondering how asking for an apology turned into you being the villain.

They don't want resolution. They want you off-balance. Because when you're scrambling to defend yourself, they're in control.

They Don't Need Closure. They Need Your Energy

A woman told me her ex would text her provocative messages, then when she responded, he'd accuse her of being "obsessed" and "unable to let go."

"He'd send something like 'I hope you're finally happy,' knowing it would trigger me. When I'd reply explaining I wasn't trying to hurt him, he'd screenshot it and tell people I was harassing him."

They bait. You bite. They flip it. You spiral.

And suddenly they're calm—the reasonable one—while you're frantically defending your tone, your memory, your intentions, your entire character.

Your frustration is their fuel. Your confusion is their victory.

The Game Ends When You Stop Playing

You try one more time. Maybe if you're calmer. Maybe if you use different words. Maybe if you show them the text where they said exactly what they're now denying.

But they won't acknowledge it. Can't. Because admitting fault would end the game. And the game is what they need—that spinning, churning dynamic where you're always reaching for solid ground that keeps shifting.

A survivor told me, "I spent three years trying to get him to admit he'd lied about one specific thing. I had proof. Screenshots. Witnesses. But he'd just keep twisting it until I looked crazy for caring so much about 'ancient history.' The day I stopped trying to make him admit it was the day I got my sanity back."

Nothing threatens them more than your refusal to engage.

Practical Step

Before any conversation, ask yourself: "What do I actually need from this exchange?"

If it's genuine understanding or problem-solving, and they've shown they can do that, proceed carefully.

If it's validation they'll never give or an admission they'll never make, don't step in. You're walking into quicksand.

Practice these phrases:
- "I need to think about that."
- "Let's talk later when we're both calm."
- "I hear you."
- "Okay."

End the exchange. Walk out if you can. You're not being rude. You're refusing to sink.

Why It Matters

Disengaging isn't weakness. It's wisdom. You're not "letting them win"—you're refusing to play a game where the only victory is exhaustion.

Quicksand Only Lets Go When You Go Still

You think if you just find the perfect words, they'll finally understand. If you stay calm enough, logical enough, patient enough, the conversation will work.

But they're not trying to understand. They're trying to confuse.

Every clarification becomes a new accusation. Every defence opens another attack. Every attempt at resolution creates three new problems.

Stop. Go still. Say only what's absolutely necessary. Then step back. Not to punish them. To preserve yourself.

If You Remember One Thing

They don't need closure. They need your energy.

Let them think they won. Let them tell their version. Let them twist the narrative for whoever still listens.

You don't need the last word. You need your peace back.

And you get it by doing the quietest, strongest, most self-respecting thing possible:

You stop giving them the reaction they came for.

They text? You don't respond immediately, or at all.
They bait? You don't bite.
They loop? You step out.

Your silence isn't surrender. It's sovereignty.

And every time you refuse to enter the quicksand, you remember what solid ground feels like.

4.10
They Couldn't Celebrate You
Without Making It About Them

Author's Note:

This chapter is about stolen moments—those small wins you couldn't share, or the big ones that were met with silence, jealousy, or criticism. If someone in your life made your pride feel like a problem, this is your reminder: Your joy was never too loud. They were just too small to hold it.

You Learned to Keep Joy to Yourself

You're practically vibrating with excitement as you walk through the door. The email came through an hour ago—you got the job. The one you've worked toward for two years. Your dream role.

"I got it!" you say, unable to contain the smile.

He looks up from his phone. "Got what?"

"The position at the university. The one I interviewed for last month."

"Oh." Back to scrolling. "How much does it pay?"

"It's not about the money—"

"Everything's about money." He's still looking at his screen. "Hope you didn't oversell yourself. These places have high expectations."

You stand there, excitement draining from your body like water from a punctured balloon. By night, you're doubting whether you even deserved it.

You learned to keep good news to yourself. Better to swallow joy than watch it get digested into disappointment.

They Withheld Praise to Keep the Power

You weren't asking for a parade. Just acknowledgment. A smile. A "well done." Something to mark the moment as real.

But every achievement was met with qualification.
"You passed your exam." "Everyone passes that exam."
"I got promoted." "About time."
"My article was published." "In that tiny journal?"

A woman told me she completed her Master's degree while working full-time and raising two children. Her partner's response? "Now maybe you can finally contribute more financially."

"I stood there in my cap and gown," she said, "holding my diploma, and felt smaller than I'd ever felt. Like I'd wasted four years on nothing."

They acted unimpressed. Framed your wins as lucky, expected, or insufficient. And if you succeeded without their help? They either ignored it or found ways to punish you for it.

This wasn't humility. It was hierarchy. And you were never allowed to rise.

They Resented Your Shine

You could feel the temperature change when something went right for you.

The flat tone when you mentioned the compliment from your boss.
The sudden bad mood after your friend praised your work.
The picking fights on days you had something to celebrate.

A survivor told me, "Whenever I had good news, he'd find something wrong with the house. Suddenly the kitchen was filthy, dinner was late, I'd forgotten something important. It was like clockwork. My joy triggered his rage."

They couldn't tolerate your confidence because confidence made you harder to control. Joy made you remember who you were before them. Success gave you options. So they dimmed it. Dismissed it. Turned celebration into something that felt selfish, excessive, embarrassing.

You Started Minimising Yourself to Keep the Peace

You stopped mentioning achievements. Stopped sharing good news. Downplayed compliments before they could.

"How was the presentation?"
"Fine. Nothing special."

But it was special. You'd worked on it for weeks. The room applauded. Your manager pulled you aside to say it was the best they'd seen.

You just knew sharing that would cost more than keeping it quiet.

A woman told me she got accepted into a prestigious programme. "I told him it was 'no big deal,' that 'lots of people got in.' I minimised it before he could. But inside, I was screaming with pride. I just couldn't let him see it."

You learned to celebrate in silence. In bathroom stalls. In your car.

Practical Step

List five achievements—big or small—that you minimised or hid. Next to each, write what response you feared or received.

Then write what you wished someone had said. Give yourself those words now. Say them out loud if you can: "I'm proud of you. You worked hard for this. You deserve to celebrate."

Why It Matters

Because recognising how your joy was systematically suppressed helps you understand why celebrating feels dangerous. It's not vanity. It's trauma from having your light repeatedly extinguished.

If You Remember One Thing

You weren't full of yourself. You were full of potential.

And they couldn't stand it.

They didn't downplay your achievements because they were humble. They did it because your growth highlighted their stagnation. Your light exposed their darkness.

But dimming yourself to make others comfortable was never your job. And it still isn't.

You get to speak about what you've built. Feel proud of what you've overcome. Celebrate without permission or apology.

Your wins matter. Your joy matters. Your light matters.
And this time, you get to shine as bright as you want.

No one gets to tell you it's too much.

Because it never was. They were just too small to stand in your light without feeling diminished.

That's their limitation, not yours.

Celebrate everything. Start today.

Part 5
Inheritance

What was passed down,
and carried forward

5.1
It Didn't Start with a Partner
It Was a Parent

Author's Note:

This chapter explores how childhood shapes what we tolerate. If you were raised in a home where love had conditions, silence meant safety, or your needs were met with guilt, this will help you understand why the relationship you ended up in wasn't random.

It was recognisable.

You Didn't Fall for an Abuser Because You Were Weak

You're sitting at the dinner table, eight years old. Your mother's jaw is tight. That particular silence fills the room—the one that means someone's about to pay.

"Who left the milk out?" Her voice is calm. Too calm.

Your stomach drops. Was it you? You can't remember. But you know better than to stay silent.

"I think it was me. I'm sorry."

She doesn't yell. She sighs. That long, disappointed sigh that makes you feel smaller than shouting ever could.

"Do you know how much milk costs? Do you think we're made of money?"

You sit there, throat burning, learning that your mistakes aren't just mistakes. They're evidence of your carelessness. Your selfishness. Your fundamental wrongness.

Twenty years later, when your partner sighs that same sigh because you forgot to turn off a light, your body remembers. That familiar shrinking. That desperate need to fix it, to be better, to prove you're not wasteful or careless or bad.

You didn't fall for them because you were weak. You fell because the pattern felt like home.

We Learn What Love Feels Like from the People Who Raise Us

If love came wrapped in criticism, silence, or conditional approval, hypervigilance feels like connection. Walking on eggshells feels like family.

If asking for help got you dismissed—"Stop being so needy," "Figure it out yourself," "I've got bigger problems"—then later, when someone withholds affection, it doesn't register as cruelty.

It registers as normal. Not good. But known.

A woman told me, "My mother would go days without speaking to me when I disappointed her. Just complete silence. I'd follow her around the house, trying to guess what I'd done wrong. Trying to fix it."

"So when my husband gave me the silent treatment," she said, "I didn't think 'this is abuse.' I thought 'this is Tuesday.' I already knew the dance."

They Made You Prove You Were Worth Loving

You became the fixer. The peacekeeper. The one who didn't ask for much.

Maybe you were the child who cooked dinner when Mum was "having a bad day" (drunk).
Maybe you were the one who kept Dad calm by never disagreeing.
Maybe you learned that being loved meant being useful.

You predicted needs before they were voiced. Smoothed conflicts before they exploded. Became smaller so everyone else could be bigger.

A survivor told me, "I was seven when I started making my father's coffee exactly how he liked it. Every morning. If I got it wrong, he'd leave for work without saying goodbye. I'd spend the whole day at school sick with anxiety, wondering if he'd come home."

So later, when a partner demanded perfection, you already knew the choreography. You'd been auditioning for unconditional love your whole life. But the audition never ended.

The Fear You Felt in Childhood Became the Compass You Followed

Your nervous system doesn't chase joy. It chases familiarity.

That's why the relationship didn't feel completely wrong—wrong enough to run immediately. Parts of it felt known. The criticism that sounded like Dad's "feedback." The withdrawal that felt like Mum's disappointment. The impossible standards that echoed childhood.

It's not wired to say, "This is good for me." It's wired to say, "I recognise this."

And if love always came with conditions—be quieter, be helpful, be less—you learned to expect pain with connection. You learned to call it normal.

You Didn't Pick Wrong. You Recognised What You Knew

You weren't attracted to cruelty. You were familiar with emotional distance.
You weren't drawn to control. You were trained to navigate it.
You didn't choose suffering. You chose what your body recognised as relationship.

A woman told me, "My stepfather never hit me. But he made sure I knew that wanting anything—new shoes, help with homework, a hug—was an inconvenience. I learned to be grateful just to be tolerated."

"So when my partner controlled the money and called me ungrateful for needing basics," she said, "it didn't feel like abuse. It felt like the love I'd always known."

Practical Step

Write down how love was shown in your childhood home:
- Did you have to earn affection?
- Were your needs treated as burdens?
- Did you feel safe being yourself, or safer being invisible?

Then write how those patterns showed up in your adult relationships. Notice the thread connecting them.

This isn't about blame. It's about understanding why you walked toward what hurt you.

Why It Matters

Because once you see the blueprint, you stop blaming yourself for following it. You weren't stupid. You were programmed. And programming can be rewritten.

If You Remember One Thing

You weren't broken. You were taught to survive.

The first person who taught you to silence your needs, apologise for existing, and earn your worth by shrinking—it may not have been your partner.

It may have been a parent. A caregiver. Someone who was supposed to protect you but taught you that love meant managing their emotions.

You didn't fail by choosing someone familiar. You survived the only way you'd been taught.

But here's what changes now:

You stop blaming yourself for walking toward pain. You were following the only map you had.

You stop confusing familiarity with love. What feels known isn't always what's good.

You stop accepting conditional love as real love. You deserve more than auditions.

The child who learned to be small to be safe? They did what they had to do.

But you're not that child anymore.

Now you get to draw a new map. One where love doesn't require performance. Where safety doesn't mean silence. Where you don't have to earn what should be freely given.

It starts with this: You were never too much. You were never not enough.

You were a child who deserved unconditional love.

And you still do.

5.2
Father Was Just the Title

Author's Note:

This chapter is for anyone raised by a father who confused control with love. If you were trained to chase approval, accept silence, or confuse fear with respect, this will help you see:

You weren't the problem. You were surviving someone who made love conditional.

Love Was Measured by How Little You Needed

You're seven, wobbling on a bike that's too big. He's standing in the driveway, arms crossed, watching. Not teaching. Just observing, like you're an experiment in disappointment.

The wheel catches. You fall hard, knee hitting gravel. Blood springs up, bright against torn skin.

"Get up," he says, not moving. "Guess you're not as tough as you think."

You stand, leg shaking, gravel embedded in your palm. The scrape burns, but not as much as the shame. You want to cry. You want him to check if you're okay. You want what other kids seem to have—a father who runs over, who helps, who cares.

Instead, you learn your first lesson about his love: needing him means failing him.

From then on, you get tough. Not because you want to. Because tenderness isn't an option he offers.

You Were Expected to Worship Him. Not Know Him

His presence changed the house before he entered it. You could hear it in your mother's voice—suddenly higher, faster, careful. The way she'd quickly turn off the TV, smooth her hair, start moving with purpose.

"Your father's home."

Those three words rearranged everything. Toys vanished. Voices dropped. Everyone became smaller, quieter, less.

You learned early that "respect" meant fear. Not curiosity about his day. Not connection over dinner. Fear dressed as reverence.

A woman told me, "I knew everything about my father's moods but nothing about his childhood. I could predict his anger to the minute, but I couldn't tell you his favourite colour. We lived in the same house for eighteen years, and he was a stranger who terrified me."

He Didn't Teach. He Judged

Report card day. You're holding it behind your back, already knowing it's not enough. Three A's, two B's. Last term you had four A's.

"Let's see it then."

You hand it over. Watch his eyes scan, stop at the B in maths.

"What happened here?"

"I struggled with—"

"I don't want excuses. I want excellence."

He drops it on the table like rubbish. Walks away. No mention of the A's. No acknowledgment of the hours you studied, the tears over homework, the trying so hard your head ached.

Your success was his proof of good genes. Your failure was your character flaw. You learned to walk into every room already bracing for judgment.

Money Was Never the Real Problem

He had money for what mattered to him. New golf clubs. The car upgrade. Expensive whiskey for his cabinet. Private lessons for your brother—the one who showed "potential."

But when you needed something? School shoes when yours had holes. The field trip everyone else was going on. The dress for the school dance.

"Money doesn't grow on trees."
"You think I'm made of money?"
"What do you expect me to do, pull a brick out of the wall?"

The week he bought a $600 leather jacket, he called your $30 school supplies "excessive." Money was never about amount. It was about worth. And you weren't worth the investment.

You Were Meant to Reflect Him. Not Outgrow Him

You got into university—first in the family. You're shaking with excitement as you tell him.

"Which one?"

You tell him.

"Not Oxford then."

That's it. Three words that drain four years of work.

You achieved something. He found the flaw.
You found joy. He found mockery.
You grew stronger. He grew colder.

He didn't raise you. He competed with you. And when you started succeeding despite him, he resented it. Because you were never allowed to be your own person. Only a better version of him, or a failure. No in-between.

Practical Step

Write two lists: "What I needed from him" | "What I got"

Be specific. Don't soften it. Include the small things—the hug after a nightmare, the "well done" after trying hard, the presence at your school play. Then look at the gap between the lists. That gap isn't your failure. It's his.

Why It Matters

Because seeing the gap helps you understand: you weren't too needy. You were neglected. And neglect is abuse, even when it comes from someone who provided a roof.

The Day You Stopped Feeding His Ego, He Let You Starve

A woman told me her father only called when he had an audience. Speakerphone on. Voice booming with false warmth. "How's my girl?"

He hadn't seen her in three years. But he told everyone they were "close."

"I stopped calling him first," she said. "Stopped thanking him for crumbs. Stopped apologising for having boundaries. And he never called back. Not once. He didn't miss me. He missed the applause for playing father."

When you stopped being useful—stopped reflecting his glory, stopped accepting his terms, stopped shrinking yourself to fit his comfort—he didn't fight for you.

He just let you go. Like you were an employee who quit. Not a child who needed a father.

If You Remember One Thing

You weren't the disappointment. He was.

Not because he didn't say the right things. But because he never saw you. Not really. Not as a whole person separate from him.

He wore the title "Father." But you paid the price—in silence, in shrinking, in never feeling quite enough.

What he gave wasn't love. It was performance. Power dressed as parenting. Control called care.

It's okay to grieve the father you needed but didn't get. It's okay to stop trying to earn what should have been freely given.

You can love the idea of him and still admit the reality fell short.

You can set down the weight of his moods, his silence, his refusal to meet you with warmth.

He may never pick any of it up. He may never acknowledge what he didn't give. But that's not your weight to carry anymore.

You were a child who deserved unconditional love. You deserved safety, warmth, celebration.

You still do.

5.3
She Called Herself Mother
But I Raised Her

Author's Note:

This chapter is for anyone who had a mother in name, but not in presence. If you were the one who cared, who carried the weight, who held everything together while she unravelled or disappeared, this will help you name what she never admitted:

The roles were reversed, and it was never fair.

You Didn't Have a Mother. You Had a Child in Her Place

You're nine years old, standing at the cooker, dragging a chair over because you can't reach the back burners. Your little brother is crying—hungry again. Mum's been in bed for three days. "Just tired," she says when you bring her tea, though the bottles by her bed tell a different story.

The school form is still on the counter, unsigned. The parents' evening she promised to attend came and went. But somehow there's always wine. Always cigarettes. Always something more important than you.

You learn to forge her signature. Pack your own lunch. Tell teachers she's "working late" when they ask why she never comes.

You hold your breath when she finally emerges from her room. Will she be crying? Silent? Looking for someone to blame? You've learned to read the air before she speaks, to gauge which version of her you'll need to manage today.

By ten, you know which bills are urgent by the colour of the envelope. By twelve, you stop expecting her to remember your birthday.

Still, she calls herself your mother. Still demands gratitude for "everything I've done." Still acts wounded when you can't give her what she never gave you.

But the truth is: you raised her. And yourself. And probably your siblings too.

You Were the Emotional Adult Long Before You Had a Choice

"Come here, sweetheart. Mummy needs a cuddle."

You're seven. She's crying again. About him. About money. About how hard her life is. You stroke her hair while she sobs into your school jumper, telling you things no child should carry.

You learn which words soothe her. Which tone keeps her stable. When to be invisible and when to perform care.

A woman told me, "I was eight when I started talking my mother out of leaving us. She'd pack a bag, cry about how we'd be 'better off without her,' and I'd have to convince her to stay. I'd promise to be better, to help more, to need less. I was eight, and I was already her therapist."

You check her breathing when she passes out. Hide the bottles before people visit. Clean up what she breaks—dishes, promises, your childhood.

You become an expert at reading micro-expressions, voice changes, the particular silence that means storm coming. You know when not to ask for dinner money. When not to mention the school play. When not to exist too loudly.

She Needed You Helpless, Then Blamed You for Being Strong

She calls you "too independent." Says you're "cold," "difficult to love," "never needed anyone."

But she only says this when you stop fixing her life. When you stop being her emotional support child. When you dare to have needs she can't meet.

A survivor told me, "She bragged I was so self-sufficient I'd raised myself. Then when I moved out at eighteen, she sobbed that I'd abandoned her. I wasn't independent by choice. I was neglected into it."

She didn't want a daughter. She wanted a parent who would never leave, never judge, never stop giving. So when you started growing—having friends, interests, boundaries—she started shrinking you. Guilt. Manipulation. Sudden crises only you could solve.

She Taught You That Love Meant Sacrifice

"I gave up everything for you."
"You don't know what I sacrificed."
"Someday you'll understand what I went through."

But you already understood. You were the one who sacrificed. Your childhood for her addiction. Your needs for her emotions. Your safety for her comfort. You were already older than her in all the ways that mattered. Cooking dinner at eight. Putting siblings to bed at nine. Lying to social workers at ten.

You didn't inherit sacrifice from her—you learned it by giving up your own childhood.

A woman told me, "She'd say 'You kids are the reason I couldn't follow my dreams.' But I wanted to scream: 'You're the reason I couldn't have a childhood.' I never said it. Even now, grown, I can't say it to her face."

Practical Step

Write two columns: "What I needed from her" | "What I gave her instead"

Include the small things: help with homework vs helping her write apology letters. Bedtime stories vs talking her through breakdowns. A packed lunch vs packing her work bag because she was too hungover.

Look at those lists. Feel the weight of that reversal. That's not normal. That's parentification. And it's a form of abuse.

Why It Matters

Because grief needs truth. And this truth—that you mothered your mother—is the one most people never let you say out loud.

If You Remember One Thing

She called herself a mother. But titles aren't earned by biology.

They're earned by showing up.

You were the child. She was the adult. And she abandoned that role so completely, so consistently, that you forgot what it felt like to be held.

You became strong because you had no choice. Not because you didn't need tenderness.

You survived her chaos. Her absence. Her endless need. But surviving isn't the same as being loved.

Now you get to mother yourself. To give that child—the one who cooked and cleaned and comforted—what she never could.

It wasn't your fault. You weren't the parent. You weren't too much or too difficult or too independent.

You were a child doing an adult's job, carrying her failures as if they were yours. You don't have to carry them anymore.

Set them down. All of them. Even if she never picks them up. Especially then.

5.4
They Protected Them. Not You

Author's Note:

This chapter is for anyone who grew up being blamed, criticised, or overlooked, while a sibling was celebrated, protected, or endlessly excused. If you were cast as the problem while someone else got a free pass, this will help you name the truth:

These weren't fair roles. They were survival dynamics, built around someone else's dysfunction.

They Got the Cover. You Got the Blame

You're fourteen, standing in the kitchen as your mother discovers the broken vase. Your brother is right there, cricket bat still in his hand from practising indoors—something you'd be screamed at for even thinking about.

"How did this happen?" she asks, but she's looking at you.

"I didn't—"

"You must have knocked it while cleaning."

"I haven't been in here—"

"Don't lie to me."

Your brother says nothing. She turns to him, voice softening. "Were you being careful, sweetheart?"

"Yeah, Mum. Must've been loose already."

She nods. Turns back to you. "You need to be more careful. That was expensive."

When they broke something, it was an "accident." When you broke something, you were "careless." When they talked back, they were "spirited." When you talked back, you were "disrespectful." Your tears were manipulation. Their tears were genuine pain.

You weren't imagining the double standard. You were living in it.

One of You Got the Spotlight. The Other Got the Shadows

Family photos tell the story. They're in the centre, smiling, arms around them. You're on the edge, slightly out of focus, like you were added as an afterthought.

They got new clothes for school photos. You got hand-me-downs that never quite fit. Their achievements got framed. Yours got a nod. Their problems got solved. Yours got dismissed.

A woman told me, "My brother could scream at our parents, throw things, fail every class—and they'd say he was 'going through something.' When I got one B instead of an A, I was 'throwing my future away.' I learned to be perfect. He learned he could do anything. Guess which one ended up in therapy—me."

You learned to shrink. To need less. To be so low-maintenance you became invisible.

And they still didn't choose you.

It Wasn't About the Sibling. It Was About the System

Your sibling didn't create the hierarchy. They were placed on the pedestal while you were handed the broom to clean up after them.

They were trained to represent the family's image—the proof that everything was fine. You were trained to absorb the family's dysfunction—the container for everything that wasn't.

A woman told me her brother crashed two cars drunk and her parents bought him a third. When she asked for help with university books, her father said, "You always have your hand out."

"For years I thought I was greedy," she said. "But I wasn't asking for more. I was asking for anything at all."

The golden child got protection. You got projection.

This wasn't about you being bad or them being good. It was about a family system that needed a hero and a villain to function.

They Didn't Just Blame You. They Trained You to Blame Yourself

When something went wrong, everyone looked at you. Even when you weren't there.

"Your sister's upset. What did you do?"
"Your brother failed his test. You should have helped him study."
"The dog got out. Why weren't you watching?"

You learned to apologise before anyone asked. Take responsibility before fingers pointed. Accept blame like breathing.

A survivor told me, "I was eight when I started saying 'sorry' at the beginning of every sentence. 'Sorry, can I have some water?' 'Sorry, I finished my homework.'

I was apologising for existing. Still do it at thirty-five."

You became the family's dumping ground. Every frustration, disappointment, and failure got swept your way.

And the worst part? You started believing you deserved it.

Practical Step

Write down the labels they gave you:
- Difficult
- Dramatic
- Selfish
- Ungrateful
- Too sensitive

Next to each, write the truth:
- "Difficult" → I had needs they couldn't meet
- "Dramatic" → I showed emotions they couldn't handle
- "Selfish" → I asked for basic care
- "Ungrateful" → I noticed the inequality
- "Too sensitive" → I felt the pain they pretended wasn't there

Cross out their lies. Circle your truths.

Why It Matters

Because scapegoating teaches you to carry shame that was never yours. Recognising the system helps you hand it back.

If You Remember One Thing

You weren't the problem child. You were the truth-teller in a family built on denial.

While they polished one child into proof of their success, they needed another to carry their failures.

You carried them. Every unprocessed emotion. Every unacknowledged problem. Every uncomfortable truth.

And despite being handed the worst role, you still turned out kind. Still turned out capable. Still turned out nothing like the story they wrote for you.

You were never the scapegoat. You were the mirror.
And they punished you for showing them exactly who they were.

But mirrors don't lie. And neither did you.
That's why they needed you gone. Because you were right.

And in families built on pretence, being right is the ultimate betrayal.

5.5
You Apologised for Them

Author's Note:

If it ever felt like your job was to smooth things over, explain someone else's outbursts, or say sorry for things you didn't even do, this chapter is for you.

You weren't "mature for your age." You were managing adults who refused to manage themselves. That wasn't your role. It never should've been. But you survived it. Let's name it now.

You Said Sorry Before You Even Knew What For

You're seven, in Woolworths with your dad. He's shouting at the cashier about the price of something. His face is red. People are staring. The cashier's hands are shaking as she scans the items.

"I'm sorry," you whisper to her when he turns to grab his wallet. "He's just tired."

She looks at you—this small child apologising for a grown man's rage—and her face crumples slightly. She knows this isn't the first time you've done this.

On the way to the car, you apologise to him too. "Sorry, Dad. I should've reminded you about the sale ending."

You hadn't even known about a sale. But somehow his anger felt like your responsibility to prevent.

You learned early that some people explode and others clean up. You became the cleaner. The smoother. The one who made it okay for everyone else.

You Thought It Was Love to Take the Blame Quietly

Your mother's crying again. She's had another fight with your stepfather. You're twelve, doing homework at the kitchen table.

"It's my fault," she says, not really to you but needing someone to hear. "I shouldn't have asked about the credit card."

"It's not your fault, Mum," you say automatically.

Later, when he comes home, you've already tidied the house, made dinner, got your siblings bathed. You know if everything's perfect, maybe he won't start again.

He finds something anyway. The tea's too weak.
"Sorry," you say quickly. "I'll make another pot."

Your mother says nothing. Your siblings stay quiet. You've learned that taking the blame quickly sometimes ends things faster.

A woman told me, "I was eight when I started apologising pre-emptively. I'd walk into a room and say sorry before anyone even looked at me. Just in case I'd done something wrong by existing."

You got brilliant at reading micro-expressions. At sensing mood shifts before they happened. At rearranging yourself to prevent storms that were never yours to control.

And You Still Do It Now, Don't You? Apologise for Being Hurt

You tell someone they upset you, and somehow the conversation ends with you saying sorry for bringing it up. Someone bumps into you, and you apologise.

Your partner's in a mood about work, and you ask, "What did I do?" Nothing. You did nothing. But your nervous system is still wired to believe that all discomfort in a room must somehow be your fault.

A woman told me she used to apologise to furniture. "If someone exploded at home, I'd literally say 'sorry' to the kitchen bench, the doorframe, anything. Like I was apologising to the universe for the tension. I was thirty-five when I realised none of it had been mine to fix."

This is what happens when your body learns that keeping peace matters more than keeping yourself intact.

You Weren't the Problem. You Were the Pressure Valve

You could de-escalate before you could spell the word. You became fluent in:
- Tone-adjusting to match what they needed
- Face-reading to predict explosions
- Topic-changing to avoid triggers
- Blame-taking to end conflicts faster

You were the translator between chaos and calm. The bridge between your parents. The buffer between volatile people and the world.

A survivor told me, "My therapist asked me to describe my childhood role. I said 'human shock absorber.' I literally positioned my body between angry people.

At seven years old."

But none of that was care. It was survival. And you don't owe the rest of your life to coping mechanisms that got you through the first part.

Practical Step

Write down three moments from childhood where you apologised for someone else's behaviour:
- When Dad yelled at the waiter
- When Mum was drunk at parents' evening
- When your brother broke something and you said you did it

Next to each, write: "This wasn't mine to fix." Then notice: How many times this week have you apologised for things that weren't your fault?

Why It Matters

Because recognising the pattern is how you break it. You're not responsible for managing other people's emotions. You never were.

If You Remember One Thing

You were a child, not a family therapist. Not a marriage counsellor. Not an emotional shock absorber.

The apologies you gave weren't kindness. They were survival.
The peace you kept wasn't harmony. It was self-protection.

And every time you said sorry for someone else's explosion, you were teaching yourself that their comfort mattered more than your truth.

But here's what's true now:

Your feelings aren't inconveniences. Your needs aren't impositions. Your hurt isn't something to apologise for.

You don't have to manage other people's emotions to earn your right to exist peacefully.

You don't have to apologise for who they were. Or who they still are.
You don't have to say sorry for taking up space, having needs, or feeling hurt.

The words "I'm sorry" can retire from active duty now.
They've done enough service. Let them rest.

And let yourself exist without apology.

5.6
You Were Gaslit as a Child

Author's Note:

They made you question what you felt. What you saw. What you knew. Long before any partner distorted your reality, you were already being trained to override your gut.

This chapter isn't about blame. It's about naming how early it started, and how quietly. Because when someone teaches you not to trust yourself, you carry that confusion into every room you enter. Let's clear it.

You Knew Something Was Wrong But They Told You It Wasn't

You're six, shivering in bed. The heating's been off for days—you can see your breath in your bedroom. You go to your mother, teeth chattering.

"Mum, I'm cold."
"No, you're not. You're fine. Go back to bed."

You stand there, confused. Your body is shaking. Ice has formed on the inside of your window. But she said you're not cold. So maybe you're wrong about what cold feels like.

The next morning, you wet the bed—your body too cold to wake you in time.
"You're too old for this," she says, stripping the sheets roughly. "Stop being a baby."

"But I was cold—"
"I said you weren't cold. Stop making excuses."

You're eight now. The shouting downstairs makes your chest tight. You cover your ears.

"The yelling hurts," you tell your dad later.

He laughs. "What yelling? We were just talking. You're imagining things."

But you heard the plates breaking. Saw your mother crying. Your ears still ring.
"Maybe you're right," you say, because arguing makes him angry. "Maybe I imagined it."

He ruffles your hair. "That's my girl. Always so dramatic."

You learn to stop trusting what your body tells you. Cold isn't cold. Scared isn't scared.
Loud isn't loud. You must be wrong about everything.

They Called It "Discipline" But It Felt Like Fear

"I'm not angry," he says, while his face is red and the veins in his neck bulge.
"This doesn't hurt," she says, while gripping your arm so tight it leaves marks.

"I'm doing this because I love you," they say, while you shake with fear.
You were told you were being dramatic. Overly sensitive. Making things up.

"We were just joking." But you weren't laughing.
"We're only trying to help." But your stomach hurt for days after.
"You're remembering it wrong." But your body remembered perfectly.

A woman told me her mother would leave the room whenever she cried, then later
deny it happened. "She never left you alone," her aunt insisted. "Your mother was
always there for you. You must be confused."

"I spent years thinking I had memory problems," she said. "Turns out I had a family
problem. They all agreed to the same lie."

You learned to doubt your instincts because believing them meant accepting that the
people who were supposed to protect you were actually hurting you.

The More You Questioned It, the More They Smiled

"Are you angry with me?"
"Of course not."

But their jaw is clenched.

"Did I do something wrong?"
"Don't be silly."

But they haven't looked at you all day.

"Why does it feel like you're upset?"
"You're being paranoid. Always making problems where there aren't any."

Every time you voiced confusion, they called you difficult. Every time you named the tension, they said you created it.

A survivor told me, "I'd ask my father if everything was okay. He'd smile this cold smile and say, 'Perfect. Why would you think otherwise?'

Meanwhile, he hadn't spoken to my mother in three days. We ate dinner in silence. I learned to stop trusting the obvious."

So you stopped asking questions. Started assuming you were always wrong. Started apologising for noticing what they insisted wasn't there.

They Didn't Just Lie. They Taught You Not to Trust Yourself

And once that seed was planted, every future relationship had fertile ground.

When a partner said, "That never happened," you already knew how to doubt your memory.

When they said, "You're too sensitive," you already believed it.

When they said, "You're overreacting," your childhood training kicked in: They must be right. I must be wrong. I can't trust what I feel.

A woman told me, "My ex would move my keys, then act concerned when I couldn't find them. 'You're so forgetful,' he'd say. And I believed him. Because my whole childhood was people telling me that what I saw and felt wasn't real. He didn't have to train me. I came pre-programmed."

Practical Step

Write down three moments from childhood that still feel wrong in your body:
—They told you you weren't hungry, but you were.
—They insisted you weren't hurt, but you were bleeding.
—They claimed nothing happened, but you remember everything.

Under each, write: "My body was right. They lied."

Then pick one memory. Close your eyes. Tell that child: "You weren't wrong. You weren't crazy. You were right."

Why It Matters

Because your body kept the receipts, even when your mind was taught to throw them away. Trusting those receipts now is how you reclaim your reality.

If You Remember One Thing

Gaslighting doesn't always start with romantic partners.
Sometimes it starts when a child says, "I'm scared," and gets told, "No, you're not."

When a child says, "That hurt," and gets told, "I barely touched you."
When a child says, "You're angry," and gets told, "I'm not angry—you're too sensitive."

That's not just dismissal. That's rewriting reality.

It's training to doubt your perceptions. Training to mistrust your instincts. Training to believe that what you feel is less real than what they need you to feel.

But your body kept score anyway. Every flinch they mocked. Every tear they dismissed. Every fear they laughed at.

Your truth survived, even when silenced. Your instincts stayed intact, even when buried.

You're listening to them now.
And that's how the cycle breaks.

Trust what you felt then. Trust what you feel now.

Your body was never wrong.

They were.

5.7
Love Meant Earning It by Shrinking

Author's Note:

If love always felt conditional, contingent on how quiet, small, or accommodating you could be, this chapter is for you. This isn't about romance. It started much earlier than that. You learned to earn love by being less. Less loud. Less needy. Less honest.

You Didn't Fail to Be Loved. You Were Trained to Perform for It

You're six, at Sunday dinner. Your uncle tells a joke and something in you breaks free— real laughter. The kind that comes from your belly, makes you snort, makes your whole body shake with joy.

SLAM.
Your father's hand hits the table. Plates jump.

"Enough. You're embarrassing yourself."
The room goes silent. Your cousins stare at their food. Your mother looks away.

You're sent to your room, where you sit on the edge of your bed, tears burning your cheeks. You replay it over and over. Was your laugh too loud? Too long? Too much?

You decide to practice being quieter. Gentler. Less.

A woman told me this story. She's fifty-two now. She still apologises when she laughs in public. Still catches herself mid-joy and pulls back, makes herself smaller.
"I monitor my own happiness," she said. "Like there's a volume control on my soul, and I'm always turning it down."

They made it clear: your real self was the problem.

Got excited? Eye rolls.
Started crying? They left the room.
Asked for what you needed? "You're being difficult."
Showed enthusiasm? "Calm down."
Expressed an opinion? "Who asked you?"

So you learned. Smaller meant safer. Quieter meant loved. Less meant acceptable.

They Rewarded You for Vanishing

They praised you for being "low-maintenance." Smiled when you didn't ask for birthday presents. Called you "mature for your age" when you never complained. But you weren't mature. You were terrified.

You learned that needing things got you rejected. Having opinions made you troublesome. Showing up fully meant being alone.

A survivor told me, "My parents bragged to everyone that I was 'so easy.' Never asked for anything. Never caused problems. They didn't realise I was dying inside, shrinking myself down to nothing because that's when they seemed happiest with me."

You became a ghost of yourself, hoping they'd love the empty space where you used to be.

You Learned to Hide Before You Knew What You Were Hiding

By seven, you're already an expert at reading rooms. You pause outside doorways, listening for the emotional temperature. You scan faces before speaking. Calculate how much of yourself is safe to reveal.

A woman told me she spent hours at twelve, practising how to enter rooms without being noticed. "Shoulders in. Eyes down. Neutral expression. If I could walk through a room without anyone reacting, that felt like victory."

"No one told me that being invisible isn't peace," she said. "It's just safety bought with pieces of your soul."

You rehearsed smallness like other children rehearsed piano scales. Perfecting the art of not being too much. Training yourself out of existence.

Their Love Was Just Conditional Tolerance

You weren't loved more when you were quiet. You were just easier to ignore. You weren't cherished when you asked for nothing. You were just convenient. You weren't valued when you shrank. You were just less threatening.

Real love doesn't require editing. It doesn't ask you to rehearse yourself in mirrors, moderate your laughter, or apologise for having needs. What you experienced wasn't love. It was conditional tolerance based on how little inconvenience you caused.

A woman told me, "I thought if I could just be small enough, quiet enough, easy enough, they'd finally love me properly. But there was never a 'enough.' The bar kept moving. The target kept shrinking. Until there was almost nothing left of me to love."

Practical Step

Write a sentence that starts with: "They liked me better when I…"
Finish it honestly. Say it out loud.
Then say this: "But I don't have to disappear to be loved anymore."
(Even if you don't believe it yet.)

Why It Matters

This uncovers how performance replaced connection, and gives you a way to start coming back to yourself.

If You Remember One Thing

They didn't love you more when you were quiet, agreeable, and easy.
They loved the version of you that didn't threaten their comfort.

The real you—with your big laugh, your strong opinions, your messy feelings—
was never too much. You were just too real for people who needed you to perform
smallness.

Love doesn't ask you to shrink. It doesn't celebrate your disappearance. It doesn't
require you to practice being less in mirrors.

What they called love was just their convenience.
And your authenticity was never part of their equation.

The parts of you they couldn't handle? Those were the parts that deserved the most
protection. The laugh that embarrassed them. The tears that inconvenienced them. The
needs that bothered them.

Those weren't flaws. They were you, trying to exist.
You don't owe anyone your disappearance.

Start with this: Let yourself laugh. Really laugh. Without apology.

It's not too much. It never was.
They were just too small to hold your fullness.

5.8
They Taught You Loyalty
Even When It Hurt You

Author's Note:

Some of us were taught that loyalty meant staying, even when it was breaking us. We learned to keep secrets. To cover for dysfunction. To protect the image of people who were hurting us.

And when it started hurting, we thought the pain was a test of our love, not a sign of something being wrong. This chapter is about that lie. And the cost of carrying it too long.

They Didn't Call It Silence. They Called It Love

You're nine, sitting in the back seat on the way to church. Twenty minutes ago, your father hit your brother in the garage. Hard. The sound still rings in your ears. Your brother sits next to you, silent, a red mark spreading across his cheek.

Your mother turns from the front seat, lipstick perfect, voice steady.
"We don't talk about what happens in this house."

At church, your father shakes hands, laughs with the minister. Your mother smiles, touches shoulders gently. Your brother sings hymns through swollen lips.

You sit through the sermon with your heart pounding, wondering how something could be so wrong and still need protecting. How love could look like this—performance on the outside, violence on the inside.

A woman told me this story. She never told anyone else. Not until she was forty. "They called it family loyalty," she said. "But it was just complicity dressed up as love."

We were taught that silence was devotion. That keeping quiet proved we cared. That protecting the family meant protecting the secret.

But silence wasn't love. It was the training ground for shame.

They Taught You Pain Was Proof of Love

They called it sacrifice. They called it putting family first. They called it loyalty.

But what they really meant was: Don't question. Don't leave. Don't name what's happening.

You kept showing up long after it stopped being safe. Long after it stopped being reciprocal. You thought being loyal meant holding on, even when they'd let go of you years ago.

A survivor told me, "I drove three hours every Sunday to visit my mother, who spent the entire time criticising me. When I finally stopped going, she told everyone I'd abandoned her. But she'd abandoned me emotionally when I was five. I just took thirty years to stop showing up for the absence."

They Demanded Unconditional Love But Never Gave It

You were taught that love meant endurance. That no matter how badly they treated you, the proof of your character was staying put.

It didn't matter if you were neglected, dismissed, or punished. The lesson was always the same: real love never walks away.

But their love had conditions. Be quiet. Be convenient. Be less. And even when you met them all, it still wasn't enough.

A woman told me her mother would disappear emotionally for days after any disagreement. She called it "needing space." But it felt like exile.

"Why do you do this?" she finally asked.

"Because family doesn't abandon each other," her mother replied, while actively abandoning her daughter in the same room.

She stayed for years after that. Quiet. Careful. Walking on glass. She thought loyalty meant never leaving, even when you were being emotionally starved from the inside.

Love Doesn't Require Your Destruction

Love doesn't require obedience. It doesn't demand silence. It doesn't shame you for having limits. It doesn't look like swallowing tears in a bathroom stall so no one sees you breaking.

If loyalty means losing yourself, it's not loyalty. It's bondage. And you don't have to keep choosing chains. Real loyalty flows both ways. It protects but doesn't imprison. It commits but doesn't consume.

What they called loyalty was just control wearing a family photo smile.

Practical Step

Write down one secret you were told to keep that made you feel sick or scared. Don't share it yet. Just name it.

Then write: "It wasn't mine to carry." Hand it back. It was never yours.

Why It Matters

Breaking the silence, even privately, is how you begin returning what was forced on you. You're not betraying them by naming the truth.

You're finally being loyal to yourself.

If You Remember One Thing

You don't have to protect what hurt you.

You can love someone and still leave.
You can care and still say no.
You can honour the good memories and still refuse to carry their shame.

The loyalty they demanded wasn't love—it was a leash disguised as devotion.

They taught you that leaving meant you never really loved them. But staying in something that destroys you isn't proof of love. It's proof of conditioning.

You were never disloyal for wanting to be treated well.
You were never selfish for having boundaries.
You were never ungrateful for refusing to carry their shame.

Loyalty is beautiful when it's mutual. When it's safe. When it honours your humanity as much as theirs.

Not when it costs you everything and returns nothing.

That's not loyalty. That's sacrifice to a god who was never listening.

5.9
You Didn't Learn Boundaries Because They Had None

Author's Note:

If saying no still feels rude, if asking for space makes you feel guilty, if you have to rehearse a thousand versions of "I need time" before actually sending the message, you probably weren't taught boundaries. You were taught access. Obligation. Merging. This chapter is for the part of you that still flinches when you assert a need, because for so long, your needs were treated like disrespect.

You Learned That Privacy Was Selfishness

You're sitting at the kitchen table, doing homework. Your diary is upstairs in your bedside drawer, under old birthday cards. You think it's safe there. Private. Yours.

Then at dinner, your mother quotes something you wrote three days ago. Word for word. "I see you're having feelings about that boy from school," she says, not even looking up from her plate. Your stomach drops.

The violation sits between you like another person at the table. When you ask how she knows, she looks offended. "We don't have secrets in this family. What kind of mother would I be if I didn't know what was going on with my own daughter?"

You learn that privacy is selfishness. That love means surveillance. That boundaries are betrayal.

They Called It Closeness But It Was Control

A woman told me her dad used to read her diary too. Never admitted it, but the things she wrote kept appearing in conversations she didn't start. "Just be careful who you trust with those feelings," he'd say, pretending it was general advice.

She started writing in code. Then stopped writing altogether.

Another survivor said she had to report her whole day to her mother. Every conversation, every interaction, every thought that crossed her mind. If she left something out, she was "hiding things" and "pulling away from the family."

They demanded emotional transparency and called it trust. They required constant access and called it care. Every moment to yourself felt like theft from them.

You Lost The Right To Say No

It wasn't just that your "no" was ignored. It was that your "no" was never allowed to exist.

A woman told me about family gatherings where she had to hug everyone, whether she wanted to or not. When she tried to refuse her uncle whose shirt always smelled of stale tobacco, whose hugs lasted too long, her mother hissed: "Don't be rude. It's family."

She learned to hold her breath until it was over. To freeze her body and count to ten. Not because she felt safe, but because saying no was treated like an act of war. Every boundary became defiance. Every need for space became rejection. Every attempt at self-protection was selfishness, rudeness, or proof you didn't love them enough.

That wasn't parenting. That was colonisation. They didn't just cross your boundaries. They colonised your entire internal landscape. Your thoughts weren't private. Your feelings needed approval. Your body wasn't yours to protect.

Boundaries Aren't Betrayal

You learned not to lock anything. To live wide open. To mistake invasion for intimacy. But unlocked isn't love. It's exposure.

Now when someone texts "we need to talk," your whole body prepares for inspection. When someone asks for emotional transparency, you hand over everything—even what isn't ready to be shared. When someone pushes past your comfort, you feel guilty for having a comfort zone at all.

Practical Step

Write this sentence: "I'm not available for that right now."

Say it out loud. To the mirror. To your pet. To the empty room. Notice how it feels in your mouth. Notice if your voice shakes. Notice if guilt rises. Then say it again: "I'm not available for that right now."

That's you drawing a line. That's you creating a door where there wasn't one. That's the beginning of taking your space back.

Why It Matters

Because boundaries aren't walls that keep love out. They're doors that let the right love in. Because the people who truly care about you want you to feel safe, not surveilled. Because your comfort was always valid, even when they taught you it wasn't.

If You Remember One Thing

They didn't respect your boundaries because they never had their own. You didn't fail to set them. You were never shown how.

You were taught that love meant total access. That care meant invasion. That family meant no doors allowed.

But your space was always yours. Your truth was always enough.

Now you get to decide where the door is. Who gets to knock. And who doesn't get to come back in.

5.10
You Didn't Miss the Red Flags
You Were Raised in Them

Author's Note:

This chapter is about how childhood trains us to normalise harm. If you've ever asked yourself, "Why do I keep ending up with people like this?" this will help you connect the dots with compassion. You weren't reckless. You were rehearsed. And now, you're unlearning the training.

You Didn't Just Fall into a Toxic Relationship. You Were Trained for It

You're eight years old, watching your mother apologise to your father for burning dinner. She's crying. He's silent. The silence is worse than yelling because you don't know when it will break. Your fork hovers mid-air, food going cold.

You learn to read his jaw muscle. The way his newspaper snaps when he turns the page. You become an expert at measuring danger in the smallest movements.

Twenty years later, you're in a relationship where you track someone else's moods like weather patterns. You apologise before they've even said what's wrong. You shrink yourself to avoid the storm.

It doesn't feel like danger. It feels like home.

You Learned Early That Your Power Was a Problem

A woman told me she remembers the exact moment she learned to be small. Seven years old, laughing too loud at her birthday party. Her father grabbed her arm, squeezed hard enough to leave marks. "Stop showing off. You're embarrassing me."

The candles were still smoking on her cake.

She learned that joy was dangerous. That taking up space was selfish. That being seen was a risk she couldn't afford.

Now she sits in meetings, brilliant ideas dying in her throat. Her partner asks why she never speaks up. She doesn't know how to explain that she was conditioned to believe her voice was an intrusion.

Practical Step

Write one belief about yourself that came from childhood—not from truth, but from survival. Something like "I'm too much" or "My needs are a burden."

Then write what's actually true: "I was a child who deserved to be heard."

Read the true sentence out loud. Let yourself hear it.

Why It Matters

Naming the lie breaks the spell. Hearing the truth starts to rewrite the story.

You Were the Regulator. The Buffer. The Peacekeeper

You weren't raised. You were recruited. You learned to scan your mother's face when she came home from work. If her mouth was tight, you'd disappear to your room. If she was crying, you'd make her tea and tell her she was beautiful.

You were nine years old, managing an adult's emotions.

A woman once told me: "My partner asked how I was and I panicked. I didn't know how to answer a question that wasn't loaded. Every question in my house growing up had a right answer, and the right answer was whatever kept the peace."

You learned that your feelings were less important than keeping everyone stable. That your needs came last, if at all.

This Wasn't Love. It Was Conditioning

The praise came with conditions: "You're such a good girl when you're quiet." The affection came with strings: "I'll hug you when you stop crying."

The rules changed with their moods. Yesterday's acceptable behaviour was today's betrayal.

Your nervous system learned to stay on high alert. Don't relax. Don't need. Don't expect comfort unless you've earned it through perfect behaviour.

That's not childhood. That's preparation for tolerating abuse.

Practical Step

Write down three things you now know were never your fault. The divorce. Their drinking. Their rage. Next to each one, write what you needed to hear instead: "That shouldn't have happened to you." "You were just a child." "I believe you."

Say these words to yourself now. Even if your voice shakes.

Why It Matters

You stop parenting yourself through guilt and start parenting yourself through compassion. You give yourself what they couldn't.

If You Remember One Thing

You weren't broken for ending up in more hurt later. You were programmed to not recognise it as hurt.

The red flags weren't flags to you. They were the landscape you grew up in.
The territory you knew how to navigate. The language you were fluent in.

But now you see it.
Now you recognise the difference between love that heals and love that demands.

Between safety and familiarity.

You stop apologising for not knowing what you were never taught.
You stop calling the fire home.

And you start choosing what doesn't require you to shrink.
What doesn't punish you for having needs.

What lets you exist without performing for your right to be there.

Part 6
Reveal

When the damage finally makes sense, and so does your pain

6.1
It Wasn't Your Fault

Author's Note:

This is one of the hardest truths to accept. You didn't just survive years of abuse. You also carried the belief that it happened because of something you did or failed to do.

Survivors don't just blame themselves by accident. They're trained to. Conditioned by family. By partners. By culture. By therapists who missed it. They're taught that if they'd just tried harder, stayed calmer, explained it better, left earlier, trusted less, trusted more, it might have been different. It wouldn't have been.

They Didn't Just Hurt You. They Made You Think You Caused It

You're standing in the kitchen, washing dishes from dinner you cooked perfectly. Nothing burned. Nothing late. Everything exactly how he likes it. He walks in. The floorboards creak. He sees one water spot on the counter—one—and that's enough.

"This is why I can't trust you with anything."

You apologise. Scrub the spot. Scrub the whole counter again. Check every surface twice. Later, lying in bed, you run through the evening: Maybe if you'd dried the counter first. Maybe if you'd used a different cloth. Maybe if you'd just been more careful.

You don't think: Maybe he's looking for reasons to be cruel. You think: What did I do wrong? And here's the truth you couldn't see: none of it was your fault.

A friend once told me she was ashamed she stayed so long. We were sitting in the corner of a café—one she'd avoided for years. Her hands trembled as she stirred her tea. "He'd do something awful," she said, "and then go silent. Just disappear. And I'd spend the whole week wondering what I'd done."

She laughed that sideways, embarrassed laugh survivors use when they're still half-convinced it was their fault. "I wasn't even mad at him. I was mad at me. For always reacting wrong. For not being easier. For not being enough."

I didn't say anything for a moment. Just let her sit with it. Then I said, "He trained you to think that. That wasn't your voice." And she cried.

The Interrogation Never Stopped

They didn't need to blame you out loud. They taught you to run the prosecution yourself.

A slammed door: "Did I say it wrong?"
The silent treatment: "What did I do this time?"
A raised voice: "How did I set him off?"

Every question turned back on you. Every scene twisted into evidence against yourself. You were living inside a courtroom where you were always the accused—and none of it was your fault.

A survivor once told me she kept a journal of her "mistakes"—things she'd said wrong, ways she'd failed to anticipate his moods. She thought if she could just identify the pattern, she could stop causing his anger.

"I had three notebooks full," she said. "Three years of evidence against myself." The pattern wasn't in what she did. The pattern was him needing someone to blame.

You Were Set Up to Fail

The rules kept changing. What pleased them Monday enraged them Tuesday. What earned affection in the morning earned contempt by night. It was a rigged carnival game—the hoop bent, the ring toss unwinnable, the bottles too heavy to fall. You couldn't win because winning was never allowed.

But instead of seeing the scam, you saw your own inadequacy. Instead of recognising the con, you tried harder.

That's how deep the lie went: you believed losing a game designed for you to lose meant you were the problem. You weren't. The failure was never yours to carry. The failure was theirs—of honesty, of stability, of love.

It wasn't you. It was never you. It was the setup.

Practical Step

Write down every blame you still carry:
"I should've known…"
"I should've left…"
"I should've seen the signs…"
"I shouldn't have trusted…"
"I should've been stronger…"

Get it all on the page. Then destroy it—rip it, burn it, bury it, throw it into the ocean. Whatever feels like release.

As you do, say: "It wasn't my fault. It was a setup." Even if you don't believe it yet.

Why It Matters

Shame survives in silence. Blame feels heaviest when you carry it alone. Destroying that list isn't giving up—it's handing back what was never yours.

So the next time you hear yourself thinking, "I should have…", you'll have something stronger than the lie: a memory of ripping it up, a voice that said, "It wasn't my fault. It was a setup."

That act carves a crack in the old story. And through the crack, truth gets in.

If You Remember One Thing

You didn't cause it. You survived it.

They needed you to fail—not because of what you did, but because blame was their weapon and confusion was their method. They built a maze where every path led back to you being wrong.

That's coercive control: create chaos, then hold you responsible for the mess. Destabilise reality, then blame you when you stumble.

You weren't too sensitive—they were deliberately cruel.
You weren't asking for too much—they were withholding on purpose.
You weren't the problem—you were the target they chose.

The voice that insists it was your fault? That's their programming still running—the interrogation they taught you to run on yourself.

But you're here. You're reading this. You're starting to see the setup for what it was.

It wasn't your fault when they hurt you.
It wasn't your fault when you stayed.
It wasn't your fault when you couldn't see it.

Each time you refuse to carry their blame, you take something back.
This is more than survival. It's the beginning of what they tried to stop: your freedom.

6.2
When Your Life
Doesn't Look Like You Hoped

Author's Note:

This chapter is for the moment you realise the relationship you're in feels nothing like the one you imagined, and the shame that comes with that. If you're starting to question whether the life you're living is really yours, this chapter won't push you to leave. It will help you name what's happening, and remind you: seeing clearly isn't betrayal. It's the beginning of getting yourself back.

You Didn't Set Out to Live Like This

You're standing in your kitchen, loading the dishwasher in silence. Again. Not the comfortable silence of people who don't need words. The thick silence of people who've given up trying. You remember imagining this kitchen once. How you'd cook together. Music playing. Wine on the counter. Stories from the day.

Now you move around each other like ghosts. Careful not to touch. Careful not to disturb. Careful not to exist too loudly. And you think: This isn't who I thought I'd be. Not just because of them. Because of who you've had to become just to survive them.

The Weight of Pretending Everything's Fine

Friends ask how things are. "Good," you say. "Busy, but good." The lie sits in your throat like acid. You post photos that look like happiness. You perform a relationship that exists nowhere except in the version you show others. Every fake smile costs you another piece of whoever you used to be. Until you can't remember who that person was anymore.

A woman told me she used to practice her "everything's fine" voice in the car before social events. "I'd rehearse answers about our weekend plans, our holiday, anything that sounded normal. By the time I arrived, I almost believed it myself."

You Keep Telling Yourself It's Not That Bad

They don't hit you. They don't scream (all the time). At least they come home. At least they're not as bad as their father. At least. At least. At least. But lying there at night, staring at the ceiling while they sleep beside you, you wonder: How did I end up in a life I barely recognise? And it's not just about them. It's about what it's doing to you. It's about the way "not that bad" still feels like drowning.

Everyone Keeps Telling You Relationships Are Work

Your mother says, "Marriage isn't easy." Your friend says, "All couples struggle." Even therapy sometimes asks the wrong question: "What's your contribution to the dynamic?" They mean well. But what they're really saying is: Try harder. Expect less. Stop complaining. So you do. You lower your standards so gradually you don't notice you're eventually grateful for crumbs. A thank you becomes an event. A kind word feels like a gift. A night without tension feels like love.

Your Body Knows Before Your Mind Admits It

That relief when they leave for work? Your body knows. The way you breathe differently when they're not home? Your body knows. That exhaustion that sleep doesn't fix? Your body knows this isn't sustainable. This isn't safe. This isn't love.

A woman once told me she knew her marriage was over when she started hoping for traffic jams. "I'd sit in my car," she said, "inching forward on the highway, and feel peaceful. Because I didn't have to go home yet."

Her body relaxed in gridlock more than it ever did in her marriage.

She kept screenshots on her phone. Apartments she'd never visit. Jobs in cities she'd never move to. "I called it my 'maybe life,'" she said. "It took me three years to realise:

love shouldn't feel like a job you hate but can't quit."

Another survivor told me she'd get migraines that mysteriously disappeared during his business trips. "My doctor kept prescribing different medications. But my body was just trying to tell me what I wasn't ready to hear."

Practical Step

Write two lists side by side:

Left: "What I hoped love would feel like"
Right: "What my relationship actually feels like"

Don't edit. Don't soften. Just write what's true. Look at the gap between the columns. Notice what your stomach, chest, or throat does as you read that gap. That's your body recognising truth.

That's not your failure. That's your clarity returning.

Why It Matters

Because once you see the gap clearly, you can't unsee it. And that's when things start to shift—not because you have to leave, but because you finally stop pretending you're satisfied with crumbs.

If You Remember One Thing

You're not crazy for grieving a relationship while you're still in it.
You're not weak for staying longer than makes sense.

The gap between what you hoped for and what you're settling for isn't proof you expect too much. It's proof you deserve more.

Love doesn't feel like disappearing. And you don't have to vanish to be worthy of it.

6.3
You Didn't Burn Out
You Were Burned Through

Author's Note:

This chapter is about exhaustion used as control. If you were constantly working, constantly doing, constantly pushed to stay "productive" just to avoid punishment or shame, this will help you understand: You didn't burn out because you weren't strong enough. You were burned through by someone who needed you too tired to resist.

They Didn't Teach You Work Ethic, They Taught You Self-Erasure

You're sitting on the sofa after work, just for a moment, and you can feel it building— that familiar knot in your stomach. Any second now, they'll walk in. Any second now, you'll hear the sigh, see the look, feel the temperature drop. So you stand up before they can catch you. Start wiping down counters that are already clean. Because sitting down isn't allowed. Not after work. Not after dinner. Not even for five minutes.

Rest was "lazy." Rest was "selfish." Rest was punished with silence that screamed louder than words ever could.

There was always The List. Written or unwritten, it hung in the air like smoke. Laundry that could wait but mustn't. Floors that were clean but needed cleaning. Gardens that were fine but required attention. Projects that appeared from nowhere, urgent and endless.

You stayed up until 3am folding clothes in perfect squares. Sometimes 4am organising cupboards that nobody would check. Sometimes you worked straight through to daylight, then showered and went to your job, running on nothing but fear disguised as determination.

When colleagues asked how you managed it all, you said, "I don't know. I just do." Because how could you explain that stopping meant consequences you couldn't afford?

That's not resilience. That's what it looks like when a body is run like a machine until the bolts start rattling loose.

You Were Trained to Keep Going Until You Collapsed

They called it having standards. They called it being responsible. They called it "how adults live." But it wasn't living—it was performing survival under surveillance.

A woman told me: "I once fell asleep standing up while washing dishes at 2am. When I jerked awake, my first thought wasn't 'I need rest.' It was 'I hope he didn't see that.'"

She'd been running on three hours of sleep for weeks because her partner insisted the house needed deep cleaning every single night.

You weren't resting between tasks. You were recovering just enough to keep functioning. Not enough to think clearly. Not enough to question why one person's standards required another person's collapse. Just enough to make it through the next impossible day.

Because when you're always moving, always doing, always proving your worth through exhaustion, you don't get the chance to stop and ask: Whose life am I living?

Control Doesn't Always Scream, Sometimes It Keeps You Busy

If they can't silence you with rage, they'll exhaust you with demands. If they can't isolate you physically, they'll keep you so occupied that you lose connection with yourself.

Control doesn't always come with raised voices or slammed doors. Sometimes it comes disguised as "high standards." A schedule that leaves no space for breathing. Lists that regenerate overnight like some domestic hydra—complete one task, three more appear.

You're vacuuming at midnight because the carpet "looks dusty." You're reorganising the garage at dawn because things "aren't quite right." You're scrubbing bathroom grout with a toothbrush while everyone else sleeps because last time you didn't, there were consequences. Not violence. Not yelling. Just that look. That tone. That withdrawal of warmth that taught you: productivity equals safety.

A man told me he worked himself into chronic migraines, chest pains that sent him to emergency twice. "The doctor said it was stress. I said it was just life. I didn't realise until years later—that wasn't life. That was her keeping me too sick to see straight."

Rest Wasn't a Right, It Was a Test

You tried sitting down once. Really tried. Picked up a book, made some tea, told yourself you deserved one quiet hour. Twenty minutes in, they appeared. Didn't say anything at first. Just looked at you. Looked at the book. Looked around the room with that particular expression that catalogued every imperfection.

"Must be nice," they finally said. "Having time to relax."

The book closed itself in your hands. The tea went cold. You found yourself scrubbing skirting boards until your knees ached, because the alternative—their disappointment, their contempt, their cold silence—hurt worse than any physical exhaustion.

A survivor told me she used to hide in the bathroom just to sit down for five minutes. "It was the only place I could rest without being seen. Even then, if I took too long, he'd knock and ask what I was doing. I learnt to rest in ninety-second intervals, like a soldier catching sleep in a war zone."

Practical Step

Tonight, sit down for ten minutes without doing anything productive. Notice what happens in your body. Does your chest tighten? Do your hands itch for something to clean? That anxiety isn't yours—it's the ghost of their control. Breathe through it. You're allowed to be still.

Why It Matters

Your exhaustion wasn't random. It was manufactured. They kept you too tired to think, too drained to plan, too spent to leave. They kept you moving so you couldn't stop and see clearly. Kept you busy so you couldn't connect with people who might notice something was wrong. Kept you exhausted so you couldn't imagine a different life.

If You Remember One Thing

You didn't burn out because you were weak. You were burned through because someone else treated your energy like their personal resource. They mined your strength until you ran empty, then blamed you for not having more to give.

Your exhaustion wasn't a character flaw. Your need for rest wasn't laziness. Your body crying out for stillness wasn't weakness—it was wisdom, trying to save you from someone who saw your depletion as their success.

You were running on empty because someone else was driving. They had their foot on your accelerator, pushing you past every red light your body threw up, past every warning sign that said: this isn't sustainable.

You're allowed to stop now. Not when the house is perfect. Not when everything's done. Not when you've "earned" it. Now.

You're allowed to rest without permission. You're allowed to sit without guilt. You're allowed to exist without producing evidence of your worth.

Your body isn't a machine that broke down. It's a living thing that was pushed past breaking.

Your fatigue isn't failure.
It's proof of how long you kept going against impossible demands.

The person who taught you that rest equals laziness was wrong. The person who made you believe your worth lived in your exhaustion was lying. The person who kept you too tired to think clearly knew exactly what they were doing.

Your time isn't theirs anymore. Your energy belongs to you. And yes, you're allowed to spend it on nothing at all.

That's not lazy. That's freedom.

6.4
Trauma Bonding Feels Like Love
Until You Know

Author's Note:

This chapter is about trauma bonding—the emotional confusion that happens when care and cruelty come from the same person. If you've ever stayed because of the good moments, or defended someone who hurt you by saying "they did their best," this is for you. Because it wasn't love. It was survival. And now, you don't have to confuse the two.

You Clung to the Good Moments to Survive the Bad Ones

You're seven years old, sitting in the back seat. The car still smells like her rage—sharp and metallic, like burnt wire. Ten minutes ago she was screaming that you're ungrateful, selfish, impossible to love. Now she's pulling into the ice cream shop, her voice suddenly honey-soft: "What flavour do you want, sweetheart?"

Your stomach hurts. Your hands are still shaking. But you say "chocolate" because maybe if you get the order right, if you smile the right way, if you're good enough now, the screaming won't come back.

She kisses your forehead at bedtime. Says "I love you more than anything in the world." The same lips that called you worthless three hours ago now whisper that you're precious. Your child-brain splits in half trying to hold both truths, so you choose the softer one. You have to. It's the only way to survive loving someone who terrifies you.

I grew up dizzy from the whiplash. Never knowing which mother would walk through the door. The one who braided my hair or the one who pulled it. The one who sang to me or the one who said I ruined her life.

When people asked about my childhood, I always said, "She did her best." Because she also packed my lunch with little notes. Because she also stayed up when I had nightmares. Because when love comes braided with harm, you hold onto the gentler strands like evidence you weren't crazy to need her.

That's trauma bonding.
Not love. Survival dressed up as attachment.

Trauma Bonding Isn't Loyalty, It's Survival

It happens when your nervous system learns to pair terror with tenderness. When the same person who makes you feel unsafe is also your only source of safety.

It wasn't weakness.
It was your body rewiring itself to survive—terror paired with tenderness, chaos fused with calm.

Your brain releases cortisol during the chaos, floods with dopamine during the calm. You become addicted to the cycle: tension, explosion, honeymoon, repeat. The relief after abuse feels like love because your body is so grateful the danger has passed.

You think the good moments cancel out the bad. The birthday cake erases the silent treatment. The apology heals the wound. The soft touch overwrites the shove. But it doesn't work that way. The good and bad don't cancel—they fuse. They create a trauma bond so strong that leaving feels like dying.

A woman told me: "He'd ignore me for days, wouldn't even look at me. Then suddenly he'd bring flowers, cook dinner, tell me I was his everything. That warmth after the cold felt like the sun coming out. I lived for those moments. I realise now—he controlled the weather."

Forgiveness Is Easier Than Admitting the Truth

You say, "They were stressed."
You say, "They had a hard childhood too."

You say, "They didn't mean it."

Sometimes it feels safer to believe it was accidental than to face the truth that it was chosen.

Because if they meant it, if they knew what they were doing, if they hurt you with awareness and kept doing it anyway—then it wasn't misunderstanding. It was betrayal. And betrayal from someone you love is a pain so deep, forgiveness feels like the only way to survive it.

The Good Moments Weren't Lies, They Were Leverage

You remember the surprise birthday party they threw you. The time they drove through the night to help you move. The perfect Christmas morning. The soft "I'm sorry, baby" after the explosion.

You say, "They weren't all bad." And you're right.
But notice when the good arrived:

After they'd pushed you too far.
Before they needed something.
During the moments you might leave.
Right when witnesses were watching.

The kindness always came with strings.
Not random acts, but carefully timed drops of sugar in poisoned tea.

A survivor told me her mother would scream at her for hours, then take her shopping the next day. "Buy whatever you want," she'd say, credit card out like an apology. "I thought it meant she loved me. I didn't realise until therapy that it wasn't a gift. It was a bribe to forget."

Practical Step

Write down five "good" memories with the person who hurt you. Then write what happened right before or after each one. Watch the pattern emerge: explosion then affection, cruelty then care, withdrawal then warmth. You're not wrong for treasuring the good moments. You're brave for finally seeing what surrounded them.

Why It Matters

When you see the pattern, you stop calling it love. You start calling it what it was: a control mechanism disguised as connection.

You Weren't Addicted to Them, You Were Addicted to Relief

You craved the calm after the storm—the way your shoulders finally dropped, your stomach unclenched, your breath came back to you. The tenderness after the attack. The "I love you" after the "You're nothing." You stayed for those rare moments when your body could soften, not realising they were deliberately rationed to keep you starving for more.

It wasn't stupidity. It was biology. Your nervous system did what it had to do to survive in an impossible situation. But now you're safe enough to see it clearly. Now you're strong enough to want more than survival.

A man told me: "After my father hit me, he'd sometimes cry. Hold me. Tell me he was sorry, that I was his boy, his pride. Those moments felt more real than the violence. I realise now I wasn't staying for him. I was staying for those ten minutes of feeling loved. Ten minutes out of thousands."

If You Remember One Thing

You weren't weak for loving them.
You weren't foolish for staying.
You were trauma-bonded—neurologically wired to confuse intensity with intimacy,

chaos with connection.

Trauma bonding doesn't feel like abuse. It feels like hope. Hope that this time will be different. Hope that the good version is the "real" them. Hope that if you just love harder, forgive faster, need less—the storms will finally stop.

But they never stopped, did they?
Because the storms weren't weather. They were weapons.
And the calm wasn't peace. It was calculated.

Real love doesn't make you grateful for basic kindness. It doesn't hurt you then heal you and call that wholeness. It doesn't make you work for warmth you should receive freely.

Real love is boring in the best way. Consistent. Present. Safe. It doesn't vanish when you have needs. It doesn't punish you for having feelings. It doesn't make you earn it back after taking it away.

You survived something that wore love's mask but carried abuse's blade. You learnt to be grateful for drops of water in a desert someone else created. You called it love because it's all you knew.

But now you know better.
Now you know that love shouldn't cost you your sanity.

And once you know, you can't unknow.
Which means you never have to call chaos love again.

You get to choose what love feels like now.
And it should feel like safety.

6.5
"I'm Fine"
Was A Full-Time Job

Author's Note:

This chapter is about the cost of holding it together when everything inside you was coming undone. If you've ever smiled at work after crying in the car, or said "no worries" while your heart raced, this is for you. Because surviving abuse doesn't always look like collapse. Sometimes it looks like showing up while quietly falling apart.

You Showed Up Like Everything Was Fine
Because Falling Apart Wasn't an Option

You're sitting in your car outside work, mascara running, chest heaving from the morning's fight. The clock says 8:58. In two minutes, you need to be at your desk, smiling, professional, "together." So you flip down the visor mirror, wipe the black streaks with a tissue that shreds against your skin, and practise: "Morning! Yeah, good weekend, thanks."

You walk through those doors like you didn't just spend twenty minutes hyperventilating in a car park. Like you didn't sleep on the sofa again. Like your phone isn't full of messages that make your stomach drop every time it buzzes.

You still made the meeting.
Still packed the lunches with shaking hands.
Still answered "How are you?" with "Fine, thanks! You?"

Even when your chest felt like a fist was squeezing it from inside. Even when the fluorescent lights felt too bright and every sound too sharp. Even when you had to excuse yourself to the bathroom just to breathe.

You didn't fake it to deceive anyone. You faked it because the alternative—letting it show, letting it spill, letting anyone see how bad it really was—would have cost you everything.

The truth was too jagged to squeeze between "Good morning" and "See you tomorrow." It would have cut the air open, bled all over the photocopier, stained the break room conversations.

What You Called Holding It Together Was Actually Survival in Disguise

You were calm at school drop-off because your children needed you to be their anchor, not their storm. You kissed their foreheads, straightened their backpacks, waved until they disappeared inside—then sat in your car and let your hands shake.

You laughed at your colleague's jokes because you couldn't afford to be the difficult one, the emotional one, the one who might lose her job if anyone knew what was happening at home. So you perfected the art of normal: coffee in hand, smile in place, while your shoulders burned from holding everything in.

You played along at family dinners, passing potatoes while your mother-in-law asked, "How's everything at home?" You said "Great!" because the truth would have blown up the table.

That wasn't strength. That was strategy.
You weren't pretending. You were protecting yourself from a world that punishes victims for not being perfect ones.

Being Civil with Your Abuser Wasn't Weakness, It Was Calculation

You smiled at handover. Said "Have a good day" when they collected the kids. Kept your voice neutral during the phone calls about schedules. People watching thought you were "handling it so well," "being so mature," "taking the high road."

They didn't see you afterwards—pulling over on the freeway because your vision blurred with rage. Throwing up in the work toilets from anxiety. Taking headache tablets that stopped working months ago because your jaw never unclenches anymore.

Your civility wasn't compliance. It was survival mathematics. Every neutral word calculated to prevent escalation. Every calm interaction a chess move to protect your children, your case, your sanity.

You didn't react to their social media posts painting themselves as the victim. Didn't correct the narrative when mutual friends said, "It's sad, but these things happen." Didn't defend yourself when they twisted every story to make you the villain.

A woman told me: "During mediation, he lied about everything. I sat there, calm, taking notes. The mediator said I was 'remarkably composed.' I wanted to scream that I wasn't composed—I was dissociated. But I just nodded and said, 'Thank you.'"

What others called grace was your body frozen in its chair, every muscle locked while your mouth smiled on cue. What looked like dignity was actually your nervous system in freeze mode, each inhale having to pass inspection before you let it out.

You Didn't Just Swallow Your Pain, You Learnt to Speak Around It

You became fluent in deflection. An expert in "I'm fine." A master of the redirect.

You stopped saying what wouldn't be heard. Stopped crying where it would be weaponised. Stopped showing hurt that would be called "manipulation" or "drama" or "attention-seeking."

You learnt that "fine" was the password to avoid deeper questions. That "busy" explained away weight loss. That "tired" covered the insomnia, the hypervigilance, the way you startled at every door slam.

The words you really wanted to say—"I'm drowning," "I'm terrified," "I need help"—stayed trapped behind your sternum like birds in a cage, wings beating against bone.

Practical Step

Tonight, find one person you trust—or even your own reflection—and say one true thing about how you're really doing. Not the whole story. Just one sentence that isn't "I'm fine." Notice how your body responds to letting even that small truth exist outside of you.

Why It Matters

Because "I'm fine" became your prison. And naming what's real—even in whispers, even to yourself—is how you start to break free.

The Performance Was Exhausting
Because You Were the Only One Who Knew It Was a Performance

Everyone else thought this was just you: capable, reliable, "together." They didn't know you were method acting your own life. That every normal interaction required a script, a costume, a version of yourself that could function in daylight.

You memorised appropriate responses. Practised facial expressions in mirrors. Calculated how much truth you could reveal without the whole facade crumbling. You became so good at performing okay that sometimes you almost convinced yourself.

A man told me: "I gave a presentation the morning after she destroyed my laptop in a rage. Stood there talking about quarterly projections while thinking about the broken glass I'd swept up at 3am. My boss said it was my best presentation yet. I went to my car afterwards and couldn't stop shaking."

If You Remember One Thing

Saying "I'm fine" when you were falling apart wasn't lying. It was survival.

It was what you said when the truth was too dangerous to speak. When honesty would cost you your job, your children, your safety. When the world demanded you be okay,

264

so you performed okay until you almost forgot what real felt like.

You weren't weak for hiding your pain. You were strategic.
You weren't dishonest for protecting your truth. You were smart.

The facade wasn't fake—it was armour. And you needed it to survive spaces that couldn't hold your reality.

But here's what changes everything: You don't have to perform anymore.

You're allowed to stop saying "I'm fine" when you're not. You're allowed to let your face show what your heart feels.

The words might shake at first. Might come out as whispers. Might need practice in safe spaces before you can say them in the world.

But they're your words.
Your truth.
Your right.

After so long of speaking around your pain, you finally get to speak it directly. Not to everyone. Not all at once. But to someone. Somewhere. Starting now.

Because "I'm fine" was never the truth. It was just what you said to survive.
And you've survived. Which means you can start telling the truth now.

Even if it's just to yourself.
Even if it's just "I'm not fine."
Even if it's just "I need help."
Those three words might be the bravest thing you ever say.

And the most honest you've been allowed to be in years.

6.6
They Didn't Defend You
They Defended Him

Author's Note:

This chapter is about the betrayal that doesn't come from your abuser—it comes from the people who watched. If someone stayed neutral, dismissed your story, or kept smiling at the person who hurt you, this will help you name it: They weren't protecting peace. They were protecting comfort. And it cost you more than they'll ever know.

I Risked Honesty, She Chose Distance

You're sitting across from your oldest friend, the one who's known you since school. Your hands are wrapped around a coffee cup that's gone cold while you search for the right words. Finally, you tell her. Not everything—that would be too much—just one incident. The time he screamed at you for forty minutes about loading the dishwasher wrong. The time he threw your phone against the wall then blamed you for "making him lose control."

She shifts in her chair. Takes a sip of her latte. Looks past you at the wall and says, "Well... I wasn't there, so I don't really know what happened."

The words land like ice water on skin. You watch her face rearrange itself into careful neutrality, see her mentally stepping back from the edge of your truth. She changes the subject to her daughter's dance recital. You nod along, but your hands tremble around the cup, heat long gone cold.

Later, scrolling through Facebook, you see she's commented on his post: "Great photo! Miss you guys!" The betrayal lodges in your throat, thick and immovable, like trying to swallow stones.

Not his silence this time. Hers.

Her neutrality closed like a door with no sound—sudden, final, shutting you out.

They Don't Need to Defend the Abuser to Wound You, Just Doubt You

You open up to your sister, voice trembling, showing her the text messages. The ones where he calls you pathetic, useless, "lucky anyone tolerates you." She reads them, eyebrows raised, then hands your phone back.

"Wow, that's... intense," she says. Then nothing. No follow-up. No "Are you okay?" No "What can I do?" Just the cold draft of discomfort dressed as neutrality.

Three weeks later at Christmas dinner, she's laughing at his jokes. Taking selfies with him. When he puts his arm around you for the family photo, she says, "You two are so cute together!" Your skin crawls but you smile too, because resistance would only make you the problem.

A woman told me: "My best friend said she believed me but didn't want to 'pick sides.' Then she went to his birthday party. Posted photos. When I asked how she could celebrate someone who terrorised me, she said I was being dramatic. That's when I learnt: neutrality is just cowardice with better PR."

They Say "There Are Two Sides" But Only One Is Weaponised

You gather your courage and tell your mother about the financial control. How he monitors every purchase, questions every receipt, makes you justify buying tampons. How he has access to all your accounts but you can't see his.

She nods sympathetically, pats your hand, then says: "Marriage is complicated. I'm sure he's stressed about money. You know how men are about providing."

You tell your brother about the rage. The holes in walls. The door he ripped off its hinges. He says: "That doesn't sound like him. Are you sure you're not exaggerating? Maybe you both need counselling."

They say they're being "fair." Being "balanced." Not wanting to "get involved."

But neutrality when someone is being harmed isn't neutral.
It's complicity dressed as wisdom.

People Don't Want to Believe the Villain Is Someone They Like

They know him as the guy who helps with moving day. Who remembers birthdays. Who tells great stories at barbecues. They see the public performance, not the private terrorism.

They don't see him counting your calories.
They don't hear him say you're disgusting.
They don't feel the temperature drop when you disagree with him in private.

So when you finally speak your truth, you're not just telling them what happened. You're asking them to shatter their comfortable illusion. To admit they were fooled. To acknowledge they might have enabled harm by their blindness.

Most people would rather protect their comfort than face that discomfort. Would rather believe you're "misremembering" than believe their judgement was so wrong.

A man told me: "When I finally told people about my wife's abuse, they said, 'But she's so tiny! She's so sweet!' As if size determines cruelty. As if public sweetness cancels private sadism. Their disbelief became another set of bars around me—invisible, but just as confining. I felt my chest tighten, as if even my lungs had been locked behind those bars."

Practical Step

Make a list of three people who believed you without question. If you can't think of three, include yourself. These are your truth-keepers. Stop wasting energy trying to convince people who've already chosen comfort over your reality.

Why It Matters

Your truth doesn't need universal approval to be true. It needs to be spoken to people who honour it, not debate it.

Betrayal by Bystanders Is a Wound with No Apology

He hurt you—they ignored it.
He lied about you—they believed it.
He played victim—they comforted him.
He rewrote history—they accepted his version.

And you're left holding the truth like a live wire no one wants to touch.

You watch them continue to invite him to gatherings. Include him in group chats. Ask "How's he doing?" as if you're the one who left destruction in your wake. Some even suggest you should "try to be friends for everyone's sake."

They smile as if nothing's wrong, while your truth sits unspoken in the room.

The loneliness of being disbelieved can be worse than the original abuse. At least with him, you knew where you stood. These people? They pretend everything's normal while you drown in their denial.

If You Remember One Thing

The hardest part wasn't always what he did to you.
Sometimes it was the silence that followed when you tried to tell.

The friend who said, "I don't want to take sides."
The family who said, "Let's not ruin Christmas."
The colleague who said, "That's between you two."

Their neutrality wasn't wisdom—it was abandonment wearing a diplomatic mask. Their silence wasn't peacekeeping—it was complicity dressed as kindness.

But here's what they'll never tell you: You don't need their validation to recover. You don't need their belief to be believable. You don't need their acknowledgement for your truth to be true.

You're allowed to call their neutrality what it was: a choice to protect themselves at your expense. You're allowed to grieve the secondary losses—the people who chose comfort over courage, who chose him over truth, who chose silence over you.

And now? Now you don't wait for validation from people who benefit from your silence.

You speak to those who listen.
You recover despite their doubt.
You rise without their permission.

Not because they finally saw your truth.
But because you stopped needing them to.

Your truth stands alone.
Even if you're the only one standing with it.

And sometimes, that's enough to begin.

6.7
They Didn't Co-Parent
They Recruited

Author's Note:

This chapter names a specific kind of heartbreak that many survivors carry in silence: the child who gets groomed by the narcissist. The one who becomes his echo, his reflection, his defender. This isn't about blame. It's about grief. The kind that doesn't come from losing a child, but from watching one disappear into someone else's story, someone else's rules. If this is your reality, you're not alone. And you're not the failure here.

She Had Dinner with Him Every Week
But She Didn't Come When It Mattered

You're lying in the hospital bed, machines beeping their quiet rhythm. The nurse adjusts your IV drip. Your phone sits silent on the bedside table—no new messages. It's been three days since the surgery. Four since you texted her: "Going in tomorrow morning. Scared."

She read it. The little tick marks tell you that much.

But she doesn't come. Not for the pre-op terror when your hands shook signing consent forms. Not for the long recovery hours when pain medication made everything blur. Not when the surgeon used words like "complications" and "concerning."

Your brother shows you Facebook on his phone, trying to distract you. There's your daughter, smiling in a restaurant booth, wine glass raised. Posted yesterday. "Love our weekly dinners! Best dad ever"

Your stomach twists—not from surgery, but from recognition.

The same booth where he's been feeding her stories for months. How you were always anxious, always difficult. How he tried so hard but you were never satisfied. How much calmer life is now without your "drama."

Your chest tightens, and it's not from the incision. It's from recognising the script. You've heard it before, in court documents, in emails to mutual friends. Now it's coming from her mouth, at their weekly dinners, while you lie here with surgical tape holding you together.

Sometimes the wound doesn't come with words at all. Just the silence where love should have been.

He Didn't Say "Don't Love Her," He Said "I Worry About Her"

The most insidious thing a narcissist does after separation isn't rage. It's recruitment.

They don't scream "Your mother is evil!" That would be too obvious. Instead, they become the concerned parent, the stable one, the victim of your instability. They shake their head sadly when your name comes up. Sigh deeply. Change the subject "for everyone's sake."

They say, "I worry about your mum. She's been through a lot."
They say, "You were young, you don't remember how hard she could be."
They say, "I don't want to speak badly of her, but..."

Then they wait. Let the child fill in the blanks with doubt.

They reward alignment with warmth. Punish questions with withdrawal. Create a climate where loving you feels like betrayal of them. Where defending you means losing their approval. Where seeing you clearly threatens their version of reality.

A woman told me: "My son started calling me Sarah instead of Mum after the divorce. His dad never told him to do it. But every time he said 'Mum' at his father's house, the temperature dropped. Kids learn fast what keeps them safe."

The child—even adult children—learns which parent is "safe" to love openly and which one must be loved in secret, if at all.

It Looks Like Rejection But It's Rehearsed

You text: "Haven't heard from you in a while. Miss you."
They reply three days later: "Been busy."
Your hand shakes as you put the phone down, as if even your body knows the words aren't true.

You call on their birthday. It goes to voicemail.
They text: "Thanks for the call. In a meeting."
It's Sunday.

It feels like rejection. But the lines have been rehearsed. They've been taught that distance from you equals loyalty to him. That your pain is manipulation. That your love comes with strings they must cut.

They think they're being "mature" by staying "neutral." But silence in the face of lies isn't neutral. It's participation, wearing the mask of maturity.

Practical Step

Write them one letter. Not defending yourself—they've heard his version too many times.

Instead, write about specific memories only you two share. The song you sang during bath time. The way they mispronounced "butterfly." The night they had that nightmare and you stayed up making stories until dawn. Keep it for yourself first.

This is about reclaiming your truth, not convincing them. Then find one person who knew you as a parent before he rewrote the story. Ask them to tell you one specific thing they remember about you with your child.

Why It Matters

Your memories are real even if your child doesn't remember. Other people saw you love them. You weren't crazy then, and you're not crazy now. Writing it and hearing it from another makes your truth concrete—evidence that his version isn't the only one.

You Can't Save Someone Who's Been Taught You're the Enemy

This might be the hardest truth to swallow: love isn't always enough.

You could have been the perfect parent—never raised your voice, never missed a school play, never forgot their favourite meal—and still, his version might win. Because he got there first with the story. Because he made himself the victim. Because he turned your love into evidence of your "instability."

You find yourself defending things that shouldn't need defending. "I did pick you up from school." "I wasn't drunk at your birthday." "I never said that." But every defence falls into the trap he built—proof, in their eyes, of what he told them to expect.

A survivor told me: "My daughter asked me to come to therapy with her. I was hopeful. Then I sat there while she read a list of things I'd supposedly done—half were complete fiction, half were his actions she'd been told were mine. The therapist looked at me like I was a monster. I realised: I was fighting his ghost wearing her face."

If this has happened to you, it isn't proof you failed. It's proof he was ruthless.

Your Love Was Real Even If They Don't Remember It That Way

There's a particular grief that comes from being rewritten in your child's story. Not just forgotten—actively revised. The nights you stayed up with their fever become "neglect." The boundaries you set become "control." The tears you cried become "manipulation."

When they start quoting his narrative as truth—"Mum was always angry," "Dad tried so hard to make it work," "She made our childhood chaotic"—something breaks inside you that might never fully mend.

But here's what remains true: The love you gave them is etched into their bones, even if their mind can't access it right now. The safety you provided lives in their nervous system, even if their words deny it. Every story you read, every meal you cooked with love, every time you chose patience over frustration—it all happened. It all mattered. It's all real.

If You Remember One Thing

You weren't hard to love.
You were easy to erase.

He needed you small because your truth threatened his fiction. He needed your child confused because clarity would expose his manipulation. He needed them aligned because their love for you was evidence you weren't the monster he painted.

But through all of it—the rewriting, the recruitment, the rehearsed rejection—you kept loving them. Even when it hurt. Even when they couldn't receive it. Even when they threw it back at you wrapped in his words.

The lullabies you sang were real.
The plasters you carefully placed on scraped knees were real.
The pride at school concerts was real.
The terror during their illnesses was real.
The joy at their first words, first steps, first day of school—all real.

None of that disappears because someone rewrote the script.
None of that becomes false because they can't see it now.

You were not the problem parent.
You were the inconvenient truth.

The one who remembered what really happened.

The one whose existence challenged his narrative.
The one who wouldn't perform in his play.

That took courage they can't recognise yet.

Maybe one day they'll see through the fog he created. Maybe they won't. But your worth as a parent doesn't depend on their awakening. Your love was real when you gave it. It's still real now—carried in memory, in your body, in the life you built around them.

You don't need their validation to claim your truth.
You don't need their memory to confirm your love.
You don't need their recognition to know who you really were.

You loved them. Fiercely. Truly. Completely.
That's enough.

Even if you're the only one who knows it.
That's enough.

6.8
You Don't Owe Reconciliation

Author's Note:

There's a pressure survivors feel that no one talks about. The pressure to "move on." To keep the peace. To make things okay again, even when nothing has been repaired. If you've ever been told to reach out, let it go, rebuild the relationship, and the person who hurt you never once apologised, this chapter is for you. Because reconciliation without remorse is just more harm, with better lighting.

They Never Said Sorry But You Were Still Asked to Fix It

You're sitting at the kitchen table, your mother across from you, stirring sugar into her tea. She's not looking at you when she says it: "Don't you think it's time you reached out to your father? Life's too short for grudges."

Your stomach drops. Three years since you went no contact. Three years since the last explosion, the final cruelty that broke something permanent. Three years of peace you fought for, boundaries you bled to build. And not once—not one single time—has he acknowledged what he did.

But here you are, being asked to be the bigger person. Again.

"He's getting older," she continues, eyes on her spoon making slow circles. "You'll regret it if something happens."

What about your regret? What about the years you already lost trying to make him love you without hurting you? What about the therapy bills, the nightmares, the way you still flinch when someone raises their voice?

A woman told me: "My sister asked if I was ready to forgive our mother for the childhood abuse. I said, 'She's never admitted it happened. She still tells people I'm making it up.' My sister said, 'But holding onto anger is poisoning you.' I realised then—I wasn't holding anger. I was holding truth. And they wanted me to drop it because it made family dinners awkward."

That's the message survivors receive over and over: Your boundaries are the problem. Your memory is the issue. Your refusal to pretend is what's tearing the family apart.

Not the abuse. Not the silence. Not the person who caused the harm and walked away clean.

You're told forgiveness is the higher path. That holding a boundary is "bitterness." That refusing to reconcile is "refusing to heal." But what about the person who never said sorry? Why aren't they asked to grow? Why aren't they pressured to reach out?

Why is the survivor the only one expected to do the emotional labour of repair?

Forgiveness Shouldn't Be a Performance

You don't owe anyone a reconciliation story to make them comfortable. You don't owe the family a happy ending for the holiday photos. You don't owe your community false peace so they can avoid taking sides. You don't owe your story a redemptive arc to prove you're "healed."

This isn't about spite or revenge. It's about reality. You cannot reconcile with someone who refuses to acknowledge what they did. You cannot rebuild trust with someone who still denies breaking it. You cannot create safety with someone who never stopped being dangerous.

They want you to build a bridge to someone who burnt the last one while you were still on it. They want you to extend a hand to someone who once used theirs to harm you.

They want you to open a door you locked for survival.

You Can Choose Peace Without Picking Up What Broke You

Your aunt calls: "But he's your father."
Your friend suggests: "Maybe write him a letter."
Your therapist asks: "Have you considered forgiveness for your own peace?"

As if you haven't considered it. As if you haven't turned it over in your mind a thousand times, wondering if you're being too harsh, too unforgiving, too much like them.

But choosing peace doesn't mean choosing them. Recovery doesn't require proximity to the person who wounded you. Forgiveness—if you choose it—doesn't mean reconciliation. You can forgive from a distance. You can recover behind locked doors. You can find peace in the space their absence created.

A survivor told me: "I forgave my ex-husband. Not for him, but to stop carrying his poison in my body. But forgiveness didn't mean I had to let him back in.

I forgave him from three thousand miles away, with a restraining order between us."

They Should Be Seeking Repair, Not Waiting for You to Fold

If reconciliation was real, it wouldn't start with you. It would start with them—on their knees, if necessary. With genuine remorse. With acknowledgement of specific harm. With changed behaviour that proves they understand the weight of what they did.

Instead, you get:
"Let's just move forward."
"Can't we put the past behind us?"
"I don't remember it that way."
"You're being dramatic."

Or worse—nothing. Silence that expects you to fill it with forgiveness they haven't earned.

Practical Step

Write down what genuine accountability would look like from them. Not vague promises or tearful manipulation. Real accountability. Would it include: Admitting specific acts without minimising? Taking responsibility without blame-shifting? Respecting your boundaries without testing them? Understanding the impact without centring their feelings? Consistent changed behaviour over time?

Now ask yourself: Has any of that happened? Even once? If not, you're not refusing reconciliation. You're refusing to participate in their fantasy where nothing happened.

Why It Matters

Because reconciliation without accountability is just giving them permission to hurt you again. And you've been hurt enough.

If You Remember One Thing

You don't have to make peace with someone who made war on you and never surrendered.

You don't have to "see both sides" when one side was abuse and the other was survival.

You don't have to prove you're not bitter by embracing someone who made you taste bitterness in the first place.

The pressure to reconcile isn't coming from love or wisdom. It's coming from discomfort—other people's discomfort with your boundaries, with your truth, with the inconvenience of acknowledging what really happened.

They want you to reconcile because your boundary holds up a mirror to their complicity. Your distance declares that actions have consequences. Your absence announces that some things can't be undone with small talk and shared meals.

But their comfort isn't your responsibility.
Their family image isn't yours to maintain.
Their denial isn't yours to enable.

You are allowed to stay gone. You are allowed to maintain distance without justifying it to anyone who wouldn't understand anyway. You are allowed to choose safety over civility, peace over performance, healing over harmony.

Some doors are meant to stay closed. Not because you're unforgiving, but because you finally learned to protect what's precious: your peace, your safety, your hard-won freedom from people who proved they couldn't be trusted with your heart.

Reconciliation is a choice, not an obligation.
Forgiveness is a journey, not a destination you owe anyone else.
And family isn't defined by blood—it's defined by behaviour.

You don't owe reconciliation to anyone.
Especially not to someone who never even said sorry.

That's not bitterness.
That's wisdom.

And it's about time someone said it out loud.

6.9
Loneliest is Loving Someone Who Doesn't See You

Author's Note:

This chapter is for the part of you that kept hoping they'd notice—if you just tried harder, explained it better, or became a version they would finally love. If you've ever been told you were too much, this is your reminder: You weren't too much. You were just unseen. And your worth was never dependent on their vision.

You Tried to Earn Love by Disappearing But They Never Noticed You Were Gone

You're standing in the kitchen, chopping vegetables for dinner. He's at the table, scrolling through his phone. You clear your throat softly—once, twice. Nothing.

You say his name. He doesn't look up. You mention the promotion you got today, the one you've worked toward for two years. "Mmm," he says, thumb still moving across the screen.

So you try differently. Make his favourite meal. Wear the dress he once liked. Laugh quieter. Stop singing in the shower because he needs quiet.

You become smaller, smoother, less complicated. Less you.

You think: Maybe now. Maybe if I take up less space—maybe then he'll finally see me. But the smaller you become, the easier you are to overlook. And one morning you realise you've disappeared so completely that even you can't find yourself anymore.

You became an expert in self-erasure—holding your breath, lowering your voice, shrinking until even your body forgot how to take up space.

These weren't flaws. They were survival skills—brilliant, exhausting strategies to stay close to someone who refused to come close to you.

They Didn't Love You, They Loved Your Compliance

You brought them coffee exactly how they liked it—half sugar, low fat milk, not too hot. They took it without looking up.

You remembered their mother's birthday when they forgot. They took credit for your thoughtfulness.

You rearranged your schedule for their convenience. They assumed that's what you were for.

They didn't want to see you. They wanted you to be a mirror, reflecting back what they needed: agreement, validation, admiration for stories told a hundred times.

When you showed up with your own opinions, your own needs, your own stories— their eyes glazed over. When you said, "Can we talk about us?" they suddenly had emails to answer. When you cried, they called it manipulation. When you laughed too loud, they called it embarrassing.

And every time you showed your humanity, they treated it like an inconvenience.

A woman told me: "I won an award at work. Came home glowing. He looked at me and said, 'The kitchen's a mess.' That's when I knew—I could cure cancer and he'd still only see what I hadn't done for him."

They Didn't Want Connection, They Wanted Control

Every time you tried to explain how you felt, they said you were "overthinking."
Every time you asked for emotional intimacy, they said you were "needy."
Every time you expressed hurt, they said you were "too sensitive."
Every time you showed joy about something they didn't care about, they said you were

"too much."

The labels stuck like stones in your chest, each one pressing down until breathing felt like betrayal. But here's what they never said: "Tell me more." "How can I help?" "I'm listening." "I see you."

They didn't want honesty. They wanted harmony—but only the kind where you harmonised with them, never the other way around. They wanted peace—but only the kind where you swallowed your truth to keep things smooth.

Practical Step

Write a letter to yourself that begins: "You are not too much. You were just..." Then finish that sentence ten different ways. Examples: "...too real for someone who needed you performed." "...too honest for someone who preferred facades." "...too whole for someone who needed you broken."

Keep writing until you feel the truth sink from your head to your bones.

Why It Matters

Because being dismissed repeatedly teaches your nervous system that you're not worth responding to. This exercise rewires that lie, one truth at a time.

You Tried to Fit Into a Story You Were Never Meant to Star In

You memorised their moods like weather patterns, adjusting yourself accordingly. Storm brewing? Become invisible. Sunny spell? Perform happiness but not too much— don't outshine them. Cold front? Wrap yourself in apologies for existing.

You edited yourself down to bullet points they might read. Simplified your complex feelings into digestible portions. Translated your needs into their language, hoping maybe then they'd understand.

But they didn't want to understand. They wanted you uncomplicated.

A man told me: "She said I was 'too emotional' every time I tried to connect. So I learnt to talk about sports, weather, anything surface. One day she said, 'You never share anything real.' I realised then—I couldn't win. The game was rigged from the start."

You became a ghost haunting your own life—present but weightless, watching yourself fade from the edges inward.

If You Remember One Thing

You were never too much.
You were just too real for someone who needed you blurry.

They didn't fail to love you because you weren't enough.
They failed to love you because they refused to see you clearly.

Real love doesn't ask you to shrink. It doesn't demand silence or apologies for existing. It sees your whole self and says, "Yes. You."

You are not a rough draft waiting for edits.
You are the whole story.

Every time you made yourself smaller, you weren't moving closer to love. You were moving further from yourself. And the self you abandoned? That's the one who deserves to be cherished.

Stop auditioning for a part in someone else's story.
Stop shrinking to fit their comfort.
Stop translating yourself into easier language.

The right person won't need you to disappear to earn their attention. They'll see you across a crowded room—not despite your intensity, but because of it.

Not in spite of your truth, but drawn to it.

Your healing begins the moment you stop trying to be loveable to someone who chose not to love you.

Start here: When you catch yourself shrinking tomorrow, pause.
Ask: "What would I do if I knew I was already enough?"

Then do that. Even if your voice shakes.
Even if they don't notice. Do it for the person you were before you learnt to disappear.

She's still in there, waiting.

And she was never too much. She was always exactly enough.

6.10
Disappointment Doesn't Have to Break You

Author's Note:

This is the chapter for when you're sitting in the aftermath of a decision you wish you hadn't made. When you're looking at your life and thinking: How the hell did I end up here? When your first instinct is to go to war with yourself. Pause. You can want change without declaring war on yourself. You can feel regret and still show yourself care. That's not softness. That's strength.

You Don't Have to Like It to Be Kind About It

You're staring at the bank statement, seeing the money you sent them last month. The money you swore you wouldn't send again. Your stomach drops. Not because of the amount—though that stings too—but because you recognise this feeling. This is disappointment wearing your own face.

You can look at your choices and say, that wasn't right for me. You can feel the sting of that without needing to numb it, explain it, or weaponise it against yourself.

You're allowed to be disappointed. You're allowed to want more. You're allowed to say, I don't like where I am right now without saying, I don't like who I am.

There's a difference. And it's everything.

Self-Hate Isn't Fuel. It's Fire

A woman told me she used to wake up every morning and list everything she'd done wrong the day before. "It was my motivation," she said. "I thought if I was cruel enough to myself, I'd finally change." She paused. "All it did was make me exhausted. And silent. And more likely to go back to him because at least his cruelty was familiar."

Hating yourself into wholeness doesn't work. Not sustainably. Not without cost. Shame can mimic motivation—getting you up, getting you moving—but it always demands payment. With burnout. With silence. With isolation. With a voice in your head that always moves the goalposts.

You don't need to punish yourself to do better. You just need to stay with yourself long enough to move forward.

When criticism was how you learnt to survive, kindness can feel foreign. That's okay. Start small.

Self-Compassion Isn't a Reward. It's a Prerequisite

You don't have to earn kindness from yourself by being perfect first. Compassion isn't for the moments you feel proud.

It's for the mornings you can barely face. The late-night spirals. The "I should've known better." The "I can't believe I did that again." The moment you find yourself googling their new partner at 2am, hating yourself for caring.

Those are the moments where compassion matters most. Because that's where you rewrite the story.

If being kind to yourself feels selfish or weak, remember: your nervous system can't heal while under threat—even from yourself. Compassion tells your body it's safe enough to change.

Practical Step

Write a letter to yourself from the version of you who understands why you did what you did. Let it begin like this: "You made the best decision you could with what you knew then. That doesn't make it easy. But it does make it human."

If writing feels too vulnerable right now, just think the words. Or write one sentence.

Or just sit with your hand on your heart and breathe. Even that counts. Don't edit. Don't analyse. Just write from care.

Why It Matters

Most people don't stay stuck because they failed. They stay stuck because they've turned the failure into a verdict. When disappointment becomes self-attack, your nervous system reads it as danger. You can't grow while fleeing from yourself.

Compassion doesn't mean you're avoiding responsibility. It means you're taking responsibility without the cruelty. It's what lets you keep moving, not because you're bypassing the truth, but because you're finally telling it with care.

If You Remember One Thing

You're allowed to hate what happened without hating who it happened to.

You can want to change without treating yourself like a mistake. Disappointment is data, not a death sentence. It tells you what you value, what you want to be different, where you want to grow.

But it doesn't tell you that you're broken. It doesn't tell you that you're beyond repair. It doesn't tell you that you deserve punishment.

You are not your worst thing. Not your poorest choice. Not your lowest moment.

You're the person who survived it all. Who learnt from it. Who's still here, still trying.

And that person, the one reading this right now, the one who cares enough to want better, still deserves gentleness. Especially from yourself.

If you can't believe you deserve gentleness yet, that's okay. Just try not blocking it when it shows up.

Part 7
Knowing

The story doesn't hold like
it used to. And neither do you

7.1
The Voice in Your Head
Isn't Yours. It's Theirs

Author's Note:

This chapter is about what happens when the gaslighting goes quiet but keeps living inside your head. If you've ever thought, "Maybe I was the problem," long after they left, this will help you see where that thought really came from, and how to start getting your voice back.

Surviving Coercive Control Isn't Just About Getting Away

You drop a plate in your new kitchen. It clatters on the floor and you apologise—out loud—to no one.Heart racing. Hands shaking. The voice arrives before you form a thought: "Can't you do anything right?"

They're gone. Maybe for months. Maybe for years. But their voice lives in you, clearer than morning light through your window.

Your lungs tighten as if apologising is the only currency you have left. Your throat goes dry—an automatic concession before you've finished thinking. You catch yourself mid-apology to the empty room. Who are you apologising to? The ghost of their criticism? The echo of their contempt?

You realise with a sick twist in your stomach: They might have left, but they're still here. Living rent-free in your head. Commenting on every move you make.

Too loud when you laugh.
Too slow when you think.
Too selfish when you buy something small for yourself.
Too emotional when you cry at a film.

Too needy when you text a friend twice.

Sometimes it takes months, even years, to notice: these aren't your thoughts. They arrived like echoes—repeated so often you began to accept them as your own. And like everything else they said, they were lies designed to keep you small.

You Were Never the Problem But They Needed You to Think You Were

That was always the game. Make you feel broken so they could position themselves as your only solution. Keep you doubting every instinct so you'd stop trusting your own perception. Convince you that you were difficult to love so you'd be grateful for scraps.

They needed you insecure. Uncertain. Always apologising. That's how coercive control works—not through chains but through doubt. Not through locks but through the voice in your head that sounds like yours but speaks their script.

They handed you their shame.
Their inadequacy. Their self-loathing.
And told you it was your reflection.

Every accusation was a confession.

Every criticism was projection. Every "you always" and "you never" was them describing themselves while looking at you.

A woman told me: "Three years after leaving, I still heard him criticising my parking. Every time I reversed, his voice: 'You're going to hit something. You can't judge distance.' One day I realised—he'd had four accidents. I'd had none. But I believed I was the bad driver because he said it so often it became my truth."

The Voice Sounds Like Yours But the Words Are Theirs

You think you're having your own thoughts. "I'm so stupid." "I can't do anything right." "No one else would put up with me." But pause. Whose vocabulary is that? When did you start describing yourself with their insults?

You never called yourself "crazy" before them.
You never thought you were "too much" before them.
You never believed you were "impossible" before them.

These aren't observations. They're infiltrations. Their voice wearing your voice like a mask.

A man told me: "I kept hearing her say 'pathetic' every time I showed emotion. Even alone, crying at my dad's funeral, I heard it. 'Pathetic.' It took therapy to realise—that word was never in my vocabulary before her. I'd borrowed her cruelty and turned it inward."

Practical Step

Write down the cruel things you say to yourself. The self-attacks that feel automatic. Then ask: Who said this to me first? When did I start believing this? Would I say this to a friend?

Next to each cruel statement, write what you were actually doing when they said it. Were you expressing a need? Setting a boundary? Having a feeling? Being human?

If any item feels too raw, stop. Put the notebook away and do a grounding exercise: five deep breaths, feet on the floor, name three objects in the room. This isn't about rushing. It's about reclaiming.

Why It Matters

Because recovery isn't just leaving physically. It's evicting their voice from your head. It's recognising that the cruelty you've internalised was never yours to carry.

You Can't Recover While Still Believing Their Version of You

You can't build self-worth on the foundation of their lies. You can't recover while measuring yourself against their impossible standards. You can't move forward if you're still seeing yourself through their distorted lens.

Every time you repeat their lines, you give their control more room. You're not a collaborator—you're a person who learnt survival scripts. Now you can unlearn them.

Recovery means dragging their words into the light and saying: "That's not mine. I'm giving it back."

A survivor told me: "I kept hearing him say I was 'too emotional' whenever I felt anything. One day, mid-cry, I said out loud: 'No. I'm having a normal human response to grief. He was too emotionally constipated to handle feelings.' It was the first time I talked back to his ghost. The first time I felt like myself in years."

The Gentleness You're Missing Is the Gentleness They Stole

A woman told me she used to flinch at the sound of her own name. "He only said it when I was in trouble. Never softly. Never with love. Just sharp and loud, like a slap." Years later, when anyone said her name gently, she still braced for impact.

She started writing her name at the top of her journal each morning. Just her name. Nothing else. "I had to teach myself," she said, "that my name wasn't a warning. That it could be soft. That it belonged to me, not his anger."

The tenderness you struggle to give yourself isn't because you don't deserve it. It's because they trained you to believe kindness was dangerous. That gentleness meant weakness. That self-compassion was selfish.

But the voice that tells you you're not worth kindness? That's their voice. The real you, the one they tried to silence, knows better.

If You Remember One Thing

Not one word they used to break you was true.

Not the names they called you in anger.
Not the flaws they insisted you had.
Not the reasons they gave for treating you badly.
Not the story they told about who you are.

They needed you to believe you were the problem because that's how they kept control.
If you knew you were good, whole, worthy, you might leave. So they rewrote you as
someone who should be grateful for their tolerance.

But you're not broken—you're breaking free from their programming.
You're not too much—you were too much for THEM to control.
You're not hard to love—you were hard to manipulate.

Every cruel thought that sounds like your voice but feels like violence? That's theirs.
Every self-attack that leaves you smaller? That's theirs. Every moment of self-doubt that
keeps you stuck? That's theirs.

Your work now isn't to fix yourself.
It's to see that nothing was ever wrong with you.

Your work is to separate your voice from theirs.
To notice when you're being cruel to yourself with their words.
To interrupt the broadcast of their criticism.
To change the channel to something kinder.

Start small. When you hear their voice, say out loud: "That's not mine." Do it once.
Twice. More. Say it until your mouth remembers how your true voice sounds.

It's still there. Waiting. And it has never once agreed with their lies about you.

7.2
Your Brain Wasn't Broken
It Was Rewired

Author's Note:

This chapter is for anyone who's ever asked, "What's wrong with me?" Who's felt foggy, numb, emotional, scattered, then blamed themselves for it. You weren't broken. You were adapting. This is where you learn how trauma rewired your brain to survive.

This Is What It Feels Like When Your Body Remembers Before You Do

You're standing in the kitchen, staring at the kettle. The water boiled dry an hour ago. The metal smells scorched, acrid smoke still rising. Keys in one hand, phone in the other, you can't remember why you're standing here.

Were you leaving? Just arriving? Have you eaten today?

Your phone buzzes. One message: "We need to talk."

Your stomach drops through the floor. Hands instantly sweating. Heart hammering so hard you can hear it in your ears. You haven't even read past those four words, but your body's already bracing for impact.

That's what coercive control does. It doesn't just hurt you. It hijacks your nervous system and turns it into an alarm that never switches off.

Your Nervous System Became a Smoke Detector
That Can't Tell the Difference

Your brain has one job: keep you alive. When you lived with someone who could explode without warning, your amygdala—the brain's alarm system—got bigger.

Meanwhile, your hippocampus—the part that helps you think clearly and remember where you put your keys—actually shrank.

Now you have a smoke detector that screams at burnt toast like it's a house fire.

The kettle clicking off makes you jump.
Keys in a door make your chest tighten.
A text notification makes you nauseous.
That heavy silence that comes before someone speaks.

You're not overreacting. You're having a normal response to an abnormal amount of danger you once lived in. Your brain learnt to scan every room, every face, every pause in conversation for threats. Because it had to.

That's why your shoulders ache even on safe days. Why your jaw hurts in the morning. Why your stomach knots before you've even read the full message.

Hypervigilance Isn't Paranoia, It's Pattern Recognition

You notice everything. The slight change in their tone. The way the air shifts when someone's mood darkens. How long it takes them to reply to a text. You read rooms like survival manuals because you had to become fluent in the language of danger.

That's not paranoia. That's pattern recognition that saved your life. The skill isn't the problem—it's just stuck on high alert.

A woman told me: "I could tell by the way he closed the car door whether dinner would be silent or explosive. The soft click meant I was safe. The slam meant I should stay in the kitchen."

Your body became a finely-tuned instrument for detecting danger. The problem is, it's still playing that song even though the concert's over.

Practical Step

When you feel your heart racing over something small, name it: "My body's having a false alarm." Then give it evidence of safety: five things you can see, four you can touch, three you can hear, two you can smell, one you can taste. You're teaching your nervous system the difference between then and now.

If grounding makes you more panicked, stop. Try something simpler—hold a warm mug, press your feet to the floor, remind yourself: "That was then. This is now."

Why It Matters

Because your brain is still trying to protect you from danger that's no longer there. Naming it as a false alarm helps your nervous system learn what's actually safe.

You Started Forgetting Because Survival Came First

You forgot appointments. Names. Where you parked. Your own postcode at the doctor's surgery. But you remembered the exact tone that meant trouble. The pause before punishment. The look that meant you'd done something "wrong."

That's not dysfunction. That's your brain being efficient with its resources. When you're in survival mode, remembering your cousin's birthday matters less than remembering what triggers danger.

A woman told me she forgot her own phone number filling out a form, but could recall the exact way her partner's jaw tightened before a fight. "My brain didn't keep the everyday stuff," she said. "It kept what might kill me."

Your Emotions Got Louder Because You'd Been Silencing Them

You cry over spilt milk—literally. Rage at a dropped spoon. Go completely numb when something actually devastating happens. It's not mood swings. It's years of suppressed feelings finally finding cracks to seep through.

A survivor told me: "I cried in a Woolworths car park because they were out of my usual yoghurt. Security asked if I was okay. How could I explain I wasn't crying about yoghurt? I was crying about years of tears I never got to shed."

When you're not allowed to have feelings, they don't disappear. They compress. Then when you're finally safe, they explode over "nothing" because your body finally has permission to feel.

You Freeze Because Every Choice Used to Have Consequences

What to eat. What to wear. Which route to take home. Simple decisions feel impossible because your brain remembers when the "wrong" choice meant hours of punishment.

A woman told me she stood in a supermarket for forty-five minutes trying to choose bread. "Not because I didn't know what I wanted. Because my ex used to mock me for buying the 'wrong' kind. I'd rather go hungry than pick wrong again."

Your chest locks, your throat tightens, your breath disappears—because every choice once carried consequences for your safety.

It's not indecision. It's trauma. Your brain is trying to protect you from dangers that don't exist anymore.

If You Remember One Thing

Your brain did exactly what it was supposed to do. It kept you alive in an impossible situation by rewiring itself for survival. The fog, the forgetting, the freezing, the flooding emotions—all of it was your brilliant brain adapting to keep you safe.

You didn't lose your mind.
You saved your life.

The hypervigilance that exhausts you? It protected you.
The dissociation that frustrates you? It sheltered you.

The anxiety that torments you? It warned you in time.

Every symptom is not proof of weakness—it's proof of survival.

Now the war's over, but your body doesn't know that yet. So give it time. Give it evidence. Give it your voice saying: "We're safe now. We don't have to be afraid."

Your work isn't to fix a broken brain.
It's to gently teach a brave one that the danger has passed.

That's how healing begins. Not by erasing what happened, but by teaching your body, day by day, that what protected you then isn't needed now.

Give it your feet on solid ground.
Give it proof, again and again, that the threat is gone.

And slowly, patiently, your brain will learn to trust calm again.

7.3
Why Did I Give Them So Many Chances?

Author's Note:

This chapter is for anyone who's ever asked themselves, "Why did I give them so many chances?" It's not about blame or judgement. It's about understanding that hope, loyalty, and love aren't weaknesses—even when they're used against you. You gave them chances because you're human. And being human in an inhumane situation doesn't make you foolish. It makes you brave.

You Didn't Give Them Chances, You Gave Them Grace

You're lying in bed at 3am, counting. First time: the shouting match about dishes. Second time: when they disappeared for two days. Third time: the affair you forgave. Fourth, fifth, sixth... The number climbs. Shame presses on your chest. Your stomach clenches with every number.

"Why did I stay?" you ask the ceiling. "Why did I keep believing?"

We grow up hearing that love is patient, that loyalty is virtue, that forgiveness proves strength. So when harm comes wrapped in apology, we don't see it as manipulation. We see it as a rough patch. A bad day. Something to work through.

You didn't give them endless chances because you were weak. You gave them grace because that's what good people do. You forgave because you'd been taught that's what love looks like.

But what no one tells you is that grace without change becomes a cage. That forgiveness without accountability becomes permission. That loyalty to someone who betrays you becomes self-abandonment. There's nothing wrong with forgiveness. But forgiveness without change stops being connection and starts being self-erosion.

A woman told me: "I forgave him for screaming at me in front of our daughter. For the affairs. For the money he stole. Every time he showed even a hint of softness—a half-smile, a 'sorry babe,' a decent week—I grabbed onto it like proof he was changing.

I wasn't giving chances to the abuse. I was giving chances to the person I desperately hoped he could become."

You Weren't Being Naïve, You Were Being Trained

They didn't just hurt you. They rewired your reality. They taught you that their good moments were their "real self" and the cruelty was somehow your fault. Too emotional. Too demanding. Too much.

So you learnt to stay calm to avoid escalation.
To explain yourself better so they'd understand.
To try differently because maybe last time you didn't say it right.

Each "chance" felt like your decision, but it wasn't. It was conditioning. They'd trained you to believe the pain was temporary and the glimpses of good were the truth.

But those glimpses weren't truth. They were bait. Carefully rationed just often enough to keep you hooked, never enough to actually feed you.

Denial Disguised as Hope Kept You There, But So Did Fear

Sometimes you gave another chance because denial felt safer than reality. You called it hope, but it was really refusing to see what was right in front of you. Because admitting it wouldn't change meant admitting you'd have to leave. And leaving meant:

Starting over when you could barely get through today.
Explaining to everyone why you "gave up."
Losing the house, the friends, the life you'd built.
Facing the world alone after they'd convinced you that you couldn't.
A survivor told me: "I stayed because I'd already invested fifteen years. Walking away

felt like admitting those years were wasted. So I gave him another chance. And another. Each one was me trying to protect my past, not my future."

You weren't stupid. You were carrying too much to risk dropping it all.

The Sunk Cost of Love

There's an economics term called "sunk cost fallacy"—continuing something because of what you've already invested, not because it's working. But when it comes to relationships, we don't call it economics. We call it commitment.

You thought: "I've given so much already."
"We have history."
"I know the real them."
"If I just try harder..."

You weren't irrational. You were trying to salvage meaning from years that already cost you so much. Each chance wasn't really about them changing. It was about you not wanting to lose what you'd already given: years, tears, trying, hope.

Practical Step

Write down why you stayed. The real reasons, not the pretty ones. Write what you told yourself at the time:

"I didn't want to be alone."
"I thought they were finally changing."
"I was scared of starting over."
"I loved them."
"I didn't think anyone else would want me."

Then beside each reason, write what you know now. Not to shame yourself, but to see how far you've come. Example: "I was scared of being alone" becomes "Being alone was safer than being destroyed."

Why It Matters

Because when you see your reasons clearly, you stop confusing survival with stupidity. You stop hating yourself for doing what you needed to do to get through.

You Gave Chances Because You're the Kind of Person Who Believes in Redemption

You gave them chances because you believe people can change. Because you've seen it happen. Because you know what it's like to need forgiveness yourself.

You gave chances because your heart is wired for connection, not abandonment. Because walking away from someone you love—even someone who hurts you—goes against every instinct you have.

You gave chances because you're the kind of person who sees potential, not just patterns. Who believes in tomorrow, not just today. Who hopes even when hope hurts.

That's not weakness. That's humanity.

The problem wasn't your capacity to forgive.
The problem was they weaponised it.

If You Remember One Thing

You didn't give them too many chances because you were foolish. You gave them chances because you loved fiercely. Because you had history. Because you believed in repair. Because you were scared. Because no one taught you that staying could become self-destruction.

Your hope wasn't stupid—it was human.
Your loyalty wasn't weakness—it was love.
Your forgiveness wasn't naivety—it was grace.

They took those beautiful parts of you and used them as weapons. They turned your strengths into chains. They made your compassion into a cage.

But here's what they didn't account for: those same qualities that kept you there are the ones that will rebuild you now.

You gave them chances because you're someone who believes in redemption. That's not the part that needs changing.

What needs changing is who you give it to.

The hope that made you stay? Let it carry you forward.
The loyalty you showed them? Pour it into yourself.
The grace you extended? Keep it—and spend it only where it's safe.

You weren't foolish for giving chances. You were human.
And from now on, that humanity belongs to you.

7.4
So Close Yet So Far Away

Author's Note:

This chapter is about emotional abandonment inside a relationship. If you ever lay beside someone and still felt completely alone, like your needs, feelings, or voice didn't matter, this will help you see the truth: You weren't asking for too much. You were asking to exist. And that's the baseline, not a burden.

You Were Inches Apart and Still Completely Alone

You're sitting on the sofa together. Your thighs touching. The TV mumbling in the background. Dinner plates balanced on knees. You take a breath, gather courage, and say something small but true: "I've been feeling really lonely lately."

The words hang in the air like smoke. He doesn't turn. Doesn't pause the show. Just shifts his weight slightly, creating a millimetre of space between your legs, and asks, "Is this the episode with the boat?" Your stomach drops. Not because he's cruel. Because he's absent. Right there, close enough to feel his body heat, yet unreachable as another continent.

That's when you understand: proximity isn't intimacy. You can share a bed, a home, a life with someone and still be screaming into the void. This isn't the dramatic loneliness of being left. It's the quiet devastation of being ignored while they're right there.

You're Together But You're Not Connected

They're in the room, but they're not with you.
You try to talk about your day—they scroll through their phone.
You mention you're struggling—they change the subject.
You cry—they sigh and ask if you're "doing this again."

Eventually, you stop trying. Start having whole conversations in your head instead, because at least there you get a response. You rehearse what you'd say if they cared. Practice arguments that never happen. Win debates they'll never hear.

A woman told me: "I used to plan entire conversations while he played video games. I'd script my feelings, his responses, our breakthrough moment. Then I'd look at him—headphones on, completely absorbed—and realise I was more alone with him than I'd ever been by myself."

You Start Shrinking Just to Take Up Less Disappointment

You stop mentioning when something hurts. Stop asking for help. Stop expecting birthday cards or anniversary acknowledgement. Not because you became "low-maintenance" but because every expressed need was met with:

"You're so needy."
"Nothing's ever enough for you."
"Why are you making such a big deal?"
Or worse—that blank stare that says they're not even pretending to listen.

So you shrink. Make yourself smaller. Need less. Want less. Until you're barely taking up any emotional space at all. Your body learns to fold in—smaller posture, quieter voice—as if being less will disappoint less. You call it keeping the peace. Really, it's slow-motion disappearance.

Practical Step

Write down the last five times you tried to connect emotionally. How did they respond? With curiosity? Care? Or deflection, dismissal, irritation? Now ask yourself: If a friend treated me this way, would they still be in my life?

Why It Matters

Because you're learning the difference between someone being physically present and someone being emotionally available. One without the other isn't a relationship—it's occupancy.

Your Loneliness Doesn't Come from Being Alone
It Comes from Being Unseen

They know your coffee order but not your dreams.
They know your schedule but not your fears.
They share your bed but not your inner world.

You could have a panic attack next to them and they'd complain about the noise. You could go silent for days and they wouldn't ask why. You could disappear into yourself completely and they'd only notice if dinner was late.

A man told me: "She lived with me for seven years. Knew exactly how I liked my eggs. Never once asked why I stopped singing in the shower. The day I left, she said she didn't see it coming. How could she? She never saw me at all."

When You're Rejected Long Enough, You Start Rejecting Yourself

At first, you fight for visibility. Leave notes. Send texts. Try to explain how abandoned you feel. But when every attempt bounces back—too dramatic, too sensitive, too much—something shifts.

You stop trusting your own needs. Start wondering if maybe you are asking for too much. If wanting someone to ask "How was your day?" and actually listen to the answer is unreasonable. If expecting emotional reciprocity is demanding.

The gaslight isn't just "that didn't happen." It's also "that doesn't matter." And when your feelings don't matter to the person who's supposed to love you, you start editing yourself out of your own story.

The Cruellest Part Is How Normal It Looks from the Outside

To everyone else, you're a couple. You show up together. Leave together. Post photos where you're both smiling. No one sees the arctic distance between you at home. The meals eaten in silence. The bed that feels like two separate islands.

People say, "You're so lucky to have each other." You think, "I don't have them at all." They see smiles in photos. They don't hear the silence after the camera clicks.

If You Remember One Thing*

There's no loneliness like being unseen by the person lying next to you. No silence like sharing space with someone who's emotionally checked out. No hurt quite like giving your whole heart to someone who can't even spare you their attention.

You weren't crazy for feeling alone in that relationship. You were alone.
You weren't asking too much by wanting conversation, connection, care.

You were asking for the bare minimum.
You weren't needy for craving intimacy. You were human.

Now you know what loneliness wrapped in companionship feels like.
And you'll never mistake it for love again.

Next time, you'll wait for someone who doesn't just share your space but meets you in it. Who hears your silence, who holds your truth, who stays present instead of just close.

Until then, you're learning your own presence is enough. Your own care is enough. Your own company is safer than begging for scraps of connection.

You're not too much.
They were too empty.

That was never your fault.

7.5
The Good Moments Were Real
But They Were Never Safe

Author's Note:

This chapter is about the moments that felt real, and were, but were never safe. If you stayed because you believed the good parts meant something, this will help you see the truth clearly: You didn't stay because you were weak. You stayed because they used hope as a tactic. And now, you get to stop mistaking relief for love.

They Led with Warmth Then Used It to Disarm You

You wake to gentleness. His hand traces your shoulder. Coffee appears on your nightstand, made exactly right—two sugars, splash of milk, in your favourite mug. He kisses your forehead, whispers, "I don't know what I'd do without you."

Your body, which had been braced all week, finally softens. You let yourself lean into him. Let yourself believe maybe the worst is over. Maybe he's realised. Maybe you're through the storm.

"I know I've been difficult," he says, eyes soft, voice breaking slightly. "But you're everything to me. You know that, right?"

You nod. Hope unfurls in your chest like a flower desperate for sun.

By dinner, he's different. The warmth evaporated somewhere between lunch and now. You said something—you can't even remember what—and his jaw tightened. Now he's listing your failures. Your tone. Your attitude. The way you "always" do this.

You're apologising before you understand what you're apologising for. The morning's tenderness feels like a dream you made up. But you didn't. It happened. The coffee cup is still on your nightstand, proof that six hours ago, he loved you.

That's what breaks you. Not the cruelty. The whiplash. The way safety turns to danger without warning. Your chest loosens at their tenderness, only to seize hours later at their sudden rage. Your body learns not to trust softness because it so often precedes the blow.

It Wasn't Fake, It Was Strategic

Those tender moments weren't imaginary. The surprise flowers. The foot massage after your long day. The night he held you while you cried about your mother. All real.

But notice when they happened:

After you mentioned feeling distant.
When you stopped responding to texts quickly.
Right before his parents visited.
The day after you said you needed space.

A woman told me: "He was most loving when I was leaving. Not metaphorically— literally. Bags packed, keys in hand leaving. That's when he'd suddenly remember how to be the man I fell in love with. He'd cry, hold me, promise everything. And I'd unpack. Every. Single. Time."

The kindness wasn't random. It was dispensed like medicine—just enough to keep you from dying, never enough to make you well.

Hope Was the Hook

You didn't stay for the pain. You stayed for the moments between it. Those glimpses of who they could be. Who you thought they really were, underneath.

Every soft moment felt like evidence: See? They do love me. They can be gentle. We can make this work.

You collected these moments like breadcrumbs leading home. Not realising they were strategically placed to keep you lost.

Practical Step

Write down three moments you still miss. The real ones, the tender ones. Then write what happened immediately before and after each one. Watch the pattern emerge: crisis, sweetness, calm, building tension, explosion, sweetness again.

Why It Matters

You're not erasing the good moments. You're seeing them in context. Real love doesn't appear only when you're about to leave. It doesn't vanish the moment you disagree.

You Kept Waiting for the Version That Seemed to Care

There were different versions of them, and you never knew which one you'd get:

The one who danced with you in the kitchen.
The one who brought you tea without being asked.
The one who looked at you like you hung the moon.

You kept hoping that version would stay. Thought if you were patient enough, understanding enough, small enough, quiet enough, they might remain that gentle person.

But that person wasn't who they were—it was a costume they wore when necessary. It appeared when they wanted sex, or money, or forgiveness, or when they sensed you pulling away.

A man told me: "She was incredible when I was broken. Lost my job? She was an angel. Got promoted? She turned cold. Took me years to realise she only loved me when I was beneath her."

You Can Grieve the Good and Still Walk Away

You don't have to pretend it was all bad to justify leaving. You don't have to hate every memory to validate your pain. The good moments were real. Your love for those moments was real. Your hope that they meant something was human.

You're allowed to miss the pancake Sundays while remembering they only happened after Saturday night fights. You're allowed to treasure the soft "I love you" while knowing it came with a price tag of silence about your needs.

A survivor told me: "What I grieved most wasn't him. It was the version of him I fell in love with. The one who showed up just often enough to keep me believing he was real. Leaving meant accepting that version was never coming back—because it was never really there."

The Cruellest Part Is How They Made You Addicted to Crumbs

They trained you to be grateful for basic kindness. To see normal affection as exceptional. To treat bare minimum effort like grand gestures.

At first, you called it grace—believing the good outweighed the bad. Over time, it became crumbs—clinging to whatever they rationed, mistaking survival for love.

A good morning text became an event.
A hug became a reward.
A calm evening became something to earn.

To the outside world, those crumbs looked like devotion. "He's so thoughtful," they'd say, seeing the flowers. To you, they were lifelines. But no one saw the starvation that came in between.

You learned to survive on emotional crumbs and call it a feast. Not because you had low standards, but because they systematically starved you until crumbs felt like abundance.

If You Remember One Thing

You didn't imagine the love. Those tender moments happened. But they were never the foundation—they were the bait. That's why leaving hurts so much. Because your heart remembers the morning coffees, even as your body remembers the evening rage.

The good moments were real.
But they were never safe.
They were bait, not bond. Strategy, not security.

It's okay to miss them. It's okay to grieve them. It's even okay to still wish they meant what you thought they did.

But now you know: Real love doesn't vanish when you need it most. It doesn't perform tenderness only to prevent your leaving. It doesn't make you pay for connection with silence, fear, or pain.

The good moments were real. But so was the harm.

And real love is consistent.
It stays.

7.6
The Abuser Isn't Powerful
They're Afraid

Author's Note:

This chapter is about seeing through the performance. If you ever found yourself shrinking around someone who seemed confident, dominant, or untouchable, this will help you understand: They weren't powerful. They were terrified of being ordinary. And control was the only thing they ever truly mastered.

It Wasn't Confidence, It Was Insecurity in Disguise

You're at dinner with friends. He's holding court, telling that story again—the one where he's the hero, everyone else is incompetent. His voice fills the room. He interrupts when someone tries to contribute. Laughs too loud at his own jokes.

But you see what others miss. The way his jaw tightens when someone else gets a laugh. The micro-flinch when a friend mentions their promotion. How he suddenly needs to leave when he's not the smartest person at the table. The way he goes coldest toward people who don't need him—who have their own money, their own confidence, their own voice.

Later, in the car, he tears apart everyone who was there. Too pretentious. Too boring. Too fake. You realise he's not critiquing them. He's defending against them. Every person who doesn't worship him is a threat.

Your body knew before your mind did. The way your shoulders would tighten when he entered a room. How you'd hold your breath during his stories, waiting for the moment he'd turn them into weapons. The knot in your stomach that never quite loosened, even during his "good" moods.

He doesn't radiate strength. He radiates panic wrapped in a three-piece suit of arrogance. For years, you thought he was powerful. Untouchable. Above you. Until you realised you'd been protecting a terrified child in a grown man's body. One who never learnt to exist without making others smaller.

They Attack What They Can't Be

You come home glowing. Got the promotion. Ran the 5K. Finally finished that project. You can't wait to share it. Their response?

"Well, don't let it go to your head."
"Anyone could do that with enough time."
"I hope you're not expecting special treatment."

Your excitement deflates like a punctured balloon. You mumble something about it not being a big deal. They nod, satisfied, and change the subject. Because the moment you felt good in your own skin, they felt smaller in theirs.

You're kind? They call you naive.
You're joyful? They call it childish.
You're growing? They call it showing off.

They don't just envy what you are. They punish it. Because your light reminds them of their darkness.

A woman told me: "Every time I achieved something, he'd find a way to make it small. Got into university? 'Standards must be dropping.' Lost weight? 'Don't get too skinny.' Made a friend? 'They probably want something.' I realised he wasn't protecting me from disappointment. He was protecting himself from feeling inferior."

Arrogance Is Just Fragility in a Loud Voice

They interrupt every sentence. Correct every opinion. Dismiss every idea they didn't think of first. In meetings, at parties, over breakfast—they must be the expert, the authority, the final word.

But watch what happens when someone gently challenges them. Even a soft "I'm not sure that's right" or "Have you considered..."

They explode. Or ice over. Or launch into a twenty-minute dissertation on why they're right and everyone else is too stupid to understand.

That's not power. That's terror.

Real strength can hear disagreement without crumbling. Real confidence doesn't need to prove itself every five minutes. Real power can say "I don't know" without feeling diminished.

What you're dealing with isn't a titan. It's a house of cards in a hurricane, desperately trying not to collapse.

Practical Step

List five qualities they tried to diminish in you. Your creativity. Your friendships. Your independence. Your joy. Then circle the ones that still live in you, despite their best efforts. Those are the parts of you they feared most—and likely the parts others cherish most about you.

Why It Matters

They saw your light and tried to extinguish it because it exposed their darkness. Reclaiming these qualities isn't just recovery—it's discovering what made you powerful all along.

They Wear Hate Like Armour

You try something new. A bold lipstick. A different hairstyle. A hobby they don't understand. You feel good. Confident. Like yourself.

They look you up and down. "That's... interesting. Bit much for you, don't you think?"

Just like that, your shoulders drop. You second-guess yourself. Maybe it is too much. Maybe you should tone it down.

But that wasn't fashion advice. That was fear speaking. Your visibility reminded them of their own invisibility. Your confidence highlighted their insecurity. Your joy exposed their emptiness.

They mock, belittle, and intimidate not because they're above you, but because they feel beneath you. And cruelty is how they try to level the field.

They Want Power Because They Feel Powerless

They don't dominate because they're natural leaders. They dominate because it's the only way they know how to feel safe. Control is their religion because chaos lives inside them.

They need your obedience to regulate their fragile sense of self.
They need you small because they feel microscopic.
They need you confused because clarity would expose them.

Everything they do is rooted in fear:
Fear of being exposed as ordinary.
Fear of being seen as they really are.
Fear of you realising you don't need them.

A man told me: "She picked fights whenever I succeeded at anything. New client? She'd find something wrong with how I handled it. Compliment from a colleague? She'd remind me of my failures.

I thought I was the problem until I realised—my growth terrified her because it meant I might outgrow her control."

The Truth They Never Wanted You to See

Behind every cruel word was someone terrified of being worthless.
Behind every controlling behaviour was someone who felt out of control.
Behind every dismissal of your dreams was someone who'd given up on their own.

They weren't powerful. They were performing power because they'd never felt it authentically. They weren't confident. They were loud because they couldn't stand the silence where their self-worth should be.

If You Remember One Thing

You spent so long shrinking in their shadow. Afraid of their rage, their silence, their ability to cut you down with a single look. You made yourself smaller to make them feel bigger. Quieter to avoid their noise. Less to accommodate their need to be more.

But here's what they never wanted you to realise:

They were never bigger than you. Just louder.
Their cruelty wasn't strength. It was fear with teeth.
Their manipulation wasn't genius. It was desperation in disguise.

The person you feared was just a frightened child in a costume of control.

So hold your ground.
Speak your truth.
Reclaim your space.

The person who seemed so powerful was terrified of being ordinary.

And now? You see through them.
That's your power.

And it's what they always feared you'd find.

7.7
You Lived the Truth While Everyone Else Clapped for the Lie

Author's Note:

This chapter is about the gap between what you know and what the world still believes. If you've ever watched people applaud the person who hurt you while you sat in silence carrying the truth, this will help you understand: Their performance doesn't erase your experience. They fooled the room. But you lived the reality. And your voice still matters, even if you're the only one who hears it.

Everyone Loved the Version You Never Got to Meet

You're scrolling through social media when you see it. Your chest goes tight, like someone has reached in and pinched the air out of you. Him. Tagged at a fundraiser. Black tie, champagne glass raised, arms around colleagues. Your stomach drops like you're falling.

The comments pour in: "Such a great guy!" "Lucky to know him!" "Always been the best!" "Role model!"

Hands trembling, throat closing around words no one would believe. Because twelve hours before that photo, he screamed at you for crying. Called you pathetic. Said you were lucky he tolerated you at all.

But there he stands. The beloved community leader. The charming colleague. The man everyone wishes they knew better. You stare at the screen like you're looking at a stranger wearing the face of someone who systematically destroyed you.

This is the particular cruelty of coercive control. Not just that they hurt you, but that they're celebrated by the same world where you're struggling to breathe. You know the truth. Your body holds it—in the way you still flinch at sudden movements, still check your phone with dread, still can't sleep through the night. But the world sees a hero. And you're left holding a truth no one wants to hear.

Your Reality vs Their Performance

What you lived was quiet cruelty: cold silences that stretched for days, rage over microscopic "mistakes," jokes that landed like knives, and so-called "communication" that felt like emotional terrorism. What the world saw was something else entirely—an inspirational leader, a devoted partner even after you left, a thoughtful friend. The mask they wore when the curtains were drawn.

Your body keeps the receipts. You still tense at the sound of a slamming door. Your stomach drops at every notification. Crowds set your nerves humming with hypervigilance. The sleep that once restored you no longer does. These are the facts you carry even when no one else asks.

Meanwhile their social media tells a different story. Perfect couple photos kept up for months after you left. Inspirational quotes about growth and healing. Carefully curated kindness. Public displays of the empathy they never once showed you.

The Performance Wasn't for You, It Was Despite You

They never bothered charming you once they had you. That energy went elsewhere—to everyone around you, making themselves indispensable at work, beloved at gatherings.

So when you finally found your voice, when you finally spoke your truth, you were met with disbelief. "That doesn't sound like them." "Are you sure you're not misremembering?" "They've always been wonderful to me." "Maybe you misunderstood?"

Each doubt another wound. Each defence another betrayal. Each "but they seem so nice" another reason you stopped trying to explain. Because how do you describe a Jekyll and Hyde when everyone else only knows Jekyll?

They Control the Narrative by Speaking First

While you were still in shock, still processing trauma, they were already spinning stories. "We grew apart." "They had some issues." "I tried everything to help." "It's sad, really." "I wish them well."

They sound reasonable. Balanced. Sad but stable. The concerned ex-partner who tried their best. Meanwhile, you can barely form sentences about what happened without your voice shaking, without sounding "emotional" or "bitter."

A woman told me: "My ex spent months telling our friends I had 'mental health issues' while he was actively gaslighting me. He was so concerned, so worried about my stability, so patient with my 'moods.' The genius was that the more upset I got about his lies, the more I proved his point. I'd try to explain what he was doing, and I'd get emotional, frustrated, desperate to be believed. And there he'd be, calm and collected, saying, 'See? This is what I've been dealing with.'"

Practical Step

If naming truth-keepers feels too risky right now, make the list for yourself. Stop trying to convince the audience. Focus on three people who believe you without needing proof. Write their names down privately and keep the list somewhere safe. Revisit when you feel stronger. These are your truth-keepers. Let them be your mirrors when the world reflects lies. Everyone else is just noise.

Why It Matters

You can't heal while fighting to be believed by people invested in the performance. Your energy belongs in recovery, not in convincing their fan club. The people who matter will see through the show without you having to prove it.

The Cruellest Part Is How They Use Your Trauma Response Against You

They create the damage, then point to it as evidence you were always damaged. They traumatise you, then use your trauma symptoms as proof you're unstable. They isolate you, then tell everyone you're antisocial.

When you try to explain what happened, your voice sounds frantic—paranoid because the manipulation was covert, obsessive because you're trying to make sense of it, bitter because you're angry about injustice, dramatic because the truth sounds unbelievable. When they speak, they sound calm, reasonable, patient, even heartbroken. The cruel irony is that the very distress they created becomes the "evidence" they use against you.

The same person who created your anxiety now uses it as evidence against you. The person who broke you gets sympathy for having to deal with someone so "difficult."

If You Remember One Thing

The hardest part isn't that they fooled you. It's that they fooled everyone. While you were drowning, they were taking bows. While you were gasping for emotional oxygen, they were giving speeches about kindness. But here's what their audience doesn't know: You saw the rehearsals. You lived backstage. You know what happens when the curtain drops.

Their standing ovation doesn't erase your truth. Their five-star reviews don't invalidate your pain. Their public persona doesn't overwrite your private hell. You're not crazy for being angry while everyone applauds. You're not bitter for remembering what they trained everyone to forget. You're not wrong for seeing through the performance.

You're the only one who knows the difference between the show and the truth. And that knowledge? That's not your burden. That's your freedom.

Because you never have to buy a ticket to their performance again. Not today, not now. Maybe not ever. But that's your choice to make when you're ready. You don't have to clap for their lies or pretend their mask is their face—not yet, not until you choose.

You know who they really are. And one day, that truth will matter more than their audience ever did.

7.8
They Didn't Fear Your Past
They Feared Your Recovery

Author's Note:

This chapter is about what happens when healing becomes a threat. If you've ever hidden your journal, downplayed your therapy, or been called "unstable" for trying to get help, you're not paranoid. You're not overreacting. You were being watched.

Because to someone who depends on control, your growth is dangerous. Not because of what you've healed from, but because of what you might see next. And if they can't stop you from getting stronger, they'll try to twist that strength into something shameful. Because the more awake you become, the more visible their behaviour becomes. And that's what they're really afraid of.

They Don't Want You Better, They Want You Dependent

You started therapy and they smirked. You bought a self-help book and they called it "woo-woo." You tried setting boundaries and suddenly you were "obsessed with psychology." Your chest tightened with each dismissal, that familiar shrinking sensation when something precious gets mocked.

Every step forward, every honest effort to repair what they broke, got twisted into evidence of instability. You weren't getting help—you were "addicted to self-improvement." You weren't healing—you were "making everything about trauma." You weren't growing stronger—you were "becoming difficult." Your waking up terrified them.

They Read Your Journal, Then Used It Against You

You tried to process. To reflect. To survive. You wrote things down to make sense of them, confided thoughts that weren't safe to say out loud. The notebook was yours, private, sacred—the one place you could be honest without consequence.

Then they found it.

Your stomach dropped when you realised they'd been through it. Your hands went cold. Not just glanced—studied it. The fears you'd written about at 2am became dinner-table mockery. The doubts you'd processed privately became "proof" you were unstable. Your most vulnerable moments, the ones you'd trusted only to paper, became weapons they'd pull out whenever you got too strong.

"You wrote that you sometimes feel crazy," they'd say with that particular smile. "Maybe you are."

They weren't looking for understanding. They were looking for leverage. And they found it in the words you'd used to try to heal.

They Called Therapy a Cult, But Watched You Like a Hawk

They said you didn't need it. Said you were exaggerating. Said you were making them look bad by "telling stories to strangers." But they watched. They listened. They tracked every appointment, every breakthrough, every medication adjustment.

The moment you cried in a session? They called you unstable. The moment you mentioned medication? They said it explained everything—not the healing, but why you were "so difficult lately." The moment your therapist helped you see a pattern? They accused you of being brainwashed. They didn't want to understand you. They wanted reasons to dismiss you.

A woman I spoke with told me her ex said therapy was "for crazy people." Then years later, he started a psychology degree. Not because he wanted healing. Because he wanted the image. The control. The language he could use to sound reflective while still being cruel. She said, "It hit me in the chest. All those years I asked for couples counselling and he laughed. Now he was doing a degree to look wise." He never apologised. He never took responsibility. He just took the language of healing and used it to keep the spotlight off the damage.

Practical Step

Protect your recovery like the sacred thing it is. Lock your journal. Password your notes. Keep therapy details vague or off-limits. If you can't store notes securely, consider an encrypted app or writing in code words only you understand. Speak freely only in spaces you know are safe. And write down three things your recovery has given you that no one can take away—inner knowing, body awareness, the ability to recognise red flags. These are yours forever.

Why It Matters

Your recovery is happening in places they can't reach. They may mock the surface, but they can't touch the roots growing deep inside you.

If You Remember One Thing

They called therapy self-indulgent, but watched it like a threat. They mocked your medication, then used it to discredit you. They said journaling was "navel-gazing," then quoted your private words without permission.

They weren't trying to help you heal. They were trying to stay in control of the version of you they could still manipulate.

But here's what they didn't count on: healing changes you at a cellular level. It rewrites your nervous system. It rebuilds your sense of self from the inside out. And no amount of mockery can reverse what's already taking root.

You're past the point of needing their permission. You're not asking for their blessing or their understanding.

You're getting your life back. And they don't get to be part of that chapter.

7.9
Part of You Always Knew
But They Taught You to Doubt It

Author's Note:

This chapter is about the aftermath of subtle abuse, the kind that doesn't scream, doesn't slam doors, doesn't leave bruises. If you still question whether what you went through "was bad enough," this will help you understand: Quiet harm still rewires your nervous system.

The Pain You Carry Isn't An Overreaction

It's a record of what they refused to name.

You never stiffened at yelling because there wasn't any. You flinched at the sound of a sigh. At the silence after a question. At the way they'd walk into a room and say nothing, but somehow still make the air feel heavy, like storm clouds gathering without thunder.

For years, you didn't call it abuse. You just thought you were anxious. Too sensitive. Bad at relationships.

But now you know: It wasn't the volume that broke you. It was the constant pressure of being too much for someone who never raised their voice but erased you anyway.

You Didn't See It Because It Didn't Look Like What You Were Taught to Fear

You weren't locked in a room. You weren't screamed at every night. But you still stopped laughing. Still stopped asking for things. Still stopped recognising yourself in the mirror.

Because their silence wasn't calm—it was control. Their stillness wasn't safety—it was strategy. Their indifference wasn't neutral—it was violent in its precision. And the reason you didn't call it abuse? Because no one told you that being systematically ignored could break you just as thoroughly as being hit.

Your Nervous System Didn't Forget Even If You Did

You wake up bracing for something you can't name. Flinch when the mood shifts like barometric pressure dropping. Feel guilty for resting, for asking, for having needs that might inconvenience someone. You still hear their voice in your head, not yelling but evaluating. Measuring your worth against your usefulness. Calculating whether you've earned the right to exist fully today.

Your body carries the weight of every time you were ignored, dismissed, or made to feel foolish for simply being human. That knot in your chest when you try to speak up. The way your shoulders rise when footsteps approach. The way your stomach clenches when someone sighs, even if it's not at you. The exhaustion that sleep never quite cures.

That's not oversensitivity. That's memory. And memory doesn't only live in the brain—it lives in the tension you carry, the space you take up, the apologies you offer for existing.

You Didn't Leave Bruised, You Left Hollow

People asked if you were okay. You smiled. Said yes. Because how do you explain grief for something so quiet you weren't even sure it was real?

You didn't have scars. You had emptiness. A slow unravelling of confidence, clarity, and self-worth that happened so gradually you didn't notice until you were already gone.

They didn't need to raise a fist to do it. They just needed you to keep doubting your right to exist fully.

A woman I spoke with once told me she Googled "emotional abuse" and closed the tab five seconds later. "It didn't apply," she said. "He didn't scream. He just made me feel invisible." Years later, in therapy, she finally understood: "The silence was what broke me—because it gave me nothing to point to."

Practical Step

Write down the rules you taught yourself to stay safe: "Don't bring it up before bed." "Don't cry in front of them." "Don't expect a response." "Keep your voice level." "Don't be too happy—it's annoying."

Then ask: Who made those rules necessary? And notice how many of them were about making yourself smaller. These aren't rules you need to keep anymore. They were never yours to begin with.

Why It Matters

Because self-blame dies when the system that created it gets exposed. Those weren't relationship skills—they were survival strategies.

If You Remember One Thing

Not all abuse looks like chaos. Sometimes it looks like order. Like politeness. Like steady silence while you slowly disappear inside it. But now you see the trace. Now you recognise the cost.

You weren't "making it up." You were adapting to survive something that refused to name itself. Something that hid behind civility while dismantling you piece by piece.

And next time, you'll listen to your body, not their calm tone. You'll trust the tension in the room. You'll trust that flutter in your chest. You'll trust your knowing.

Because now you understand: It didn't have to be loud to be real. It just had to make you disappear.

And you're done disappearing.

7.10
They Hurt You
Then Called You The Abuser

Author's Note:

You say, "You hurt me," and the room changes. The person who abused you for years suddenly claims they're the victim. Of YOU.

They race ahead—while you're still reeling—to tell another story. They file restraining orders. They tell the court they're afraid. They sob to your family about your "abuse." They post on social media about surviving domestic violence—meaning you.

There's a name for this reversal: DARVO. Deny. Attack. Reverse Victim and Offender. It happens when exposure threatens them. When consequences loom. When their image is at stake. That's when they take your entire history of suffering and claim it as their own.

The confusion isn't about whether something happened—it's about watching your life story get stolen and reversed. Watching the person who hurt you wear your pain like a costume. Watching systems designed to protect victims get weaponised against you instead.

This chapter is about recognising that reversal for what it is: not confusion, but strategy. Not misunderstanding, but a deliberate attempt to escape accountability by becoming you.

The Day Everything Flipped

For years, you lived it. The fear. The exhaustion. You have the texts calling you worthless. The medical records from anxiety so severe you couldn't eat.

Then you leave. Or speak up. Or someone notices.

Within days—sometimes hours—they're on the phone to everyone you know. "I'm scared," they say, voice breaking. "I don't know what they might do." They file for an emergency protection order, claiming you're the threat. They post cryptic messages about "surviving abuse" and "finding strength." They show up to court with printed emails—your desperate attempts to explain the hurt—presented as evidence of YOUR harassment.

The person who made you afraid to exist in your own home now claims they're afraid of you. And people believe them.

They Don't Just Deny the Abuse—They Steal It

This isn't simple denial. They don't just say "that never happened." They take the exact things they did to you and claim you did them.

They isolated you from family? Now they say you kept them from their loved ones.
They controlled the money? They claim financial abuse.
They screamed at you daily? They tell the mediator about your "rage."
They threatened to take the children? They file emergency custody citing your "instability."

They memorise your symptoms and perform them. They take the language you finally found to describe your suffering and speak it back reversed, with them as protagonist.

A woman told me: "He googled 'signs of abuse' and then accused me of every single one. The same man who'd thrown me against walls was now telling the judge he feared for his safety."

Why Courts and Therapists Fall for It

Systems trust composure. They trust paperwork. They trust whoever speaks first and speaks calmest.

If children are involved, they will weaponise your love—knowing you'll doubt yourself before risking them.

You walk into court carrying years of trauma. Your hands shake. Your voice cracks. You sound "emotional" because you ARE emotional—you're trying to get someone to see the truth through years of systematic gaslighting.

They walk in rehearsed. Calm. Concerned. They've had time to prepare their performance while you were still in shock from escaping. They speak in therapy language they learned from self-help books: "I'm just concerned about their mental health." "I want what's best for the children." "I tried so hard to help them heal."

She sat in court while his lawyer handed the judge a folder labelled "safety concerns"—made entirely from her own desperate emails begging him to stop.

Your trauma symptoms—the shaking, the panic, the desperate need to be believed—become their evidence. Your medical records for anxiety and PTSD get twisted into proof you're unstable. The fact that you're in therapy becomes confirmation you're the problem.

Meanwhile, they've never seen a therapist. Never admitted fault. Never shown distress. To the court, they look like the stable one. The reasonable one. The one who's been "dealing with" your issues.

The Preparation You Never Saw

DARVO doesn't happen spontaneously. While they were still actively abusing you, they were already preparing alibis.

Those times they provoked you into yelling, then recorded only your response.
The texts where they pushed you to the breaking point, then saved only your desperate reaction.

The months of telling mutual friends you were "struggling" while never mentioning what they were doing to cause it. The careful cultivation of their public image as patient partner to someone "difficult."

They were building their case long before you even knew there would be a trial.

Practical Step

Start documenting NOW, even if you're not ready to leave. Email yourself. Keep a hidden journal. Save screenshots in a secure cloud account they don't know about. Include dates, exact words, witnesses. Focus on patterns, not just incidents. Document the calm times too—the cycles, the honeymoon periods, the calculated nature of it all.

If you can't document now, that's okay—document when you can. Your notes still matter, even if they come later.

If you're already out and facing DARVO, find a domestic violence advocate immediately. Not just a lawyer—an advocate who understands this specific reversal. They've seen it before. They know how to help courts recognise the pattern.

Most importantly: stop trying to convince people who've already chosen their side. Focus your truth on professional systems—therapists trained in coercive control, judges educated about DARVO, advocates who understand that the calmer party isn't always the victim.

Why It Works So Well

DARVO works because it exploits society's difficulty with complex truth. People want victims to be perfect and villains to be obvious. When an abuser claims victimhood convincingly, it's easier for others to believe "it's complicated" or "there are two sides" than to recognise sophisticated manipulation.

It works because it turns your authentic distress into evidence against you. The more upset you get about being called an abuser, the more "unstable" you appear. The harder you fight to prove your truth, the more "obsessed" you seem. It's a trap designed to tighten the more you struggle.

It works because they're performing calm while you're living trauma. They can rehearse their lines because they're lying. You stumble over yours because you're trying to convey years of complex psychological torture in a few minutes to strangers.

If You Remember One Thing

When someone who abused you for years suddenly claims to be your victim, that's not confusion. That's confession.

They know exactly what they did—that's how they know which costume to wear. They know exactly what abuse looks like—they've been doing it. They know exactly how victims sound—they've heard you.

DARVO is the last gasp of an abuser about to face consequences. It's the nuclear option when exposure threatens. It's what happens when someone who needs control at all costs realises they're losing it.

You're not crazy for being devastated when your abuser calls you abusive. You're not wrong for feeling like reality has been turned inside out. You're not overreacting to having your own story stolen and worn against you.

This is what they do when they're cornered. This is what they do when truth threatens their image. This is what they do when the person they broke starts to heal and speak.

But here's what they can't steal: your body knows what it survived. Your nervous system remembers who made it afraid. Your truth exists whether they acknowledge it or not.

Their performance might win them an audience, but it doesn't erase what happened. And every time they work this hard to reverse the story, they reveal their fear that the real story is coming out.

The truth doesn't need a costume. It just needs time.

Part 8
Aftermath

This is what the damage looks like
And it makes perfect sense

8.1
When Someone You Love
is Being Shouted At

Author's Note:

This chapter is for the ones watching it happen. For the parents, siblings, friends. For the people who see someone they love go quiet when their partner enters the room. If you've ever had that sick feeling that something's wrong, but no one else seems to say it, this is for you.

The person doing the shouting might be any gender. So might the person being shouted at. But the dynamic is the same: shouting doesn't need fists to be abuse. And just because they're still defending their partner doesn't mean they feel safe.

He Wants Obedience, Not Resolution. And Definitely Not Love

You're sitting at dinner when it happens. The raised voice from the kitchen. The sudden silence. Your stomach clenches as you recognise the pattern—he shouts, she folds, then they both walk back into the room like nothing happened. She's smiling but her hands are shaking as she sets down the plates.

You want to say something but you're not sure what. You don't want to make it worse for her. So you stay quiet, complicit in the pretence that this is normal.

You're not imagining it. You're not overreacting. You're not being dramatic.

You're witnessing someone being slowly worn down by a person who wants obedience, not love. You see how she goes quiet mid-sentence when his car pulls up. How she watches his face before she speaks, gauging the temperature of his mood.

A mother told me: "I watched my daughter shrink every time he walked into the room. She was so quick to agree with him. So careful. And when he raised his voice, she just froze. Not like she was scared of getting hit, like she was scared of being wrong. For a while I told myself it was just how they argued.

"But one night I heard him shouting through the phone, and she just sat there, staring at the wall. After he hung up, she said it was fine. That he was just tired. And that's when I knew she wasn't allowed to have needs anymore."

Shouting Isn't Passion. It's Power

It's not about what he says. It's about how the air changes when his voice rises. It's about when he chooses to explode—right when she's trying to explain something, right when she disagrees, right when she has a need.

You've noticed how her voice has changed. How she explains herself like she's already guilty of something she hasn't done yet.

That's not sensitivity. That's survival. That's what happens when someone learns that their thoughts, needs, and feelings trigger rage.

Your body knows something's wrong too. You feel the tension rise when he's around. The relief when he leaves the room. The way everyone breathes differently when he's not there.

You Don't Need Bruises To Believe It's Abuse

He doesn't need to hurt her physically for it to be coercion. He just needs to make her stop asking. Stop objecting. Stop existing too loudly.

That's what shouting does. It doesn't communicate—it conditions. Each raised voice teaches her that disagreement is dangerous. Each outburst trains her that her needs cause problems. Until her silence becomes the only safe answer.

The shouting might not leave marks you can photograph, but you can see the damage in how she moves through the world now—smaller, quieter, constantly apologising for taking up space.

What You Can Say (And What Not To)

Here are some things that help: "I've noticed how he speaks to you. I don't think that's okay." Or try: "You're not overreacting. I've seen the way he talks to you." Sometimes the simplest is best: "You don't deserve to be shouted at. No one does." You might say: "Whenever you're ready to talk about it—no pressure—I'm here." Or even just: "I'm worried about you. You seem different lately."

But be careful. It's best to avoid confronting him directly—this often makes the abuse escalate in private, where you can't see it. Try not to push her to leave before she's ready or ask "Why don't you just leave?"—leaving is often the most dangerous time. And please, keep inviting her to things even if she keeps saying no. Isolation makes everything worse.

You don't need the full story. You don't need her to agree that it's abuse. You just need to plant a different voice than the one she hears at home.

If You Remember One Thing

Shouting isn't just noise. It's a weapon. A warning. A way to erase someone in plain sight.

So keep seeing it. Keep noticing. Keep being the one who doesn't pretend it's normal.

Even if they can't name it yet. Even if they still call it love. Your quiet noticing might be the only truth they have left to hold onto.

You might feel helpless watching it happen. But your witnessing matters. Your refusal to normalise it matters. Sometimes the only thing standing between someone and complete isolation is one person who sees and refuses to look away.

8.2
If Your Body Still Remembers
It Was Real

Author's Note:

This chapter is about jumping when the toaster pops because your body learned that sudden sounds meant danger. If you've ever gone rigid at a sigh, jolted at footsteps, or apologised for nothing, this is for you. Your body isn't betraying you. It's bearing witness. It remembered when no one else did. And that testimony is enough.

Your Nervous System Was the First One To Know

You jolted when someone raised their voice in the next room. Not because they were yelling at you. Not because it was loud. But because your body went cold, fast, like it remembered something your brain couldn't quite name.

That's the thing about psychological abuse. You don't always remember the exact words. But your nervous system remembers exactly what it felt like to be under attack. The hollow feeling in your ribs when their voice changed pitch. The way your stomach dropped when you heard their key in the door. How your muscles locked when they started that particular tone.

And it reacts the same way it would if you'd been slapped. Because to your nervous system, threat is threat. Whether it comes from a fist or a voice doesn't matter. The danger was real. The impact was real. Your body knows this, even when your mind doubts.

Your Body Catalogued What Words Couldn't Capture

Your mind might have forgotten the arguments, but your body kept detailed records. It documented which floorboard creaks meant trouble. The exact tone that preceded an explosion. How danger smelled like their morning coffee mixed with that particular silence.

Your nervous system became an involuntary historian, archiving threats in muscle memory, storing warnings in your startle response. It learned that Tuesday evenings were dangerous. That happiness triggered punishment. That asking for anything meant hours of cold silence.

You might not remember their exact words, but your body remembers the barometric pressure of their rage. The way the air got thick before they exploded. The specific quality of quiet that meant you'd done something wrong but wouldn't find out what until later.

Emotional Abuse Hits The Same System

They didn't raise a hand. They didn't break plates or leave bruises. But your heart still races when their name appears on your phone. You go rigid when someone exhales disappointment—that particular breath that meant you'd failed again. You still apologise automatically, reflexively, even when you've done nothing wrong.

Your skin prickles at certain tones of voice. You wake with your teeth pressing into your tongue from clenching all night. Your breathing goes shallow when asked a simple question, as if the wrong answer might still have consequences.

Your nervous system doesn't grade trauma by visibility. It doesn't care whether anyone else would call it abuse. It just responds to what it learned: that you weren't safe. That vigilance was survival. That peace could shatter without warning.

But here's what you might not realise: your body isn't overreacting. It's being loyal to you. It's protecting you the only way it knows how—by remembering danger and trying to keep you ready for it. The problem isn't your body's memory. The problem is that everyone else forgot to notice what you survived.

Emotional Abuse Doesn't Fade. It Echoes

You're years out. You're safe now. You know you're safe. You can list all the reasons you're safe.

But your sleep is still broken, waking at 3am with your heart pounding for no reason you can name. Your digestion never quite recovered—anxiety took up residence there and won't leave. Your jaw aches from a night of grinding. You script basic interactions before they happen. You apologise for having opinions, for needing things, for being noticed at all.

That's trauma. That's your nervous system still fighting a war that ended years ago, still protecting you from dangers that aren't there anymore. Your body hasn't gotten the message that the threat has passed. It's still standing guard, exhausting you with its vigilance.

Practical Step

Start with simple body awareness. Once a day, do a five-second scan: Where are you holding tension? Is your jaw locked? Shoulders raised? Stomach tight? Don't try to fix it yet—just notice.

When you catch yourself going rigid, fawning, or apologising for nothing, pause and ask: "Is this now, or is this then?" Help your body learn the difference between past danger and present safety. This takes time. Be patient with yourself.

Why It Matters

Your body is trying to protect you from something that already happened. Teaching it that the danger has passed is how healing begins.

Trauma Is Measured by Impact, Not Method

They didn't hit you. They didn't scream. But you lost your voice somewhere along the way. You stopped feeling joy—it just drained away so gradually you didn't notice until it was gone. You forgot what it felt like to be believed, to trust your own perceptions, to exist without constantly monitoring yourself. You started asking permission to take up space in your own life.

That's trauma.

Your body doesn't care whether it came through fists or silence, through violence or neglect, through explosion or erosion. It only knows that you got hurt. That you had to adapt to survive. That you had to make yourself smaller to stay safe.

A woman once told me she was more shaken by her emotionally abusive relationship than by being mugged at nineteen. "At least when I got mugged," she said, "no one made me question whether it actually happened. No one suggested I was being dramatic. No one told me I should be grateful it wasn't worse."

If You Remember One Thing

There's no hierarchy of valid pain. No award for surviving a "lesser" kind of abuse. No prize for downplaying what your body still jolts from.

Abuse doesn't have to be loud to be real. It doesn't have to be visible to be valid. It doesn't have to leave marks that others can see.

If it changed the way you breathe, if it rewired the way you exist in the world, if it made you doubt your own reality—it was real.

Your body's memory is evidence enough. Your nervous system's hypervigilance is proof enough. The way you still brace for impact when someone's mood shifts—that's testimony enough.

You don't need to convince anyone. You don't need to justify why "just words" or "just emotions" could leave you this altered. You don't need to minimise it to make others comfortable.

Your body has already testified. That testimony is enough to deserve healing.

8.3
You Didn't Say Yes
You Just Couldn't Say No

Author's Note:

This chapter is about the shame survivors carry after abuse, the belief that staying meant agreeing. If you've ever asked yourself why you didn't leave sooner, or wondered if you "allowed" what happened, this will help you see it clearly: Staying wasn't saying yes. It was saying: this is the safest I can be right now. You didn't consent to control. You adapted to survive it. And that's not the same thing.

It Wasn't Consent. It Was Survival

You've asked yourself a thousand times: How did I let this happen? Why didn't I see it sooner? Why didn't I leave the first time, the fifth time, the fiftieth?

And buried underneath that relentless questioning is the lie that you somehow "consented" to coercion. That staying meant agreeing. That not fighting meant accepting.

But here's the truth: You don't consent to coercive control. You adapt to survive it.

When leaving feels more dangerous than staying, when resistance triggers worse punishment, when you've been systematically stripped of resources and support—that's not a choice. That's a cage with invisible bars.

Coercion Isn't a Choice. It's a Trap Designed to Look Like One

You were vulnerable when they found you. Maybe you were lonely after a loss. Maybe you were hopeful after heartbreak. Maybe you were young and believed in the good in people. That's not weakness—that's human.

You'd been trained, long before they arrived, to overlook red flags. Taught that love meant sacrifice. Conditioned to believe that patience could fix people. They didn't create these beliefs—they exploited them.

They built conditions where resistance felt impossible. They isolated you so slowly you didn't notice until everyone was gone. They exhausted you until fighting took more energy than you had. They made the cost of leaving higher than the cost of staying— not through one big threat, but through a thousand small erosions.

Your hand hovered over the doorknob a hundred times, but never turned it. Not because you wanted to stay—because you couldn't see a door you were allowed to walk through.

A woman told me: "People ask why I didn't just leave. They don't understand—by the time I realised I needed to, I had no money, no friends left, three kids, and absolutely no belief I could survive on my own. That wasn't my failure. That was his success."

You Weren't Naive. You Were Systematically Groomed

The beginning wasn't abuse—it was intoxication. You were love-bombed with attention that felt like finally being seen. You were mirrored so perfectly you thought you'd found your soulmate. The connection felt instant, intense, inevitable.

You were sold a future and then punished for believing in it. The person who promised you everything slowly took everything away, but so gradually you didn't notice until you had nothing left.

That's not foolishness. That's what grooming looks like in adult relationships. It's not just for children—it's a systematic process of building dependence before revealing control.

A survivor once told me: "I wasn't weak. I just didn't know what slow, healthy love looked like. I thought intensity meant intimacy. I thought jealousy meant caring. Now I know those were warning signs dressed up as romance."

What You Didn't Know Then Doesn't Mean You Were Complicit

You didn't have the language for coercive control. You didn't have the education about trauma bonds. You didn't have someone holding up a mirror saying: "This isn't love. This is ownership."

So you stayed. You tried harder. You explained yourself better. You navigated every word like a minefield. You held your breath through entire conversations. You made yourself quieter, smaller, less threatening to their ego.

That's not compliance. That's what a nervous system does when it's trapped—it adapts to survive. Your brain was doing exactly what brains do under sustained threat: finding ways to minimise harm when escape feels impossible.

Practical Step

Write a letter to the version of you who stayed. Not with blame, but with the compassion you'd show a friend. Tell them what they couldn't have known. Thank them for surviving however they could. Let them know that staying alive was enough, even if it meant staying in hell.

If writing feels too hard, just say it out loud: "You did the best you could with what you knew then. Surviving was enough."

Why It Matters

The guilt you carry was never yours to hold. It belongs to the person who created conditions where staying felt safer than leaving.

If You Remember One Thing

You didn't let it happen. You didn't ask for it. You weren't choosing trauma.

You were navigating life with a nervous system shaped by old wounds, and someone weaponised that. They saw your loyalty and called it weakness. They saw your hope and called it naivety. They saw your love and turned it into a chain.

Coercion isn't consent. Confusion isn't weakness. Adaptation isn't agreement.

You didn't need to be smarter, stronger, or more aware. They needed to be better. They needed to not be predators.

And now you do know. Now you have the words. Now you can see the cage they built bar by bar.

So offer yourself what they never did: Grace for not knowing then what you know now. Truth about what really happened. And a way forward that doesn't begin with the shame they left you holding.

Your survival was never shameful. It was miraculous.

8.4
They Took More Than Time

Author's Note:

This chapter is about the invisible aftermath of abuse. If you ever thought the pain would end when they left, but still find yourself flinching at kindness, doubting peace, or rebuilding what they quietly destroyed, this will help you name it: They didn't just take time. They took parts of you. If you look at your life now and see gaps you can't explain, this chapter will help you name where they came from. And naming the cost is how you start getting them back.

It Wasn't Just The Time. It Was the Loss Of You

You thought the worst part would be the time you lost. The years you gave. The birthdays spent crying in locked bathrooms. The holidays where you performed happiness while dying inside.

But it wasn't. The worst part was looking in the mirror after they left and not recognising who stared back. The person in the reflection had your face but none of your ease. Your body but not your confidence. Your voice but not your conviction.

It was the doubt that infected every decision you tried to make. The way you flinched when someone simply asked, "What do you want for dinner?" because choosing had become dangerous. The paralysis when faced with any preference, any opinion, any need.

Abuse doesn't just steal time. It systematically dismantles who you are, piece by piece, until you're not sure what's left is even you.

Self-Doubt Is What Stays Long After They Leave

You finally escaped. The door closed behind them for the last time. But their voice didn't leave with them—it moved into your head.

You still ask "Am I overreacting?" when your gut screams that something's wrong. You triple-check your texts for anything that could be "misinterpreted." You rehearse phone calls before dialling. You apologise before you speak, during, and after.

You question whether that thing that happened was "really that bad." Whether you're remembering it right. Whether you're being dramatic. Whether everyone else is right and you've just learned to erase anything they could weaponise.

Because they didn't just make you question their behaviour—they trained you to edit yourself down to fit inside their comfort. And that internal editor doesn't leave just because they did.

Peace Feels Unsafe Because Your Body Doesn't Trust It Yet

The house is quiet now. No footsteps to track. No mood to monitor. And still, you brace. Your shoulders stay raised. Your jaw stays clenched.

Because your body learned that calm wasn't real—it was the held breath before the storm. The setup before the explosion.

A woman told me the first time her new partner responded to disagreement with curiosity instead of rage, she completely shut down. "He asked what was wrong," she said. "I couldn't explain that I didn't know how to be treated well without waiting for the punishment that always followed kindness."

They Poisoned Your Relationships Then Played the Victim

While you were trying to survive them, they were already rewriting history. They talked to your friends with concern in their voice. Dropped subtle lines: "I'm worried about them." "They've been so volatile lately." "I've tried everything to help."

And suddenly, people you'd loved for years looked at you with that particular expression—part pity, part suspicion. Not because you'd changed. But because they'd been given the edited version of your story, with you cast as the problem and them as the long-suffering hero.

A woman told me she lost two decades-long friendships after her ex told them she'd been "controlling and unstable." She said, "They never asked me what happened. They just stopped calling. He took them too."

Kindness Feels Foreign Because You Were Trained to Fear It

You meet someone new who actually listens when you speak. Who pauses before responding. Who asks, "Do you want comfort or solutions?" Who remembers things you mentioned weeks ago.

And your chest tightens. Not from joy—from suspicion. When will this kindness turn sharp? What's the price? What do they want?

Because your body doesn't know what to do with gentleness that stays gentle. With consistency that doesn't come with conditions. With love that doesn't hurt. So you flinch at softness. You question genuine care. You wait for the trap.

Even when there isn't one. Especially when there isn't one.

Practical Step

Start documenting your instincts. Write down your gut feelings about situations, then note what actually happened. Track the times you thought "something feels off" and were right. Track the times kindness stayed kind.

Begin with small acts of receiving: Let someone buy you coffee. Accept a compliment without deflecting. Allow help without immediately repaying it. Notice when the sky doesn't fall.

Each small act of receiving is proof that the part of you that can trust hasn't been erased—only buried.

Why It Matters

You're not rebuilding logic—that was never broken. You're rebuilding trust in your own perceptions. And that requires evidence that your instincts were right all along.

If You Remember One Thing

What they took wasn't just years. It was your ease in your own skin. Your trust in your own thoughts. Your belief that love could be safe. Your confidence that you knew reality when you saw it.

And when they left, they didn't return what they'd stolen. They left you holding the bill for damage you didn't cause. Left you questioning whether the theft even happened.

But here's what they didn't take: Your capacity to rebuild. Your ability to relearn. The parts of you that survived by going underground, waiting.

You're allowed to name every single thing they destroyed without apologising for the inventory. You're allowed to grieve the person you were before they systematically dismantled you. You're allowed to be furious about the reconstruction you now have to do alone.

Because what they broke wasn't your fault. But what's left—the core of you that survived—that's yours. And it's stronger than you know. Strong enough to rebuild everything, differently this time.

The person in the mirror might be unfamiliar now. But they're not permanent. They're transitional. They're the bridge between who you were forced to become and who you're choosing to be.

And that person you're becoming? They're already beautiful.

8.5
Being Seen Shouldn't
Feel Like Danger

Author's Note:

This chapter is for Georgie. And for every woman like her, who trembled when the camera came out, who never felt at home in her own reflection, who carried shame in her skin that never belonged to her.

If you've ever turned away from a lens, avoided mirrors, or felt exposed instead of cherished when someone looked at you—this is for you. The unease wasn't vanity. It wasn't weakness. It was the residue of being measured, corrected, and controlled until visibility felt like danger.

You were never the damage. The harm lived in what was done to you, not in who you are. And now, you deserve to reclaim your body—not as a performance to satisfy others, but as a place you get to live freely.

When You're Told You're Never Enough
Being Seen Feels Like Exposure

She was breathtaking. Strangers would say it. I would think it every time I looked at her.

But when the camera came out, she tensed. Her shoulders pulled up. Her smile became calculated. One day I asked to take her photo. She said no. I paused, confused. Then she started shaking. Not gently. Not emotionally. Physically. Her whole body trembled like a trapped animal sensing danger.

I didn't take the photo. But I'll never forget the tremor. Later, she said quietly, "I've just never felt good enough." Not pretty enough. Not thin enough. Not composed or calm or acceptable enough.

That's what decades of coercive control does. It doesn't just change your mind about yourself. It burrows under your skin and teaches you that visibility equals vulnerability. That being seen means being judged. That the camera doesn't capture—it exposes.

Her Body Was A Battleground Long Before The Illness

She wasn't allowed to relax in her own skin. To indulge without commentary. To take up space without apology. Her appearance was policed with surgical precision. Her appetite scrutinised like evidence of moral failure. Her natural softness treated as something to correct, to discipline, to overcome.

She learned to hide. To present only the version that might be acceptable—neutral, careful, controlled. To pre-emptively excuse her own presence before anyone could object to it. To dim her light before anyone else could extinguish it.

And when she couldn't meet those impossible standards—because no one could—she felt ashamed. Not because she'd failed at something worth doing, but because someone else had decided what her worth was made of, measured it, and found her lacking.

Years Of Criticism Taught Her That Being Seen Was Unsafe

It wasn't about the photo. It was never about the photo. It was about control. About how many times her body had been commented on, picked apart, reshaped into something she couldn't recognise as her own.

Every meal became a performance of restraint. Every outfit a negotiation with imaginary critics. Every mirror a courtroom where she was both defendant and prosecutor.

When I asked to take her picture, I thought I was loving her. Celebrating her. But what I didn't understand—not until her body started to shake—was that she'd spent a lifetime being looked at without care. Being evaluated instead of seen.

The lens didn't feel like love. It felt like scrutiny. Like another test she was about to fail.

Shame Doesn't Just Live In The Mind
It Lives in the Immune System

Chronic trauma doesn't fade. It burrows deep. It dysregulates your stress response until your body can't tell the difference between a camera and a weapon. It floods you with cortisol every time you're perceived. It weakens your immune system until your cells mirror your hypervigilance.

When you live like that—always braced, always monitoring, always pre-emptively excusing your presence—your body pays the price. The inflammation. The autoimmune responses. The illnesses that make perfect sense when you understand that shame is stored in tissue, not just thought.

A woman once told me she spent most of her adult life apologising for being "too much"—too curvy, too loving, too visible. She learned to stop asking for help because help came with a side of judgment. When she got sick, really sick, she delayed getting treatment because she didn't want to be seen. "I didn't want to sit in another waiting room," she said, "and be looked at like I caused it."

Practical Step

Write down one way your body still recoils at being seen. Maybe it's photos. Maybe it's compliments. Maybe it's being noticed at all. Then ask yourself: where did that fear come from? A comment someone made? A look that cut? A rule you were taught about what bodies deserve?

Trace it back. Name it. And recognise that it didn't start with you. Releasing it isn't about pretending it never happened. It's about refusing to let their judgment live in your skin any longer.

Why It Matters

Trauma isn't just the harm that was done to you. It's the habits and rules that remain long after, the ones that taught you to shrink yourself before anyone else could. Naming them is the first step to breaking them.

If You Remember One Thing

Some survivors learn to disappear in silence. Others disappear in shame. Georgie carried both.

But I saw her. Not the version she thought she had to be. Not the careful construction designed to avoid criticism. I saw her—brilliant, tender, fierce, exhausted from performing acceptability.

I saw what the shame had cost her. And I see it in you, too.

If you're reading this, maybe you were her. Or maybe you still are. Maybe you still tense when someone looks too long. Maybe you still apologise for taking up space you have every right to occupy.

So here's what I want you to remember:

It's not vanity to want to be seen with kindness. It's not selfish to exist fully in your own skin. And it's not weakness if your body broke under the weight of being judged, shamed, or controlled.

That wasn't your fault. That was what survival looked like in a world that made your worth conditional.

But maybe now, gently, carefully, you get to stop hiding. You get to be seen, not as a problem to be fixed, but as a person worth cherishing. Not as a body to be evaluated, but as a whole human being deserving of witness.

Because being seen shouldn't feel like danger. It should feel like recognition. Like someone saying: "There you are. I've been waiting for you to arrive."

It should feel like coming home.

8.6
They Didn't Want You Whole
They Wanted You Manageable

Author's Note:

This chapter is for anyone who finally felt joy, only to have someone close to them withdraw, criticise, or walk away. If your recovery was met with punishment instead of pride, that wasn't proof you did something wrong. It was proof they never wanted you whole—they only wanted you manageable.

You Were Finally Okay and That Made You Inconvenient

You came home from therapy smiling. Actually smiling. Not the careful one you'd practised for years, but the real one that reached your eyes and softened your shoulders. "You seem different," they said. Not warmly. Suspiciously. Like you'd broken an unspoken contract.

Your chest tightened like you'd stepped out of line in a play you didn't know you were in. That signal meant you'd done something wrong. But all you'd done was heal. You were happy. Maybe for the first time in years. Not perfect, not finished, but finally breathing on your own.

And instead of celebrating with you, they pulled away. Made snide comments about your "new personality." Got quiet when you laughed too freely. Acted like your joy was a personal attack on them. Not because you were unsafe. Not because you'd done anything wrong. But because they lost their leverage when you no longer hurt. Your recovery had disrupted the ecosystem they'd built around your pain.

Your Pain Had Been Their Power

When you were broken, they were needed. When you doubted yourself, they were the authority. When you were drowning, they were the rescuer. The wise one. The stable one. The hero of your story. But what happens to the rescuer when you learn to swim? They lose their role. Their purpose. Their sense of superiority. The careful hierarchy built on your suffering collapses.

So they respond to your healing like it's betrayal. Your joy becomes "selfishness." Your boundaries become "attacks." Your growth becomes "abandonment." Your happiness gets reframed as cruelty to them.

Because some people don't actually want you broken. That's too simple. They want you functional enough to appreciate them, but damaged enough to need them. They want you manageable. And wholeness? Wholeness can't be managed.

They Were Comfortable With Your Suffering

You were easier when you needed constant reassurance. Easier when your pain made them feel superior, stable, necessary.

But recovery changed the script. You stopped apologising for existing. Started choosing joy without committee approval. Started trusting your own judgement without their input.

And instead of being proud, they turned cold. Less enthusiasm for your good news. More criticism disguised as concern. Distance when you needed support for growth instead of crisis management.

Your body noticed before your mind did. The tension when you mentioned feeling good. The shift when you set a boundary. The disappointment when you handled something alone.

They Preferred You in Pieces They Could Rearrange

They didn't have to say it outright. The punishment was in the withdrawal. The sudden busy schedule when you needed celebration but immediate availability when you were in crisis. The forgotten calls when things were good. The subtle digs at your "changes." The nostalgic references to who you "used to be"—meaning who you were when you were suffering.

They made your happiness feel like betrayal. Your peace feel like selfishness. Your wholeness feel like you'd abandoned them—when really, you'd just abandoned the role they'd assigned you.

A woman told me that when she finally left her abusive marriage and found peace, her adult daughter stopped speaking to her. "Six months," she said. "No calls. No texts. She walked past me at the shops like I was invisible."

"At first I thought I'd done something terrible. I apologised for everything. For leaving her father. For changing. For being happy without him. For finding someone kind." She showed me the messages she'd sent. Dozens. All variations of "I'm sorry" and "Please talk to me" and "What did I do wrong?"

"Then my therapist asked me something that changed everything: 'What if she's not angry that you left him? What if she's angry that you're okay without him?'"

"That's when it clicked. She'd spent years being my caretaker, my counsellor, my rescuer from her father's abuse. When I was crying daily, she had a role. When I was happy? She didn't know who to be. My pain had been her purpose. My healing took that away."

Practical Step

Think of someone who got weird when you got better. Maybe they said things like: "You've changed" (accusingly). "I liked the old you better." "You don't need me anymore" (as manipulation). "Must be nice to be so happy" (bitterly).

Now ask yourself: When I was struggling, what did they get from that? The role of wise advisor? The stable one by comparison? The hero? The one with all the answers? The needed one?

That's what they lost when you healed. Not you—just their role in your suffering. Write it down. Name what your pain gave them. It helps you see their withdrawal for what it is: grief over lost control, not proof you've done something wrong.

Why It Matters

Recognising their withdrawal as loss of control rather than proof of your wrongness frees you from the urge to shrink back into suffering just to restore their comfort.

If You Remember One Thing

Your happiness doesn't require approval. Your peace doesn't need permission. Your wholeness isn't a betrayal of anyone, no matter how much they act like it is.

If someone walks away from your recovery, that wasn't love. That was management. They didn't want you well—they wanted you dependent. They didn't want you whole— they wanted you in pieces they could rearrange to suit their needs.

You didn't lose them by healing. You revealed them. You revealed that their care was conditional on your crisis. That their love required your limitation. That their presence depended on your pain.

And the next time someone punishes you for finding peace, remember this: You don't have to break again to keep anyone comfortable. You don't have to perform suffering to maintain relationships. You don't have to apologise for becoming whole.

Let them go. Let them grieve the version of you that needed them to survive. That version served its purpose—it kept you alive. But it's not who you are anymore.

You're not too much now that you're happy. You're finally enough. And anyone who preferred you broken was never really for you—they were for what your brokenness gave them.

Your wholeness is not negotiable. Not anymore.

8.7
Your Body Couldn't Feel Safe Because It Wasn't

Author's Note:

This chapter is about nervous system regulation, and why it's nearly impossible when you're living under coercive control. If you've ever felt stuck in fight, flight, freeze, or fawn, if you've felt like you were always bracing, always listening for the shift, always trying to manage someone else's mood, this will help explain why.

You weren't weak. You were overwhelmed by constant threat. Your nervous system couldn't settle because the danger was real—emotional, psychological, everywhere. That wasn't failure. That was protection. Your body bracing for danger it couldn't leave but couldn't afford to miss.

You Can't Regulate in a Relationship That Isn't Safe

You tried everything. You journaled until your hand cramped. You did breathwork until you were dizzy. You listened to every podcast about anxiety. You repeated affirmations in the mirror each morning. But your chest still tightened when their car pulled up. Your shoulders still rose when their mood shifted. Your breath still went shallow when they entered the room.

Because your body knew what your mind couldn't yet admit: this wasn't safe. It's not a mindset issue. It's not a lack of tools or willpower. You can't regulate your nervous system in a relationship driven by coercive control. The threat is constant. The hypervigilance is justified. The tension is a rational response to an irrational situation.

You weren't failing at calm. You were succeeding at survival in an environment where calm could be dangerous. Where missing a mood shift meant hours of punishment. Where relaxing meant being caught off guard.

The Consequences Aren't Just Emotional. They're Physical

When your nervous system stays in survival mode for weeks, months, years, your entire body starts to pay the price. Sleep becomes impossible—you wake at 3am with your heart racing, scanning for threats that aren't there but used to be. Your digestion shuts down because your body thinks you're being chased and decides eating can wait. You develop mystery symptoms that no test can explain: the headaches, the joint pain, the fatigue that sleep doesn't cure.

Your immune system weakens from the constant flood of stress hormones. You catch every cold, every flu, everything going around. You feel tired but wired, exhausted but unable to rest, because your body doesn't remember how to stand down. Your memory starts failing—where did you put your keys, what were you just saying, why did you walk into this room? Your focus scatters because a brain on high alert can't concentrate on one thing when it's monitoring everything for danger.

The fatigue feels like walking through wet sand—every movement takes three times the effort it should. You start wondering what's wrong with you. Why you can't just relax. Why you can't just let things go. Why your body seems to be betraying you. But it's not betrayal. It's protection. It's your body screaming "This isn't safe" in the only language it knows: symptoms. And when no one listens—not doctors, not friends, not even you— it screams louder.

This is what coercive control does. It doesn't just break your spirit. It hijacks your nervous system until you forget what peace feels like in your bones.

Practical Step

Instead of asking "How can I calm down?" ask: "What is still making me feel unsafe?" Is it their number in your phone? The possibility they might show up? The way certain tones of voice still make you brace? Name the ongoing threats, even the "small" ones. Notice how your body reacts when you name them. Your jaw might tighten. Your chest might loosen. Your shoulders might drop or rise. Your body is helping you find what still feels unsafe.

Why It Matters

When you stop blaming your body for reacting normally to an abnormal environment, you can start working with it instead of against it.

If You Remember One Thing

You weren't meant to feel calm in chaos. You weren't broken for staying activated. You were responding to constant threat exactly as you were designed to.

The solution was never to force yourself to relax in danger. The solution was to get to safety first, then teach your body the danger has passed.

Your nervous system wasn't overreacting. It was accurately reading an environment where emotional violence could erupt at any moment. Where love came with conditions that changed without warning. Where peace was just the pause before the next storm.

Even now, in safety, your body might still be bracing. Still reading the air. Still protecting you from threats that feel current even though they're in the past.

That's not weakness. That's loyalty. Your body is still trying to keep you safe the only way it learned how.

The goal isn't to force calm. It's to slowly, gently teach your nervous system that the war is over. That it's safe to stand down. That peace isn't a trap anymore. Even just noticing your breath without trying to change it—that's a beginning. That's your nervous system learning it's safe enough to be witnessed.

Coming home to your body after coercive control isn't about perfecting your stress response. It's about befriending it. Understanding it. Thanking it for keeping you alive when calm could have killed you.

That's not too much to ask. That's the beginning of coming home to yourself.

8.8
When The Reflex Is to Turn on Yourself. Don't

Author's Note:

The person who hurt you often leaves a voice in your head that keeps working long after they're gone. This chapter is for that moment when you hear them in your own words—the instant you scold yourself for a small mistake. Here you'll find a simple way to recognise that reflex and a small practice to interrupt it. This isn't about perfection. It's about reclaiming conversation with yourself.

You Were Conditioned to Turn on Yourself

You sit in the car after the interview, palms damp on the wheel. Before you can even name the feeling, the voice shows up: "You stuttered. You rambled. They saw straight through you." Not encouragement. Not kindness. Just the familiar blade of self-attack. "You should've prepared better." "You always freeze up." "No wonder you're still nowhere."

You don't realise you're repeating exactly what they used to say. Word for word. The same tone. The same disgust. Their voice has become so embedded in your head that you think it's your own thoughts, your own standards, your own truth.

The control didn't stop when they left. It migrated. Their criticisms became your checklist. Where once you waited for their rebuke, you now beat yourself to it—minimising, rehearsing apologies, scouring your tone for faults. That self-policing wasn't born in you; it was handed down as a survival skill. Now it's outdated, but it still runs on habit.

And even now, years after they're gone, that conditioning kicks in automatically. One mistake, one perceived failure, and their voice appears, wearing your voice like a costume.

The Reflex Isn't the Truth

You weren't born cruel to yourself. Think about it—did you speak to yourself this way as a child? Before them? Did you tear yourself apart for spilling juice or getting a sum wrong? Of course not. This internal cruelty was installed, not innate. You were made this way to survive someone else's control.

You learned to monitor your tone before speaking, rehearse your feelings before expressing them, pre-empt their reactions by punishing yourself first. You learned that getting it wrong meant consequences, so you started delivering those consequences to yourself in advance. Better to hurt yourself first than wait for them to do it.

A woman told me she still catches herself in the bathroom mirror before dates, picking apart her appearance before anyone else can. "If I say it first, it won't hurt when they do," she explained. "Except now there's no 'they.' It's just me, doing their work for them."

A man described replaying every conversation from dinner parties, cataloguing his mistakes: "I talked too much about work. I should've been funnier. They probably think I'm boring." He's been divorced for two years, but his ex-wife's criticisms still narrate his social interactions.

These aren't character flaws. They're survival strategies that outlived their purpose. The taskmaster has left, but you're still following their rules.

Triggers Don't Mean You're Broken
They Mean You're Human Responding to Trauma

A survivor told me about dropping a glass in her kitchen—just water, just an accident. But she found herself on her knees, crying as she picked up the pieces, hearing: "You can't do anything right. You're useless. You ruin everything."

She'd been living alone for two years. The person who used to say those things was gone. But his voice was still there, sharp as the glass in her hands, cutting just as deep.

Sometimes the spiral still happens—you freeze, you clam up, you bite off your own praise. That response is not the problem. The problem is the follow-up: the story you tell yourself afterward, the sentence you deliver as punishment. So practice one small interruption: notice the thought, label it as "their voice," and answer it with one kinder line. The spiral loses momentum if you don't feed it.

When you feel the urge to collapse inward, to shrink, to scold yourself for reacting—that's when recognition can begin. Not with perfection. Not with never being triggered. But with interrupting the self-attack that follows.

The Voice That Stays

A woman told me she spent a whole day in bed after sending a text to her ex that she immediately regretted. Not because it hurt him—he didn't even reply. But because she'd broken her own rule: "No more reaching out."

"I punished myself for days," she said. "I kept hearing his voice: 'You're pathetic. You're weak. No one else would put up with you.' Even though he wasn't there anymore, I'd become my own warden."

That's what coercive control does at its most insidious level. It doesn't just control you while it's happening. It teaches you to continue the control long after it's over. To keep yourself small. To stay in line. To punish yourself for stepping outside the invisible boundaries they drew around your life.

Even when there's no one watching. Especially when there's no one watching.

Practical Step

Immediate: (10 seconds): When the self-attack starts, place your hand on your chest. Breathe in for four, out for six. Say out loud, "Not my voice." Then add one true, brief line: "I tried my best." "I'm allowed to be imperfect." Repeat until the reflex pauses.

Later: (10 minutes): Journal the incident. Write what you did, what the critic said, and one fact that disproves it. Keep this log; over time you'll see patterns and proof that the attacks are not reality.

Why It Matters

Because recovering from coercive control means learning to speak to yourself like someone who deserves gentleness. Because the person who hurt you doesn't get to keep hurting you through your own voice. Because you've been your harshest critic long enough, and it hasn't made you stronger—it's just kept you trapped.

If You Remember One Thing

You were trained to believe that harshness makes people better. That punishment means progress. That shame is the price of growth.

But watch a child learning to walk. Do they improve through criticism? Or through trying again, with encouragement, with someone saying "You're doing so well, try once more"? The voice that tears you apart—that's not wisdom. That's residue. That's the echo of someone who needed you to doubt yourself so they could control you.

The real work isn't being harder on yourself. It's refusing to continue their cruelty in their absence. It's interrupting the pattern they installed. It's choosing, over and over, to speak to yourself with the kindness they never offered.

When the reflex is to turn on yourself, stop. Breathe. Put your hand on your heart. Choose differently. That's the moment you interrupt the pattern. That's the moment their hold weakens. That's the moment you start to break free from the prison they taught you to build around yourself.

Interrupting this voice is small work with big returns. Each time you refuse to answer with self-punishment, you teach your nervous system a new rule: you are an ally, not a jailer.

Freedom begins in the pauses you choose.

8.9
Survival Wired You for Safety, Not for Rest

Author's Note:

If your brain feels scrambled, your body's always buzzing, and you can't seem to switch off even when you know you're safe, this chapter is for you. You're not broken. You're not lazy. You're not too sensitive. You're a survivor whose nervous system got rewired for war.

Coming back from coercive control isn't just mental. It's physical. If you're exhausted, forgetful, or can't relax, stop judging it. Your body's not betraying you. It's still protecting you. Now it needs your patience as it learns safety again.

You're Not Failing. You're Still Bracing

She stands in the supermarket cereal aisle, staring at boxes she can't read. The words swim. Her mind went blank somewhere between the pasta and the bread. Yesterday she forgot her own postcode at the pharmacy. Last week she drove to work on her day off.

This isn't just tiredness. It's the bone-deep exhaustion of a body that hasn't stopped scanning for danger in years.

You know the feeling—when you're so tired your teeth hurt, but sleep won't come. When you walk into rooms and freeze, forgetting why you entered. When you replay a conversation from weeks ago at 2am, searching for the threat you might have missed.

Your body feels heavy as concrete but your mind races like a hamster wheel. Foggy but wired. Exhausted but on edge. Because even though you've left, even though it's over, your nervous system hasn't got the memo yet. It's still standing guard, waiting for the next attack that your mind knows isn't coming but your body can't quite believe.

Abuse Rewires Your Whole System

They didn't just break your heart. They broke your body's regulation.

Every fight that stretched until dawn—your cortisol spiking, never dropping. Every silent treatment—your adrenaline pumping while you tried to decode what you'd done wrong. Every gaslighting spiral—your stress hormones flooding as reality shifted beneath you.

When he slammed the door, your heart pounded for hours afterwards. When she gave you that look before guests arrived, your stomach dropped and stayed clenched through dinner, through dessert, through the goodbye hugs. When they started with "We need to talk," your whole body went rigid before the words even landed.

That's cortisol flooding your system. That's adrenaline with nowhere to go. That's your survival system firing again and again until it forgot how to stop.

Your nervous system got stuck on high alert like a smoke alarm that won't stop shrieking even after the fire's out. And now, months or years later, your body still jolts at notification sounds. Still tenses when someone sighs. Still treats silence not as peace but as the calm before the storm. You get a metallic taste in your mouth when the phone rings, that copper penny flavour of old fear.

Your Body Is Still Tensing Even When It's Sitting Still

A woman finally gets her own flat after escaping abuse. First night of freedom. She triple-checks the locks, leaves every light on, sits on the sofa until 4am because lying down feels too vulnerable.

"I thought freedom would feel peaceful," she tells me. "But at first, it just felt foreign. Like my body didn't trust the quiet. Like it was waiting for something bad to happen because something bad always happened."

You're out. You're safe. You know that intellectually. But your jaw still clenches while you sleep. Your shoulders stay hunched like you're expecting a blow. You startle when the neighbour's door closes. Your heart races when a car pulls up outside.

Quiet feels dangerous because it once was. In your old life, silence meant the storm was building. Calm meant the explosion was coming. Peace was just the pause while they reloaded.

Your body memorised those patterns for survival. It doesn't forget them just because your mind understands you're safe now. Your muscles remember. Your nerves remember. Every cell that kept you alive remembers.

Survival Mode Makes It Hard to Think, Sleep, and Breathe

You read the same email four times and the words won't stick. You cry when you drop your keys but feel nothing at actually sad moments. You lose words mid-sentence, forget names of people you've known for years, walk into rooms with purpose then stand there blank.

This isn't weakness. It's a brain that's been in emergency mode so long it's forgotten how to process normal life. When you're constantly scanning for threats, there's no bandwidth left for remembering where you put your phone or what you needed from the shops.

Sleep becomes its own battlefield. You're exhausted but wide awake, body humming with invisible electricity. Or you fall asleep but wake gasping from dreams where you're late, lost, being chased by something you can't see. Even unconscious, your brain whispers: Don't get too comfortable. Remember what happened last time you relaxed.

A man tells me he hasn't slept properly in two years since leaving his partner. "I'm safer than I've ever been," he says, "but my body acts like I'm still in danger. I wake up at 3am ready to run, and I don't even know what from anymore."

You Don't Need to Push Through. You Need to Come Down

She sits in her therapist's office, frustrated to tears. "I should be better by now. I should be over this. I have my life back, so why can't I function?"

She tries to force herself back to normal—be productive at work, keep up socially, tick off lists like before. But her body crashes at 2pm. She panics in crowds. She forgets where she put her phone thirty seconds after setting it down.

This isn't failure. It's a nervous system in overdrive finally realising the war is over.

When soldiers come home, we don't expect them to snap back into civilian life overnight. We understand they need decompression, time to adjust. But survivors of coercive control? We expect them to bounce back the moment they're "free."

Your exhaustion isn't laziness—it's your body finally safe enough to stop running. That brain fog isn't weakness—it's your mind processing years of suppressed fear. When you crash—and you will—it's not regression. It's your system saying: We survived. Now we need to rest.

Practical Step

Start small. Five minutes of deliberate slowness a day. Drink your tea without scrolling. Walk without podcasts. Eat one meal without distraction. You're teaching your nervous system that stillness doesn't mean danger anymore.

When anxiety buzzes out of nowhere, pause. Put your hand on your chest and say out loud: "Thank you for protecting me. We're safe now." It may sound simple, but you're literally rewiring your brain's threat detection system.

Keep a trigger log—write down what makes you jump: notification pings, footsteps, sighs, silence. Seeing them on paper helps you recognise them for what they are: a nervous system still doing the job it learned, even though the shift has ended.

Why It Matters

Because recovery isn't just processing what happened emotionally. It's rehabilitating a body that was conscripted into constant warfare. Your hypervigilance wasn't paranoia— it was adaptation to a genuinely dangerous environment. And now you need to adapt again, this time to safety.

When you understand the biology, you stop blaming yourself for being "weak" or "broken." You're neither. You're a human whose body did exactly what it needed to survive.

Now it needs your patience as it learns to live.

If You Remember One Thing

That exhaustion that feels like a lead blanket. The fog that makes you forget your own postcode. The jumpiness at quiet rooms. The racing heart at innocent sounds.

None of it is permanent. It's your body still protecting you from a danger that's gone but not forgotten.

You weren't just emotionally manipulated. You were neurologically rewired for survival. Your entire system reorganised itself to keep you alive in an impossible situation. That's not dysfunction. That's brilliance. That's your body's love for you, expressed in the only way it knew how.

So don't rush recovery. Don't bully yourself into "better." Your nervous system is slowly learning that it's safe to stand down, safe to rest, safe to trust quiet again.

And when it does—when your shoulders finally drop, when sleep comes easily, when silence feels like peace instead of threat—you'll know what safety feels like in your bones.

That day is coming. Your body just needs time to believe it.

8.10
It Wasn't Your Fault for Trusting
It Was Their Plan to Deceive

Author's Note:

You didn't miss the signs because you were foolish. You missed them because they were hidden, on purpose. This chapter is for every survivor who still feels ashamed for trusting, loving, or hoping. You weren't weak. You were targeted. And it's time to return that shame to where it belongs. Not yours. Never was.

It Wasn't Naivety. It Was a Setup

You're sitting across from someone you trust—maybe your sister, your best friend, your therapist—and the words tumble out like a confession: "I feel so stupid. Three years I stayed. How did I not see it? Everyone else saw it. Even his mother tried to warn me."

The shame burns in your throat like acid. You can't meet their eyes. You pull away when they reach for your hand because you don't deserve comfort. You should have known better.

This is the confession that lives in every survivor's throat. The burning shame of having trusted. The humiliation of having loved someone who was destroying you. But here's what that shame obscures: you weren't stupid. You were systematically deceived by someone who made deception an art form.

They didn't stumble into your life by accident. They arrived dressed in everything you needed. Remember those first weeks? The good morning texts. How they remembered exactly how you took your coffee. The way they leaned in when you talked about your mother's death, holding space for your grief like no one else had. How they shared their own wounds at just the right moments, creating intimacy that felt earned.

They made you feel safe. Seen. Special. Like you'd finally found someone who understood the parts of you others overlooked.

And when they had you—when you'd reorganised your life around them, when your friends knew them as your other half, when you couldn't imagine Sunday mornings without them—that's when they changed. Not because you did something wrong, but because that was always the plan.

You Didn't Fall for the Truth. You Fell for the Performance

Think back to the beginning. Remember how they watched you at parties, noting what made you laugh? How they asked about your childhood dreams and suddenly shared the same ones? How they hated the same films you hated, loved the same obscure band you loved, even developed a sudden interest in that hobby you'd mentioned once?

A woman told me about her ex-husband who claimed to love hiking when they met. "I was passionate about it, spent every weekend on trails. He bought all the gear, learned the terminology, planned elaborate camping trips. Two years after our wedding, he admitted he'd always hated the outdoors. Laughed it off, as if years of deception had no cost."

They studied you like anthropologists study cultures—careful, patient, hunting for patterns. Catalogued your responses. Memorised your triggers. Reflected your values back at you until you saw yourself in them.

It wasn't coincidence. It wasn't fate. It was calculated mimicry designed to bypass your defences.

You didn't fall for who they were. You fell for who they pretended to be. And that performance was crafted specifically, methodically, brilliantly to appeal to you. That doesn't make you naive. It makes you human, responding normally to what appeared to be genuine connection.

The Lie Was Designed to Work on You

You're not foolish for missing the red flags. You were systematically conditioned to see green.

Every manipulation came wrapped in just enough sweetness to confuse your gut instinct. Every cruel comment was followed by "I'm just kidding, you know I love you." Every withdrawal of affection was followed by a crumb of tenderness, perfectly timed to keep you hoping.

A survivor described the pattern: "He'd ignore me for three days—no texts, cold shoulder in bed, eating dinner in silence. Then on day four, he'd bring home my favourite Thai food from that place across town. Leave a note on my pillow. Pull me close and whisper that he was sorry, that work was stressing him, that I was his everything. The formula never changed. Withdraw, return with gift, repeat."

"I used to think he just didn't know how to love properly. Now I realise he knew exactly what would keep me coming back."

It wasn't your failure to leave. It was their expertise at keeping you psychologically destabilised while maintaining just enough intermittent reinforcement to keep you invested.

Trauma bonding isn't weakness. It's biochemistry. It hijacks your brain's reward pathways so you literally wait for relief after pain, like an addiction to the cycle itself.

Would You Blame a Gazelle for Being Hunted?

Picture a nature documentary. The camera follows a gazelle grazing near the river. In the tall grass, a lion crouches, invisible. Patient. Calculating distance, wind direction, the gazelle's escape routes.

The gazelle doesn't see the danger until the lion explodes from cover. Sometimes the gazelle escapes. Sometimes it doesn't.

Do you watch that scene and think, "That gazelle was so stupid for drinking water"? Do you blame it for not detecting a predator specifically evolved to be undetectable?

Of course not. We understand that predators are designed to hunt. That prey animals aren't foolish for being targeted. They're simply living while something else plans their destruction.

So why do you keep blaming yourself for being targeted by someone who approached you with the specific intent to use your trust against you? You weren't stupid for drinking water. You were human, seeking connection, offering trust, believing in love. And someone weaponised those normal, healthy impulses against you.

Shame Isn't Yours to Carry

You make lists in your head of everything you're ashamed of: "I gave him my grandmother's inheritance. I forgave him after he cheated. Twice. I believed him when he said his ex was crazy. I defended him to my father. I let him convince me my friends were toxic. How did I not see it?"

But you were groomed. Slowly. Methodically. Intentionally.

They didn't break down your boundaries all at once—that would have sent you running. Instead, they tested each boundary like a burglar checking windows. A small push here. A little guilt there. Gradually expanding what you'd tolerate, what you'd excuse, what you'd forgive.

A woman told me she kept a journal during her relationship. Reading it afterwards was shocking: "I could see myself making excuses for smaller and smaller things. First month: 'He was late but he's so busy.' Sixth month: 'He forgot my birthday but he's stressed.' Second year: 'He pushed me but he didn't mean it.' I watched myself disappear one excuse at a time."

That's not weakness. That's what grooming looks like from the inside. It's trauma engineering, specifically designed to bypass your rational mind and hook your emotional brain.

The shame you carry for "letting it happen"? It belongs entirely to the person who orchestrated it, not to you for being human enough to trust.

Practical Step

Write down everything they mirrored back to you. Your kindness. Your interests. Your dreams. Your wounds.

Look at that list and recognise: these were your beautiful qualities they borrowed to bait the hook. The things that made you vulnerable to them are the same things that make you capable of real love. Don't let their exploitation make you ashamed of your capacity for connection.

Take a piece of paper and write in large letters: "It was their deception. Not my failure." Put it somewhere you'll see it daily—bathroom mirror, car dashboard, phone wallpaper. Every time shame whispers that you should have known better, look at those words. Say them out loud if you need to.

If you're still dealing with shared assets, children, or ongoing contact, start an evidence log. Document interactions, save messages, note dates. Get independent legal or financial advice if needed. Your safety and clarity matter more than keeping peace.

Why It Matters

Because the shame you carry about trusting them slowly teaches you not to trust yourself.

Every minute you blame yourself for being deceived lets the manipulation do its work. You can't recover while carrying shame that never belonged to you.

If you're reading this convinced you were the only one who "fell for it," please know this: being targeted by a predator does not make you prey. It makes you a survivor — someone who lived through predation and is learning how to live again.

If You Remember One Thing

You weren't blind. You were hopeful.

You were sincere. They made that sincerity into a blueprint for deception.

You weren't foolish—you were being targeted. They learned how you loved and used it as a map.

They studied you, mirrored you, and exploited your capacity for love and trust.

The embarrassment you feel for having loved them? That's what they counted on to keep you silent. The shame about staying too long? That's what they installed to make you blame yourself instead of them.

But now that you see it clearly—now that you can name their tactics and recognise their strategy—let this be the moment you finally stop carrying shame that was never yours.

You don't owe anyone an apology for being systematically deceived. Not your friends who "saw it coming." Not your family who tried to warn you. Not even yourself.

You only owe yourself the grace of saying: "I was targeted by someone who made destroying me their goal. And I survived."

That's not stupidity. That's strength. That's courage. That's the truth.

Part 9
Release

You stop holding what
was never yours to carry

9.1
You Weren't the Problem
You Were the First to Spot It

Author's Note:

This one's for every time you saw them smiling online and thought, "Maybe it was me." It wasn't. What you're seeing isn't healing. It's acting. This chapter is here to remind you that walking away was the win. And no filtered photo will ever change that.

They Didn't Change. They Just Changed Audiences

You saw the photo. Them smiling, arm around someone new. Looking happy. Healed. Finally being the partner you'd begged them to be. Your stomach dropped like you'd been punched. "Why didn't they treat me like that? What did I do wrong? What does this person have that I didn't?"

You replay everything—what you said, what you didn't say, where you must have failed. Maybe if you'd been less anxious. Maybe if you'd needed less. Maybe if you'd loved them differently. But you didn't go wrong. They didn't become better. They just found someone who hasn't seen behind the curtain yet. Someone who's still in Act One of a play you know ends badly.

It Looked Like Love. So Did Yours at First

Remember your beginning? The attention that felt like finally being chosen. The promises that sounded like forever. The way they looked at you like you were their whole world.

Their new relationship looks exactly like that because it is exactly that—the same opening scene, just with a different co-star.

They didn't become a better partner. They became more strategic, more polished. They adjusted the script based on what worked and what didn't with you. You were their rehearsal. This is just the same show with a new co-star.

But underneath the updated performance, it's the same pattern. The same inevitable ending. And if their new partner hasn't figured that out yet? It's not because you were harder to love. It's because you were the first to stop applauding a performance that was hurting you.

What You're Seeing Now Is the Love-Bombing Phase, Again

The gifts posted on Instagram. The surprise weekend trips. The "can't believe I found you" captions. It all looks warm and genuine and everything you'd wanted. But so did your beginning. Remember? Before the silence started. Before the criticism crept in. Before you learned to make yourself smaller to avoid their moods.

They haven't evolved. They've just restarted the same cycle with someone new. And that person is exactly where you were—intoxicated by attention, not yet aware it comes with a price.

A woman told me her ex got engaged six months after their breakup. The ring was bigger. The proposal more elaborate. The social media posts gushing with love. "It felt like he became the man I always begged him to be," she said.

Then, a year later, his new fiancée reached out to her. "She wanted to know if what she was experiencing was normal. The silent treatments. The gaslighting. The same exact things he'd done to me. Different woman. Same script."

Abusers Don't Improve. They Adapt

They mirror what each new person wants until trust is established. Then the mask slips. Then the tests start. Then the withholding begins. Then the person you fell for disappears, replaced by someone you don't recognise.

By the time the new partner sees it, they're already trauma-bonded, already doubting themselves, already wondering what they did to make the "good version" go away.

And if their current partner hasn't reached that part yet? That doesn't mean your ex changed. It means the countdown hasn't finished. The honeymoon phase has an expiration date. It always does.

Their Glow-Up Is Your Freedom

They'll post love notes you never received. Holidays you begged for. Quotes about growth and healing. And it'll sting, until you remember: They never stopped performing. They're just performing for someone else now.

If they finally look like the person you always wished they'd be, it's because you taught them exactly what to pretend. Your pain became their education. Your feedback became their script revision.

That's not your loss. That's your escape.

A woman once told me her ex posted about "doing the work" and "gratitude for growth" the week after she left. "He was quoting therapy concepts he'd mocked when I suggested them. He never did the work. He just used my pain as his social media rebrand."

Practical Step

When you catch yourself thinking "Maybe it was me," write down three specific times they hurt you. Not the maybe-moments. The clear ones. The ones you'd never do to someone you loved.

Then write this beneath them: "They didn't become better. They became more convincing."

Keep this list somewhere accessible. Read it whenever their new "happiness" makes you doubt your decision to leave.

Why It Matters

Because every moment you spend wondering if you were the problem is a moment their abuse is still working. Because you need to remember that leaving wasn't giving up—it was waking up.

If You Remember One Thing

No, they didn't change. They reset. They restarted the cycle with a fresh audience who doesn't know the show's ending yet.

They're not better now. They're just not exposed yet.

What looks like love from the outside is just the honeymoon phase of the same nightmare you survived. The love-bombing that precedes the devaluation. The pedestal that comes before the fall.

You weren't too much. You weren't impossible. You weren't the problem.

You were the one who finally said, "This isn't love." You were the one who saw through the performance. You were the first to spot what was really happening.

And now? You're free.

They're just starting over with someone who doesn't know yet what you know. Someone who will, eventually, be exactly where you were—wondering why the person who promised them everything became someone who gave them nothing but pain.

Your story with them is over. Theirs is just repeating.

9.2
They Were Never Going to Change

Author's Note:

This chapter is for the moment it clicks—not just that it was abusive, but that nothing you could've done would have changed it. If you're holding guilt for not trying harder, staying longer, or loving better, this is where you let that go. Because once you see they were never going to change, everything else starts to make sense.

When the Question Changes, So Does Everything

There wasn't a big fight. No dramatic ending. Just a moment, quiet and sharp, where something finally landed. They weren't confused about what you needed. They weren't trying to do better. They weren't going to change.

And in that moment, the question shifted. It stopped being "How do I fix this?" and became "Why am I still trying to?" That shift—from fixing to seeing—changed everything. Because you can't repair something that was never broken. It was working exactly as they intended.

You Didn't Leave Too Soon. You Left After the Spell Broke

You tried everything. You stayed through countless "last chances." You adjusted your approach, explained your needs differently, made yourself softer, smaller, easier to love. You convinced yourself the next conversation would be the breakthrough. The next apology would stick. The next promise would be different.

You lived on that hope like a drug, always one more try away from the relationship you thought you were in. But the person you kept reaching for—they weren't evolving. They were recycling the same apologies, the same promises, the same temporary changes that lasted just long enough to keep you hoping. Eventually, you stopped seeing potential.

You saw a pattern. And patterns don't change just because you love them harder.

You Weren't in a Relationship. You Were in a Cycle

They hurt you. Then apologised. Then blamed you for being hurt. Then needed comfort for having hurt you. Then started over.

Monday's cruelty. Tuesday's remorse. Wednesday's excuse. Thursday's deflection. Friday's reset. The weekend's honeymoon. Repeat. That wasn't miscommunication. It was choreography. The same steps in the same order, so predictable you could set your watch by it.

A woman told me she kept thinking, "If he just understood how much this hurts me, he'd stop." She explained everything—with words, with tears, with letters, with therapy language.

"Then one day I was sobbing, really breaking down, and I looked at him. He wasn't concerned. He wasn't confused. He looked bored. Like he was waiting for me to finish so we could move on. That's when I realised: he already knew exactly how much it hurt. He just didn't care."

You Didn't Fail Them. They Failed to Choose Growth

You were willing to change. To examine yourself. To do the work. You bought the books they wouldn't read. You found the therapists they wouldn't see. You did the emotional labour for two people while they did none.

A relationship only transforms when both people are invested in becoming better. And they weren't. They didn't want healing—that would require accountability. They didn't want growth—that would mean changing. They just wanted you more manageable, more accepting, more willing to live with less.

The Moment You Stopped Waiting for Change

There's a specific kind of grief when you realise someone you love is choosing not to change. Not unable. Not confused. Choosing. All those times they said they didn't understand what you needed? They understood. They just decided your needs weren't worth meeting. All those promises to do better? They knew how. They just didn't want to. All that potential you saw in them? It was real. They just chose not to reach for it.

Practical Step

Write down each time you thought, "Maybe this time will be different." Then note what actually happened—not the promise, not the hope, the reality. Look at the list. That's not failure. That's data. Proof you weren't the problem. End with this: "They weren't going to change. And it was never my job to make them."

Why It Matters

Because when you see the pattern in black and white, it stops being a blur of doubt. That list shows the truth: they repeated the harm, not you. Accepting they were never going to change isn't giving up—it's finally seeing clearly.

If You Remember One Thing

You didn't leave because you gave up on them. You left because you finally stopped giving up on yourself. They were never going to change. Not because they couldn't— they had every resource, every chance, every bit of your patience and love. They chose not to.

You didn't walk away too early. You walked away when you finally understood that waiting for them to change meant agreeing to never change yourself. Meant accepting less forever. Meant dying slowly in a relationship that was never going to become what they kept promising.

That's not failure. That's clarity. And now you get to change—not to become worthy of love, but to become who you were before you started making yourself smaller for someone who was never going to make room for all of you anyway.

9.3
You're Not Indecisive
You're Rebuilding Self-Trust

Author's Note:

This one's for the moments you stared at a menu, a message, or a mirror and thought, "Why can't I just decide?" You're not defective. You're not lost for good. You're just recovering from a world that trained you to doubt your own voice. Your instincts are still there. Buried, not gone. And you're already on your way back to them.

This Isn't Indecision. It's Recovery from Being Undermined

You stand in front of the fridge and can't decide what to eat. Everything feels wrong or too much or not worth the effort.

You scroll through five delivery apps. Read every review. Check every menu twice. Nothing feels right. An hour passes. You eat crackers instead.

You panic at small choices—which shirt, which route, which brand of coffee. You freeze at big ones—the job offer, the apartment, the invitation. And you hate yourself for it.

You used to be decisive. You used to trust your gut. Now even choosing a podcast feels like it could be the wrong move.

That's not indecisiveness. That's what it feels like to recover from someone who made you question every thought, every preference, every instinct you had. Your brain is still waiting for someone to tell you you're wrong.

Every Choice Became the Wrong One

They didn't scream at every decision. That would have been too obvious. Instead, they sighed. They questioned. They second-guessed your tone, your timing, your reasoning.

They waited until after you'd acted, then explained what you "should" have done. How you "could" have handled it better. Why your way was "interesting" but ultimately flawed.

"Why did you go that way? Traffic's always bad there." "That's what you're wearing?" "You really think that's the best option?" "I would have done it differently, but okay."

Death by a thousand corrections. Until eventually, you stopped deciding altogether. Because no matter what you chose, it would be wrong in their eyes. And slowly, inevitably, your inner voice went quiet.

You Learned to Outsource Your Voice

You started asking for permission for things that didn't need permission. You softened your opinions with "I don't know, but maybe..." You began sentences with "This might be stupid, but..."

Not because you lacked clarity, but because clarity had become dangerous. Because knowing what you wanted made you a target. Because having preferences meant having something they could criticise.

So you started asking, "What do you think I should do?" even when you already knew. You crowdsourced decisions that used to be instinct. You polled friends about things that didn't matter, just to avoid being wrong alone.

A woman told me she used to send outfit photos to her ex for approval before going anywhere. "He'd say things like, 'If you want that kind of attention, sure.' I started dressing to avoid his reactions, not to express who I was.

Even now, two years later, I still hear his voice when I get dressed."

The Fog You Feel Is Manufactured

That cloudy, hesitant, anxious brain that can't pick a restaurant or commit to weekend plans? That's not who you are. It's the aftermath of being systematically undermined.

That fog was built, brick by brick, over years of corrections and contradictions. Years of being told your instincts were wrong, your preferences were stupid, your choices were flawed.

But here's what they never told you: You're not confused. You're recovering. The fog isn't permanent. It's your brain's protective response to years of criticism. And protection can be unlearned once safety is established.

Your Instincts Are Still in There. They're Just Quiet Right Now

That little twinge you feel when something's off? That spark of recognition when something feels right? That's still you. It never left.

It just got buried under layers of fear. Fear of being wrong. Fear of being mocked. Fear of choosing something that would become ammunition later. Fear of trusting yourself and being betrayed by your own judgment.

But your inner compass isn't broken. It's just waiting for you to trust it again. Every small decision you make without asking for permission, every preference you honour without apology, every instinct you follow without second-guessing—that's you excavating yourself from the rubble.

Practical Step

Make one decision today without checking with anyone. Pick lunch without reading reviews. Take a different route without explaining why. Say yes or no to an invitation based solely on how you feel.

Start small. The size of the decision doesn't matter. What matters is the practice of trusting yourself without external validation.

Then, at the end of the day, write down what you decided and how it went. Not to judge it, but to notice: you decided something, the world didn't end, and your instincts were probably right.

Why It Matters

Because every time you decide something without seeking approval, you rebuild the connection between your gut and your actions. You teach yourself that your voice matters. That your preferences are valid. That you can be trusted with your own life.

If You Remember One Thing

That fog you're in? That hesitation that makes you question everything? It doesn't mean you're broken.

It means you survived someone who trained you to disconnect from your gut, and now you're slowly, carefully, bravely tuning back in.

Your instincts didn't disappear. They went underground to survive. They're still there, whispering beneath the doubt, waiting for you to remember that they've been right all along.

You're not learning how to trust yourself. You're remembering how.

That knowing was always yours. No one could take it, only teach you to doubt it. And doubt can be unlearned, one small decision at a time.

You don't have to hear your instincts perfectly yet. You don't have to trust them completely. You just have to believe they're real. And they are.

9.4
Your Success Was Never the Problem
It Was Their Trigger

Author's Note:

If your wins were met with silence, sarcasm, or sabotage, this chapter is for you. You were never too much. Your growth exposed what they refused to face in themselves. That was never your burden to carry.

Your success was never the problem. It was the proof they were losing control.

When Pride Threatens Power, They Shame You Back into Place

You got the job. You were excited, nervous, proud. You'd worked for this. You'd earned it. You couldn't wait to share the news.

You told them. They paused. Not the pause of someone processing good news, but the pause of someone calculating a response. Then: "Don't get cocky."

Just like that, your pride turned to shame. Your excitement curdled into something you had to apologise for. Not because you were arrogant—you were just happy. But your joy made them feel smaller. And their power depended on you staying dim.

They Don't Celebrate You. They Shrink You

You win something. They change the subject to their bad day. You hit a goal you've been working toward for months. They say, "Must be nice to have that kind of free time."

It's not bad timing. It's by design.

They need your spotlight to feel like a threat, because anything that reminds you of your worth makes you harder to control. So they interrupt your momentum with their chaos. They make your success feel selfish.

They Shift the Focus So You Forget You're Winning

You share something you're proud of—a compliment from your boss, a personal breakthrough, a small victory. Before you can finish the sentence, they interrupt with their own story. Or they get sick. Or angry. Or deeply offended by something unrelated.

Somehow, your moment becomes about them. And you end up comforting them about your good news, apologising for taking up space with your joy.

That's not coincidence. That's sabotage.

A woman told me she got a promotion she'd worked toward for two years. She told her partner over dinner, practically glowing. He went quiet. Pushed his food around his plate. Then said, "I guess I'm the only one stuck in the same place."

"I spent the rest of the night comforting him about my promotion," she said. "By the end, I felt guilty for succeeding. I actually apologised for getting it."

Your Independence Makes You Unmanageable. That Scares Them

The more confident you became, the more "jokes" they made about you getting "too big for your boots." The more self-sufficient you got, the more resentful they became about your "selfishness."

Your independence wasn't just threatening—it was dangerous to their control. You no longer needed their approval to feel valid. You no longer looked to them to define your worth. And that made you harder to manipulate, harder to diminish, harder to keep small.

So they escalated. The put-downs got sharper. The sulking lasted longer. The "emergencies" during your important moments became more frequent.

Coercive Control Isn't Always Forceful
Sometimes It's Just Subtle Erosion

They didn't need to forbid your dreams. They just taught you that joy wasn't safe.

They didn't stop you from succeeding. They just made you feel guilty for wanting more than what you had. They sighed heavily when you talked about your goals. They sulked until you dimmed yourself to avoid their mood. They made celebrating feel like betrayal.

Eventually you stopped sharing your wins because their reaction hurt more than the victory felt good.

That's not support. That's control wearing a polite face.

A woman told me her ex used to mock her artwork—nothing cruel, just little comments. "Interesting choice." "That's... different." "Is that supposed to be a tree?" She stopped showing him her work. Stopped talking about her exhibitions. Eventually stopped painting altogether.

"Later, he told people I 'lost my passion,'" she said. "Like it just disappeared on its own. He didn't kill it directly. He just kept turning off the light until I forgot where I'd left it."

Practical Step

Make two lists. First: accomplishments they downplayed, disrupted, or dismissed. Second: everything you achieved without their support—despite their doubt, during their sulking, in spite of their sabotage. Look at that second list. That's not just success. That's success under hostile conditions. That's strength most people never need to find.

Why It Matters

Because recognising the pattern breaks its power. Because reclaiming your achievements—even retroactively—reminds you that your instincts were never wrong.

They just weren't convenient for someone who needed you manageable.

If You Remember One Thing

You were never too proud. Too ambitious. Too much.

You were becoming whole. And that wholeness threatened the person who needed you fractured to maintain the power dynamic.

So they disrupted your joy. Dismissed your progress. Diminished your light. They made your growth feel like betrayal and your success feel like selfishness.

But here's what they couldn't erase: You still succeeded. Despite their sulking. Despite their sabotage. Despite having to navigate their emotions about your achievements while processing your own.

And now that you see the pattern—now that you understand your success was never the problem, just their trigger—you get to start celebrating without apology. Without dimming. Without checking anyone's emotional weather before you shine.

Because the only approval you ever needed was your own. And you've had that all along.

9.5
You Deserve the Love
You Were Always Waiting For

Author's Note:

This chapter is about what happens when real love finally shows up and you don't know how to let it in. If you've ever tensed at kindness, questioned someone's patience, or braced for punishment even when no one was angry, this is for you. This isn't a flaw in you. It's what coercive control taught your body to expect. This chapter will help you name why safety feels foreign, and why you deserve it anyway.

Coercive Control Taught You That Crumbs Were a Feast

They trained you to be grateful for scraps. A text back became proof they cared. A day without yelling meant kindness. A remembered birthday passed for love.

You learned to clutch at crumbs as if they were a banquet. To celebrate the bare minimum like it was extraordinary. To be pathetically grateful for treatment that should have been baseline.

A woman told me her partner brought her flowers once in five years. "I kept those dead flowers for months," she said. "Pressed them in a book. Photographed them. I thought it meant he was finally changing. Looking back, I realise I was so starved for basic affection that one bouquet felt like proof of love."

Coercive control doesn't just steal your present. It recalibrates your expectations so low that normal kindness feels suspicious and basic decency feels overwhelming.

You Became Afraid of Real Love

When someone shows up consistently, your trauma brain whispers: "What do they want? What's the catch?"

When someone respects your boundaries without sulking, you wonder: "When will they snap? When will the punishment come?" When someone apologises without drama, without making you comfort them for hurting you, you think: "This feels wrong. Too easy. Where's the three-day fight?"

Coercive control conditioned you to believe that love requires suffering. That care comes with invoices. That peace means something terrible is building.

A woman told me her new partner never raised his voice. "For six months, I kept waiting for the explosion. When he disagreed with me, he just... talked. No screaming. No silent treatment. No punishment. Just conversation."

"I almost left him because the calm made me anxious. I was so conditioned to intensity—to the highs and lows—that steady kindness felt like boredom. I'd been taught that drama meant passion, that chaos meant caring. Peace felt like he didn't care enough to fight."

The Love You Trained Yourself Not to Expect

You stopped expecting good morning texts that weren't demands. You stopped expecting affection that didn't come with strings.

You trained yourself to need less and less. To be grateful for absence of cruelty rather than presence of kindness. Your standards didn't lower themselves. They were systematically pushed down by someone who benefited from you expecting nothing.

You're Not "Too Damaged" for Healthy Love

Your hypervigilance isn't a character flaw—it's your nervous system still protecting you. Your need for reassurance isn't neediness—it's learning to trust after betrayal. Your triggers aren't defects—they're your body's memory of danger. These aren't things that make you unloveable. They're normal responses to abnormal treatment.

And the right person won't see your recovery journey as something to tolerate or fix. They'll see it as proof of your strength. They'll understand that loving you means loving all of you—including the parts still healing, still learning what safety feels like.

The Love You Were Always Waiting For Already Exists

It's the love that doesn't require you to walk on eggshells, monitoring every word for potential landmines. The love that doesn't punish you for having needs or boundaries or bad days. The love that doesn't disappear when you're inconvenient, imperfect, or human.

You spent so long waiting for your abuser to love you properly that you forgot proper love was never going to come from them. You can't squeeze blood from a stone. You can't extract empathy from someone who sees you as an object to control.

But real love already exists in the world. Not as something you have to create, teach, or earn through suffering. It exists in people who choose care without keeping score. In relationships where peace is the baseline, not the exception.

A man told me he makes sure his partner never comes to a cold bed. Every winter night, he turns on her side of the electric blanket before she comes in. "She tears up sometimes when she slips under the covers," he said. "Not because of the warmth, but because she can't believe someone thinks about her comfort when she's not even in the room."

That's love. Not grand gestures. Not drama. Just consistent care that doesn't need to be begged for.

Practical Step

Write down three ways coercive control taught you to accept less than you deserved. Maybe you learned that jealousy meant love. That anger meant passion. That control meant care. Then write what healthy love in those areas actually looks like. Not perfect love—just healthy. The kind where disagreements don't become wars. Where needs aren't weapons. Where kindness doesn't have a price tag attached.

Why It Matters

Recovery means unlearning the lie that you have to earn basic human decency through perfect behaviour. You deserve love that doesn't require you to shrink, perform, or beg.

If You Remember One Thing

Coercive control taught you to work for love. To bend yourself into impossible shapes. To keep proving your worth through endless emotional labour. It told you care had to be earned through suffering. That peace was suspicious. That affection could vanish the moment you stopped performing.

But real love doesn't need you to audition for it. It doesn't test you with manufactured chaos. It doesn't keep score of your mistakes.

Real love just arrives. Steady. Safe. Present in the small things you don't have to beg for: The pre-warmed bed. The text that says, "Running late, miss you" because your time matters. The voice that stays calm even in disagreement.

You don't have to shrink for it. You don't have to perform for it. You don't have to fear losing it for simply being human.

You were never too much. You were never asking for too much. You were always worthy of the love you kept waiting for someone incapable of giving.

And now, the only work left is learning to recognise real love when it shows up. Learning to let it in without suspicion. Learning that you deserve warmth without having to suffer for it first.

The love you need already exists. You just have to stop accepting anything less.

9.6
You Don't Need Their Apology to Close the Door

Author's Note:

This one's for the survivor still waiting for the moment that never comes—the apology, the recognition, the accountability. If they never own it, never admit it, never say they were wrong, you can still recover. You can still close the door without hearing it latch.

You Keep Checking for Signs They Finally Get It

You scroll their profiles looking for posts about growth, healing, accountability. You search for coded messages in their captions, evidence they've finally understood the damage they caused.

You ask mutual friends if they've mentioned you. Not because you want them back, but because you need to know: Do they feel bad? Have they changed? Do they finally see what they did?

You rehearse conversations in your head where they finally say the words: "I was wrong. I hurt you. I'm sorry." You imagine their face when they say it. You imagine how it would feel to finally, finally be validated by the person who invalidated everything.

You're not waiting for them to come back. You're waiting for them to acknowledge what they did. To admit you weren't crazy. To confirm that yes, it was that bad, and yes, you deserved better.

A woman told me she kept her ex's number unblocked for three years after leaving. "I told myself it was because I wasn't bitter, because I was healed enough not to need to block him.

But really, I was hoping he'd text something—anything—that proved he finally understood what he'd put me through."

The text never came.

They Trained You to Need Their Approval

For years, they made you doubt every perception, every feeling, every memory. They rewrote conversations. They denied events. They told you that you were too sensitive, too dramatic, too much.

They trained you to need their confirmation before trusting your own reality. And now, even after leaving, part of you still believes that their acknowledgment is the only way to know you're not crazy.

But here's what they won't tell you: They know exactly what they did.

They remember the silent treatments. They remember the threats. They remember how small they made you feel. They're not confused about what happened. They're not waiting for clarity.

They're just not willing to admit it. Because admission would mean accepting you were right. And they can't afford for you to be right about anything—not then, not now, not ever.

They're Not Confused. They're Protecting Themselves

Their refusal to apologise isn't about not understanding. It's about maintaining control of the narrative.

If they admitted what they did, they'd have to face who they are. They'd have to surrender the story where they're the victim, the misunderstood one, the person who "tried so hard" but you were "impossible."

A woman told me her ex-husband finally admitted he was abusive—to his therapist, to his new partner, to his friends. Everyone except her. "He could own it everywhere except the one place where it mattered most," she said.

"I realised he wasn't protecting his reputation. He was protecting his control. If he admitted it to me, I'd finally have permission to trust myself completely. And that was the one thing he could never allow."

Craving Their Admission Keeps You in the Trauma Bond

Every time you check if they've posted about personal growth. Every time you analyse their words for hidden acknowledgment. Every time you hope this will be the day they finally see the damage they caused.

You're still giving them power over your recovery.

You're making your healing contingent on their evolution. You're letting your peace depend on their awakening. You're keeping yourself tethered to someone who will never give you what you need.

The recognition you're longing for would feel like proof that you're not crazy, that your pain was real, that you deserved better. But you already know these things. Your body knows. Your sleepless nights, your startle at footsteps, the way you still check locks twice—all of it is evidence enough.

Practical Step

Write the apology you wish you'd receive. Include everything—the acknowledgment, the accountability, the specific admissions. Write it all out.

Then beneath it, write what you know to be true, regardless of whether they ever admit it. Write your truth without needing their signature. This is your story. You don't need their permission to own it.

Why It Matters

Because waiting for their words keeps you frozen. Because your healing can't depend on someone else's willingness to be honest. Because you deserve to move forward whether they catch up or not.

If You Remember One Thing

The apology you're longing for isn't the key to your freedom. Your self-trust is.

You don't need their words to validate your experience. Your body remembers what happened. Your sleepless nights, your startle at footsteps, the way you still check locks twice—all of it is proof enough.

You don't need their permission to know it was abuse. You don't need their admission to trust your memories. You don't need their apology to take your life back.

They may never say they're sorry. They may go to their grave insisting they were the victim. They may rewrite history until even they believe their version.

None of that changes what happened to you. None of that makes your truth less true.

The door closes when you stop waiting for them to shut it. When you stop needing their acknowledgment to trust your own experience. When you realise that their refusal to apologise is just their final act of control—and you don't have to let it work.

Your recovery was never in their hands. It was always in yours.

And you don't need their words to live your freedom.

9.7
You Can Grieve the Years Without Blaming Yourself

Author's Note:

This chapter is for the survivor who stayed too long, gave too much, and now keeps replaying the years wondering how they didn't see it sooner. If you've ever carried guilt for what you didn't know then, this is where you stop punishing yourself for trying. You didn't fail. You did your best. And that's enough.

Those Aren't Shame Questions. They're Grief

"Why did I put up with it for so long?"
"Why didn't I leave after the first time?"
"How did I not see what everyone else saw?"

These questions loop in your head at 3am. They follow you into the shower. They interrupt your workday. You replay the years like a detective looking for the moment you should have known, the sign you should have seen, the exit you should have taken.

But those aren't shame questions. They're grief dressed up as self-blame.

You didn't stay because you were weak. You stayed because you loved—not wisely but completely. Because you hoped—not foolishly but courageously. Because you saw glimpses of who they were in the beginning and held onto those moments like evidence that the real person was still in there, waiting to return.

You stayed because leaving felt like giving up on someone you loved. Because you'd already invested so much that walking away felt like admitting it was all for nothing. Because they convinced you that you were the problem, and if you could just fix yourself, everything would be better.

You Stayed Because You Were Hooked, Not Weak

Trauma bonding isn't love. It's biochemical addiction wired into you.

They hurt you, then comforted you. Destroyed you, then rebuilt you. Your nervous system learned to need them like a drug—the source of both wound and relief.

You stayed because your brain was hijacked by a cycle that creates dependency. The intermittent kindness was more addictive than constant affection. The unpredictability kept you hooked.

A survivor told me, "I stayed for twenty-two years. By year five, I couldn't imagine life without him. Not because I loved him, but because he'd become my entire nervous system."

You Weren't Blind. You Were Invested

You saw the problems. Named them, fought about them, tried to fix them. But you also saw potential—who they could be in good moments.

That's not stupidity. That's hope.
That's not weakness. That's commitment.

You weren't blind to abuse. You were invested in the person you thought existed underneath it.

When you love someone—really love them—you want to believe they'll change. When you've given years, walking away feels like betraying not just them but the version of yourself who chose them. The sunk cost feels unbearable. Starting over feels impossible.

That's not blindness. That's commitment weaponised against you. It's your capacity for loyalty turned into a cage.

A woman told me she was with her partner for twenty-two years before she left. "I used to think I wasted my life. Now I realise: I gave everything I had to someone who just kept taking. That doesn't make me weak. It makes him unworthy of what I offered."

Grieving the Years Is Part of Recovery, Not a Sign You Failed

You're allowed to grieve the time. The decades you can't get back. The dreams that died slowly. The holidays that felt like minefields. The birthdays you spent crying in bathrooms.

You're allowed to mourn the person you were before they systematically dismantled you. The confidence you had before they made you question everything. The friends you lost because they isolated you. The opportunities you missed because you were too exhausted from surviving to thrive.

This grief doesn't mean you shouldn't have stayed. It means your life matters to you now. It means you're finally valuing what was taken. And that's not weakness—that's awakening.

The Years Weren't Wasted. They Were Survived

Every year you stayed was a year you kept yourself alive in an impossible situation.

You managed. You coped. You protected what you could.
You raised children who saw you endure.
You held jobs while drowning.
You kept some part of yourself intact despite daily erosion.

That's not wasted time. That's strength no one saw because it happened in private. It's the endurance of someone refusing to let another person completely erase them, even when erasure felt easier than resistance.

Those years taught you what you'll never accept again.
They showed you your capacity to survive.
They proved something in you always refused to die.

Practical Step

Write a list of every reason you stayed. Not with judgment—with compassion. Include everything: the financial fears, the threats, the children, the shame, the hope, the exhaustion, the glimpses of good times, the promises of change.

Then look at that list and ask yourself: If your best friend had stayed for those reasons, would you call them stupid? Or would you understand? Finally, write yourself a letter of forgiveness. Not for staying—you don't need forgiveness for trying to love someone. But for blaming yourself for not knowing what you couldn't possibly have known.

Why It Matters

Because those reasons don't prove you were weak. They prove you were human. The shame isn't yours to carry. Once you see that clearly, the blame shifts back where it belongs—on the person who exploited your love and your trust.

If You Remember One Thing

You didn't fail. You didn't waste your life. You weren't stupid, weak, or blind.

You were surviving something orchestrated to keep you trapped. You did your best with the tools you had, the information you believed, the hope you carried, and the love you gave.

So if the guilt still whispers, if you still catch yourself wondering why you didn't leave sooner, remind yourself of this:

You couldn't see it then because they made sure you couldn't. You see it now because you survived long enough to get distance, clarity, and safety.

That growth isn't something to be ashamed of. It's something to honour.

The years you "lost" taught you what you'll never accept again. The time you "wasted" showed you your own strength. The love you "threw away" proved your capacity for commitment—it just landed on someone who didn't deserve it.

You don't need to apologise for how long it took to leave. You need to celebrate that you left at all. Because leaving takes a kind of courage that people who've never been systematically broken down can't imagine.

Those years are yours to grieve. But they're not yours to be ashamed of.

They're proof that you can survive anything. And now, finally, you get to live.

9.8
Your Pain Was Their Pleasure

Author's Note:

This chapter names something most people avoid: the truth that some abusers don't just want power. They want to see you suffer. If you've ever felt like they enjoyed watching you cry, freeze, or beg, this chapter will help you trust that instinct. Because you were right.

It Wasn't Just That They Hurt You. It's That They Liked It

There was a flicker of satisfaction when you broke.
A calmness when you panicked.
A slight smile at the exact moment you started to cry.

The cruelty wasn't always obvious. Sometimes it was a "joke" that hit too hard, delivered with perfect timing. Sometimes it was silence that dragged out just long enough to make you squirm. Sometimes it was the smallest betrayal, done slowly, with calculation, and a look that said: "There it is."

That's when you stopped thinking it was about control. It wasn't just about winning. It was about watching you lose.

They Don't Just Want Power. They Want the Reaction

They poke you. Dismiss you. Humiliate you. And when you flinch, when you fall apart, when you break down—they relax.

That's the part no one warns you about. They don't get anxious when they see you cry. They get calm. Your pain confirms what they were hoping: "I can still get to you."

A survivor told me, "He'd start fights right before important events—my birthday, job interviews, family gatherings. Always perfectly timed. And when I'd finally break down, there was this... satisfaction in his eyes. Like he'd won something."

They Call It "A Joke", But It's Meant to Hurt

The comment lands sharp. The room goes quiet. They smirk. Maybe laugh. And if you react? You're "too sensitive."

But you weren't confused. You felt the deliberate tone, the sting, the precision. These aren't clumsy partners making mistakes. They're snipers. Every word aimed to wound.

There Was Pleasure in the Control. That's What Made It Worse

When you froze. When you cried. When you begged—there was something behind their eyes. Not empathy. Not regret. Satisfaction.

They liked watching you twist. Liked the slow build to your collapse. Liked that they were the only one who could calm the storm they created.

A woman once told me, "He used to withhold affection for days. Then when I finally broke down sobbing, he'd hold me. And he'd smile while I cried. I didn't know what was wrong with me. But now I do. Nothing was wrong with me. He was just getting exactly what he came for."

This Isn't Just Abuse. It's Sadism

There's a word for people who take pleasure in hurting others. It's not "misunderstood." It's not "troubled." It's sadistic.

But most of the world won't call it that, especially when it comes wrapped in charm or success or a good public image. So they sanitise it. They use clinical terms that sound detached from the reality you lived through. They say "anger issues" or "communication problems" or "toxic dynamics."

But you know better. Because you've lived it. You've seen the satisfaction in their eyes. You've felt the deliberate nature of the cruelty. You know the difference between someone losing control and someone enjoying themselves.

Practical Step

Choose three moments when you saw calm or satisfaction in their eyes while you were in pain. Write them down exactly as you remember them. Don't edit or excuse. When you're ready, read those words out loud—once—ending with: "They enjoyed it."
This isn't about convincing anyone. It's about letting your own nervous system register what your eyes already knew.

Why It Matters

Because naming deliberate cruelty pulls it out of the fog of "maybe I'm overreacting." Survivors are trained to downplay what they've experienced. Writing and speaking these moments breaks that training. It shifts the shame off you and onto the person who chose to harm. And it reminds your body that you're not imagining things—you're telling the truth.

If You Remember One Thing

This wasn't just control. This wasn't insecurity. This wasn't "how they were raised." This was someone who hurt you and liked it. And that doesn't make you paranoid. That makes you a witness.

You saw the smile when you cried. You felt the calm when you panicked. You noticed the satisfaction when you broke.

Now you get to call it what it was: Cruelty that wasn't accidental—it was recreational. And now? Now you stop pretending it wasn't that bad. Now you name what they didn't think you'd ever survive long enough to say:

They enjoyed your pain. And you're still here. That truth itself is defiance.

9.9
The Shame You
Carried Was Never Yours

Author's Note:

This chapter is for the survivor who still feels embarrassed for staying, apologetic for reacting, or ashamed of what was done to them. If you're still walking around with guilt you never earned, this will help you lay it down. That shame? It was never yours. You just carried it because someone else refused to.

The Weight in Your Chest

You're sitting across from your friend, and she asks how things really were. Your chest tightens. You start to speak, then stop. Start again. Your voice drops to almost a whisper. "It wasn't that bad," you hear yourself say. "I mean, compared to what other people go through..." You watch her face, searching for judgement. Not about what he did—about why you stayed. Why you didn't see it sooner. Why you let it happen at all.

A woman told me she rehearsed her story twenty times before her first support group meeting. "I kept editing it, making it sound less pathetic. I was so ashamed. Not of him hitting me—of me not leaving the first time."

You know that feeling. The hot flush when someone asks why you didn't just leave. The way you rush to explain, to justify, to make them understand you're not stupid, you're not weak, you tried. You minimise what happened because somehow his cruelty became your embarrassment.

How They Made Their Shame Yours

You're in the kitchen after another explosion. He's storming around, slamming cupboards. "Look what you made me do," he says, gesturing at the hole in the wall.

"You know how you get me. You push and push until I snap." Your mind races. Maybe you did push too hard. Maybe you should have seen the signs. Maybe if you'd just backed down sooner...

By morning, you're the one apologising. You're the one promising to do better. You were the one carrying the weight of his violence like you threw the punch yourself.

That's how it works. They refuse to hold their own shame, so they hand it to you. Make you the keeper of their conscience. You become responsible for their choices, their reactions, their cruelty.

"You're too sensitive."
"You always overreact."
"You make everything so difficult."

Each accusation is shame being transferred. Each blame is them refusing to carry what belongs to them. And you, trying to make sense of the chaos, trying to keep the peace, trying to survive—you pick it up. You carry it. You wear it like it's yours.

The Apologies That Pour Out of You

You apologise to the doctor for crying during the exam. You apologise to your friend for needing to talk again. You apologise to your therapist for taking up their time with "the same old story."

You say sorry for having needs. Sorry for remembering. Sorry for not being over it yet. Sorry for the space you take up, the feelings you have, the healing you need.

A man told me he apologised to his new partner every time he flinched. "She'd reach over to touch my face, and I'd pull back. Then I'd spend ten minutes saying sorry, explaining I wasn't scared of her, I was just... broken. I was apologising for my own trauma responses. For the damage my abuser did to me."

You've been trained to feel like a burden. To believe your pain is an inconvenience.

To think your healing is asking too much. But those aren't your thoughts—they're his words, still echoing in your head. Those aren't your apologies. They're echoes of his refusal to own what he did.

The Moment You Hand It Back

You're in therapy, telling the story again. But this time, something shifts. You're describing the night he threw the plate, and instead of rushing to explain what you did to trigger him, you stop. You sit with the silence. Then you say, "He threw the plate. That was his choice."

Your therapist nods. "His choice," she repeats. "His choice," you say again, and something loosens in your chest. For the first time, it didn't feel like your failure. It felt like his. The shame you've been carrying—for staying, for not seeing it sooner, for "letting" it happen—it starts to feel foreign. Like wearing someone else's coat. Heavy and ill-fitting and not meant for you.

Because it never was meant for you. It was always his. The shame of hurting someone who loved him. The shame of breaking someone who trusted him. The shame of being cruel to someone who was kind to him. He just refused to wear it, so he convinced you it was yours.

Practical Step

Take a piece of paper and write down three things you still feel ashamed about. Maybe it's staying. Maybe it's how you reacted. Maybe it's something you did to survive that still makes your stomach turn. Write them down, even if your hand shakes. Especially if your hand shakes.

Now beside each one, write the truth of whose choice it really was: "The shame of hurting someone who loved him belongs to [their name], not me." Keep going until each piece of shame is sitting where it belongs.

Then read your list out loud — to the mirror, to the empty room, even to the cat in the doorway. Say: "I don't have to keep apologising for what they did to me." Say it until your voice steadies. Because truth spoken aloud settles in your body in a way it never does on the page.

Why It Matters

Those aren't your failures. They're their actions you've been hauling like stones in your pocket. Naming whose shame it really is hands it back—even if they won't take it. Refusing what was never yours is how you reclaim yourself, and how your body learns to stop absorbing blows that don't belong to you.

If You Remember One Thing

You walk a little taller now. Not because you've forgotten what happened, but because you've remembered whose shame it really was. You stop softening the story. Stop editing out the cruel parts. Stop protecting them from the truth of what they did.

You were never the one who should have been ashamed. You were brave for staying as long as you did, trying to love someone who wouldn't love you back. You were strong for surviving what you survived. You were resourceful for finding ways to cope, even if those ways weren't perfect.

The shame was always theirs—for hurting you, for breaking your trust, for refusing to change. You just got tricked into carrying it because they needed you to be wrong so they could avoid being accountable.

But you can put it down now. All of it. The embarrassment, the humiliation, the guilt you never earned. You can hand it back, even if they won't take it. You can leave it behind, even if they won't own it.

Your survival was always yours to claim.
Their shame was always theirs to carry.

You get to keep one and leave the other behind.

9.10
"Maybe If I'd Handled It Differently". Nope

Author's Note:

This chapter is for the moments you thought, "Maybe if I'd just handled it differently..." You weren't overreacting. You weren't too silent. You weren't too much or too little. You were set up to fail. Every choice was a trap, designed to keep you off balance. And seeing that clearly is how you finally step free.

Nothing You Said Was Ever Right Enough

You're standing in the kitchen, heart racing, trying to explain why you're hurt. Your voice catches. "When you said that thing at dinner—"

"Oh my God, you're so dramatic," he cuts in. "It was a joke."

The next week, same kitchen, different hurt. This time you say nothing. You keep chopping vegetables, swallowing the sting of his comment about your sister.

"What's wrong with you?" He slams the fridge. "You're giving me the silent treatment again. So fucking cold."

A month later, you try meeting in the middle. Calm voice, measured words. "I feel hurt, but I want to understand your perspective too."

He laughs. Actually laughs. "Listen to you. So manipulative. You've been reading those self-help books again, haven't you? Trying to therapise me."

Every road led to blame. The destination was always your fault.

You lie awake at 3 AM, replaying the conversation. Maybe if you'd said it differently. Maybe if you'd waited until morning. Maybe if you'd been less emotional. More emotional. More direct. Less confrontational.

Your chest tight, your mind racing through alternatives that might have worked better. But there was no better. There was no right answer. Because they weren't looking for resolution—they were manufacturing reasons to be disappointed in you.

The Double-Bind That Drove You Mad

You're at dinner with friends. He makes a cruel joke about your promotion—how you "probably slept your way up." Everyone goes quiet.

Later, in the car, you say, "That hurt me."

"You're being oversensitive," he says. "Learn to take a joke."

Next dinner party, he mocks your cooking. This time you say nothing, just smile and change the subject.

In the car: "You never stand up for yourself. It's pathetic. No wonder people walk all over you."

You try setting a boundary. "I need you to stop making jokes about me in public."

"You don't care about this relationship," he snaps. "You're trying to control me."

So you give in. "Okay, I'm sorry. You're right."

"Jesus, you're weak," he says. "You have no backbone. No self-respect."

A woman told me her ex called her "selfish" for not cancelling a work trip, then mocked her as "clingy" for wanting time together the next week. "I finally realised," she said, "he didn't want connection. He just wanted control over how and when I felt guilty."

They Kept You So Busy Doubting Yourself

You're typing a text. Delete. Retype. Delete again. It's about groceries, but somehow even this feels like a minefield. Will "Can you grab milk?" sound demanding? Will "If you have time, could you maybe get milk?" sound passive-aggressive?

You rehearse conversations in the shower. Practice your tone in the mirror. If you say it this way, maybe he won't explode. If you wait until after he's eaten, maybe she'll actually listen.

You've become a scientist of their moods. A scholar of their triggers. You map their emotions like weather patterns, trying to predict which version of them you'll meet today.

You soften your voice until it's barely a whisper. Choose your words like you're defusing a bomb. Plan your emotions like walking through a minefield where every feeling could be the wrong one.

And still, Saturday morning, you set something off. You smiled too much. Or not enough. You made breakfast too early. Or too late. The eggs are wrong, even though you made them the exact same way you did last week when they were perfect.

Because they weren't confused by your communication. They were creating chaos to keep you unsteady. When you're constantly trying to figure out what you did wrong, you don't have energy to notice what they're doing.

This Was Never a Conversation

You thought you were working through problems together. You'd sit on the couch, tissues between you, trying to understand each other better. But watch what actually happened:

"I felt hurt when you ignored me at the party," you say.

"What party?" they ask.

"Tom's birthday. Last week."

"I didn't ignore you."

"You literally walked away when I was mid-sentence."

"That never happened."

"It did. I was telling the story about—"

"Why are you always making things up? This is why I can't trust you."

"What? No, I just—"

"You know what? I'm done with this conversation. You're obviously having some kind of episode."

You sit there, tissues untouched, wondering how trying to discuss being ignored became you being called crazy. They'd corner you with contradictions, then act wounded when you couldn't find your way out.

You tried staying calm—they accused you of being cold.
You showed emotion—they called you unstable.
You used logic—they said you were heartless.
You brought evidence—they said you were obsessive.

This wasn't miscommunication. This was psychological warfare disguised as relationship conflict.

Practical Step

Take a piece of paper and make two columns. In the first, write "What I was accused of when I spoke up." Fill it in: dramatic, oversensitive, demanding, difficult. In the second column, write "What I was accused of when I stayed quiet": cold, withholding, passive-aggressive, emotionally unavailable.

Now look at those contradictions. Speaking up made you too much. Staying quiet made you not enough. That's not your communication failing—it's evidence of their manipulation. Evidence the game was rigged.

Keep that page somewhere close. When your brain whispers that you could have handled it differently, look at it. Then ask yourself: "Who taught me that expressing normal feelings was a crime?" Say their name out loud. Because naming the source of the lie breaks the spell they cast.

Why It Matters

That list isn't just paper and ink. It's evidence. Evidence that you weren't crazy. Evidence that you weren't the problem. Evidence that no amount of perfect communication could have fixed what was deliberately being broken. When you see the pattern laid out like that, you stop searching for the right words you never said. You stop believing there was a magic combination that would have made them happy. You see the trap for what it was.

If You Remember One Thing

"Maybe if I'd handled it differently?" Nope. The game was rigged.

You're not overthinking anymore. Well, you are, but now you catch yourself. Now when your brain starts the familiar loop—"Maybe if I'd said it differently"—you remember the list. You remember the trap.

That overthinking you do? That wasn't weakness. It was your nervous system trying to solve the unsolvable. To survive the unsurvivable. To find the magic combination that would finally make them happy. Your brain was doing exactly what brains do: looking for patterns, trying to predict danger, attempting to keep you safe.

But there was no combination. No perfect response. No right way to be.

They moved the target every time you got close.
They changed the rules every time you learned them.
They twisted every word, every silence, every tear.

Not because you were doing it wrong.
Because keeping you confused kept them in control.

And now you see it clearly. The game was rigged from the start. So you stop playing. You stop trying to win an unwinnable game. You stop measuring yourself against their shifting standards.

Your feelings were always valid.
Your responses were always human.
Your confusion was never the problem—it was the point.

You handled it the only way anyone could have: imperfectly, humanly, while under siege.

There's no different way you could have handled it that would have changed them.

There's only this: You survived it. You saw through it. And now you're free of it.

Part 10
Indisputable

This is the part where
you stop doubting yourself

10.1
If They Didn't Care Then They Don't Care Now

Author's Note:

This one's for when they show back up, sounding tender, using all the right words, maybe even crying. If they didn't care when it counted, they don't care now. That's not growth. It's bait.

You don't owe anyone a second chance to destroy you slower.

They Didn't Miss You. They Missed Control

Your phone lights up at 11pm. Your body knows before you look—that specific ringtone you never changed. Your hands shake as you read:

"I've been thinking about us."
"I miss what we had."
"I know I hurt you, but I've changed."

Your chest goes tight. Not with love. With memory. The last time you saw them, you were on the kitchen floor, sobbing, begging them to care. They stepped over you to get a beer from the fridge. Didn't even look down.

Now they miss you?

No.

They miss the version of you that kept trying. The one who apologised for having needs. The one who made excuses for their cruelty. The one who always picked up the phone at 11pm.

They Watched You Break and Felt Nothing

They saw your hands shake as you tried to pour coffee. Heard your voice crack mid-sentence. Watched you stare at the wall for hours. You gave them access to your deepest wounds, and they pressed harder. You showed them exactly where it hurt, and they aimed for those spots. You begged for basic kindness, and they called you needy.

And now they "understand"? Now they "get it"? No. What they get is that you're gone, and with you went their supply of attention, forgiveness, and second chances.

Their Regret Isn't Emotional. It's Strategic

They want you back in the cycle. Explaining. Doubting. Bending yourself into shapes that might finally earn their approval.

That "I've changed" message? It's not because they woke up transformed. It's because they woke up alone. Or their new supply isn't working out. Or they're bored and want to see if you'll still jump.

A woman told me her ex sent a long apology email six months after she went no contact. He said all the right things—took responsibility, promised change, even quoted her favourite poem. She replied. Within a week, he was back to the same patterns. She said, "That email wasn't remorse. It was a test to see if I'd still respond. And I failed."

Real Remorse Shows Up in Actions, Not Convenient Timing

Regret isn't texting when they're lonely at midnight. It's respecting your boundaries when you set them. It's consistency over months, not words over minutes. It's changed behaviour without you having to coach them through it.

If they only feel sorry after you're gone, they're not sorry about what they did. They're sorry about what they lost—access to someone who tolerated their cruelty.

They Want Back In Because the Game Stopped Working

They didn't have an epiphany. They had a power outage.

You stopped chasing. You stopped explaining. You stopped trying to decode their moods and manage their emotions. You stopped playing the role they wrote for you.

And now they're throwing out lines to see if you'll bite. Testing whether the old buttons still work. Checking if you're still programmable.

Practical Step

Make two lists:
1. What you did to try to fix things (apologised, went to therapy, changed yourself)
2. How they responded at the time (mocked you, dismissed you, blamed you)

Then write what real change would actually look like—not words, but consistent actions over time. Compare what they're offering now to what genuine remorse requires. Keep these lists.

When the "I've changed" messages come, read them. Remember who they were when you needed them to be different.

Why It Matters

Because seeing it written down breaks the spell. The pattern becomes undeniable: no matter how hard you tried, they kept moving the target.

And if they didn't care then—when you were right there, breaking—they don't care now. They just care that you're gone.

If You Remember One Thing

Regret doesn't arrive late. It shows up in the moment, when someone sees your pain and chooses to stop causing it.

If they didn't care when you were crying into your cereal, they don't care now that you're healing without them.

They care about access, not about you.
They care that their usual tricks don't land anymore.
They care that you're finally silent, and silence means their power is gone.

So let them send the texts. Let them leave the voicemails. Let them cry about losing the best thing they ever had.

Just don't let them back in.
They're not sorry. They're circling.
And you? You're already gone.

You don't owe them a response.
You don't owe them forgiveness.
You don't owe them another chance.

The person who breaks you doesn't get to be the person who puts you back together. Not now. Not ever.

10.2
A Thousand Small Cuts Still Bleed

Author's Note:

This one's for the quiet grief. The tiny losses no one else saw. The joy you muted. The stories you stopped telling. The way you changed your laugh, your clothes, your voice. You weren't overreacting. You were slowly diminished. And now, you get to reclaim every inch of yourself they tried to wear down.

It Wasn't One Thing. It Was Slow Erosion

It wasn't one thing. It was the comment about your outfit. The look when you laughed too loud. The way they walked out of the room mid-conversation. The sigh when you shared something vulnerable. The times they "forgot" to say sorry. The moments you swallowed your voice just to avoid another fight.

Not bruises, not broken bones. Just a slow undoing that left no evidence except inside you. A thousand small cuts that told you, again and again, you were too much, or not enough.

The Damage Didn't Start Big. It Started Subtle

They didn't come in swinging. They came in sweet. Charming. Patient. Then came the soft digs. The long silences. The double standards. And you stayed. Because none of it looked like abuse. But your body kept the score. And your confidence paid the price.

Practical Step

List the things you started doing differently just to keep the peace. The way you laughed. Spoke. Dressed.

Why It Matters

You're not crazy. You were adapting. And adaptation is proof you were surviving something real.

This is how confidence disappears without you noticing. This is why so many survivors say, "I don't know who I am anymore." You didn't lose yourself in one traumatic moment. You were edited out of your own life, word by word, choice by choice, until you couldn't recognise the person in the mirror.

They Didn't Steal Your Joy Loudly. They Took It Quietly

They didn't forbid happiness. They just rolled their eyes when you were excited. They acted bored when you had good news. They made you second-guess your pride, your light, your laughter.

And over time, joy became something you filtered. Measured. Withheld.

A woman once said to me she stopped singing in the car because her ex once said, "You sound like a dying animal." She laughed it off. And never sang again. She said, "It wasn't a big deal. Until I realised how many small joys I stopped reaching for."

A man told me he stopped wearing his favourite purple shirt after his partner said it made him "look gay." Just once. That shirt sat in his closet for three years. He said, "When I finally left, I put it on and cried. One comment. Three years. That's how it works."

Another survivor stopped telling stories at dinner. "Every time I'd start, she'd pick up her phone. Not dramatically. Just... disinterest. After a while, I stopped having anything to say. To anyone."

Different survivors, same pattern: one small cut, then another, until joy felt dangerous.

They Rewrote Your Reality. One Lie At A Time

You remembered it one way. They insisted it didn't happen. You asked a question. They changed the subject. You told your truth. They made it sound irrational. It wasn't one gaslight. It was a slow, silent campaign to convince you that your instincts couldn't be trusted.

Practical Step

Write down a moment you remember clearly that they tried to deny. Even if it feels small. Especially if it feels small.

Why It Matters

Every memory you reclaim is a thread back to yourself. But more than that: documenting these "small" moments shows you the architecture of control. How they built a cage out of sighs and silence. How they trained you to police yourself so they didn't have to.

Their Silence Wasn't Peace. It Was Punishment

You needed support. They gave you distance. You were scared. They got cold. You reached out. They disappeared. They didn't yell. They just withheld. And that silence didn't feel calm. It felt like being locked outside your own house while they watched from the window.

If You Remember One Thing

You weren't shattered by one moment. You were frayed by a thousand.

They didn't scream. They sighed at your joy.
They didn't hit. They walked away mid-conversation.
They didn't forbid. They just made everything cost too much.

The world may not see those wounds. But your body remembers every single one. The way you hesitate before laughing. The pause before you speak. The automatic "sorry" when you take up space.

So give yourself permission to grieve the small things. The songs you stopped singing. The pride you stopped claiming. The joy you muted to stay safe.

Because those weren't little things. They were your life. Bit by bit, they took who you were and replaced it with who they could tolerate.

It wasn't the big moments that broke you.
It was the small ones that stole you.

And now recovery means collecting yourself back, piece by piece, until the person who stopped singing in the car is singing again. Until the one who stopped wearing bright colours pulls them from the closet. Until the one who stopped telling stories finds their voice at the table.

You deserve to take it all back, one breath, one truth, one reclaimed joy at a time.

10.3
They Didn't Have Empathy
They Used Yours Against You

Author's Note:

This one's for the kind-hearted. The ones who stayed too long not because they didn't see the damage, but because they kept seeing the hurt behind it. You weren't blind. You were manipulated through your empathy. And now, it's time to use that same empathy to protect yourself instead of excuse them.

You Felt Bad for Them

You're sitting on the bathroom floor at 2am, holding them while they sob about their childhood. Twenty minutes ago, they were screaming at you about the dishes. Now you're stroking their hair, whispering "it's okay," while the words they just called you still ring in your ears.

"My dad used to scream about the dishes too," they're saying. "I'm so sorry. I'm just like him."

Your chest tightens with their pain. You hear yourself saying, "You're nothing like him. You're trying." Your own hurt evaporates. By morning, you'll have forgotten you had a right to be upset.

They Hurt You, Then Made You Feel Guilty

"Can we talk about last night?" you say carefully.

Their face crumples. "I knew you'd throw it in my face. After everything I told you about my past, you still can't forgive me for one mistake."

"It's not about forgiveness, I just need—"

"You need me to be perfect. But I'm broken, okay? I'm doing my best." Tears that always work. Pain that always wins.

You feel it in your stomach—that familiar twist of guilt. How can you add to their suffering?

A woman told me her partner smashed her phone in a rage. When she tried to talk about it the next day, he broke down completely. "He was on the floor, sobbing about his father beating him, saying he was turning into a monster. I ended up on the floor with him, rubbing his back, telling him he wasn't a monster, that I knew he didn't mean it. My hands were still shaking from fear, but I was comforting him. I was comforting my abuser for abusing me."

They Wanted Forgiveness, Not Growth

You've had this conversation fifty times. Different triggers, same ending. They hurt you, they spiral into self-hatred, you comfort them, nothing changes.

"I'll go to therapy," they promise through tears.
"I'm getting better," they insist after each episode.
"You're the only one who understands me," they say when you try to leave.

But they never book the appointment. Never follow through. Never actually change. Because why would they? The current system works perfectly—they get to explode and you get to clean it up. They get to be broken and you get to be their eternal forgiver.

A survivor told me, "I spent three years being his unpaid therapist. Every cruel thing he did came with a tragic backstory. I thought if I loved him enough, he'd heal. But he didn't want to heal. He wanted permission to stay broken at my expense."

Your Empathy Was Beautiful. But It Was Also the Hook

Another woman stayed through five different rock bottoms. "This time was always going to be different. He'd cry real tears, make real promises. I'd feel his desperation in my bones. How could I abandon someone in that much pain? By the end, I couldn't tell where his suffering ended and mine began."

You're not weak for caring. You're not foolish for believing people can change. But empathy without boundaries becomes a weapon in the wrong hands.

They didn't exploit your weakness. They exploited your strength.

They learned exactly which wounds to show you. Which tears worked. Which stories made you soften. They turned your compassion into the cage that kept you.

Practical Step

Write this down: "I can care about someone's pain and still leave when they cause mine."

Then list three times your pain was replaced by theirs. Notice how your needs vanished? How the conversation always became about their trauma, their struggles, their pain?

That pattern isn't coincidence. It's strategy.

Why It Matters

Seeing the pattern breaks the spell. You weren't having conversations about harm—you were being manipulated into silence through sympathy.

If You Remember One Thing

You're standing in the doorway with your bags packed. They're crying again. Tears that once worked. Anguish that once hooked you. "How can you leave when I need you most?"

Your body wants to drop the bags. Your arms ache to comfort them one more time. This is the moment that broke you before—their pain calling to your empathy like a siren song.

But this time you know: Their pain is real. And it's also not your responsibility.

You didn't cause their trauma.
You can't cure it.
And you don't have to burn yourself down to keep them warm.

Walking away from someone's pain doesn't make you cruel. Refusing to be manipulated through sympathy doesn't make you heartless. Choosing your safety over their comfort doesn't erase your compassion.

It means you finally understand: Your empathy was never broken. It was just aimed at someone who consumed it without ever reciprocating.

Now you get to point it where it always belonged—toward yourself first, then toward people who honour it rather than weaponise it.

That's not selfish. That's survival.

10.4
You're Not an Imposter
You Were Taught to Doubt Yourself

Author's Note:

This one's for the survivor who still feels like they're faking it, like any minute now, someone will find out they don't belong. You weren't an imposter. You were made to question yourself by someone who needed you uncertain. They called your clarity arrogance. Your joy, attention-seeking. Your intuition, overreacting. But that doubt? It's not your truth. It's residue. And you're allowed to outgrow what they planted.

Imposter Syndrome Hits Harder
When You Were Taught to Doubt Your Worth

You're standing at the podium, about to give the presentation you've prepared for weeks. Your manager just introduced you as "our expert on this." The room is waiting.

And all you can hear is their voice: "Don't embarrass yourself. You always think you know more than you do."

Your hands shake as you shuffle papers. These people are about to find out you're a fraud. Any second now, they'll see what they saw—that you're not as smart as you pretend to be. That you got lucky. That you don't deserve to be here.

But here's what's actually happening: You're not an imposter. You're a qualified professional standing in earned success, while ghosts from your past try to pull you back into smallness.

Success Felt Like Betrayal

"Who do you think you are?" they'd say when you got the promotion.

"Must be nice to think you're so special," when you shared good news.

"Don't get too big for your boots," when you dared to feel proud.

A woman told me her ex would go silent every time she achieved something. "Not angry silent. Worse. Disappointed silent. Like my success was a betrayal. I started hiding my wins. Then I started avoiding opportunities altogether. It was easier than dealing with his reaction."

Another survivor said, "She'd laugh—this specific laugh—whenever I was excited about something. Not cruel, exactly. Just dismissive. Like I was a child playing dress-up. Twenty years later, I still hear that laugh when something good happens."

When You Start Doing Well, the Doubt Creeps In

You get the job offer. Your first thought: "They made a mistake."

Someone compliments your work. You think: "They're just being nice."

This isn't humility. It's conditioning. You were trained to see your achievements as flukes, your talents as delusions, your worth as temporary.

A man told me he turned down three promotions before his therapist helped him see the pattern. "Every time opportunity knocked, I heard my father's voice: 'Don't kid yourself. You're not management material.' I was forty-five years old, excellent at my job, and still believing the opinion of someone who hadn't spoken to me in a decade."

The Voice in Your Head Isn't Yours

You're at dinner with new friends. Everyone's laughing at your story. For a moment, you feel it—belonging. Then the whisper starts:

"They're laughing at you, not with you."
"You're talking too much."

"They're just being polite."

You excuse yourself to the bathroom. Stare at yourself in the mirror. Try to see what they must see—the faker, the pretender, the one who doesn't belong.

But that voice? That's not your intuition. That's not reality checking in. That's years of someone needing you to stay small, uncertain, dependent on their version of who you were.

Practical Step

Start keeping a "truth file"—a notes app folder, a physical shoebox, or both. Every compliment, every achievement, every moment someone chose you—save it. Screenshot the kind email. Print the promotion letter. Keep the thank-you card. Include the presentation that went well, the friend who said you changed their life, the project you completed.

On the days when the old voice gets loud, read your truth file. Let evidence drown out conditioning.

Why It Matters

Their voice had years to dig in. Your truth needs practice to grow louder. This file becomes your proof that the imposter feeling is a lie they planted, not a truth you discovered.

You're Not Faking It. You're Recovering Into It

Every achievement feels unearned because you were taught you didn't deserve achievement. Every compliment feels false because you were trained to distrust kindness. Every moment of belonging feels temporary because they convinced you that you didn't fit anywhere except with them.

But watch what happens when you push through the doubt. The presentation ends

434

and people applaud—genuinely. The promotion sticks—you don't get "found out." The friends keep inviting you back—because they actually like you.

The imposter syndrome doesn't go away immediately. It fades slowly, each success weakening its grip, each moment of genuine connection proving it wrong.

If You Remember One Thing

You're sitting in your car after the interview. It went well—really well. They loved your ideas. They laughed at your joke. They said they'd be in touch soon.

And part of you wants to email them: "I'm not as good as I seemed. You should know that before you hire me."

That impulse? That's not honesty. That's sabotage. That's the voice of someone who needed you to fail because your success made them feel small.

You're not an imposter. You're someone who had their confidence systematically dismantled and is now rebuilding it, piece by piece, achievement by achievement.

The doubt you feel isn't evidence that you don't belong.
It's evidence that someone worked very hard to make you believe that.

And now? Now you get to prove them wrong. Not through grand gestures or perfect performances. But through showing up, even when the voice says you shouldn't. Through accepting the compliment, even when it feels unearned. Through taking the opportunity, even when you're sure you'll fail.

Because imposter syndrome isn't your truth.
It's just the echo of someone who needed you small.

And you? You were never small.
You were just taught to crouch.

10.5
It Wasn't Confidence
It Was Entitlement

Author's Note:

This one's for every time you mistook their certainty for strength. You weren't weak for second-guessing yourself. You were up against someone who never paused to reflect, because they didn't care who they steamrolled. It wasn't confidence. It was entitlement. And now, you know the difference.

They Said It Like a Fact

"We're selling the house and moving to my mother's town."

You're standing in the kitchen, coffee mug halfway to your lips. This is the first you're hearing of it.

"Wait, what? We haven't discussed—"

"There's nothing to discuss. It makes financial sense." They're not even looking at you, already scrolling through real estate listings on their phone.

"But my job is here. The kids' school—"

"You'll adapt. You always do." Said with a smile. Not warm. Strategic.

Your stomach drops. Not because of the move—because of how they announced it. Like your life was theirs to rearrange. Like your opinion was an afterthought, not a factor.

That wasn't confidence making decisions. That was entitlement assuming compliance.

Rules Were for You, Not Them

They checked your phone daily. "If you have nothing to hide, you have nothing to worry about."

But their phone? Face down, password changed weekly. "You're being paranoid. Why don't you trust me?"

They demanded to know where you were every minute. But disappeared for hours without explanation. "I don't need to report to you. You're not my parent."

A woman told me her ex required her to share her location at all times but refused to share his. "He said it was different because he was 'trustworthy' and I had 'anxiety issues.' He actually said that with a straight face. Like the rules of a relationship only applied to me."

Another survivor said, "She read my journal, confronted me about private thoughts I'd written. When I found out she was texting her ex, she said I was 'violating her privacy' by being upset about it. The sheer audacity—using my reaction to her betrayal as the crime—left me speechless."

They Lied and Demanded Trust

You're holding the credit card statement. The paper trembles slightly in your hand. There it is—the charge they swore they didn't make.

"You said you didn't buy anything last week."

"I didn't." Not even a flicker of hesitation.

"It's right here. Tuesday. Three hundred dollars."

"That must be a mistake." They take the paper from your hands, study it like they're confused too. "I'll call the bank."

The audacity of it—lying while looking at the proof. They never call the bank. A week later, you see the item in the garage.

"Oh that? I forgot. Why are you making such a big deal about it?"

And suddenly you're defending why lying matters. You're explaining why trust needs truth. You're the one who sounds unreasonable while they stand there, calm and dismissive, like you're having a breakdown over nothing.

A man told me, "She cheated, I caught her, and she looked me in the eye and said, 'I can't believe you don't trust me.' Not 'I'm sorry.' Not 'Let me explain.' Just instant outrage that I would dare question her, even with evidence in my hand."

Their Calm Wasn't Peace. It Was Indifference

You're crying, trying to explain how their words hurt you. They're sitting across from you, checking their watch.

"Are you done?" they ask, like you're a child having a tantrum.

Another time, you're trying to discuss the relationship. They're scrolling their phone. You ask them to put it down. They sigh, set it face-down, then drum their fingers on the table while staring past you.

When you finally broke down completely—that night you couldn't stop sobbing—they shrugged. Actually shrugged. "I don't know what you want me to say."

You mistook their composure for emotional regulation. But they weren't grounded— they were absent. They didn't get flustered because they didn't care enough to engage. Your pain was white noise to them, your tears an inconvenience, not a concern.

That steady voice you admired? It wasn't wisdom. It was detachment wearing a mask of maturity.

The Audacity Was the Point

They contradicted themselves mid-sentence and didn't blink.

Monday: "I never said that."
Tuesday: "You misunderstood what I said."
Wednesday: "Why are you still talking about this?"

They rewrote history while you were still living it. And because they did it with such certainty, such unshakeable conviction, you started doubting your own memory.

They didn't need to be right—they just needed to sound right. That's not confidence. That's shamelessness.

Practical Step

Write down the double standards they enforced. In one column, list what they required from you—transparency, loyalty, accountability, instant responses, detailed explanations. In another, list what they gave—secrets, lies, dismissal, disappearances, "I don't have to explain myself."

Look at those columns. That imbalance isn't a personality quirk. When you see it on paper, you realise it wasn't miscommunication—it was entitlement, plain and simple.

Why It Matters

Once you see the pattern of entitlement, you stop mistaking it for confidence. Real confidence includes accountability. Entitlement never does.

If You Remember One Thing

You're at a party. Someone's talking over everyone, dismissing other opinions, acting like their experience is the only valid one. Everyone seems impressed by their "confidence."

But you feel it in your body—that familiar tightness. You recognise it now. It's not confidence. It's the same entitlement that once had you questioning your own reality.

Real confidence can admit mistakes.
Real strength can say "I don't know."
Real power doesn't need to diminish others.

You weren't weak for doubting yourself around them. You were responding normally to someone who weaponised certainty like a bludgeon. They weren't assertive—they were entitled. They weren't self-assured—they were self-absorbed.

And now? Now when someone demands respect without offering it, dismisses your boundary as "oversensitive," or announces decisions about your life without consultation, you recognise it.

That's not leadership. That's dominance.
That's not confidence. That's control.
And you don't have to mistake one for the other ever again.

10.6
You Weren't Crazy
You Were Responding to Crazy-Making

Author's Note:

This chapter is about the moment you stop questioning your sanity and start recognising the deliberate chaos you were forced to navigate. If you ever felt like you were losing your mind, if you questioned your memory, your perceptions, your basic grasp on reality, this is your validation. You weren't going crazy. You were being driven there, systematically, by someone who needed you unstable to stay in control.

They Built the Maze. Then Called You Lost

You're standing in the kitchen, staring at the coffee maker. It's not where you left it. Yesterday it was by the window. Now it's next to the microwave.

"Did you move the coffee maker?"

"What? No. It's always been there." They don't even look up from their phone.

You know—you know—it was by the window. You made coffee there this morning. But now you're doubting. Maybe you're remembering wrong. Maybe you're the one who moved it and forgot.

Later, you find your keys in the bathroom. You never take keys to the bathroom.

"Why are my keys in here?"

"How would I know? You're always losing things."

By evening, you're apologising for being scattered. For being forgetful. For wasting their time with your confusion. But something in your stomach knows: this isn't right. Things don't just migrate on their own.

They weren't helping you find things. They were hiding them. They weren't concerned about your memory. They were dismantling it. This wasn't confusion—it was chaos as strategy.

They Called Your Clarity Paranoia

You notice the phone bill is higher. Ask about it.

"Why are you going through the bills? That's my department."

You see lipstick on their collar. Mention it.

"You're being paranoid. It's probably yours."

You don't wear that shade. Haven't for years.

"Then it's from the dry cleaner. Why are you always looking for problems?"

You find messages. Deleted but recoverable. Confrontation time.

"This is insane. You're literally spying on me. You need help."

They weren't defending themselves. They were manufacturing doubt in you. Making you question your right to notice, to ask, to know. The issue was never the lipstick or the messages—it was making you feel crazy for seeing what was right in front of you.

A man told me, "She had me convinced I was dangerously jealous. I went to therapy for it. Took medication for anxiety. Apologised constantly for my 'trust issues.' Two years after our divorce, her affair partner contacted me. They'd been together our entire marriage. I wasn't paranoid. I was perceptive. And she knew it."

Your Reactions Were Proportional to the Insanity

You're at dinner with friends. They ask about your weekend plans.

"We're going to the coast," your partner says confidently.

This is the first you're hearing of it.

"I thought we were visiting your parents?"

They look at you with genuine confusion. "We talked about this yesterday. The coast. Remember?"

You don't remember. Because it didn't happen. But their certainty is so complete, their confusion at your confusion so convincing, that you start wondering if maybe you're having memory problems. At thirty-two. You excuse yourself to the bathroom. Splash cold water on your face. Try to piece together yesterday's conversations. But the harder you try, the more everything feels like fog.

A woman told me she started recording conversations on her phone because she kept "forgetting" things. "He'd tell me we'd discussed something—major things, like selling my car or lending money to his brother. I had no memory of these conversations. I thought I was developing early-onset dementia. Then I listened to one of my recordings. The conversation he swore we'd had? Never happened. That's when I realised I wasn't losing my mind. He was stealing it."

Gaslighting Isn't Confusion. It's Warfare

You're looking at a photo from last Christmas. You're wearing the blue dress. You remember that day clearly—the fight in the car, the silent dinner, the way they ignored you all evening.

"That was such a lovely day," they say, looking over your shoulder. "Remember how happy we were?"

"We had that huge fight. You didn't speak to me for hours."

"What? No, that was Easter. Christmas was perfect. You wore that blue dress I love, we laughed all day. You're mixing things up again."

You stare at the photo. You know what happened that day. The dress doesn't change the memory. But their voice is so sure, so gentle, so concerned about your "confusion."

By bedtime, you're googling "memory disorders young adults."

They Needed You Unstable to Stay Stable

A woman told me her ex would change plans constantly but never tell her. "I'd get dressed for dinner, he'd be in sweats watching TV. 'I told you I was tired. We discussed staying in.' We hadn't discussed anything. But he'd describe the conversation in such detail—where we were standing, what I was wearing when we 'talked'—that I'd start thinking maybe it happened and I just... lost it somehow."

Another survivor said, "She'd hide my wallet in the freezer, then hand it back to me with this concerned sigh, like I was falling apart. My medication would end up in the garage. She'd 'find' it and suggest maybe I needed professional help for my 'increasing forgetfulness.'"

Practical Step

Start a reality journal. Not to prove anything to them—they'll call it obsessive. But for you. Write down conversations, decisions, where things are placed. Date everything. When they tell you something different happened, check your notes. Trust your documentation over their revision.

This isn't paranoia. It's protection. Your memory isn't failing. It's under attack. And you don't need to keep this forever—it's a temporary tool to retrain your trust in your own memory.

Why It Matters

When you see the patterns documented, you stop questioning your sanity and start questioning their motives. The "confusion" isn't yours—it's manufactured.

If You Remember One Thing

You're not crazy for feeling crazy in a crazy-making environment.

The anxiety wasn't weakness—it was your nervous system accurately detecting danger. The confusion wasn't your failure—it was their weapon. The exhaustion wasn't laziness—it was the natural result of constantly defending your reality against someone determined to rewrite it.

You kept notes because you needed evidence. You questioned everything because nothing was stable. You felt paranoid because you were actually being deceived.

That's not mental illness. That's mental clarity fighting to survive in deliberately created chaos.

The most sane thing you ever did was trust yourself enough to know something wasn't right. Even when they worked overtime to convince you the problem was in your head, some part of you held onto the truth.

Your reality was real.
Your perceptions were accurate.
Your responses were appropriate.

You weren't the problem. You were the witness they needed to silence.

And now? Now you know the chaos wasn't coming from inside you. It was being carefully orchestrated around you. You weren't losing your mind. You were finding your voice. And that voice—the one that kept whispering "this isn't right"—that was your sanity, refusing to surrender.

10.7
You Weren't Loved.
You Were Used to Avoid Their Shame

Author's Note:

This one's for anyone who kept shape-shifting, shrinking, and trying harder, not to feel loved, but to feel safe. You weren't the problem. You were the solution to their need to avoid responsibility. They trained you to chase their approval so they'd never have to face themselves. And now that you see the setup, you get to stop working to solve a problem that was always theirs.

They Needed You to Feel Like the Flawed One

You're standing in the bedroom doorway, trying to explain why their comment hurt you.

"I just felt dismissed when you—"

"Here we go again," they interrupt. "You're so sensitive. Everything I say is wrong. I can't do anything right, can I?"

Now you're comforting them. "No, that's not what I meant. I'm sorry. I know you're trying."

Twenty minutes later, you're the one apologising. For bringing it up. For your tone. For making them feel bad about making you feel bad. Your original hurt? Never addressed. It vanished the moment they flipped the script.

This happened every time. They'd hurt you, you'd try to address it, and somehow you'd end up being the one saying sorry. Not because you were weak. Because they trained you to believe their comfort mattered more than your pain.

A woman told me, "I kept a tally once. In six months, I apologised 247 times. Him? Three times. And those three were followed by 'but you...' Every single one."

The Goal Wasn't Love. It Was Your Obedience

Saturday morning. They've been cold all week—one-word answers, turned backs in bed, leaving rooms when you enter. You don't know what you did wrong. You've been replaying every conversation, every moment, trying to find your mistake.

Then they walk in with coffee and a smile. "Morning, beautiful."

Your whole body floods with relief. Whatever you did, you're forgiven. You're good again. You're chosen again.

You don't bring up the week of silence. You don't ask what changed. You're just grateful the conditional approval is back. You'll do anything to keep this version of them here— the one who sees you, chooses you, wants you.

But by Tuesday, they're cold again. The warmth was just a reset button, not reconciliation. And the cycle starts over.

A woman told me, "He'd ignore me for days, then bring home flowers like nothing happened. I'd be so relieved I never asked why he'd been cruel. I just thanked him for the flowers. Looking back, I wasn't his partner. I was his emotional yo-yo—pulled close when he was bored, pushed away when I had needs."

They Used You to Avoid Their Own Reflection

"You're impossible to please," they say after you mention they forgot your birthday.

"You expect too much," when you ask for a phone call during their trip.

"Nothing's ever good enough for you," when you point out they promised to help with the house but spent the day gaming instead.

447

Every legitimate need you expressed got reframed as a character flaw. You weren't asking for basic consideration—you were "needy." You weren't expecting partnership—you were "demanding." You weren't hurt by neglect—you were "impossible."

They couldn't tolerate being wrong, so they made you wrong for noticing. They couldn't handle accountability, so they made you feel guilty for expecting it.

A man told me his ex would scream at him, then say he "made her" do it by being so difficult. "She'd throw things, break things, say horrible things. Then she'd cry about how I 'drove her' to act that way. I spent years believing I was toxic, that I brought out the worst in people. Therapy helped me see—I didn't make her violent. She just couldn't face that she was."

You Chased Love That Was Never Coming

You changed your hair because they mentioned preferring it different.

You stopped seeing friends they didn't like.

You learned to laugh quieter, even at movies, because they said it drew attention.

You monitored your tone, your timing, your needs, your wants, your dreams.

And after all that reshaping, all that shrinking, they still weren't satisfied. Because satisfaction was never the goal. The goal was keeping you trying. Keeping you off-balance. Keeping you so focused on earning their approval that you'd never notice they weren't earning yours.

A survivor told me, "I wrote down everything he said he wanted me to change. I did all of it. Lost weight, dressed different, spoke softer, gave up my weekend hobby. When I'd completed the whole list, he made a new one. That's when I knew—there was no version of me that would be enough. He just needed me chasing."

Practical Step

Make a list of five times you carried their blame. Write what actually happened, what you apologised for, and what the truth really was. For example: "They screamed at me about dinner. I apologised for not being clearer about timing. Truth: They forgot we had plans."

Look at that list. See how you were trained to carry their shame? That weight was never yours.

Why It Matters

When you see the pattern written down, you stop believing you were the problem. You were the solution—to their inability to face themselves.

If You Remember One Thing

You're packing the last box. They're standing in the doorway, suddenly soft.

"I know I wasn't perfect, but you weren't easy either."

For a moment, you almost agree. Almost take half the blame. Almost believe that love is supposed to feel like constantly failing someone.

But then you remember: You weren't hard to love. You were just trying to get love from someone who could only offer transactions. Who needed you small so they could feel big. Who required you broken so they wouldn't have to look at their own cracks.

They were never going to love you the way you deserved. Not because you weren't lovable, but because real love requires seeing another person as whole and separate. And they could only see you as an extension of their needs.

You weren't too much or not enough.
You were just the only one trying to love with both hands.

And now you're done begging for crumbs from someone who ate at your table every day.

You thought you were in a relationship. You were in an audition that was rigged from the start. And walking away isn't giving up—it's finally understanding that the game was never meant to be won.

Your love was real.
Theirs was just management.

And now you know the difference.

10.8
You Weren't Too Sensitive
They Were Too Cruel

Author's Note:

This one's for the part of you that still hears their voice saying "you're overreacting" or "you're too emotional" when you remember what they did. For the part that wonders if maybe you really were too much, too needy, too intense. Here's what I wish someone had told me earlier: when someone consistently hurts you and then tells you that your pain is the problem, that's not feedback.

That's strategy. They weren't helping you grow thicker skin, they were training you to accept their cruelty as your sensitivity. Your sensitivity was the proof you weren't numb—it was the part of you still fighting to notice what was wrong.

They Called Your Accuracy "Overreacting"

You're in the car after dinner with friends. Something's wrong. They haven't looked at you once since you laughed at Tom's joke. Their jaw is tight. Their responses are clipped.

"Is everything okay?"

"Fine." The word cuts like ice.

"You seem upset—"

"Oh my God, here we go. You're so paranoid. Everything's always a crisis with you. I'm just tired, but you have to make it into some big drama."

You spend the rest of the ride silent, questioning yourself. Were you imagining the coldness? Creating problems where none existed? Being "too sensitive" again?

Three days later, they explode: "You were flirting with Tom. Don't deny it. I saw how you laughed at his stupid joke."

You weren't paranoid. You were perceptive. Your sensitivity had detected exactly what was happening—punishment for a crime you didn't commit. But they'd already convinced you that noticing their mood changes was a character flaw.

What They Called "Too Emotional" Was Normal Human Response

You're crying in the bathroom after they walked out mid-conversation. Again. You were trying to discuss the credit card bill, and they just... left. Went to watch TV like you weren't even speaking.

Later, they find you with red eyes.

"Seriously? You're crying about this? I just needed a break. You're so emotional about everything."

A woman told me her ex would give her the silent treatment for days, then mock her for crying about it. "He'd say, 'Look at you, falling apart over nothing. No wonder you can't handle life.' But I wasn't falling apart over nothing. I was having a normal response to emotional abandonment. It took me years to understand that crying when someone hurts you isn't weakness—it's human."

The Hurt Wasn't the Cruelty. The Blame Was

"You're too sensitive" when they yelled at you in public.

"You're overreacting" when they forgot your anniversary.

"You're being dramatic" when they lied about where they'd been.

He made a cutting joke about your weight at the party. When you went quiet, he laughed louder. "Relax, you can't take a joke. Everyone knows I'm kidding." But everyone saw you shrink. And he saw it too. That was the point.

They didn't just hurt you. They conducted a campaign to convince you that being hurt by hurtful things was your personal failing. They broke things then blamed you for bleeding.

A man told me, "She'd insult me in front of people—real cutting stuff about my job, my family, my body. When I'd bring it up later, she'd say I was 'too sensitive for adult relationships.' I started believing maybe I was too soft for love. Now I know—love isn't supposed to require armour."

Your Body Was Trying to Save You

That anxiety when their car pulled up? Your nervous system preparing for unpredictability.

That knot in your stomach during conversations? Your body bracing for gaslighting.

That prickle on your skin when their voice shifted tone? Your body alerting you to danger.

That exhaustion after seeing them? The toll of hypervigilance.

You weren't "too emotional." You were having appropriate physiological responses to psychological danger. Your sensitivity was your alarm system, and it was working perfectly.

What Healthy People Do When You're Hurt

You're sitting across from a friend, explaining how their comment stung.

"I had no idea it came across that way. I'm really sorry. That must have felt awful. I'll be more mindful."

No deflection. No minimising. No attacking your right to feel. Just acknowledgment, apology, adjustment.

That's what emotional maturity looks like. That's what your sensitivity deserves. Not "you're too sensitive," but "I'll be more careful with your heart."

A survivor told me, "My new partner accidentally triggered me—used a phrase my ex always said. I tensed up, started crying. Instead of calling me too sensitive, they held me and said, 'Tell me what words to avoid. Your feelings make sense.' That's when I realised my sensitivity wasn't the problem. The problem was being with someone who weaponised it."

The Sensitivity They Feared Most

That "overreaction" when they crossed your boundaries? That was self-preservation.

That "drama" when you called out their lies? That was truth-telling.

That "too much" feeling in your gut? That was wisdom.

Your sensitivity wasn't a weakness they had to endure. It was a strength they had to destroy. Because sensitive people notice things. Feel inconsistencies. Detect deception. And that threatened someone whose entire relationship strategy required you numb and confused.

Practical Step

Pull out three examples when they called you "too sensitive." Write what actually happened—their action, your response, their accusation.

Look at that evidence in black and white. See the proof: your feelings made sense, their cruelty didn't.

Why It Matters

When you see it written down, the pattern becomes clear: they weren't trying to help you. They were trying to silence you.

If You Remember One Thing

You're at the door, keys in your hand. They lean against the wall, throwing one last jab.

"No one else will put up with how emotional you are."

For a second, that old fear flickers. Maybe they're right. Maybe you are too much. Maybe you'll be alone because you feel too deeply.

But then you remember: You cried when they hurt you. You got angry when they lied. You felt anxious when they were unpredictable. You had feelings about being mistreated.

That's not too sensitive. That's human.

You weren't too emotional. They were too cruel.
You weren't too sensitive. They were too callous.
You weren't broken. They were destructive.

And the fact that you can still feel deeply after everything they did to shut you down?

That's not weakness.
That's triumph.

Your sensitivity survived their cruelty. And now it guides you toward people who see it not as a flaw to exploit, but as the strength that kept you alive.

10.9
You Were Called What They Couldn't Face in Themselves

Author's Note:

This one's for the part of you that still wonders if maybe they were right, if maybe you were selfish, unstable, or hard to love. You weren't. You were being projected on by someone who couldn't carry their own shame. That wasn't your reflection. That was their mask slipping. And now you get to leave it behind.

They Accused You of What They Were Actually Doing

"You're so selfish," they say, after you ask them to pick up milk on their way home.

This from the person who hasn't asked about your day in six months. Who forgot your birthday but raged when you didn't plan their party perfectly. Who takes the last of everything without asking if you wanted some.

"You never listen," they snap, cutting you off mid-sentence. Again.

You've been trying to tell them about your mother's diagnosis for three days. Each time you start, they interrupt with work drama, phone scrolling, or sudden urgent tasks. But somehow you're the one who doesn't listen.

"You're always starting fights," they accuse.

You brought up the credit card bill. Calmly. With receipts. They screamed for an hour, threw a glass, stormed out. But in their retelling, you're the aggressive one.

That's projection—accusing you of exactly what they're doing while they're doing it. It's so brazen, so backwards, that you stand there stunned, wondering if somehow you've misunderstood reality itself.

The More Specific the Accusation, the More It's About Them

"You're having an affair."

You're not. You haven't even thought about it. But they accuse you with such certainty, such detail—they know exactly how you'd do it, who with, when it's happening. They check your phone obsessively. Track your location. Interrogate you about every conversation.

A woman told me her ex accused her of cheating constantly. "He'd describe my 'affair' in detail—where we met, what we did. It was so specific I started doubting myself. Was I giving off signals? Was I doing something unconsciously? Two months after I left, his girlfriend called me. They'd been together our entire relationship."

The accusation wasn't insight. It was confession.

You're Not Defending Yourself. You're Being Baited

"You're emotionally unstable!"

This after they've been provoking you for two hours. Moving goalposts, denying things they just said, smirking when you get frustrated. You finally raise your voice, and they go calm.

"See? This is what I'm talking about. You can't control yourself."

You spend the next hour explaining that you're not usually like this, that they pushed you, that anyone would react this way. But the more you explain, the crazier you sound. Because that was the point—to get you defensive, emotional, proving their accusation right.

A man told me, "She'd needle me for hours—little digs, eye rolls, sighs. When I finally snapped, she'd record me on her phone. 'Evidence' of my anger issues. She had dozens of videos of me at my breaking point. None of the hours of provocation before."

Projection Is Their Escape Route from Accountability

You: "You lied about where you were last night."

Them: "You're so controlling. This jealousy is toxic."

You: "You spent our savings without telling me."

Them: "You're obsessed with money. It's all you care about."

You: "You hurt me when you joked about my weight in front of your friends."

Them: "You're too sensitive. Everything hurts you."

Notice the pattern? Every time you name their behaviour, they make you the problem. The conversation shifts from their actions to your character.

That's not accident. It's strategy.

The Truth Lives in What They Can't Stop Accusing You Of

They call you a narcissist? Look at how they need constant admiration.

They say you're controlling? Notice how they monitor your every move.

They insist you're crazy? Watch how they manufacture chaos.

A survivor told me, "Everything he accused me of was a confession. He called me a gold digger while draining my savings. Said I was manipulative while gaslighting me daily. Accused me of being cold while withholding affection for weeks.

It was like living with a mirror that only reflected his own image back at him, but somehow I was supposed to see myself in it."

Practical Step

Write down their three most common accusations about you. Next to each, write examples of them doing exactly that behaviour.

See the pattern? Those weren't truths about you—they were truths about them they couldn't face.

Why It Matters

When you see projection for what it is, you stop carrying blame that was planted in you but never belonged. Their accusations were never about you—they were confessions dressed as criticisms.

If You Remember One Thing

You're in the kitchen, making dinner. They walk in.

"You know what your problem is? You're incapable of love. You're emotionally dead inside."

Six months ago, this would have destroyed you. You'd have cried, begged them to see how much you love them, listed all the ways you show care.

But now you see it. You haven't been cold—you've been self-protecting from their cruelty. You haven't been withholding love—you've been rationing it for someone who never reciprocates.

The accusation isn't about you. It's about them. They're the one who can't love properly, so they accuse you of their limitation.

You don't defend. You don't explain. You just keep chopping vegetables, knowing that their projection is their problem, not your truth.

Let them throw their shame at you.
You don't have to catch it anymore.

Their accusations weren't about you—they were confessions in disguise.

You weren't what they called you.
You were what they couldn't face in themselves.

And now? Now you're free from carrying their shadow.

10.10
How Did They Ever Think It Was Okay

Author's Note:

This chapter is about the question that stayed with you the longest. Not why they did it. But how they ever thought it was okay. If you've ever sat in the wreckage of someone else's cruelty and realised they felt justified, this is for you.

They Called Cruelty Reasonable

You're standing in the kitchen at midnight, paint roller in hand. The walls are half done. You started at 6am, went to work, came home, and have been renovating since. Your back screams. Your hands shake from exhaustion.

"Why isn't this finished?" They're standing in the doorway, surveying your work with disgust.

"I've been going for eighteen hours. I need to sleep."

"Other people would have it done by now. You're just lazy."

They go to bed. You keep painting until 2am because the alternative—their disappointment, their rage—is worse than the exhaustion. And in the morning, they complain the coffee is weak, like you're the inconsiderate one.

How did they think this was okay?

They Didn't Lose Control. They Just Didn't Care

You're in the emergency room. Stress-induced chest pains. The doctor is asking about your home life, your stress levels. Your partner sits beside you, holding your hand, looking concerned.

"She worries too much," they tell the doctor. "I keep telling her to relax."

Three hours ago, they were screaming at you about the grocery bill. Throwing things. Calling you worthless. The chest pains started during their tirade, but they didn't stop. They saw you clutching your chest, gasping, and kept going.

Now they're the concerned partner. Tomorrow they'll tell friends you're "having anxiety issues" like it's a character flaw, not a consequence.

A woman told me, "I collapsed at work. Full breakdown. My boss called an ambulance. When my husband arrived at the hospital, he was furious—not worried, furious—that I'd 'made a scene' at my job. I was hooked to monitors, and he was worried about his reputation."

They Watched You Break and Felt Nothing

"Please, I need a day off. Just one day."

"We don't have time for your weakness."

You haven't had a break in three months. Every weekend is their project, their schedule, their demands. You're so tired you can't think straight. You've lost weight. Your hair is falling out.

"I'm getting sick. I need rest."

"Stop being dramatic. Other people handle more than this."

Two days later, you're in bed with pneumonia. They stand in the doorway, annoyed.

"I suppose you expect me to take care of everything now."

A man told me, "She worked me into the ground—literally. I had a stress-induced stroke at thirty-eight. When I woke up in intensive care, her first words were, 'This is really inconvenient timing.' Not 'Thank God you're alive.' She was upset about having to cancel dinner plans."

They Justified It. And That's What Haunts You

It's 3am. You're googling "emotional abuse" again, trying to understand. The worst part isn't what they did. It's that they felt entitled to do it.

They took your savings and called it "our money."
They read your diary and called it "openness."
They isolated you from friends and called it "loyalty."
They controlled your every move and called it "care."

And when you finally said, "This is abuse," they laughed. Actually laughed.

"Abuse? I'm the one dealing with your mental problems. If anything, you're abusing me with these accusations."

That's what haunts you—not just the cruelty, but the righteousness. They didn't just hurt you. They felt justified. They slept soundly while you lay awake trying to understand how someone who claimed to love you could treat you like that and feel nothing.

The Truth You Need to Accept

They knew it was wrong. That's why they hid it from others.
They knew it was cruel. That's why they only did it in private.
They knew it hurt you. That's why they did it.

The control, the power, the ability to break you down—that wasn't a side effect. That was the point. And they felt entitled to that power because they didn't see a partner. They saw a tool. Something to use, not someone to protect.

Practical Step

Write this sentence and complete it five different ways: "They thought it was okay because..."

Maybe: "They thought it was okay because they never saw me as equal."
Maybe: "They thought it was okay because no one ever stopped them."
Maybe: "They thought it was okay because my pain didn't register as real to them."

Look at what you wrote. Notice how none of those reasons say anything about your worth? Their justifications reveal them—not you.

Why It Matters

When you understand they felt justified, you stop waiting for remorse that's never coming. You stop hoping they'll suddenly "get it." They got it. They just didn't care.

If You Remember One Thing

They look at you, almost indignant.

"You're really doing this? After everything I've done for you?"

Everything they've done. The control framed as care. The cruelty framed as tough love. The abuse framed as sacrifice.

They still think they're the victim in this story. They still believe you owe them gratitude for the suffering they caused. They still feel justified.

And that tells you everything you need to know.

You weren't hurt by accident or in moments of lost control.
You were hurt by someone who believed they had the right.

They thought it was okay to break you because they never thought you mattered enough not to break.

That's not a misunderstanding. That's the core of coercive control.

And now? Now you know: Their lack of remorse isn't about your worth. It's about their fundamental inability to see you as deserving of basic human consideration.

You don't need them to admit it was wrong.
You don't need them to finally feel guilty.
You don't need their recognition of the damage.

It was never okay.
And you deserved better—always.

Part 11
Return

Not to them, but to you

11.1
You Deserve Love
That Doesn't Come With Rules

Author's Note:

This one's for the person who learned to read another's moods like a weather report, who apologised before they were accused and measured joy like a risk. You weren't failing at love—you were being coached out of existing. This chapter is your permission to stop performing. To mess up. To ask for what you need. To take up space without negotiation.

You Thought You Were Building a Bridge

You set the table carefully. Mug on the right, paper folded to the crossword, pancake stack centered on their favourite plate.

They come downstairs. Survey the spread. Say nothing.

"Good morning," you try, voice bright but careful.

"Why are you so cheerful? It's annoying."

You lower your voice immediately. Lower your smile. You've learned the exact frequency that won't trigger their irritation. You whisper the rules to yourself while cooking: "Not too happy. Not too quiet. No pulp in the juice. Don't hum."

You thought you were building connection through these gestures. But you were just learning to fold yourself away so someone else could feel bigger.

The Rules You Never Knew You Were Following

Don't laugh too loudly—it's attention-seeking.
Don't cry when hurt—it's manipulative.
Don't ask for help—it's needy.
Don't succeed too much—it's threatening.
Don't struggle too much—it's pathetic.

You could never win because the rules kept changing. Tuesday's requirement became Wednesday's violation. What pleased them in January enraged them by March.

A woman told me she kept a notebook tracking her partner's preferences. "Coffee black on Mondays, with milk on Thursdays. Never talk during the game. Always talk during dinner. Don't touch him when he's stressed. Always touch him when he's happy. Three pages of rules I'd whisper to myself while driving so I'd be ready when tested. I thought I was being thoughtful. I was actually documenting my erasure."

They Weren't Playing the Same Game

You're in therapy together. You've prepared, as always. You have examples, dates, specific requests for change. You're ready to work.

They sit back, arms crossed. "I don't see what the problem is. They're just never satisfied."

The therapist asks what you need from the relationship.

"I just want to feel loved," you say. "I want to feel like I matter."

"See?" they say to the therapist. "So needy. This is what I deal with."

You spend the rest of the session defending your right to have needs. By the end, you're apologising for taking up time. The therapist suggests you work on your "communication style."

Later, in the car, they say, "Even the therapist thinks you're the problem."

You shrink a little more.

What Love Without Rules Actually Looks Like

Your new partner burns dinner. Completely. Smoke alarm screaming, pasta turned to charcoal.

"I'm so sorry," they laugh. "I got distracted. Pizza?"

You freeze, waiting. For the anger. The sulking. The three-day punishment.

Instead, they're already pulling up delivery apps. "What do you feel like? And don't say 'whatever you want'—what do YOU actually want?"

What you want. When did someone last ask that without it being a test?

A man told me, "Six months into my new relationship, I dropped a glass. Shattered everywhere. I immediately started apologising, explaining, promising to be more careful. My boyfriend just grabbed the broom and said, 'It's just a glass, love. You okay?' I cried. Because I'd forgotten that mistakes could be just mistakes, not crimes."

The Permission You Never Needed

You can cry in the kitchen and not apologise for having feelings. You can order exactly what you want from the menu without checking if it's "reasonable." You can rest without producing receipts for your exhaustion.

These aren't privileges to be earned:
- Feel your feelings without editing them
- Have needs without apologising for them
- Take up physical and emotional space
- Change your mind without a tribunal
- Be imperfect without punishment
- Rest without earning it first

Someone just convinced you these were negotiable. They're not.

Practical Step

Write yourself a permission slip: "I am allowed to take up space. I am allowed to have needs. I am allowed to rest without earning it. I am allowed to be imperfect. I am allowed to be myself, fully and without apology."

Put it somewhere you'll see it daily. Read it until you believe it.

Tonight's practice: Order exactly what you want from a menu—no pre-checking, no polling others. Say "I want the salmon" or "Actually, I'd prefer tea." Notice your body's surprise. Notice that nothing terrible happens. Write how it felt. Repeat tomorrow.

Why It Matters

They conditioned you to believe you needed permission to exist authentically. Recovery means taking that permission back. You're not asking for too much. You're remembering you're allowed to ask at all.

If You Remember One Thing

You're at dinner with someone new. You order what you actually want, not what seems "reasonable." You laugh at your full volume. You share an opinion without checking their face first.

And they smile. Not despite your fullness, but because of it.

"I love how passionate you are about this," they say.

You wait for the "but." It doesn't come.

This is what love without rules looks like. No scoreboard. No performance metrics. No constant adjustments. Just two people, being themselves, choosing each other. Someone

470

hands you the blanket without comment when you shiver. They say "What do you actually want?" and mean it.

You weren't too much. You weren't too needy.
You were just with someone who made love conditional.

Real love doesn't come with terms and conditions.
Real love doesn't require you to shrink.
Real love celebrates your expansion.

You deserve someone who wants all of you—the messy, imperfect, takes-up-space, has-needs, fully-human you.

That's not asking for too much.

That's asking for exactly what love is supposed to be.

11.2
I Know What Happened
And I Still Miss Them Sometimes

Author's Note:

This one's for the part of you that knows exactly what happened, yet still finds yourself missing them. Still wondering. Still aching. You're not failing. You're recovering. This is the in-between, where your body hasn't caught up to your truth. And every time you stay with your truth, even when it hurts, you practice loyalty to yourself instead of to their memory.

It's Not Confusion. It's Collateral Damage

Three months since you left. You're at the supermarket, reaching for pasta, when you see it—their favourite brand. The one you always bought. Your hand hovers.

For a second, you almost grab it. Muscle memory. Then deeper—you miss making their dinner. You miss knowing exactly how they liked things. You miss having someone to cook for, even someone who never said thank you.

You know what they did. You have the therapy notes, the journal entries, the friends who held you while you sobbed about the cruelty. You've named it: abuse. Control. Manipulation.

And yet here you are, crying in aisle seven because a box of rigatoni reminded you of Tuesday nights when they'd actually smile at dinner. When things felt almost normal. Almost like love.

That's not weakness. That's trauma bonding—your body still chasing the scraps it was trained to mistake for love.

You Didn't Just Lose Them. You Lost Who You Were Trying to Save

It's 2am. You're scrolling through old photos. There—that one from the beach last summer. They look happy. You look exhausted but you're smiling because they're smiling and that was so rare.

You're not missing them, exactly. You're missing the them you thought existed underneath all the anger. The one you glimpsed on good days. The one you spent years trying to excavate from the rubble of their rage.

A woman told me, "I grieved him like a death. Not because he was gone, but because I finally had to accept that the person I loved had never actually existed. I'd been in love with potential, with glimpses, with who he could have been if he'd just tried. That's what I miss—the imaginary version I spent five years trying to rescue."

Your Nervous System Is Still Bracing for the Pattern

Your phone buzzes. Different name, different person, but your whole body tenses. They used to text at this time. Usually something cruel disguised as concern.

"Just checking in," this new message says. From a friend. A real friend.

But your chest is tight. Your shoulders are up. Your body is preparing for combat that isn't coming. You draft three different responses, editing for tone, checking for anything that could be misread, anything that could start a fight.

Then you remember: this person has never punished you for being yourself.

That's trauma echo—your body still protecting you from dangers that have passed. You lived in hypervigilance so long that peace feels like the calm before a storm, even when there's no storm coming.

This Is the Push-Pull That Keeps Survivors Stuck

Monday: You're clear. You write in your journal about all the manipulation, the gaslighting, the cruelty. You feel strong.

Tuesday: You drive past the coffee shop where you had your first date. Your chest aches. Were you too harsh? Maybe you're remembering it wrong.

Wednesday: You unblock them at midnight. Just to check. They've posted a photo with someone new. Smiling. The smile you worked years to earn. You block them again. Call your therapist. Feel ashamed for looking.

This isn't backsliding. This is what recovery looks like when the person who hurt you also trained you to need them. The zigzag isn't weakness—it's your brain trying to reconcile two truths that shouldn't exist together: they hurt you and you loved them.

Your Body Remembers Before Your Mind Does

A man told me, "Six months out, I was at a wedding. Slow song came on—our song. My body just... reacted. Started crying. Couldn't stop. Not because I wanted him back, but because my nervous system remembered slow dancing in our kitchen, back when I still believed he'd change. My mind knew better. My body was still catching up."

Another survivor said, "I kept buying his coffee brand for three months after I left. Kept putting it in my trolly without thinking. My hands knew the routine even though my heart knew better."

Practical Step

Write two truths side by side: "I know it was abuse" and "I still miss them sometimes." Let them exist together without trying to resolve the contradiction.

When the missing hits, ask yourself: What am I actually missing? Them? Or the hope I had for them? The routine? The familiar? Write the real answer.

Tonight, create one new routine that's just yours. Make coffee differently. Take a new route home. Claim one small thing they never touched.

Why It Matters

Your recovery isn't linear. Recognising the push-pull as normal, not failure, keeps you from shame-spiralling when the missing hits. And creating new patterns helps your body learn that safety exists without them.

If You Remember One Thing

In the car, their song comes on. For thirty seconds, you let yourself feel it all. Then you change the station.

That's recovery. Not the absence of feeling, but choosing what to do with the feeling. Not never missing them, but missing them and staying gone anyway.

You're not weak for having loved someone who hurt you.
You're not broken for still feeling the echo.
You're not failing for grieving something that was both real and terrible.

This is what recovery looks like when trauma was delivered with tenderness, when harm was mixed with hope, when the person who broke you also made you feel chosen.

Every time you feel the pull and don't go back, you're rewiring years of conditioning. Every time you miss them and stay away anyway, you're choosing yourself.

The missing might not stop today. Or tomorrow. Or next month.

But one day you'll realise you haven't thought of them in a week. Then a month. Then you'll hear their name and feel... nothing. Or everything. Or something in between.

All of it is okay.
All of it is recovery.
All of it is yours to feel, at your own pace, in your own way.

11.3
When Kindness Feels Like a Setup

Author's Note:

This one's for anyone who pulled away the first time someone was kind, because it felt like bait. You're not broken. You're just used to love that came with conditions, control, or chaos. Let the quiet feel strange for now. That's not a red flag. It's your body learning how to feel safe again.

Real Safety Feels Suspicious When You've Lived in Emotional War Zones

Your new partner brings you tea without being asked. Just sets it on the table beside you while you're reading. No comment. No expectation. No "you're welcome" waiting to be earned.

Your whole body tenses.

What do they want? What's the catch? Why are they being nice?

You overanalyse the gesture, searching for the catch. Was the tea too hot—a subtle message you're too cold? Too sweet—suggesting you're bitter? Are they trying to make you feel guilty for not making them tea first?

"Everything okay?" they ask, noticing your stillness.

"Fine," you lie, already calculating what this kindness will cost you. Because in your experience, every gift had a price tag. Every gesture came with interest. Every kindness was a debt you'd have to repay with compliance, gratitude, or silence about something worse.

That's not paranoia. That's pattern recognition from someone who lived through transactional love.

You Keep Looking for Red Flags Because You Don't Trust Green Ones

They text: "Running late, be there in 20. Sorry!"

Your brain: They're lying. They're with someone else. This is how it starts—the excuses, the distance, the slow fade.

They arrive in 20 minutes, apologetic, holding your favourite coffee as a peace offering for being late.

Your brain: Love bombing. Manipulation. They're setting me up for something.

They ask about your day and actually listen to the answer.

Your brain: Information gathering. They'll use this against me later.

A woman told me she spent six months waiting for her girlfriend to "drop the mask." "She was kind, consistent, communicated clearly. I kept detailed mental notes of every interaction, looking for the pattern, the tell, the moment she'd flip. It took me a year to realise I was looking for danger that wasn't there. I was so ready for war, I couldn't recognise peace."

Testing for Cracks That Aren't There

Saturday night. They suggest dinner out. You say you'd rather stay in.

"Sounds perfect," they say. "Want to order Thai?"

You push: "Actually, maybe we should go out."

"Sure, wherever you want."

You push harder: "You don't actually want to go out, do you?"

They pause, confused. "I want to spend time with you. Location doesn't matter."
You snap: "Just say what you actually want instead of trying to manage me!"

They're not managing you. They're being flexible. But flexibility feels like manipulation when you're used to everything being a strategy. So you test. You change plans to see if they'll punish you. You pick fights to see their "real" face. You push them away to see if they'll chase you or let you go—both feel like proof of something sinister.

A man told me, "I kept starting arguments with my boyfriend just to see how he'd react. Would he yell? Storm out? Give me the silent treatment? He'd just say, 'Let's talk about what's really bothering you.' It took me months to stop treating his stability like a trick."

The Absence of Drama Feels Like Absence of Love

It's been three months. No explosive fights. No silent treatments. No walking on eggshells.

And you're restless.

Where's the passion? The intensity? The feeling of being desperately needed?

They love you calmly, steadily, without crisis. And part of you wonders if they love you at all. Because your nervous system learned that love is loud—either worship or warfare. This quiet consistency feels like indifference.

You find yourself creating small dramas. Withdrawing to see if they'll chase. Picking fights to feel something familiar. Not because you want chaos, but because chaos is the language you learned to speak, and this new dialect of peace feels like being in a country where you don't understand the words.

Learning to Receive Without Defending

They compliment your presentation at work.
Your immediate response: "It wasn't that good. I messed up slide seven."

They bring you flowers.
Your immediate response: "You didn't have to do that. These are expensive."

They say "I love you." Your immediate response: "Why?"

A survivor told me, "My partner had to teach me to just say 'thank you.' Not 'thank you but,' not 'you shouldn't have,' just 'thank you.' It felt like swallowing glass at first. Two years later, I can accept kindness without flinching. Most days."

Practical Step

When someone is kind, notice your first impulse. Do you deflect? Minimise? Look for the catch? Prepare to pay them back?

Practice this response instead: "Thank you." Full stop. No additions. No explanations. No debt. No repayment. Just thank you.

Tonight, try receiving one thing—a compliment, a gesture, a text—without defending against it. Notice how your body wants to reject it. Breathe through the discomfort.

This week, keep a kindness log. Write down each kind gesture you received and how your body reacted. Was there tightening? Deflection? Suspicion? Name it without judgment.

This is how you rewire: tracking the pattern, then gently practicing something new.

Why It Matters

Your nervous system learned that kindness was a trap. Every time you accept kindness without bracing for impact, you teach your body that safety can be real.

If You Remember One Thing

You're lying in bed next to someone who's never raised their voice at you. Never punished you with silence. Never made you earn their affection.

And it feels wrong. Too easy. Too quiet. Your body keeps waiting for the crash. For the real them to emerge. For the kindness to evaporate.

But maybe—just maybe—this is what love without conditions actually feels like. Not fireworks and freefall. Not passion and panic. Just someone choosing you, steadily, without making you audition for it daily.

You're not too damaged for healthy love.
You're just learning a new language.

And yes, safety feels unsafe when chaos was home. Yes, kindness feels suspicious when love came with invoices. Yes, peace feels wrong when you're still dressed for war. But that doesn't mean you're broken. It means you're transitioning.

From survival to living.
From vigilance to rest.
From earning love to simply receiving it.

It's okay if it takes time. It's okay if you test it. It's okay if you pull away and come back, checking if it's still there.

One day, kindness won't feel like a setup.
It will just feel like kindness.

And you'll receive it without flinching, without calculating the cost, without waiting for the catch.

That day might not be today.
But every time you practice receiving without defending, you get closer.

480

11.4
You're Done Playing Along

Author's Note:

This one's for the part of you that played along at dinner tables and family barbecues, smiling while they sparkled and you shrank. You weren't complicit. You were surviving. But now? You don't have to cover for their script. You don't have to prop up their performance anymore. You don't have to play along.

They Performed Warmth While You Lived the Fallout

The dinner party. They're holding court, telling that story about their volunteer work at the shelter. Everyone's captivated. They reach over, squeeze your shoulder affectionately.

"Couldn't do it without this one," they say, smiling at you.

The room awws. You force a smile back. Because three hours ago, in the car, they called you pathetic for crying about your mother's illness. Said you were "always looking for attention with your drama."

Now they're the devoted partner. The good person. The one who volunteers, who cares, who loves so deeply.

You excuse yourself to the bathroom. Splash water on your face. Try to reconcile the person in that dining room with the one who screamed at you until 3am last Tuesday, then told you the next morning that it never happened.

When you return, quieter, flatter, someone asks if you're feeling okay.

"They're just tired," your partner answers for you, rubbing your back. "Works too hard. I keep telling them to slow down."

Everyone nods sympathetically. You're the overwhelmed one. They're the caring partner trying to help. The story writes itself, and you're too exhausted to correct it.

You Were Honest, So You Looked Broken

At the neighbourhood BBQ, someone asks how you've been.

"It's been tough," you say honestly. "Really tough."

Your partner laughs, that light, dismissive laugh. "They're being dramatic. We're great. Just bought that new patio set!"

Later, they corner you: "Why would you say that? Now everyone thinks we have problems."

You do have problems. You're living them. But they've turned your honesty into betrayal, your exhaustion into exaggeration, your pain into performance.

A woman told me, "I stopped talking at social events. Not because I had nothing to say, but because everything true was considered a violation of our 'privacy.' But our privacy was just their reputation management."

They Turned Your Breaking Point Into Proof

The birthday party where you finally snapped. Months of needling, dismissing, subtle put-downs in front of everyone, and you finally said, "Stop treating me like this!"

The room went silent. They looked wounded, confused.

"I don't know what's happening," they said softly to the group. "They've been like this lately. I think they're struggling with some things."

And just like that, you became the unstable one. The one with issues. The one who ruined the party. They became the patient partner dealing with your difficulties.

A man told me, "She'd provoke me quietly—little whispers no one else could hear—until I'd explode. Then she'd look around the room with this concerned face, like she was worried about my mental health. Everyone thought I was losing it. She was just better at hiding her cruelty than I was at hiding my response to it."

Public Adoration Was Part of the Manipulation

Their Instagram: Couple photos. Anniversary posts. "So grateful for this one."

The comments: "You two are perfect!" "Relationship goals!" "So lucky to have each other!"

Meanwhile, you haven't been touched affectionately in months. Haven't heard "I love you" without sarcasm. Haven't felt safe in your own home.

But pointing out the disconnect makes you look jealous. Petty. Like you can't let them have nice things. Back then, you stayed quiet while they built a public shrine to a relationship that was killing you privately. Now you don't have to.

"Everyone loved them," a survivor told me. "The charismatic one, the funny one, the thoughtful one. I was the lucky one who got to be with them. No one saw that at home, I was their emotional punching bag. Their charm was for everyone else. Their cruelty was just for me."

The Gap Between Public and Private Is the Evidence

They brought flowers to your office. Made a big show of it. Your coworkers gushed about how romantic they were.

That night at home: "Did you see how everyone looked at me? They know I'm too good for you."

They planned elaborate date nights—when others would see. Posted about them immediately. But private anniversaries? Forgotten. Your birthday at home? Ignored.

The performance wasn't love. It was reputation management. And you were just a prop in their one-person show.

Practical Step

Make two lists. First: their public gestures—the flowers, the posts, the dinner party charm. Second: their private treatment—the silent treatments, the cruel words, the coldness.

Look at the gap. That distance between public and private? That's not love having an off day. That's someone who knows exactly what they're doing and chooses when to do it.

This week, tell one person one true thing about your experience. Not to convince them, just to practice speaking truth without editing it for their comfort.

Why It Matters

The performance only works if you stay silent. Every time you speak truth, you take back power from their narrative.

If You Remember One Thing

You're sitting in your car after another event where they sparkled and you shrunk. They're inside, probably telling another charming story, being the life of the party.

And you're exhausted. Not from the event, but from the pretense. From watching them be loving in public and cruel in private. From being gaslit into silence about your own life.

You weren't crazy for seeing the gap.
You weren't dramatic for being hurt by it.
You weren't difficult for wanting authenticity.

You were trapped in someone else's performance, expected to play a role that was killing you—the grateful partner, the lucky one, the one who had it so good.

But you know the truth. Behind the charm, behind the public displays, behind the carefully curated image, was someone who counted on your silence to keep their reputation intact.

You don't need everyone to believe you.
You don't need to prove the private cruelty to people dazzled by the public performance.
You just need to stop protecting their image at the cost of your truth.

Your story doesn't need to be polished or perfect or easy to hear.
It just needs to be yours.
And it needs to be told—even if only to yourself at first.

Because every time you name the gap between their public face and private cruelty, you reclaim a piece of reality they tried to steal. And that's not instability. That's integrity.

You don't have to nod along anymore.
You don't have to smile for their audience.
You're done playing their part.

And that's not loss—that's freedom.

11.5
You're Not Fragile
Just Fluent in Survival

Author's Note:

This one's for the part of you that thinks surviving made you brittle. For the part that wonders if all the hypervigilance, all the caution, all the deep feeling is proof you're damaged. It isn't. It's proof you learned to move through fire without turning to ash. You're not fragile. You're fluent. In danger. In silence. In survival. And now you get to use that fluency for yourself, not against yourself.

They Call You Fragile, But You've Already Walked Through Fire

"You're too sensitive," your sister says when you flinch at the door slamming.

She doesn't know that sound used to mean he was home drunk. That you'd learned to gauge his mood by how hard the door hit the frame. Soft close: manageable. Medium: walk carefully. Slam: hide.

"You overreact to everything," your coworker says when you triple-check the meeting time.

They don't know you once showed up five minutes late and paid for it for three days. Silent treatment. Belongings hidden. Food thrown away. "If you can't respect my time, you don't deserve dinner."

You're sitting in therapy, and even your well-meaning therapist says, "You seem hypervigilant."

Yes. You are. Because hypervigilance kept you alive when relaxation meant ambush. When letting your guard down meant missing the warning signs. When trust meant danger.

You weren't trained to be anxious. You were trained by danger to read it perfectly. What they call fragile is actually mastery—you became an expert at survival in conditions that required constant vigilance. You didn't break under pressure that would have shattered most people. You developed skills they'll never need.

That's not weakness. That's specialisation.

You Feel Deeply Because You Had to Read Danger in Microexpressions

You notice everything. The slight change in tone. The pause before answering. The way someone's energy shifts when they're about to explode.

"You're reading too much into things," friends say.

But you're not. You're reading exactly what's there because you became an interpreter of subtext to survive. You learned that "I'm fine" meant "I'm about to punish you for three days." That "whatever you want" meant "choose wrong and suffer." That silence meant storm brewing.

You developed a skill set most people never need—the ability to detect danger in a pause, aggression in a smile, threat in a tone shift. You became fluent in the language of warning signs.

A woman told me, "People think I'm psychic because I can predict when someone's upset before they know it themselves. I'm not psychic. I just spent ten years having to anticipate his moods to protect myself. Now I can't turn it off. But lately, I'm learning to use it differently—I help friends navigate difficult conversations, I'm excellent at negotiation, I read rooms like a professional. My trauma gave me a superpower. I'm just learning to aim it."

What They Call Overreacting
Was You Finally Breaking After Years of Restraint

The breaking point at the restaurant. When you "suddenly" walked out after he made another joke about your appearance.

It wasn't sudden. It was joke number 847. You'd smiled through 846 of them. Explained why they hurt. Asked him to stop. Accepted his "you're too sensitive" response.

Number 847 just happened to be the one that broke through your capacity to absorb any more.

A man told me, "She tells everyone I 'exploded over nothing' when I finally yelled back. She doesn't mention the two years of her screaming at me while I sat silent. The one time I matched her energy, I became the aggressive one."

They don't count your restraint. Only your release. They don't see the hundred times you held it in. Only the one time you couldn't.

You Keep Functioning While Carrying Weight That Would Crush Others

Tuesday. You're at work, leading a presentation. Professional. Composed. Clear.

No one knows you had a panic attack in the bathroom ten minutes before. That you haven't slept properly in three weeks. That you're navigating divorce proceedings, trauma therapy, and the complete upheaval of everything you thought your life would be.

You answer emails while grieving. You make dinner while dissociating. You help your friend with their crisis while managing your own PTSD.

"You're so strong," people say, not knowing that strength is just what survival looks like when you have no other choice.

A survivor told me, "I ran a marathon six months after leaving. Everyone was impressed. They didn't know I'd been running on empty for years. A marathon was nothing compared to surviving each day in that house."

You Weren't Born Guarded
You Were Taught That Openness Was Dangerous

You used to trust easily. Share freely. Love openly. Then someone used your trust as a weapon. Your sharing as ammunition. Your love as leverage.

Now you verify everything. Question motives. Keep an exit strategy. And people call you paranoid, closed-off, hard to reach.

A woman shared, "I used to be the person who hugged everyone, trusted immediately, assumed the best. Now I'm calculating escape routes and testing people with small truths before sharing anything real. I'm not cold. I'm careful. There's a difference."

That guardedness isn't damage. It's wisdom. You learned that not everyone deserves access to your softness. That's not fragility. That's boundaries born from experience.

Practical Step

Write down three traits you've been criticised for (too sensitive, too careful, too guarded). Next to each, write what danger it protected you from.

For example: "Too sensitive" = early warning system for aggression. "Too careful" = avoiding manipulation. "Too guarded" = protecting yourself from people who hadn't earned trust.

Look at that list. Those aren't flaws. They're survival skills.

This week, when someone calls you "too much," ask yourself: Too much for what? For their comfort? For their convenience? Or just too much truth for them to handle?

Why It Matters

Reframing your "fragility" as fluency in survival stops you from pathologising your adaptations. You're not broken. You're experienced.

If You Remember One Thing

You're standing in your kitchen, making tea. Simple task. Ordinary moment.

But you're here. After everything that tried to break you. After the gaslighting that made you question reality. After the cruelty that made you question your worth. After the exhaustion that made you question if you'd survive.

You survived it all.

You're not fragile for feeling deeply—you feel deeply because you stayed human through dehumanisation.

You're not weak for being careful—you're careful because you learned that trust must be earned.

You're not too much—you're exactly the right amount for someone who walked through hell and kept their heart intact.

They can call you fragile. They can misunderstand your caution as coldness, your sensitivity as weakness, your boundaries as walls.

Let them. You know what you are. Fire-tested. Battle-proven. Still standing.
You're not fragile. You're fluent in survival.

And that fluency? You get to keep it. Redirect it. Use it for building instead of bracing. For creating instead of calculating escape routes. For loving with the same intensity you once used to survive.

Your skills aren't symptoms.
They're superpowers waiting to be repurposed.

And now you get to aim them toward living, not just surviving.

11.6
Everything Happens for a Reason Is a Lie

Author's Note:

This one is about the lie that pain must have a purpose. Abuse wasn't a lesson. It was harm. And you don't need to dress it up to deserve healing.

Some Things Break You and That's All They Do

Six months after leaving, you're at lunch with your mother. You're telling her about the nightmares, the flashbacks, the way you still check locks three times before bed.

"Everything happens for a reason," she says, reaching for your hand. "You'll see. This will make you stronger."

You pull your hand back. Stronger? You were already strong. You had to be, to survive what you survived. You don't need abuse to teach you strength you already possessed.

"Maybe you needed this to find yourself," she continues.

No. You needed safety. You needed respect. You needed love that didn't come with bruises—emotional or otherwise. You didn't need trauma to become whole. You were whole before they systematically took you apart.

That's not comfort. That's asking you to be grateful for harm. To thank the knife for teaching you how to bleed.

Turning Trauma into a Lesson Is Another Form of Silencing

Your therapist leans forward: "What do you think this experience was meant to teach you?"

Your stomach drops. Meant to? As if there was intention behind someone choosing to terrorise you for three years. As if the universe conspired to break you for your own education.

"It wasn't meant to teach me anything," you say. "It was someone hurting me because they could."

The therapist shifts, uncomfortable with the rawness. They want you to find meaning because meaning makes trauma manageable—for them.

A woman told me, "My church group kept saying I needed to forgive him to heal. That holding onto anger was poisoning me.

But my anger was the only honest thing I had left. It was the only thing saying 'this was wrong.' Everyone wanted me to let it go so they could feel better about my story."

You're Not a Better Person Because of Abuse

"But look how strong you are now," your coworker says when you mention your past.

You were strong before. You just didn't have to prove it daily by surviving someone's cruelty.

"You're so resilient," they add.

You're resilient because you had no other choice. Not because abuse is some kind of strength training program. You developed coping mechanisms, not character improvements.

A man told me, "People keep telling me I'm inspirational for surviving my ex. I'm not inspirational. I'm exhausted. I didn't overcome adversity—I survived terrorism in my own home. Stop making it sound noble. It was hell."

The Pressure to Make Meaning Is Its Own Violence

You're in group therapy. Everyone's sharing their "growth" from trauma.

"It made me more empathetic."
"It taught me boundaries."
"It showed me my worth."

Your turn. Everyone's waiting for your redemption arc. Your silver lining. Your wisdom gained.

"It taught me nothing," you say. "It just hurt."

The room goes quiet. The facilitator shifts uncomfortably. "Perhaps you're not ready to see the lessons yet."

No. Perhaps there are no lessons. Perhaps some things just damage you, and the only "meaning" is that someone chose to cause harm and you survived it.

Real Recovery Doesn't Need a Justifying Narrative

You don't need to transform pain into purpose to deserve recovery.

You don't need to become an advocate, write a book, start a nonprofit, or inspire others.

You don't need to make your trauma "worth it" by helping other survivors.

You can just recover. Quietly. Privately. Without making your pain productive.

A survivor told me, "I spent two years trying to figure out the 'reason' I went through what I did. What was I supposed to learn? How was I supposed to grow?

Then my therapist asked, 'What if there's no cosmic reason? What if someone just hurt you because they chose to?' It was the most freeing thing anyone ever said."

Practical Step

Write down three things people have said to comfort you that actually minimised your pain ("Everything happens for a reason," "You're stronger now," "It could have been worse").

Next to each, write what you needed to hear instead. Maybe: "This shouldn't have happened to you." "You deserved better." "Your pain is valid."

This week, when someone tries to silver-line your trauma, practice saying: "I don't need this to mean something. I just need it to be acknowledged as wrong."

Why It Matters

You deserve validation, not transformation. You deserve to have your pain witnessed without having to make it useful.

If You Remember One Thing

You're at a dinner party. Someone's talking about their "journey" through trauma, how it made them who they are today, how grateful they are for the growth.

Everyone nods. Inspiring. Beautiful. What a gift hidden in pain.

They turn to you. "What about you? What did your experience teach you?"

You could play along. Give them the comfortable answer. Make your trauma palatable.

Instead, you say: "It taught me that some people will hurt you if they can. That's it. That's the only lesson."

The table goes quiet. Someone changes the subject.

And you feel something shift. Not because you found meaning in meaninglessness, but because you finally stopped pretending there was meaning to find.

Everything doesn't happen for a reason.
Some things just happen because people make terrible choices.
Some pain doesn't have purpose.
Some wounds don't carry wisdom.

You didn't suffer to become wise—you became wise despite suffering.
You didn't need abuse to grow—you grew around the damage.
You didn't require trauma to find yourself—you found yourself in spite of someone trying to erase you.

Your recovery doesn't need a redemption arc.
Your survival doesn't need to inspire others.
Your pain doesn't need to be productive.

You don't owe anyone a story where trauma made you better.
You're allowed to say: This broke things in me that are still broken.

And still be worthy of recovery, still be whole, still be here.

11.7
You Miss the Story. Not the Person

Author's Note:

This chapter is for the ache that confuses you—the one that makes you wonder if you miss them. You don't. You miss the story you were told. You miss the dream you invested in. That grief is real, even if the person never was.

You Miss the Start. Not the Whole Story

You're scrolling through old texts at 2am. The early ones. When they called you "beautiful" every morning. When they sent paragraphs about how you changed their life. When every message ended with hearts.

"I've never felt this way before."
"You understand me like no one else."
"I can't imagine life without you."

Your chest aches reading them. Not because you want them back—you know what they became. But because this version, this person who wrote these words, felt so real. So present. So yours.

Six months later, those same hands that typed "you're everything" were typing "you're crazy." The voice that whispered "I'll never hurt you" was screaming "this is all your fault."

You're not missing them. You're missing who they pretended to be in the opening chapter, before the mask cracked, before the real show began.

You Fell for the Character. Not the Consistent Person

First month: They love hiking because you love hiking. They're suddenly into your favourite band. They want kids—the same number you want. They've always dreamed of living where you want to live.

"It's like we're the same person," they say, and you believe it's fate.

But it wasn't synchronicity. It was mimicry. They mirrored you until you couldn't tell where you ended and they began. Not because they were your soulmate, but because they needed you hooked before they could drop the act.

A woman told me, "He literally became me. My interests, my dreams, my vocabulary. I thought we were perfectly matched. Then once I was committed, he slowly revealed he actually hated everything I loved. The hiking bored him. My music was 'noise.' The life I wanted was 'basic.' He'd been performing compatibility for months."

You're Mourning the Future That Was Never Coming

Sunday morning, three months in. You're lying in bed, planning next Christmas together. Where you'll spend it. What traditions you'll start. They're stroking your hair, adding details to the fantasy.

"We'll get a place with a garden."
"Sunday dinners with your family."
"Maybe a dog next year."

You built an entire future in those conversations. Decorated imaginary homes. Named unborn children. Planned trips that would never happen.

When it ended, you didn't just lose them. You lost the next forty years you'd already lived in your mind. The wedding that was never proposed. The home that was never bought. The life that existed only in promises they never intended to keep.

A man told me, "I grieved harder for the future than the relationship. I'd already imagined growing old with her. When she left, I had to mourn a whole lifetime that never existed."

Grief Isn't a Sign You Were Wrong. It's a Sign You Were Real

You're at their favourite restaurant—the one you can't go to anymore. Your friend says, "Why do you still miss someone who treated you so badly?" Because you don't miss them. You miss the story. The one where they were kind. Where they meant what they said. Where the beginning was real and sustainable.

You gave everything to someone performing intimacy. You loved fully while they loved strategically. Your grief isn't weakness. It's proof that your love was real, even when theirs was a performance.

"I kept trying to remember what we had," a woman told me, "until I realised I was the only one who believed we had it. I was in a relationship. They were running a con."

The Ache Is Real Even Though They Weren't

You dream about them. Not the fights. Not the cruelty. But that first month. That first kiss. That first "I love you" that felt like coming home.

You wake up grieving. Not for who they became, but for who they never really were. For the person you thought you'd found. For the love story that was actually a horror story with a beautiful opening chapter.

Practical Step

Write a eulogy for the illusion. Not for them—they're still alive somewhere, probably performing for someone new. But for the character they played. The one you fell in love with. The one who never existed after month three.

"Here lies the person who loved my laugh, who wanted my dreams, who promised safety. They died when the real person emerged. I mourn the fiction, not the fact." Let yourself grieve what you thought you had. Then bury it.

This week, when the ache hits, remind yourself: "I'm missing a story, not a person. The story was beautiful. It was also fiction."

Why It Matters

Naming what you're actually grieving—the performance, not the person—lets you mourn without going backward. You can miss the story without wanting the storyteller back.

If You Remember One Thing

You're looking at a photo from the beginning. Both of you smiling. You look happy. They look... like they're playing happy. You can see it now, the performance in their eyes.

You don't hate them. That would require believing they were real enough to hate. You don't forgive them either—that would require them to acknowledge what they did.

You just understand now: You were grieving a ghost. Missing a mirage. Mourning a future that was never on the table, with a person who was never who they said they were.

The ache you feel isn't for them.
It's for the story you believed.
The home you almost had.
The safety you almost felt.
The love that almost was.

It's okay to miss that story. Just remember—stories end. And the person you're mourning never got past chapter one because they were never written to last.

You weren't wrong to believe.
You were just loving someone fictional.
The story is over. And you don't have to keep waiting for a rewrite.

11.8
Learning Who You Are Without Permission

Author's Note:

This one's for anyone who spent so long adapting, they forgot who they were without someone else's expectations. If you've ever sat in a quiet room and wondered what you even like, what you want, what you believe in, this chapter is yours. Because recovery isn't just healing. It's discovering. And you're allowed to begin again, even if it feels strange.

You Were So Busy Surviving You Never Got to Begin

You're standing in the coffee shop, and the barista asks what you'd like. Simple question. But your chest tightens. Because for years, someone else decided. "She'll have a skinny latte," they'd say, before you could open your mouth. Or worse: "You don't really like coffee, remember?"

Now it's just you and twenty choices on a board, and you realise: you have no idea what you actually want.

A woman told me she cried the first time she ordered for herself after leaving. "The barista was so patient," she said. "I stood there for five minutes, paralysed. I'd never been allowed to want anything without checking first."

She ordered a hot chocolate with extra marshmallows. Something her ex would have mocked. It tasted like rebellion.

You Were Taught to Be Who They Needed

You learned early that having preferences was dangerous. You watched their face change when you suggested Italian instead of Thai. Felt the temperature drop when you reached for the remote. Heard the sigh when you played your music.

So you stopped suggesting. Stopped reaching. Stopped playing anything at all.

A survivor once told me: "I became a human mirror. Whatever he liked, I liked. Whatever he hated, I hated. By year three, I couldn't remember if I actually hated seafood or if I just knew he did."

Now, sitting alone at a restaurant, you get to ask a question they never let you ask: What do I actually want?

Practical Step

Start a notebook called "What If It Was Just About Me?" Each day, write down one thing you'd choose if no one was watching, judging, or commenting.

What would you eat for breakfast if no one called it weird? What colour would you paint your bedroom if no one said it was too bold? What music would fill your car if no one was there to critick the lyrics?

Don't overthink it. Just let your real preferences whisper back to life.

Why It Matters

You're not selfish for wanting. You're reawakening a self that was never allowed to form.

Recovery Isn't a Return. It's a Becoming

A woman spent her first year of recovery trying every food she'd never been "allowed" to like. She'd stand in the grocery store, heart racing, reaching for things that felt forbidden. Sourdough with real butter. Full-fat yoghurt. Chocolate for breakfast.

"I made a list called Things That Are Mine," she said. "Turns out, I hate boiled chicken. But I love smoked paprika. And almond croissants. And eating dinner at 9 PM. And wearing red lipstick to the supermarket."

Each discovery felt like finding a piece of herself that had been in storage. You can't go back to who you were before them. That version never got to stretch, or want, or wander. You're not reclaiming. You're creating. One preference. One boundary. One "actually, I'd rather" at a time.

Knowing Yourself Is The Ultimate Exit

They wanted you small so they could feel big. They wanted you indecisive so they could lead. They needed you unsure so they could define you.

But now you're asking questions that don't revolve around anyone else's comfort. What makes you lose track of time? What films make you cry the good kind of tears? What does your body feel like when it's not braced for impact?

A man told me it took him six months to realise he actually loved reading. "She always said books were boring, that I was wasting time. Now I read for three hours every Sunday. Science fiction. The kind she called childish. Turns out, I'm not boring. I was just bored."

This isn't indulgent. It's the work.

Practical Step

This week, try one thing that isn't productive, that doesn't help anyone else, that can't be justified as useful.

Take a pottery class even if you'll never sell a single bowl. Walk through a museum just to see what catches your eye. Sit in a park and watch clouds without checking your phone.

The point isn't what you choose. It's that you're choosing without needing anyone's permission or approval.

Why It Matters

The more you follow what moves you, the more you realise: this is what was missing all along. Not the perfect hobby or the right preference. Just the freedom to explore without consequence.

If You Remember One Thing

You don't have to justify joy. You don't need approval to explore what calls to you.

You're not selfish for discovering what you like, want, need, or believe in when no one else is in the room.

Getting to know yourself isn't indulgent. It's the foundation of everything that comes next.

And now, finally, you're allowed to find out who you are without asking for permission.

Even if your hands shake the first time you choose for yourself. Even if you stand in that coffee shop for five minutes, paralysed by possibility.

That's not weakness. That's the beginning of freedom.

11.9
You Knew
They Just Needed You to Forget

Author's Note:

This one's for anyone who felt the shift in the air long before they could explain it. Who picked up on the vibe, the tone, the warning, but got talked out of it. If you've ever told yourself "I'm probably overreacting," this chapter is here to say: No. You weren't. They just needed you to believe that gut-deep knowing was a glitch, instead of your compass. You were right all along.

Your Gut Knew. You Just Got Conditioned to Doubt It

You're sitting at dinner, and something shifts. Can't name it. Their smile's the same. Their voice hasn't changed. But your body reacts before you have words. Shoulders pull up. Breathing goes shallow. The air between you suddenly feels electric, dangerous.

"What's wrong?" you ask.

"Nothing's wrong." They keep cutting their steak. Normal. Calm. "Why would you think something's wrong?"

But you can feel it. The way they're gripping the knife just a fraction too tight. The pause before they answered. The smile that doesn't reach their eyes.

"You seem upset," you try again.

Now they look up. "I'm not upset. You're imagining things. Again."

A woman told me she used to document these moments in her phone. Hidden notes, timestamped. "7:23 PM - He says nothing's wrong but slammed the car door. Won't look at me." Later, when he'd explode about that exact thing, she'd check her notes. Her body knew first. She was never wrong. Not once.

"I thought I was going crazy," she said. "Turns out, I was just being gaslit by someone who needed me to doubt what my body felt first."

Trauma Teaches You to Scan for Threat

You walk into the living room and your body does the calculation before your brain catches up. Where is he sitting? What's his posture? Is that his third drink or his fourth? You catalogue the signs: jaw clenched, fingers drumming, TV too loud.

You know what's coming. You've mapped this territory a thousand times.

"You're being paranoid," they say when you mention it. "I'm just watching television. Not everything's about you."

Three hours later, they're screaming about something you did last Tuesday.

A survivor once told me: "I could predict his moods better than the weather. I knew Tuesday's tension would become Thursday's rage. But when I'd try to address it early, prevent it, he'd make me feel insane for even noticing."

That's not paranoia. That's pattern recognition. Your body keeping track when your mind's being told the scoreboard doesn't exist.

They Needed You to Doubt Yourself

"That's not what I said."

You're standing in the kitchen, and your brain feels like it's splitting. Because you remember exactly what they said. You can hear it, clear as day. But they're looking at you with such conviction, such disbelief at your "misremembering."

"You said I was stupid for forgetting the milk," you insist.

"I never said stupid. I said it was frustrating. You always exaggerate."

But you know what you heard. The word 'stupid' is still ringing in your ears. Yet here you are, doubting your own memory, your own ears, your own experience.

A woman told me she started recording conversations on her phone. "Not for court. For sanity. I needed to know I wasn't making things up." She played one back for me once. Her ex saying exactly what he later denied. Word for word.

"The scariest part?" she said. "Even with the recording, I still doubted myself. That's how deep the conditioning went."

Your Instincts Don't Need to Be Perfect to Be Valid

A man told me about the moment he knew his marriage was over. "She was laughing at her friend's joke, but something in her laugh was different. Hollow. My chest went cold before my brain caught up. I couldn't explain it, had no proof, but my body knew. I just knew she was already gone."

Six months later, he found out about the affair. It had started the week before that laugh.

"Everyone told me I was reading too much into things," he said. "But my gut knew what my eyes couldn't see yet."

You don't need evidence that would hold up in court. You don't need to explain the shift in molecular weight when they walk into a room. You're allowed to trust the tightening in your chest, the alarm in your belly, the inexplicable certainty that something's wrong. Your body's signals are valid, even when your mind's been taught to override them.

Practical Step

Start keeping an intuition journal. Not to analyse or judge, just to notice. Write down those moments when something feels off, even if you can't explain why. Note the time, what you felt in your body, what your gut was telling you. Don't try to be right or wrong. Just practise listening to yourself again. Over time, you'll see how often your body knew before your brain caught up. This isn't about proving yourself right. It's about giving your body back the microphone.

Why It Matters

You're retraining your nervous system to value what you feel in your body, not just what you can prove with your mind. Every time you document instead of dismiss, you're choosing to believe your body's wisdom.

If You Remember One Thing

That feeling in your gut when they said "nothing's wrong" but everything felt wrong? That wasn't paranoia. That was recognition.

You knew when the energy shifted. You knew when the words didn't match the tone. You knew when their story didn't add up.

They just needed you to forget you knew.

But your body remembered everything. Every flinch, every held breath, every moment your shoulders crept toward your ears. That was your intuition trying to protect you, even when your mind was being taught to betray it.

You don't have to be perfect to be right. You don't need surveillance footage to trust your gut. You just have to stop abandoning your body's signals in favour of someone else's version of the truth.

The knowing is still there, under all that doubt they layered on top. It never left. It just got very, very quiet.

It's still yours. Still real. And you're allowed to listen again.

11.10
Safe People
Don't Rush Your Recovery

Author's Note:

This one's for the part of you that needs more time—time to speak, decide, trust. If anyone ever rushed you through recovery, shamed you for slowing down, or punished you for pausing, this chapter is for you. Because your pace is not the problem. It's the protection.

You Hesitated. They Took It Personally

You're sitting across from your new partner, three months in, and they ask about your past relationship. Your throat closes. Your hands find each other under the table. You need a minute to find the words that won't unravel you.

"I..." you start, then stop. Breathe. Try again. "It's hard to talk about."

Their face changes. The warmth drains out. "We've been together three months. Don't you trust me by now?"

The familiar pressure builds in your chest. The one that says: hurry up, perform openness, prove you're healing right.

"I do trust you," you say, the words tumbling out too fast now. "It's just complicated—"

"Everything's complicated with you." They lean back, arms crossed. "My ex would have told me everything by now."

A woman told me she knew her relationship was unsafe the moment her new boyfriend said, "If you really loved me, you'd be over this by now." Six months out of a decade of abuse, and he was timing her grief with a stopwatch.

"I tried to explain that healing isn't linear," she said. "He called me dramatic. Said I was using trauma as an excuse to stay closed off." She paused. "The safe person I'm with now? When I go quiet mid-sentence, she just puts her hand on the table between us. Not touching me. Just there. Like a bridge I can cross when I'm ready."

Real Safety Doesn't Require Speed

A survivor told me about the first time she felt truly safe with someone new. "We were having tea, and she asked about my family. I froze. Completely. Just stared at my mug for maybe two full minutes. She didn't fill the silence. Didn't prompt. Didn't sigh. Just sipped her tea and looked out the window like we had all the time in the world."

"When I finally spoke, all I managed was 'They weren't kind to me.' She nodded and said, 'Thank you for trusting me with that.' That's it. No questions. No 'want to talk about it?' No wounded look that I hadn't shared more."

"Six months later, I told her everything. But it was because she'd already shown me she could hold my silence without making it about her."

That's what safety looks like. Not the absence of curiosity, but the presence of patience.

Shame Is a Red Flag, Not Motivation

You're in therapy, and you're trying to explain why you can't just "let go and move on." Your friend interrupts: "It's been a year. You need to stop living in the past."

Your stomach drops. Because you're not living in the past. The past is living in you. In your startle response when doors slam. In your body's refusal to relax when someone stands too close. In the way you still check your phone with shaking hands.

A man once told me, "Everyone kept saying I should be further along. My brother actually said, 'Other guys would have bounced back by now.' But trauma doesn't have a deadline. I wasn't being deliberate. I was being thorough. I was making sure that when I said I was okay, I actually meant it."

The people who shame your pace have never had to rebuild from rubble. They mistake their ignorance for wisdom, their impatience for help.

You Don't Have to Earn Belonging by Racing Through Recovery

A woman described her recovery timeline to me: "Year one: learning I wasn't crazy. Year two: learning to feel anger instead of shame. Year three: discovering who I was without them. Year four: believing I deserved better. Year five: actually accepting better."

"People kept asking why it was taking so long. But I wasn't behind. I was precise. Every stage mattered. Every pause was purposeful."

You're not behind schedule. There is no schedule.
You're not closed off. You're selective.
You're not broken because you need time. You're healing because you're taking it.

Practical Step

Think about one area where you feel rushed—maybe it's dating again, or forgiveness, or "getting back to normal." Write yourself a permission slip: "I give myself permission to take as long as I need with [specific thing]. My timeline is valid. My pace is protective.

Anyone who can't honour that is showing me they're not safe." Put this somewhere you'll see it daily. Let it remind you that your tempo is not a defect to fix but a boundary to honour.

Why It Matters

When you honour your own pace, you teach others how to honour it too. The ones who can't? They're telling you everything you need to know about their capacity for real intimacy.

If You Remember One Thing

The person who said "Why can't you just trust me already?" was never trustworthy. The one who said "You're taking too long to heal" was never healing.

Safe people don't watch the clock on your recovery. They don't compare your progress to others. They don't make your pace mean something about their worth. They wait— the kind of waiting that says: your timeline is yours, and I'm honoured to witness whatever you choose to share.

They say things like: "Take all the time you need." "Thank you for sharing what you can." "I'm here whether you talk or not."

Because safe love waits. Not passive waiting, not resentful waiting. But patient presence that honours your tempo.

Real safety never shames you for needing time. It thanks you for taking it.

Part 12
Recovery

This is a recovery
Raw, slow, liberating, and yours

12.1
You Don't Have to
Recover First to Deserve Love

Author's Note:

This one's for the part of you that keeps postponing your worth. That says, "Maybe when I'm more healed." "Maybe when I've done the work." "Maybe when I feel more whole." This chapter is here to end that lie. You are not a project. You are a person. And you don't have to earn love to be worthy of it.

You've Done the Work But the Voice Still Says "Not Yet"

You're scrolling through dating apps, and your thumb hovers over "create profile." You've been hovering for months. The voice in your head lists reasons to wait: finish therapy first, lose the anxiety weight, stop flinching when doors slam, learn to trust again.

A woman told me she kept a list titled "Things to Fix Before Dating." It had twenty-three items. "Number seven was 'stop crying randomly,'" she said. "Number fifteen was 'be able to watch romantic films without panic attacks.' Number twenty-three was just 'be normal.'"

She showed the list to her therapist, who asked one question: "Would you tell your best friend she needed to complete this list before deserving love?"

"Of course not," she said.

"Then why are you telling yourself?"

The woman sat there, list in her lap, and for the first time realised: she'd been treating herself like a renovation project that needed completion before going on the market.

You've unpacked the trauma. Survived the gaslighting. Rebuilt so many pieces. But there's still that whisper: Not yet. Not until you're more grounded. More whole. More something you can't quite name.

Worth Isn't Something You Earn

A man told me about his first relationship after abuse. "I kept apologising for everything. For needing reassurance. For checking texts twice. For asking if we were okay. One night, after my fifth apology of the evening, my partner took my hands and said, 'You know you don't have to earn my patience, right? It's not a favour. It's just love.'"

He started crying. "No one had ever just... loved me without me having to perform for it."

They taught you love was a reward for being easy, quiet, small enough. That safety had to be purchased with silence. That belonging was for people who didn't have baggage, triggers, or bad days. But they were wrong. You're not behind because you still have nightmares. You're not broken because crowds make you anxious. You're not too much because you need extra reassurance.

You're just remembering what should never have been taken: the knowledge that you deserve care simply because you exist.

Trauma Brain Tells You You're a Burden

You're at your friend's house, and they ask if you want tea. Simple question. But your brain runs calculations: Will it be too much trouble? Are they just being polite? Should I say no to be easier?

"No thanks, I'm fine," you say, throat dry.
"You sure? I'm making some anyway."
"Well, if you're already making it..."
A survivor once told me, "I whisper 'thank you' when someone is kind to me, like

I'm getting away with something. Like someone's going to notice I'm receiving care I haven't earned and take it back."

This isn't humility. It's conditioning. You were taught your needs were impositions. That your emotions were manipulations. That your very existence required justification. But needing care isn't weakness. It's human. And you've always had the right to be human, even when someone tried to convince you otherwise.

You Don't Have to Be Healed to Be Held

A woman described her moment of revelation: "I was sobbing on my kitchen floor, full panic attack, when my neighbour knocked. I tried to pull myself together, fix my face, pretend I was fine. She took one look at me and said, 'Honey, you don't have to be okay for me to care about you.'"

"She sat on my kitchen floor for two hours. Didn't try to fix me. Didn't need me to explain. Just sat there, handing me tissues and making really bad jokes until I could breathe again."

"That's when I understood: love isn't waiting for you on the other side of healing. It's allowed to find you exactly where you are."

Practical Step

Tonight, find a quiet moment with yourself. Place your hand over your heart—feel it beating steadily, reliably, keeping you alive without you having to earn it. That rhythm doesn't care if you're healed or hurting, perfect or struggling. It just keeps going, because you're deserving of life itself.

Say these words aloud, even if they feel foreign: "I am worthy of love right now. Not when I'm better. Not when I'm whole. Right now, exactly as I am." The words might feel like lies at first. That's okay. Trauma taught you to distrust your worth. Each time you say them, you're laying new pathways over the old grooves of shame.

Why It Matters

Your nervous system doesn't know the difference between your voice and the voices that hurt you. When you speak kindness to yourself, you're literally rewiring what trauma tried to break.

If You Remember One Thing

You are lovable even when you're anxious, even when you're triggered, even when you need to check the locks three times before bed.

You are deserving even when you cancel plans because crowds feel unsafe, even when you need subtitles because you can't focus, even when you sleep with lights on.

You don't need to transform to be held. You don't need to heal completely to deserve care. You don't need to reach some imaginary finish line where you're "normal" enough for love.

The woman with the twenty-three-item list? She went on a date at number four. "I told him I had PTSD on our second coffee," she said. "He said, 'Okay, what does that mean for you?' Not 'when will you be over it?' Just 'what do you need?'"

This world taught you to doubt your worth, to postpone your deservingness, to treat yourself like a project instead of a person.

But you—messy, healing, remarkable you—are not up for debate.

You're already enough. You always were. Even reading this with shaking hands. Even with tomorrow feeling uncertain. Even with healing still ahead.

Love isn't waiting for you to be ready. It's waiting for you to let it in, exactly as you are, right now.

12.2
Recovery Isn't Linear
And That Doesn't Mean You're Failing

Author's Note:

This one's for the part of you that panics when old feelings resurface. The moment you think, "I was doing so well, why am I here again?" This chapter is here to remind you: you didn't fail. You didn't fall back. You just hit turbulence. And that doesn't mean you're broken. It means you're still in motion. Recovery isn't linear. But it is happening. Even here. Even now.

You Were Doing Well and Then It Hit You Again

You're at the grocery store, humming along to the music, reaching for tomatoes. Six months since you left. Six months of sleeping through the night, eating full meals, laughing without checking over your shoulder first.

Then you see them. Not your ex—their new partner. Choosing avocados like it's nothing. Like your world didn't implode in produce aisles just like this one.

Your body remembers before your brain catches up. Heart hammering. Hands trembling. The tomatoes slip from your grip, roll across the floor. You're on your knees, scrambling to collect them, and suddenly you're crying. Right there by the organic vegetables. After six months of being "fine."

A woman told me she went six months without a panic attack. Then she walked past a man wearing her ex's cologne—that specific blend of sandalwood and something sharp—and had to sit on the curb, shaking, breathless, sure she'd failed.

"I called my sister sobbing," she said. "'I thought I was past this. I thought I was better.' And she said, 'You are better. Six months ago, that cologne would have ruined your whole week. Today it ruined twenty minutes."'

Healing doesn't move in straight lines. It circles back to check what's still tender. Not because you're failing. Because you're human.

Struggling Doesn't Mean You're Not Recovering

A man told me about his recovery timeline: "Month one, I couldn't leave my apartment. Month three, I was going to work, seeing friends. Month six, I thought I was cured. Then month seven, I had a dream about her, and spent three days in bed. I thought I'd lost everything."

"But then I realised—those three days? The first time, it was three weeks. Before that, three months. I wasn't going backwards. I was just... processing at different speeds."

You had a bad Tuesday. That doesn't erase six good Mondays. You cried in your car after seeing their social media. That doesn't undo the morning you woke up without checking it first. You're not back at the beginning. You're just being reminded that healing isn't a performance with a perfect final act.

A survivor once said to me: "I kept a calendar. Green days were good. Red days were hard. I expected to see all green by month six. Instead, I had green, green, green, green, RED, green, green. I wanted to quit. Then I looked back at month one: red, red, red, red, red, red, green. The red days weren't gone. But look how much green had grown between them."

Grace Over Guilt Every Single Time

You swore you'd never check their Instagram again. It's 2 AM, and you're scrolling through their stories. Your thumb moves without permission, and suddenly you've liked a photo from six weeks ago. Panic floods your chest. You unfollow, refollow, unfollow again. Screenshot to ask your friend if they'll get a notification.

You feel pathetic. Weak. Like you've undone months of progress with one late-night moment of curiosity.

A woman told me: "I messaged him. After four months of no contact. Just 'Thinking of you.' I wanted to crawl into the earth. My therapist asked, 'Did you invite him back? Did you apologise for leaving? Did you take back your boundaries?' No, no, and no. 'Then you didn't fail. You just had a human moment. And you're allowed those.'"

When it happens—and it will—you don't need punishment. You don't need to restart some imaginary recovery clock. You need to put your hand on your chest and say: "I'm learning. This is part of it. I'm still okay."

Incremental Doesn't Mean Insignificant

Recovery doesn't announce itself with fanfare. It shows up in moments so small you might miss them:

The morning you make coffee without checking if someone's mood shifted overnight. The text you don't send explaining why you need space—you just take it. The apology that rises in your throat when you have an opinion, but you swallow it and speak anyway.

A man described his breakthrough: "It wasn't some big moment. I was at dinner, and someone asked what restaurant I wanted. And I just... said it. Didn't check anyone's face first. Didn't say 'whatever you want.' Just said 'Thai food sounds good.' My friend didn't even notice. But I sat there thinking: a year ago, I couldn't even choose my own breakfast."

These aren't the victories you post about. But they're the ones that stick. The ones that slowly, quietly, rebuild you from the inside out.

Practical Step

Keep a note in your phone called "Proof I'm Healing"—or if that feels too loaded, call it "Evidence I'm Moving" or simply "My Reminders." Not the big moments—the tiny ones. The day you didn't apologise for crying. The morning you chose what to wear without wondering if someone would criticise it. The text you didn't feel compelled to answer immediately. The opinion you shared without cushioning it with "maybe I'm wrong, but..." Update it whenever you notice these small acts of reclamation. On the hard days, when you feel like you're sliding backwards, read it. Let it remind you that healing isn't always visible, but it's always happening.

Why It Matters

Recovery isn't the absence of setbacks. It's the speed at which you return to yourself. And each time you return—even if it takes hours, days, weeks—you're strengthening that path back home.

If You Remember One Thing

You didn't drown. That's what matters.

You didn't go backwards when you cried at the grocery store. You didn't undo your work when you checked their profile. You didn't fail when the nightmare came back.

You hit turbulence. But six months ago, that turbulence would have crashed you for weeks. Yesterday, it shook you for an afternoon. That's not failure. That's progress.

Recovery isn't the water becoming still. It's learning to swim in rougher seas with stronger strokes.

And the fact that you're still here—still reading, still trying, still showing up even when you don't want to—that means it's working.

Messy. Non-linear. Imperfect. Real.

And that's exactly how it's supposed to be.

12.3
You Tried So Hard to Be Easy to Love

Author's Note:

This one's for the survivor who stayed agreeable, helpful, soft, and still got called too much. You tried to make it easier for them to love you. Tried to be less. Need less. Shrink faster. But it was never about you. It was about their limitations. This chapter is here to remind you: what they taught you about being "difficult" was never the truth. You were always loveable. They just weren't capable of love that deep.

You Were Quiet. Helpful. Low Maintenance. And Still It Wasn't Enough

You're making dinner, and you've cooked their favourite again. The third time this week. You don't even like lasagne, but you know they do, so you layer the pasta carefully, making sure the edges are perfect, the way they prefer.

"What's for dinner?" they call from the living room. "Lasagne," you say, trying to sound cheerful. They sigh. That specific sigh that makes your stomach drop. "We just had Italian on Tuesday."

But Tuesday was your suggestion that got shot down. You remember because you wrote "spring rolls" on the grocery list afterwards, thinking maybe next time you could make them at home. Maybe homemade would be better. Maybe then there wouldn't be that sigh.

A woman told me: "I kept a mental spreadsheet of his preferences. Coffee: two sugars, never milk. Eggs: fried, never scrambled. Music in the car: his playlist only. I memorised every like and dislike, adjusted every preference, muted every opinion that might clash with his. I became a human algorithm designed to prevent disappointment."

"One day, after I'd spent three hours making his favourite meal from scratch, he looked at the plate and said, 'You're so needy. Always trying too hard.' That's when I realised: I could have been perfect, and it still wouldn't have been enough. Because the problem was never my effort. It was his inability to receive it without feeling obligated to give something back."

You Were Trying To Be Chosen
By People Who Couldn't Choose Themselves

You learned that having preferences was dangerous. Opinions were arguments waiting to happen. Needs were burdens. So you became an expert at wanting nothing. At being grateful for crumbs. At celebrating the bare minimum like it was a feast.

A survivor described the moment she understood: "I was at his parents' house, and his mother asked what I wanted to drink. Before I could answer, he said, 'She'll have water. She doesn't really like anything else.'

I sat there, throat dry, wanting tea but unable to correct him. Because earlier that week, when I'd asked for tea at a restaurant, he'd rolled his eyes and said, 'Why do you always have to be different?'"

"I drank that water and smiled. Made myself smaller with every sip."

A man told me: "I stopped suggesting restaurants because she'd say I was controlling. Stopped choosing movies because she'd call me selfish. Stopped expressing preferences entirely because any desire I had was 'pressure.'

By the end, I couldn't even tell you what kind of music I liked. I'd forgotten I was allowed to like things."

But no matter how agreeable you became, how flexible, how accommodating, it was never enough. Not because you were too much, but because they had no room for anyone real.

Neglect Taught You That Love Was Earned Through Erasure

You're sitting on the couch, and they're talking about their day. Twenty minutes about their horrible boss, their annoying commute, their exhausting meeting. You listen, nod, validate. When they pause, you start to share about your presentation—the one you've been preparing for weeks.

"God, not now," they say. "I'm too tired for your work drama."

Your work drama. The promotion you've been working toward for two years. But you swallow the words, tuck them away with all the other things you've learned not to share.

Your excitement about the book you're reading. Your worry about your mother's health. Your joy about reconnecting with an old friend. All "too much" for someone who has no room for you.

A woman once said to me: "I spent so long making myself digestible that I forgot I was allowed to be a full meal. I was serving myself in bite-sized pieces, hoping that if I was small enough, they might actually consume me."

You Didn't Fail at Being Loveable. They Failed at Loving

A survivor told me about the first time someone loved her without edits: "I was crying about something stupid—a commercial with a dog—and I started apologising. 'I'm sorry, I know I'm being too emotional.' My new partner looked confused. 'Too emotional for what? You're having a feeling. That's what humans do.'"

"I sat there stunned. No sigh. No eye roll. No 'you're so sensitive.' Just... acceptance. That's when I realised I'd been trying to earn something that should have been free."

You can stop performing now. Stop shrinking. Stop rehearsing your sentences before you speak them. Stop running your feelings through a filter to make them more palatable.

The right people won't need you to be easy. They'll need you to be real. They'll want your complicated feelings and your specific coffee order and your opinion about where to eat dinner. They'll want you full-sized, full-volume, fully present.

Practical Step

Start a list with two columns. On the left: "I was told I was too..." Fill it with all the accusations. Too emotional. Too sensitive. Too needy. Too intense. Too much. On the right: "What I actually was..."

Then translate the truth. Emotional becomes "Deeply feeling." Sensitive becomes "Attuned to energy." Needy becomes "Human with normal needs." Intense becomes "Passionate about life." Look at this list when the old voices try to shrink you.

Remember: those weren't accurate assessments. They were someone else's limitations dressed up as your flaws.

Why It Matters

The words they gave you were never true measurements of who you are. They were measuring their own capacity and finding it lacking.

Every time you reclaim the real definition of who you are, you're taking back space they tried to steal.

If You Remember One Thing

You weren't too much. You weren't impossible to love. You weren't the problem.

You were just surrounded by people who couldn't hold something so honest. So real. So beautifully, impossibly, wonderfully alive.

The woman who kept the mental spreadsheet? She's with someone now who makes her coffee wrong every morning—too much milk, not enough sugar—and she loves him for trying.

Their discomfort with your fullness was never your reflection. It was their admission that they couldn't love something they couldn't control.

And now? You don't shrink to fit into spaces too small for your spirit.
You expand. You unfold. You take up the space you were always meant to fill.

And you let the love that can handle all of you—every overwhelming, sensitive, intense, beautiful inch—finally find you.

12.4
Not Everything
Has to Become a Lesson

Author's Note:

This one's for the part of you still trying to turn hell into wisdom. Still trying to find meaning in what broke you. Still trying to make it "worth it." You don't have to. You don't owe anyone a takeaway. You don't have to grow from it. You don't have to be grateful for it. You can just let it hurt. And that doesn't make you weak. It makes you real.

Some Things Just Hurt and That's All

You're at a dinner party, and someone asks how you've been. You mention, carefully, that you left a difficult relationship. Their face lights up with that specific expression— the one that precedes unsolicited wisdom.

"Everything happens for a reason," they say, touching your arm. "You'll see. This will make you stronger." Your jaw tightens. Your wine glass suddenly feels heavy. Because last night you sobbed on your bathroom floor until 3 AM, and this morning you couldn't eat breakfast, and "stronger" isn't what you feel when you still flinch at footsteps that sound like theirs.

A woman told me: "At my support group, everyone kept sharing their 'growth moments.' How abuse taught them boundaries. How trauma made them resilient. When it was my turn, I said, 'It taught me nothing. It just hurt. And I wish it never happened.' The room went silent. Like I'd failed some unspoken recovery exam."

She paused. "But afterwards, three women came up to me privately and said, 'Thank you. I feel the same. I'm just tired of pretending it was worth it.'"

It wasn't a lesson. It was a violation. It wasn't character building. It was character demolishing. And the pressure to spin it into gold? That's just another weight on top of what you're already carrying.

Trying to Make It Meaningful Can Delay the Grief

You keep telling yourself there must be a purpose. Not because others say so—though they do—but because randomness feels worse than reason. If it meant something, at least the pain would have a point.

You're scrolling through Instagram, and there it is: another post about "finding the gift in the wound." The woman in the photo is glowing, hashtagging her trauma transformation. #traumatotriumph.

You look at your reflection in your phone screen. Unwashed hair. Tired eyes. Still in yesterday's clothes because today was hard enough without adding laundry.

A survivor once told me: "I spent two years trying to write a book about what I'd learned from abuse. I had chapters about resilience, growth, finding myself. But it was all bullshit. I was performing recovery for an audience, trying to make my pain productive. The real truth? It sucked. It stole years. And I'm not grateful for any of it."

"The day I admitted that was the day I actually started healing."

You keep saying "I'm stronger now" when your hands still shake opening emails. You keep saying "It taught me boundaries" when you're really just too scared to trust anyone. You keep saying "Everything happens for a reason" because the alternative— that sometimes terrible things happen to good people for no reason at all—feels too chaotic to hold.

You're Allowed to Leave the Rubble Without Mining It

A woman described her breaking point: "My therapist kept asking, 'What did you learn from this experience?' And I finally snapped. 'I learned that some people are cruel. I learned that love can be a lie. I learned that I can survive things I shouldn't have to. Are those the lessons you want? Because those aren't lessons. They're just facts about a terrible thing that happened.'"

"She was quiet for a moment, then said, 'You're right. Sometimes things just hurt. And that's valid too.'"

You don't have to sift through the wreckage looking for wisdom. You don't have to turn your scars into teaching moments. You can walk away from the devastation without checking if there's anything worth salvaging.

A man told me: "People keep asking what my 'takeaway' was from being abused. Like I went to some terrible conference and should have notes. My takeaway? Don't date people who hurt you. Revolutionary, right? Sometimes the only lesson is that it shouldn't have happened."

You Don't Owe Anyone a Redemption Arc

You're at coffee with a friend who says, "You should write about this. Help other people. Turn it into something positive." Your stomach turns. Because you can barely talk about it without losing your breath. Because "helping others" sounds like another job when you can barely help yourself. Because why does your pain need to serve a purpose for it to be valid?

A survivor once said to me: "I'm not a phoenix. I'm not rising from ashes. I'm a person who got burned and is trying to heal. That's it. No metaphors. No mythology. Just a human who went through something horrible and is still here." You're not required to be inspirational. You're not obligated to find meaning. You're allowed to say: "That sucked, it still sucks, and I'm just trying to get through today."

Practical Step

Take a piece of paper and write the story you've been telling—the polished one, the one with lessons and growth and silver linings. Then burn it, flush it, or tear it into pieces.

Now write the real story, the messy one: "It hurt. It was unfair. I didn't deserve it. I'm still angry. I'm still sad. And that's okay." This isn't about finding closure or wisdom. It's about stopping the performance of having to make your pain meaningful. Your pain is valid exactly as it is—raw, purposeless, human.

Why It Matters

Every time you admit the truth without dressing it up as wisdom, you're giving yourself permission to be human instead of heroic. And humanity, not heroism, is where real healing lives.

If You Remember One Thing

You don't have to find the lesson. You don't have to make it meaningful. You don't have to transform pain into purpose or trauma into triumph.

Some things just hurt. Some experiences just take. Some years are just lost.

And admitting that—without apology, without searching for silver linings, without performing recovery for anyone else—isn't giving up. It's being honest.

You can heal without becoming inspirational. You can recover without writing a redemption story. You can survive without thanking your trauma for the "gifts" it gave you.

You're allowed to look at what happened and say: "That should never have happened to anyone. It taught me nothing I needed to know. And I refuse to be grateful for pain I didn't deserve."

That's not bitter. That's not stuck. That's just true.

And sometimes the truth doesn't uplift. Sometimes it just sits there, heavy and real, refusing to be transformed into anything prettier.

12.5
What Doesn't Kill You Still Hurts Like Hell

Author's Note:

This one's for the survivor who's sick of hearing how "resilient" they are. Who's tired of being praised for surviving what should've never happened. You didn't get stronger. You got scarred. And this chapter isn't here to reframe that. It's here to name it. Because not every injury makes you wiser. Some just hurt. And that matters too.

What Didn't Kill You Still Changed Everything

You're at your work leaving party, and your boss raises her glass. "We'll miss you, but mostly we'll miss your incredible resilience. The way you handled that difficult client situation last year? Amazing strength."

Everyone nods, smiling. They're talking about the months you worked eighteen-hour days because going home meant being alone with memories. The "difficult client" who reminded you of your ex, whose emails made you vomit in the office bathroom. The "strength" of showing up when your hands shook so badly you could barely type.

You smile back. Say thank you. Don't mention that you're leaving because you can't do it anymore. That "resilient" feels like another word for "convenient." That you're not standing taller—you're walking with a limp they've all learned to ignore.

A woman told me: "Everyone kept saying how strong I was for 'bouncing back so quickly.' But I wasn't bouncing. I was dissociating. I'd perfected the art of looking functional while being completely absent. They saw composure. I felt nothing. That's not strength. That's a trauma response wearing a blazer."

You're not "better for it." You're still flinching when the phone rings at certain times. You're still second-guessing when you laugh too loud. You're still learning how to exist in a room without apologising for the space you take up.

They Call It Growth. You Call It Exhaustion

Your friend says, "You've grown so much. You can read people so well now. You always know when something's off."

You don't tell them it's because you had to. That you learned to track micro-expressions like your safety depended on it—because it did. That you can predict someone's mood by their footsteps, their breathing, the way they close a door.

A survivor once described it: "My therapist called it 'hypervigilance.' My friends call it 'intuition.' But I know what it really is—a nervous system that never learned how to rest. I'm not insightful. I'm traumatised. There's a difference."

You learned to scan every room for exits. To have three different responses ready for any question. To disappear emotionally while maintaining eye contact. To make yourself smaller before anyone could ask you to shrink.

A man told me: "People say I'm such a good listener. But I'm not listening out of kindness. I'm listening for danger. Every conversation is threat assessment. That's not a skill. That's survival programming that won't shut off."

You're Not Lucky You Survived. You're Unlucky You Had to

You're at therapy, and the therapist says, "You should be proud of how far you've come."

Proud. Of surviving something that nearly killed you. Like you won some terrible lottery where the prize is being alive but altered.

A woman once told me she was at her book club discussing an abusive marriage storyline when someone said, "At least experiences like that teach you who you really are, right?"

She looked up from her coffee. "It didn't teach me who I was," she said quietly. "It taught me to question everything I thought I knew about myself. I still Google things I'm certain of because he convinced me I was always wrong. I check weather apps three times because I don't trust my own eyes to know if it's raining."

"I didn't find my strength. I lost my ability to trust my own mind. I already knew who I was before him. What I needed was for someone to stop telling me I was crazy."

Let them call you strong. But you know what it cost. The years of sleep. The spontaneity. The ability to receive a compliment without wondering what they want. The simple pleasure of a surprise without panic.

Strength Was Never the Prize

A survivor told me: "Someone said I must be so much stronger now. I said, 'No, I'm so much more tired.' They looked confused. Like exhaustion couldn't coexist with survival. But I'm not stronger. I'm depleted. There's a difference between building muscle and breaking bones."

You didn't come out of this with superpowers. You came out still shaking, still rebuilding, still trying to believe your own instincts about whether it's Tuesday or Wednesday, whether you locked the door, whether that tone meant danger or nothing at all.

You don't owe anyone gratitude for your pain. You don't owe your abuser credit for your "growth." You don't owe the world an inspirational comeback story.

Practical Step

Write yourself a different kind of list. Not what you learned or how you grew, but what it actually cost you. The sleep you lost. The friends you couldn't explain it to. The jobs you left because you couldn't concentrate. The relationships you sabotaged because safety felt like suffocation. The simple pleasures—surprise parties, unexpected phone calls, someone walking behind you—that now trigger panic.

Don't try to find meaning in these losses. Just acknowledge them. Say: "This is what it took from me. I didn't need to lose these things to become 'stronger.' I just needed to not be harmed."

Why It Matters

Because the world keeps trying to package your pain as progress, your trauma as transformation. But you're allowed to refuse the reframe. You're allowed to say it just hurt.

If You Remember One Thing

What didn't kill you still tried to. And you don't have to dress that up as wisdom or wear it like a badge of honour.

You're not better because of what happened. You're better despite it. Every good thing in your life now isn't because of the pain—it's in defiance of it.

You're not a phoenix. You're not a warrior. You're not an inspiration.

You're a person who lived through hell and is tired of being congratulated for not dying in it.

And finally—finally—you get to stop pretending the burns made you beautiful. They just made you burned. And that's allowed to be the whole truth.

12.6
You Feel Too Much? Good
That Means You're Still Here

Author's Note:

This one's for the survivor who keeps trying to "get over it," to stay calm, to move on. But recovery doesn't begin with numbing. It begins with honesty. The first, most paradoxical step to feeling less overwhelmed is to stop fighting what you already feel. Let it in. Let it breathe. You're not weak for feeling deeply. You're still alive, and that's where recovery begins.

You Can't Heal What You Refuse to Feel

You're in the supermarket car park, and it's happening again. That wave of grief that comes from nowhere—or maybe from the song on the radio, or the couple holding hands by the trolleys, or just Tuesday existing when they're not in it anymore.

Your throat tightens. Eyes burn. You grip the steering wheel and think: "Not here. Not now. Get it together."

You do the breathing exercise. Count to ten. Think of three things you can see, two you can hear, one you can smell. Anything to push it down, pack it away, get through the door without falling apart.

A woman told me: "I spent six months perfecting the art of not crying. I'd bite my tongue until it bled. Dig my nails into my palms. Recite multiplication tables backwards. I thought if I could just stop feeling so much, I'd be okay."

"Then one day, I couldn't hold it anymore. Sobbed in a petrol station bathroom for twenty minutes. And you know what? After I stopped fighting it, I could actually breathe for the first time in months. The tears weren't drowning me. The effort of holding them in was."

You're not drowning in emotion. You're suffocating from the effort of containing it.

Pain Doesn't Leave Just Because You Ignore It

A man described his breaking point: "I kept telling myself I was fine. Threw myself into work, the gym, anything to stay busy. I thought if I just kept moving, the grief couldn't catch up."

"One night, I'm brushing my teeth, and I see her toothbrush holder—empty, but still there. Six months after she left. And I just... collapsed. Right there on the bathroom floor. All that running, and the grief had been waiting in my bathroom the whole time."

You don't get less sad by scheduling your days so full there's no room for sadness. You don't get less angry by smiling through meetings while rage sits like acid in your stomach. You don't heal by perfecting the performance of being okay.

A survivor once told me: "Everyone kept saying 'You're doing so well!' because I never cried at work. But I was crying in my car every lunch break. In disabled toilets. In the freezer aisle at Tesco because no one goes there to buy frozen peas at 9 PM."

"The grief didn't get smaller because I hid it. It just got lonelier."

You Don't Need to Explain the Feeling to Let It Move

You're lying in bed at 3 AM, and the sadness is there again. Heavy. Wordless. You try to trace it back—was it the email? The dream? The way the light hit the kitchen counter?

But there's no clear reason. Just this weight on your chest that has no story, no timeline, no neat explanation. Your body holding something your mind can't name.

A woman once told me: "I used to torture myself asking 'Why am I like this? Why can't I just be normal?' Then my therapist said, 'What if instead of asking why, you asked what? What does this feeling need? What is it asking for?'"

"So I started asking. The anger needed to be heard. The sadness needed to be held. The fear needed to be told it was safe now. I stopped needing reasons and started offering responses."

You don't need to understand why Thursday feels impossible. You don't need to justify why certain songs make you nauseous. You just need to stop demanding receipts from your own grief. Your body knows things your mind hasn't caught up to yet.

The Relief Comes From Admitting, Not Avoiding

A survivor described the moment she stopped fighting: "I was at work, and someone asked if I was okay. Usually I'd say 'fine!' But that day, I just said, 'No. I'm not okay. I'm sad and I don't know why and I'm tired of pretending otherwise.'"

"They didn't run. They didn't judge. They just said, 'That sounds really hard.' And somehow, naming it out loud made it... smaller. Like it had been this huge shadow, but when I turned on the light, it was just sadness. Just human sadness that was allowed to exist."

Practical Step

Find somewhere private—your car, your room, the shower. Pick the emotion you've been fighting hardest. Say it out loud, even if your voice shakes: "I'm angry." "I'm heartbroken." "I'm terrified." "I'm lost." Don't explain it. Don't justify it. Don't fix it. Just let it exist in the air for a moment.

Notice what happens in your body when you stop holding the door closed. The relief might not be immediate, but notice: does your chest feel slightly less tight? Does your jaw unclench even a little? That's your body recognising you're finally on the same team.

This isn't about understanding your feelings or making them go away. It's about letting them exist in your body without wrestling them into silence.

Why It Matters

Every feeling you suppress takes energy to hold down. That's energy you need for healing, for rebuilding, for getting through Tuesday. When you name what you feel, you stop spending strength on denial and start spending it on recovery.

If You Remember One Thing

It's not the tears that exhaust you. It's the muscle tension of holding them back. It's not the anger that depletes you. It's the smile you force over it until your face aches.

Every feeling you've tried to bury is still alive in you, taking up space, using your energy to stay hidden. They're not asking to consume you. They're asking to move through you.

The woman who sobbed in the petrol station? She told me: "I thought if I let myself cry, I'd never stop. But I did stop. Twenty minutes. That's all it needed. Twenty minutes of honest tears instead of six months of pretended strength."

The moment you stop fighting what you feel—the moment you say out loud, "I'm still hurting," "I'm still grieving," "I'm still angry and that's okay"—something shifts.

Not all at once. Not clean. Not fixed.

But you stop drowning in the effort of not drowning. You stop exhausting yourself with the performance of being fine.

And maybe, for the first time in months, you take a breath that actually reaches your lungs.

That's not weakness. That's the beginning of coming back to life.

12.7
You're Allowed to Cry
Without Explaining Why

Author's Note:

This one's for the part of you that still freezes when the tears come. The part that apologises for crying. That turns away. That hides. Not because the grief isn't real, but because somewhere along the way, you learned that being seen in pain meant being punished, mocked, or dismissed. This chapter is your permission slip. You don't have to justify your tears. You just have to let them come.

You Don't Cry for Attention. You Cry Because It Hurts

You're washing dishes, and your neighbour's wind chimes start singing. Same notes they always play. But today they sound like the ones from your childhood home, before everything went wrong, and suddenly you're sobbing into the sink.

Your partner walks in. "What's wrong? What happened?"

You try to explain: wind chimes, childhood, the way morning light used to hit the kitchen table when you felt safe. But it sounds ridiculous. How do you explain crying about wind chimes to someone who needs logical reasons for tears?

"I don't know," you finally say, ashamed of the non-answer.

A woman told me: "My ex would interrogate my tears. 'Why are you crying? What specifically triggered this? Is this about me? About us? About your mother?' Like I needed to submit a report with citations before I was allowed to feel anything."

"Now I'm with someone who just hands me tissues and sits nearby. No questions. No timeline. Just presence. First time it happened, I cried harder—because I'd never been allowed to just cry without defending it."

The tears aren't performative. They're evidence. Your body releasing what it held when it wasn't safe to feel.

You Learned That Tears Were Weapons Against You

You cried once during an argument. They said, "Oh, here come the waterworks. Trying to manipulate me with tears?"

You cried when they hurt you. They said, "You're too sensitive. It was just a joke."

You cried from exhaustion. They said, "Other people have real problems."

So you learned. Bathroom with the tap running. Car parked three streets away. Shower with music loud enough to cover the sound. You became an expert at silent crying, at crying that leaves no trace, at tears that don't inconvenience anyone.

A survivor told me: "I trained myself to cry without making sound. Without letting my face change. I could sit through dinner with tears rolling down my cheeks, and no one would notice because I'd learned to keep my expression completely neutral. I called it 'stealth crying.'"

"Even now, years later, when I cry alone, I still muffle it. Like someone might hear and punish me for having feelings."

Every Tear You've Hidden Is Still Waiting

A woman described unpacking in her new apartment, the first place that was truly hers: "I found a photo of myself from years before, smiling at some work event. And I just… broke. Standing there in my own living room, completely alone, and my hand shot up to cover my mouth."

"I was muffling my own crying in my own home where no one could hear me. That's when I realised—I'd been trained to hide evidence of my own pain. Even from myself."

She practised crying with her hand down. Just standing there, letting the sound exist. "It felt like breaking a rule. Like any second someone would burst in and tell me to stop being dramatic. But no one came. It was just me and my tears and my own permission."

A man told me: "First time I cried in front of my new therapist, I immediately started explaining—sorry, I don't usually do this, I'm not trying to be difficult, I know it's not that bad. She stopped me. 'You're allowed to cry here. No explanation needed.' I cried harder then. Twenty years of defended tears, finally unnecessary."

You Don't Need a Reason That Makes Sense

You're in the cereal aisle, and you see the brand your grandmother used to buy, and your eyes fill. You're driving and that song comes on—not even a sad song, just one that existed during a sad time—and you have to pull over. You're getting dressed and the soft fabric of your jumper reminds you of being held when you still trusted holding, and you're crying before you understand why.

A survivor once said: "People want tears to make narrative sense. Beginning, middle, end. Clear trigger, logical response. But trauma tears don't work that way. Sometimes you cry because it's Tuesday and your body remembers Tuesday. Sometimes you cry because you're finally safe enough to. Sometimes you cry because you couldn't for so long that now you need to, even when nothing's wrong."

Practical Step

Choose one safe space—your car, your shower, your bedroom. Next time tears come, go there and let them happen completely. No hand over mouth. No muffling. No apologies, even to yourself. Set a timer for ten minutes if you're afraid you'll never stop.

Most tears, when truly allowed, complete themselves in less time than we think. Notice what your body does when it's allowed to release without resistance—the shoulders that finally drop, the breathing that finally deepens, the strange peace that comes after.

This isn't about understanding why you're crying. It's about letting your body do what it needs without requiring justification.

Why It Matters

Every tear you don't apologise for is reclaiming your right to feel. Every cry you don't muffle is telling your nervous system: we're safe enough now to have emotions without consequences.

If You Remember One Thing

Tears aren't proof you're not recovering. They're proof you're finally safe enough to feel what wasn't safe to feel before.

The woman who practised crying with her hand down? She told me: "Now I cry freely. At films. At kindness. At nothing. And no one dies. No one leaves. No one punishes me. Turns out tears are just salt water, not weapons."

You're not weak for crying on a good day. You're not unstable for crying at wind chimes. You're not manipulative for crying when someone hurt you.

You're allowed to weep for the years you couldn't. You're allowed to sob without a PowerPoint presentation explaining why. You're allowed to cry because it's Tuesday and your body remembers.

You're allowed.

And you don't need anyone's permission—not even your own perfectly logical explanation—to let your body release what it's been holding.

The tears know what they're doing. Even when you don't.

12.8
When The Reflex
Is to Turn on Yourself. Don't

Author's Note:

This chapter is about what happens when you leave a coercive relationship, but the voice that punished you keeps living inside your head. The abuser might be gone. But their rules remain: how you speak to yourself, how you judge yourself, how you react when you fall short. It's not discipline. It's conditioning. And now, your recovery depends on breaking that reflex. Not by being harder on yourself. But by learning to stop becoming their voice.

You Were Trained to Turn on Yourself

You drop a glass in your new kitchen, and before the pieces hit the floor, the voice starts: "Clumsy. Useless. Can't even hold a fucking glass properly."

Your hands shake as you clean up. Not from the accident—from the words. Because that's not your voice. It's theirs. Word for word, tone for tone, the exact script they used when you spilled wine three years ago.

They're gone. Blocked number, different city, no contact for months. But here you are, alone in your kitchen, punishing yourself with their words.

A woman told me: "Six months after I left, I burnt toast and called myself stupid for twenty minutes straight. His exact words, his exact tone. That's when I realised—I'd learned to do it for him."

You were told you were too much, too emotional, too sensitive, so you became your own monitor. Measuring every response. Muting every reaction. You were told your needs were inconvenient, so you learned to shame yourself before anyone else could.

And even now, after they're gone, that training kicks in instantly. One mistake, and their voice appears in your mouth.

The Reflex Isn't the Truth. It's Muscle Memory

You're running late for coffee with a friend. Traffic, parking, everything conspires against you. You text an apology, and they respond: "No worries! I'm just reading, take your time."

But in your head: "They're lying. They're angry. You're always late. You're selfish. Inconsiderate. This is why people leave you."

You arrive to find them genuinely unbothered, actually reading, actually fine. But you spend the first ten minutes apologising anyway, punishing yourself for a crime that only exists in your conditioning.

A survivor described it: "I was trained to pre-punish myself. If I thought I might have upset someone, I'd attack myself first—harder than they ever would. It was like paying a tax in advance, hoping it would protect me from their anger. But most of the time, they weren't even angry. I was just bleeding from wounds I kept giving myself."

A man told me: "My therapist asked me to write down what I say to myself when I make mistakes. When I read it back, I started crying. Because I realised—I would never speak to another human being that way. I wouldn't speak to an animal that way. But I'd been speaking to myself like that for years."

Recovery Doesn't Mean You Never Hear Their Voice

You're cooking dinner for your new partner, and you oversalt the pasta. The voice starts immediately: "You ruin everything. You can't do anything right. They're going to realise you're worthless."

Your partner tastes it, shrugs. "Bit salty. Got any butter? That usually helps."

No anger. No contempt. No "How could you be so careless?" Just... problem-solving. Together.

A woman once told me she spent a whole day crying after sending a message to her ex that she regretted. Not because it hurt him, but because she'd broken her own rule: "No more reaching out."

"I didn't even get a reply," she said. "But I punished myself for days. I kept hearing his voice: 'You're pathetic. You're weak. No self-control.' Even though he wasn't there anymore. Even though he'd never know I'd done it."

That's what coercive control does. It installs a critic that doesn't need the original source anymore. It keeps you under surveillance in your own mind.

The Moment of Interruption Is Everything

A survivor described her breakthrough: "I was berating myself for forgetting to buy milk. Really vicious stuff—'You're useless, you can't even handle basic tasks.' Mid-sentence, I stopped. Out loud, I said: 'Wait. That's not me. That's him.'"

"I stood in my hallway and said it again: 'That's his voice, not mine. I don't talk to myself like that.' It felt insane. But also like... revolution."

She started catching it more often. The voice would start—"You're so stupid"—and she'd interrupt: "That's him." Not arguing with it. Not analysing it. Just naming it as foreign.

"Sometimes I'd catch it immediately. Sometimes not until I'd been spiraling for an hour. But each time I interrupted it, it got a tiny bit quieter. Like it knew it had been caught."

Practical Step

When you catch yourself using cruel words you'd never say to a friend, stop mid-thought. Say out loud, even if it feels strange: "That's not my voice. That's theirs." Then, speak to yourself the way you'd speak to someone you love who's struggling: "You're doing your best. It's okay to make mistakes. You're still learning how to be gentle with yourself."

This isn't about positive thinking or affirmations. It's about recognising which thoughts actually belong to you and which ones were installed by someone who benefited from your self-hatred. Even if you only catch it once in ten times, that's not failure. That's progress. Every interruption matters. Even if the voice comes back five seconds later. You're teaching your brain that this critic is an intruder, not an authority.

Why It Matters

Because recovering from coercive control means learning to speak to yourself like someone who deserves kindness. Because the voice that attacks you isn't trying to help you improve—it's trying to keep you small, scared, and controllable, even from a distance.

If You Remember One Thing

You were trained to believe that harshness makes people better. That punishment means progress. That shame is the price of growth. But that's not recovery. That's residue.

The woman who caught herself mid-criticism? She told me: "It's been a year. The voice still shows up sometimes. But now I recognise it immediately. Like hearing a song from a nightmare—familiar but not welcome. And I don't let it finish its sentence."

The real work isn't being harder on yourself. It's refusing to keep doing their job for them. When the reflex is to turn on yourself, that's your moment. Not to be perfect. Not to never struggle. But to interrupt the transmission.

Every time you catch that voice and say "That's not mine," you're reclaiming territory in your own mind.

That's the moment you stop being their echo. That's the moment you become your own.

12.9
Recovery:
It's Quiet. It's Lonely. It's Brave as Hell

Author's Note:

This one's for the survivor who gets up, gets through the day, and goes to bed still carrying everything, without anyone noticing. You don't get applause. You don't get check-ins. You don't get meals dropped at your door or people texting to say, "I'm proud of you." But you're still doing recovery. Still showing up. Still choosing not to give up. And that? That deserves respect.

You're Recovering Without Witnesses and That Counts

It's 11 PM on a Friday, and you're sitting on your bathroom floor with scissors, cutting up the shirt they bought you. The one that still smells like their cologne. The one you've kept folded in your drawer for eight months because throwing it away felt like admitting something you weren't ready to admit.

No one's here to see you do it. No friend holding your hand. No therapist nodding approval. Just you, alone, cutting fabric into pieces small enough that you can't put them back together when the 2 AM regret hits.

Your chest feels hollow and full at the same time.

A woman told me: "I deleted our entire message thread at 3 AM on a Tuesday. Two years of conversations. Thousands of photos. Gone. My finger hovered over the delete button for twenty minutes. No one was awake to talk me through it. No one saw me sob afterwards. But I did it. And the next morning, I woke up and the world hadn't ended."

You're not performing recovery for anyone. You're living it in the spaces between what people see. In the car park where you sit for ten minutes after therapy, too drained to drive. In the shower where you practise conversations you'll never have. In the grocery store where you walk past their favourite wine without buying it, and no one knows that's a victory.

Just Because It's Quiet Doesn't Mean It's Not Progress

You're at work, and a colleague mentions they're getting divorced. Everyone rallies—offers of help, checking in, "How are you holding up?" You smile, offer support too. Don't mention that you've been rebuilding from abuse for two years and no one's asked you that question once.

Not because your pain is less real. But because coercive control doesn't leave visible bruises. Because "my ex was controlling" doesn't get the same response as "my ex hit me." Because emotional violence doesn't get casseroles and care packages.

A survivor told me: "I watched my coworker get flowers after her breakup. Everyone knew her story—he cheated, it was public, dramatic. Meanwhile, I was having panic attacks in the supply cupboard because someone walked like my ex. But my trauma was invisible, so my recovery had to be too."

You didn't relapse today. Didn't text them back even though their birthday notification made your hands shake. You made dinner instead of skipping another meal. You breathed through the panic in the cereal aisle when someone wore their perfume. You asked for help—maybe just once, maybe just for directions, but you asked.

And no one clapped. No one noticed. But you did it anyway.

You're Rebuilding Without Reinforcement

A woman once told me she was at her sister's birthday dinner when someone made a joke that sounded exactly like something her abuser used to say. The same tone, same timing, same cruel punchline dressed as humour.

"I felt myself starting to leave my body," she said. "That floating feeling where you're watching yourself from above. But I stayed. Pressed my feet into the floor. Dug my nails into my palm. Counted the candles on the cake. Stayed present."

She finished her meal. Sang happy birthday. Hugged everyone goodnight. No one noticed she'd just won a battle that took every ounce of strength she had.

"I used to think recovery had to be witnessed to count," she said. "Now I know the most important battles happen where no one can see. In the pause before you respond. In the breath you take instead of running. In the moment you choose to stay in your body when every cell wants to leave."

Your Recovery Isn't Less Real Because It's Unseen

You're recovering in a thousand tiny moments no one sees. The morning you play music they hated. The afternoon you wear the colour they said looked terrible on you. The evening you cook the meal they called "disgusting" and enjoy every bite.

A survivor told me: "My biggest recovery moment happened in my kitchen at 6 AM. I was making coffee the way I like it—too much sugar, the way my ex said was 'childish.' And I realised I hadn't thought to make it their way first. For the first time in three years, I just made my own damn coffee. I cried. But they were good tears. And no one saw them but me."

Practical Step

Create a private recovery record just for you. Not a journal—that can feel too heavy. Just a note in your phone where you write one line each day: "Today I survived the grocery store." "Today I didn't check their Instagram." "Today I said no to something." "Today I chose myself."

Don't share it. Don't post it. This isn't content—it's evidence. Evidence that you're doing the work even when no one's watching. On the hard days, scroll back through it. See how many invisible battles you've already won.

Why It Matters

Because you deserve to witness your own courage. Because recovery without recognition is still recovery. Because someone needs to see what you're doing, and that someone can be you.

If You Remember One Thing

You're doing this without backup. Without a cheer squad. Without someone reaching across the table to squeeze your hand and say, "I see how hard you're fighting."

Your recovery doesn't trend. Doesn't get liked or shared. Doesn't come with a certificate of completion.

The woman cutting up the shirt alone? She told me later: "I kept one button. Put it in a box labeled 'Things I Survived.' It's not inspiring. It's not beautiful. It's just proof that I did the hardest thing—I let go, alone, at 11 PM on a Friday when no one was watching."

That's what courage actually looks like.

And if no one else says it, I will: I respect the hell out of what you're doing. Every invisible victory. Every silent boundary. Every time you choose yourself when no one's there to see it.

You're pulling off something most people will never understand—healing without witnesses, recovering without recognition, rebuilding without reinforcement.

And that's more than enough. That's everything.

12.10
If It Was That Easy
You Would've Left

Author's Note:

This one's for the survivor who's sick of hearing, "If it was that bad, why didn't you leave?" You didn't stay because you enjoyed the pain. You didn't stay because you were naive. You stayed because leaving wasn't simple, not emotionally, not financially, not physically. And the people who ask why you stayed have no idea what it costs to walk away.

"Just Leave" Isn't a Plan. It's a Fantasy

You're standing in the bathroom at 2 AM, staring at the bruise on your arm that looks like fingerprints. Your sister's number is in your phone. She lives three hours away. She'd come get you if you called.

But your name isn't on the lease. Your paycheck goes into their account. Your son is asleep in the next room, and the custody papers they made you sign say you can't take him out of state.

You dial the first six digits of your sister's number. Then delete them.

A woman told me: "Everyone asks why I didn't just pack a bag and go. I did pack a bag. Three times. But where was I supposed to go with two kids, no money, and a partner who'd convinced everyone I was unstable? The women's shelter was full. My family said I was overreacting. I had a bag but nowhere to take it."

You didn't have money stashed—they checked the statements. You didn't have friends left—they'd isolated you slowly, fight by fight. You didn't have proof—emotional abuse doesn't photograph well.

You Were Trapped By More Than Just Fear

You're at the bank, trying to open your own account. The teller smiles. "Will this be joint with your spouse?"

"No, just mine."

She needs your address. The one they know. She needs your phone number. The one they monitor. She needs an initial deposit. Money you don't have because they handle the finances.

A survivor told me: "I tried to leave six times. First time, they'd cancelled my credit cards. Second time, they'd called my job saying I was having a mental breakdown. Third time, they showed up at my friend's house with flowers and tears, and my friend let them in because 'they seemed so sorry.'"

"Fourth time, I made it to a hotel, but they'd frozen our joint account. Fifth time, my mother called me selfish for 'breaking up the family.' Sixth time worked because I'd spent a year secretly planning. A year. That's what it took."

You're googling "how to leave abusive relationship" on incognito mode at the library because they check your browser history. The list says: gather important documents. But they keep those locked up. Save money. But they monitor every penny. Tell someone. But they've convinced everyone you're the difficult one.

Even When You Leave, You're Not Free

A woman described her escape: "I left with my daughter at 4 AM while he was passed out. Drove to another state. Got a restraining order. Changed our names. That was three years ago. I still check my rearview mirror constantly. Still panic when I see his car model. Still wake up at 4 AM sometimes, ready to run again."

"People say 'Why didn't you leave sooner?' They don't understand—I'm still leaving. Every day, I'm still choosing to stay gone, and it's still hard."

You finally get out, and they become the victim. Post about their broken heart. Tell everyone you abandoned them. Your mutual friends don't know what to believe. Some choose them because their story is simpler—you're crazy, they're heartbroken. Case closed.

Meanwhile, you're sleeping on couches. Rebuilding credit they destroyed. Fighting for custody they're contesting. Explaining gaps in employment. Starting therapy you can't afford. And everyone wants to know why it took you so long.

It Wasn't That You Didn't Want To Go

A man told me: "I stayed three extra years because leaving meant my kids would be with him unsupervised every other weekend. At least when I was there, I could be a buffer. Protect them. Document everything. Build a case."

"My lawyer said judges don't like to believe mothers can be abusive. Said I needed overwhelming evidence. So I stayed and gathered proof while everyone wondered why I didn't 'just leave.' Those three years nearly killed me. But now I have full custody. My kids are safe. That's why I stayed."

You needed childcare they'd sabotaged. You needed money they'd hidden. You needed documents they'd destroyed. You needed a world that believes survivors without requiring them to be perfect victims. But you got judgment. "I would never stay." "The first time someone raised a hand to me..." "You must have liked something about it."

A woman once said to me: "I left with a backpack and $50. Everyone said I should've gone sooner. They asked why I stayed. No one asked how I survived."

Practical Step

Write a letter to the version of you who stayed. Not with shame or anger, but with compassion.

Thank them for keeping you alive when leaving could have meant worse. Thank them for buying time to plan. Thank them for protecting what they could—your children, your sanity, your life.

Tell them: "You weren't weak. You were strategic. You left when you could leave and survive it. That took more strength than anyone will ever understand."

Keep this letter somewhere you'll see it—your favourite bag, phone notes, bedside drawer—so it interrupts the old reflex to shame yourself for not leaving sooner.

Why It Matters

Because survival isn't just about escaping danger. It's about escaping in a way that doesn't destroy everything else. Sometimes staying was the safest choice until it wasn't.

If You Remember One Thing

You didn't stay because you were weak. You stayed because leaving meant losing everything at once—your home, your children, your financial stability, your safety, maybe your life.

The woman with the backpack and $50? She's housed now. Has a job. Her kids are with her. But it took five years to rebuild what leaving cost her. Five years. And she's the success story.

You stayed because escape wasn't just walking out a door. It was a complex extraction from a life they'd wrapped around you like wire. Every attempt to leave drew blood.

Freedom isn't always fast. It's slow, expensive, dangerous, and layered.

You left when leaving wouldn't kill you. You survived however you needed to. And that's the only timeline that ever mattered.

No one gets to judge how long it took you to save your own life. Not even you.

Part 13
Reveal

This isn't a comeback
It's a becoming

13.1
Reclaiming Your Inner Knowing

Author's Note:

This chapter is about reclaiming something you were trained to doubt: your own knowing. If you've ever found yourself frantically searching for answers everywhere but inside yourself, because someone convinced you that your gut couldn't be trusted, this is where we start undoing that damage.

You Keep Looking for Answers Like They Live Somewhere Else

You're scrolling through your phone at 2 AM. Another article about narcissism. Another quiz about toxic relationships. Your search history reads like a desperate prayer: "How to know if..." "Signs that someone is..." "Am I crazy or..."

Your finger hovers over the call button. Maybe your sister will know. Maybe this therapist on TikTok has the answer. Maybe if you just find the right book, the right expert, the right diagnosis, you'll finally understand what happened to you.

But here's what happened: You didn't lose your knowing. You were taught to distrust it.

Your breath caught for a reason. Your skin flushed for a reason. Your pulse quickened when they entered the room for a reason. Your whole body was carrying the truth long before you could put words to it.

Remember that moment when you first said, "Something feels off about them"? Before they laughed and called you paranoid. Before they rolled their eyes and said you were being dramatic. Before they convinced you that your concern was actually your problem.

You knew. Your body knew. That tight feeling in your chest when they walked in the room—that was knowledge. That sick feeling when they smiled at others while crushing you privately—that was truth. Until you stopped listening to the voice that was trying to protect you.

You Weren't Born Doubting Yourself

Watch a toddler for five minutes. They know exactly what they want. They trust their hunger, their tiredness, their joy, their fear. No committee meetings in their head. No second-guessing their tears.

You were that certain once. Before someone taught you that your tears were manipulation. That your anger was too much. That your needs were exhausting. That your boundaries were selfish.

A woman told me she remembers the exact moment she stopped trusting herself. "I was seven. I told my mum that Dad scared me when he drank. She said I was being silly, that Daddy just got louder when he was happy. I learned that day that my fear was wrong. It took me thirty years and an abusive marriage to realise my seven-year-old self had been right all along."

That knowing didn't disappear. It just learned to whisper because speaking up wasn't safe.

Your Instincts Weren't Paranoia. They Were Pattern Recognition

You felt it in your bones before you could name it. The way conversations with them felt like walking through a minefield. The way their "I'm sorry" always came with a "but" that erased the apology. The way you started making yourself smaller, quieter, less problematic.

A survivor told me she'd been second-guessing herself for months about ending a friendship. "Everyone said I was being dramatic. This person was 'harmless', just 'a bit intense'. But I dreaded their calls. My stomach would drop when I saw their name on my phone."

One day, instead of asking for more opinions, she sat in her car after work and asked herself: "How do I actually feel when I'm with them?"

"The answer hit me like a train," she said. "Exhausted. Erased. Like I was performing a version of myself that kept them happy. I'd been looking for permission to trust what my body had been screaming for months."

This isn't about becoming someone new. It's about returning to the self you were taught to bury.

The Second-Guessing Isn't a Personality Trait

You text three friends the same question. You rehearse conversations in the shower, preparing defences for feelings you haven't even expressed yet. You screenshot messages to analyse them later, searching for proof that you're not imagining things.

This isn't because you're naturally indecisive. Someone systematically dismantled your trust in your own perceptions. They edited your memories. They rewrote your experiences. They convinced you that your feelings were symptoms of your problems, not responses to theirs.

But underneath all that learned doubt, your knowing is still there. It's the nausea when you see their name. It's the relief when they cancel plans. It's the way your shoulders drop when they leave the room.

Starting to Listen Again

This week, try something small. When your body reacts to someone or something—that tension in your jaw, that heat rising in your chest, that sudden need to hold your breath—don't immediately talk yourself out of it. Don't search for articles about why you might be wrong. Just sit with it for thirty seconds and ask: "What is this trying to tell me?"

You might hear: "This person isn't safe." Or "This boundary needs to exist." Or simply:

"No." Whatever you hear, don't dismiss it. Write it down—even just one word. "Tired." "Angry." "Trapped." "Safe." Over time, those scraps of truth will start to pile up into a map you can trust.

Your body kept the receipts even when your mind was told to forget them.

Start with tiny decisions. Choose what to have for lunch without asking anyone. Pick a film without checking reviews. Say no to one thing without explaining why. Each time you trust yourself with something small, you rebuild the bridge back to your own wisdom.

If You Remember One Thing

The voice you're searching for at 2 AM isn't in another article about trauma bonds. It's not in your friend's opinion about whether you're overreacting. It's not in that therapist's Instagram post that might finally explain everything.

It's the quiet knowing that makes your chest tighten when something's not right. It's the relief that floods your whole body when you finally say no. It's the way you can suddenly breathe again when you make the decision that's true for you, even if nobody else understands it.

You don't need to learn how to trust yourself. You need to unlearn why you stopped.

Your instincts weren't wrong. They were inconvenient for someone who needed you to doubt them. Every time you listen to what you already know—even when your hands shake, even when people call you difficult—you take back a piece of yourself they tried to convince you never existed.

That knowing is still there. It never left. It's been waiting all this time for you to remember that it was right all along.

Each time you trust it, you're not just surviving—you're becoming. And that is what they can never take back.

13.2
Bring Back Softness

Author's Note:

This chapter is about recovery, not the polished kind, but the messy, honest kind. If you've ever felt like healing meant becoming tougher, stronger, or "above it all", this will help you come back to something softer. You don't need to become untouchable. You just need space to feel what they never let you feel.

You Were Taught That Feeling Made You Weak

You're in the bathroom at work, pressing toilet paper against your eyes, willing the tears to stop before someone notices. Your throat burns from swallowing everything down. Again.

Remember when you used to cry freely? Before someone rolled their eyes and said, "Here we go again." Before they walked out mid-sob, leaving you alone with your "drama." Before you learned that tears were ammunition they'd use against you later.

That crying made you manipulative. That needing a moment made you lazy. That showing hurt made you pathetic. That softness made you prey.

So you got sharp. You became the one who could handle anything. The one who never needed help. You started thinking recovery meant building higher walls, thicker skin, becoming impossible to wound.

But it doesn't. It's about becoming safe enough to feel again.

You Got Strong Because You Had To, Not Because You Wanted To

You're sitting in a meeting, and your colleague is crying about a deadline. Everyone rushes to comfort her. You watch, confused. When did crying become something people responded to with kindness instead of contempt?

You didn't choose this kind of resilience. You performed it to survive.

You held it together while they fell apart, because someone had to keep the household running. You swallowed your grief when your parent died because they said you were "dwelling on it." You laughed off the cruel comment at dinner because fighting back only made it worse.

Your jaw still aches from years of clenching. Your shoulders, your breath, even your stomach learned to brace. Your hands forgot how to be still—always fidgeting, picking, staying busy. Your skin went numb in places, like it was trying to protect you from feeling anything at all. Whole parts of your body rehearsed toughness as if it was the only way to stay alive.

A woman told me, "I thought I was healing every time I got through something without crying. I'd actually count the days—like sobriety chips, but for not feeling anything. Then one day, I was at my friend's house and her kid spilled juice on my shirt. I just started sobbing. Real, ugly crying. About juice. About everything."

She waited for her friend to get uncomfortable, to make a joke, to change the subject. "But she just sat there with me. Put her hand on my back. Said, 'I know it's not about the juice.' That's when I realised—I didn't need to toughen up. I needed to find people where tenderness wasn't dangerous."

The Goal Isn't to Rise Above. It's to Return to Yourself

You see those social media posts about "unbothered queens" and "choosing peace" and you wonder why you can't get there. Why anger still flares when you remember. Why certain songs still make your chest cave in. Why you can't just "let it go" and "move on."

Here's what they don't tell you: Being "unbothered" when you've been systematically bothered for years isn't healing. It's another performance. You don't need to meditate your way into tolerance for mistreatment. You don't need to breathe through boundary violations. You don't need to find the spiritual lesson in your suffering.

You need to know that anger is information, not failure. That grief means you're finally processing what you couldn't process then. That fear makes sense when trust was used against you. That feeling anything—even if it's messy, even if it's "too much"—means you're not dissociating anymore.

Learning to Let Feelings Move Through

This week, when a feeling rises—anger at the grocery store, sadness during a film, fear when someone raises their voice—try something different. Don't push it down. Don't talk yourself out of it. Don't scroll your phone to escape it.

Just name it quietly to yourself: "I'm angry." "I'm sad." "I'm scared." Put your hand on your chest and let it be there for thirty seconds. Not to fix it. Not to process it. Just to acknowledge: this feeling is real, and I'm allowed to have it.

If the feeling lingers, let it. If it passes, let it. Either way, you honoured it. You might notice your breath naturally deepens. Your shoulders might drop half an inch. Or you might feel nothing different at all. That's okay too. You're teaching your nervous system that emotions don't have to be emergencies anymore.

If You Remember One Thing

You're standing in your kitchen, and suddenly you're crying about something that happened three years ago. Your body is shaking with the force of what you never got to feel then. This isn't regression. This is your nervous system finally believing it's safe enough to process what it had to store.

You don't need to become unbreakable. You survived being broken and kept functioning anyway—that was the performance. Now you get to stop performing.

You don't need armour anymore. You need boundaries. You don't need to be untouchable. You need to choose who gets to touch you. You don't need to rise above your feelings. You need to feel them in spaces where they won't be weaponised against you.

Feeling isn't the failure. It's the return.

Your tears aren't weakness—they're defrosting. Your anger isn't toxic—it's clarity. Your sadness isn't wallowing—it's grieving what you deserved and didn't get. Your tenderness isn't what made you a target. It's what kept you human through dehumanisation.

And now, it's what you get to protect, nurture, and choose who deserves to witness. That softness they mocked? That's your compass back to yourself. Each feeling you allow is a small revolution against everyone who taught you that numbness was strength.

This is what becoming looks like: not the hard shell you built to survive, but the soft truth you finally get to live in. it.

13.3
You're Not Who You Were
Before Them and That's The Point

Author's Note:

This chapter is about the grief that hits when you realise you can't go back to who you were before the abuse. If you've ever caught yourself saying, "I just want to feel like myself again," you know that ache. But here's what no one tells you: that version of you wasn't built to survive what came next. And trying to resurrect them keeps you stuck in the past instead of stepping into who you actually are now.

You Keep Looking for the Old You Like They're Lost Property

You're sitting on your bedroom floor with a shoebox of photos. There you are at your friend's wedding, head thrown back, laughing at something you can't remember. There you are at the beach, unselfconscious in your swimming costume, not yet trained to hide. There you are at Christmas, leaning into someone's hug without calculating exit strategies.

Your finger traces that face. When did your eyes stop lighting up like that? When did your smile become something you practise in mirrors? You think: if I just rest enough, heal enough, meditate enough, maybe that person will come back. Maybe you can excavate them from under all this rubble.

But here's what you're starting to understand: that person lived in a different universe. One where "I love you" meant what it said. Where concern wasn't surveillance. Where you could disagree without consequences that lasted for days.

That version of you was never built for the world you know now.

You Weren't Supposed to Stay the Same

You're at a family dinner and your cousin is telling a story about her "crazy ex" who checks her phone. Everyone laughs. "Just change your password," your aunt says, like it's that simple. You feel yourself floating above the conversation, watching from somewhere outside your body.

The person you were before might have laughed too. Might have thought it was that simple. That person hadn't learned yet that changing passwords leads to interrogations. That privacy becomes "hiding something." That every boundary you set becomes evidence of your guilt.

The person you were before hadn't been systematically taught that love meant surveillance. Hadn't learned to scan faces for mood changes. Hadn't memorised the sound of angry footsteps versus disappointed footsteps versus the dangerous silence that meant you'd done something wrong but wouldn't know what until later.

Your stomach still drops at unexpected doorbells. Your legs get restless when conversations feel like interrogations. Your skin prickles when someone's energy shifts, even slightly, even if they claim nothing's wrong.

That version of you was whole. This version of you is forged.

You changed because surviving that changes everyone. Your nervous system rewired itself. Your brain developed new pathways. Your body learned to read danger in a shifted jaw muscle, a certain quality of silence, the way someone said "fine."

Who You Are Now Has Wisdom They Never Needed

You can spot manipulation in its infancy now. That subtle shift when someone's story doesn't quite track. The way they test your boundaries with "jokes" first. The calculated vulnerability that always somehow ends with you apologising.

You know what love-bombing feels like—that dizzy rush that feels like fate but is actually strategy. You recognise future-faking when someone paints elaborate dreams without ever taking a single concrete step. You can feel the moment concern crosses into control, when "I'm worried about you" becomes "You're worrying me."

A woman told me she ran into an old friend at a coffee shop. "You've changed," he said, frowning. "You used to be so easy-going. Now you're so... careful."

She stirred her coffee for a moment. "The person you miss would have stayed with someone who was killing her slowly. She would have called it love. I can't be her anymore. I won't."

He looked uncomfortable. "But don't you want to get back to normal?"

"This is my normal now," she said. "I know the difference between being loved and being consumed. The old me didn't even know there was a difference."

Stop Apologising for Your Evolution

Evolution isn't a flaw. It's the evidence you adapted when someone was trying to destroy you.

You're having coffee with someone new and they reach for your phone to look at a photo. Your whole body tenses. They notice. "Sorry," you say automatically. "I'm just weird about my phone."

You're not weird. You're someone who learned that phones become weapons. That message histories become prosecution evidence. That innocent friendships become affairs in the wrong hands. That privacy itself becomes proof of betrayal.

You're not paranoid for checking exits when you enter rooms. You're not difficult for needing to know plans in advance. You're not broken for tensing when someone's energy suddenly shifts. You're awake. And you don't have to apologise for the wisdom your survival gave you.

Learning to Honour Who You've Become

This week, write one sentence: "The person I am now knows..." and finish it with something you learned through surviving. Not something you lost—something you gained.

Maybe it's: "The person I am now knows that real love doesn't require surveillance." Or: "The person I am now knows the difference between compromise and erasure." Or simply: "The person I am now knows I deserve peace."

Stop trying to excavate who you were. Start celebrating who you became. Every boundary you have now, every moment of hesitation that keeps you safe, every instinct that proves correct—that's not damage. That's intelligence earned through survival.

If You Remember One Thing

You're standing in your kitchen at 2 AM, unable to sleep because you're replaying a conversation from three years ago. You're searching for the moment you should have known. The red flag you missed. The sign that could have saved you from all of this.

But you couldn't have known then what you know now. The person you were before hadn't learned yet that someone could dismantle you while saying they were helping you heal. Hadn't discovered that "I'm just trying to understand you" could mean "I'm gathering ammunition." Hadn't realised that some people study your vulnerabilities not to protect them but to exploit them.

The person you are now has walked through calculated psychological warfare and found the exit. You didn't just leave—you escaped someone who was rewriting your reality one "you're remembering it wrong" at a time. You survived someone who turned your own thoughts against you, who made you doubt your own perceptions until you couldn't trust your own mind.

You didn't lose yourself. You saved yourself from someone who was systematically erasing you.

You're not broken for being different now. You're alive because you're different now. The soft, trusting person you were before—they were beautiful. But they couldn't have survived this. You had to become someone who could.

And the fact that you're still here, still capable of recognising real love when you find it, still able to laugh even if your body stays half-braced—that's not just recovery. That's evolution.

You're not who you were before them. Thank god. That person wouldn't have survived. This person—the one reading this, the one who knows too much, the one who sees too clearly—this person did.

This isn't about going back. It's about becoming the person who could walk out and stay gone.

That's not damage. That's becoming exactly who you needed to be.

13. 4
They Count on Your Fear Of Being Alone. Disappoint Them

Author's Note:

This chapter is about how fear, especially the fear of being alone, is used to keep survivors tethered to harm. If you've ever stayed too long because silence felt scarier than mistreatment, this will help you name the trap and walk out of it. Loneliness isn't the danger. Staying lost in their noise is.

They Said You'd Be Lost Without Them

You're sitting in your flat at 7 PM on a Friday. The silence is so loud it hurts. No texts lighting up your phone. No plans. No voice filling the space. Just you and the sound of neighbours living their lives through thin walls.

You remember when Friday nights meant walking on eggshells at dinner parties, laughing at jokes that cut you, pretending everything was fine while they humiliated you with "funny stories" about your flaws. But at least you weren't alone. At least someone wanted you there, even if it was just to be their audience.

For a while after you left, they were right—you did feel lost. Because the silence after abuse is deafening, especially when the abuse came wrapped in company. Family dinners where you were the punchline. Holiday photos where you're smiling but your eyes are somewhere else. Warm voices on speakerphone that turned cold the second you disagreed.

It didn't look like violence. It looked like belonging. But belonging shouldn't cost your voice. Or your boundaries. Or your sense of self. They were never worried you'd be harmed without them. They were worried you'd realise you were being harmed with them.

Because nothing threatens an abuser more than your ability to sit with yourself and not run back to them for comfort.

They Weaponised Belonging

You used to have a full calendar. Birthdays, gatherings, group chats that never stopped pinging. Then you set one boundary—maybe you said no to lending money again, or stopped laughing at jokes about your trauma, or asked them not to share your private stories at parties.

Suddenly, the invitations stopped. The group chat went quiet when you typed. Mutual friends started having "scheduling conflicts" when you made plans. They didn't just punish you—they orchestrated your isolation.

They made themselves the centre of your social world. Your emotional hub. Your only source of "family," even when they were the ones drawing blood. So when you pulled away, it felt like being expelled from the only tribe you'd ever known.

A woman told me she spent Christmas alone for the first time after cutting contact with her family. "I sat there with my microwave meal, scrolling through everyone's family photos on Instagram. I'd never felt so wrong for choosing peace over performance.

But then I realised—this was the first Christmas I wasn't anxious. The first one where I wasn't bracing for the cutting remarks disguised as 'concern.' The silence was lonely, but it wasn't violent."

They Knew You Feared Isolation, So They Made Themselves the Cure

They studied your fears like a curriculum. Noticed how your voice got higher when you were alone too long. How you'd apologise for things that weren't wrong just to end the cold shoulder. How you'd rather be screamed at than ignored.

So they became your only medicine for the sickness they created. They'd withdraw until you were desperate for connection, then return with just enough warmth to make you grateful. A kind word after days of silence. A "How are you?" after weeks of punishment. A gift after they'd torn you down.

You'd feel your whole body relax when they finally acknowledged you again. That relief felt like love. But it wasn't—it was conditioning.

A survivor told me about a friendship that drained her for years. "Every time I tried to step back, she'd somehow know. A care package would arrive. A heartfelt text about how much I meant to her. She'd organise a surprise visit, bring my favourite coffee, listen like she actually cared. I'd think maybe I was being too sensitive, too demanding."

"One day I realised the pattern: she only showed kindness when I was leaving. The sweetness wasn't love—it was a leash, just long enough to make me think I was free."

Loneliness Isn't a Sign You Were Wrong. It's a Sign You're Finally Free

You're grocery shopping alone on a Sunday. You see couples picking out vegetables together, families filling their trolleys, friends laughing over wine selections. Your single basket feels like evidence of failure.

Your brain whispers: "At least when you were with them, you had someone to shop with. At least you weren't this alone."

But remember what shopping with them was really like. The comments about everything you chose. The sulking if you took too long. The way they'd make you feel guilty for buying the brand you preferred. The arguments in the car park. The silent treatment on the drive home.

Your nervous system was trained to associate their chaos with connection. Your body learned that anxiety meant someone cared. That walking on eggshells meant you mattered to someone. That being controlled meant being chosen.

But now, standing alone in that grocery store, you can buy the expensive coffee without justification. You can take your time in the produce section. You can change your mind without consequence. Your hands aren't shaking as you unpack the groceries. Your stomach isn't tight from waiting for the next explosion.

The loneliness isn't the danger—it's the detox.

Learning to Sit with the Silence

This week, when the loneliness hits—and it will—try something different. Instead of scrolling through their social media or reading old texts, write down what you're actually missing. Not the fantasy of who they could be, but the reality of who they were.

Write: "I miss having someone to eat dinner with" then add: "who criticised how I cooked." Write: "I miss having weekend plans" then add: "where I was always anxious." Write: "I miss feeling wanted" then add: "by someone who only wanted to control me."

Then write one thing you're free to do now that you couldn't before—no matter how small. Maybe it's watching a film they hated. Taking a long bath without being rushed. Calling a friend they didn't like. Eating cereal for dinner without commentary.

Finally, write this truth and put it somewhere you'll see it daily: "Loneliness isn't the price of recovery. It's the proof I'm no longer betraying myself to stay connected."

Because recovery can feel like abandonment when toxic people fall away. Your phone goes quiet. Your weekends empty out. The holidays get smaller. This reminder helps you flip the story: your solitude isn't punishment for leaving. It's evidence that you're no longer trading your peace for the performance of connection.

If You Remember One Thing

They built a world where being chosen by them—even badly—felt better than being alone. Where their criticism felt more bearable than silence. Where their conditional love seemed better than no love at all.

They taught you that alone meant abandoned. That quiet meant forgotten. That solitude meant you were too difficult to love. They made you believe that being controlled was the same as being cared for, that being surveilled meant you mattered.

But here's what they didn't expect: that you'd survive the silence they threatened you with.

That you'd sit in your empty flat on Friday night—the same Friday night from before—and realise the only voice criticising you now is the one they left in your head. That you'd learn to cook dinner for one without apology. That you'd discover that loneliness is temporary, but staying with someone who diminishes you leaves permanent marks.

They counted on your fear of being alone to keep you tethered. They built their whole strategy on the belief that you'd rather be destroyed together than whole alone. They expected you'd crawl back.

Disappoint them by thriving alone first. Choose the silence over the circus. Choose the empty flat over the full theatre where you're always the villain. Choose rebuilding alone over being demolished in company.

The loneliness will ease. Your peace won't.

Keep walking.

13.5
Leaving Isn't the End
It's When the Danger Peaks

Author's Note:

Leaving an abuser isn't freedom right away. It's the point where danger peaks. That's not to scare you. It's so you don't doubt yourself when things get louder after you finally go.

This chapter is here to steady you through it, so you can see the patterns clearly and take the steps that keep you alive.

The Escalation

Your phone lights up at 1:07 AM. Your hands tremble as you reach for it. The screen shows six missed calls. Three voicemails. You don't need to listen to know they're each a different version of reality—first desperate, then angry, then sickeningly sweet.

By morning, your stomach flips when your boss forwards you an email. "Just got this," she says, looking uncomfortable. "Thought you should know." It's from them, written in that concerned tone they perfected. "Just worried about her stability. She hasn't been herself lately. I thought you should know, as someone who cares about her career."

That same week, your card gets declined at the grocery store. The joint account you haven't touched—suddenly frozen. The streaming service logs you out mid-episode. Your location still showing on their phone through the family sharing you forgot to disable. The maps app, the cloud storage, the shared calendar—digital breadcrumbs you never knew you were leaving, all leading straight back to you.

A friend sends a screenshot of a social media post. Your name carefully not mentioned, but everyone knows. "Some people destroy everything good in their life and blame others for the wreckage." Seventeen mutual friends have already liked it.

Then the text: "I was at that coffee shop you love. The one near your sister's place." They know where you are, even when you haven't told them.

From the outside, it all looks petty—declined cards, vague posts, concerned emails. From the inside, it's suffocating. Each small invasion designed to make you feel there's nowhere they can't reach you. That's not coincidence. That's strategy.

Make staying gone feel harder than going back.

The Trap

You're lying on your friend's couch at 3 AM, scrolling through eighteen new messages. Your mind whispers: "It was easier when I stayed."

And in some ways, it was. Because they trained it that way. The house was quiet when you complied. The meals were peaceful when you agreed. The weekends were calm when you didn't question where they'd been. Chaos only came when you resisted. Peace was the reward for handing over control.

A woman told me that two weeks after she left, her ex had already threatened to take the dog, report her to child services for "mental instability," and tell her employer she was "having a breakdown."

"He was calmer when I stayed," she said, pressing her palms against her eyes. "God, it was so much easier when I stayed."

But that wasn't peace. That was captivity dressed up to look like calm. The exhaustion you feel now isn't proof you made a mistake. It's proof your body is finally processing what it couldn't when survival meant staying quiet.

The Switch

Monday morning: "I miss you so much I can't breathe."
Monday afternoon: "You're going to regret this."

Monday evening: "Please, just ten minutes. For what we had."

Tuesday dawn: "I'll destroy you."

Tuesday noon: "I'm sorry. I'm just in so much pain."

The whiplash isn't accidental. They know exactly which version of themselves will make you respond. The broken one who needs saving. The dangerous one who needs appeasing. The loving one who reminds you of the beginning.

Your daughter comes home from the weekend visit. "Daddy says you're sick. Daddy says you need help." She's seven. Her eyes are confused, searching your face for the truth.

Your throat closes. Every instinct screams to defend yourself, to explain the complexity she's too young to understand. But you don't need to argue with the script they gave her. You just pull her close and say: "That isn't true, sweetheart. I love you. You're safe here."

Then Wednesday: "Let's be civil about this. For the kids."

Thursday: "You've turned into someone I don't recognise."

Friday: "Can we just talk? Like adults? Ten minutes."

It feels like chaos, like they're spinning out of control. They're not. Each message is calculated bait. The hook is in making you engage, making you explain, making you step back into the dynamic where they lead and you follow.

The moment you recognise it as bait is the moment it starts losing power.

Why You Need Support

After the third night without sleep, after the fifteenth blocked call, after finding them parked outside your work "just wanting to talk," you finally stop pretending you're fine.

You send your cousin three words: "I'm not okay."

She doesn't ask for the whole story. Doesn't demand a timeline or an explanation for why you stayed so long. She shows up with milk and bread and a phone charger. Sits on your floor while you shake. Holds your phone while you breathe through another wave of messages.

Together, you pick a code word that means "call the police now." Write it on a sticky note hidden behind the spice rack. She programmes her number into your phone under "Pizza Delivery" in case they check. These aren't paranoid gestures. They're life-saving strategies.

The room still spins, but less. Your chest still tight, but breathing. Connection doesn't fix everything, but isolation is how abuse wins. And right now, not being alone is enough.

Why No Contact Saves You

You type a paragraph explaining why you left. Delete it. Type a single sentence defending your decision. Delete that too.

Finally, you send only: "Pickup 3pm at the library."

Their reply arrives in seconds—a wall of text about your selfishness, your mental state, your failures as a partner and parent. Your finger hovers over the keyboard. Every cell in your body wants to defend yourself, to make them understand, to have the last word.

You don't respond.

An hour later, a softer message. "I'm sorry. I just love you so much."
Then a heart emoji.
Then: "Please. Just say something."

Your silence holds. For the first time, you feel the unexpected power of not walking back into a fight you've already left. Every unanswered message is a boundary. Every ignored call is freedom. Every time you refuse to reply, you disappoint the script they wrote for you.

Documentation Matters

You screenshot the 47 messages from Tuesday night. The ones that swing from "I'll kill myself" to "You're dead to me" to "Baby, please come home." You print the emails. Note the times they drove past your sister's house. Save the voicemail where they sob, then threaten, then sob again.

Even when you want to delete it all and pretend this never happened. Even when it feels petty to keep count. Even when friends say, "Just move on."

Every note you keep is evidence that protects your truth later. Because they will stand calm in a courtroom while you shake. They will say it never happened. They will paint you as vindictive, unstable, bitter. The paper trail is your witness when others are too afraid to be.

But documentation doesn't just guard your future case. It steadies your present self. On the days when they're being so reasonable that you question your own memory, you can look at the screenshots and remember: this happened. I didn't imagine it. I'm not crazy.

Building Your Safety Week by Week

At your friend's place, the kettle clicks off without anyone flinching. No footsteps are being monitored. No moods are being tracked. You hide a spare key where only you and she know. Park your car two streets over. Set a lamp on a timer so the flat doesn't advertise your absence.

You sleep on the couch with your shoes by the door and your phone charging within reach. The go-bag sits in the wardrobe: IDs, cash, medications, change of clothes, phone charger, copies of court orders, a small toy your daughter loves. This isn't paranoia. This is what safety looks like after abuse.

This week, choose one safety measure to put in place. Change one password. Share one code word with someone you trust. Move one important document somewhere secure.

Small steps stack into safety.

Change your route to work. Stop posting your location. Tell someone where you're going and when you'll be back. Notice if the same car appears twice. Install new locks. Change every password. Remove them from every account. These aren't excessive precautions. They're survival strategies.

If You Remember One Thing

This isn't just a breakup. It's an escape from someone who built their life around controlling yours.

The explosion after you leave isn't proof you were wrong to go. It's proof you were never safe there. They will use systems meant to protect you. Police who ask "what did you do to make them angry." Courts that grant them visits despite your documentation. Friends who say "it takes two to tango."

They will drain accounts, cancel cards, leave you stranded. They will turn your children into messengers, your workplace into a battleground, your family into flying monkeys.

Through all of it, your body will shake. Your mind will fog. You'll forget words, drop things, walk into walls. This isn't weakness. It's what happens when a nervous system finally starts to uncurl from years of hypervigilance.

You don't owe them grace. You don't owe them explanations. You don't owe them another chance. You owe yourself safety.

Whatever keeps you alive, that's what you choose now. Again tomorrow. And the day after. Until the quiet you live in is the kind you chose, not the kind you paid for with pieces of yourself.

The storm will pass. Your freedom won't.

13.6
Still Startled, Still Becoming

Author's Note:

This one's for the part of you that keeps thinking, I should be past this by now." You're not behind. You're not failing. You're just in the thick of it.

Recovery isn't some big, cinematic breakthrough. It's not a lightbulb moment that makes everything easier. It's day after day of doing what you can, some days feeling strong, some days feeling wrecked, and showing up anyway.

You don't get to tell your nervous system you're safe now. You have to show it. In how you move, how you rest, how you speak to yourself when the old stuff flares up again.

It's slow. It's boring. It's real. And if you're still here, still trying, you're already doing the hardest part.

You're Still Jumping at Shadows. Still Forgetting. Still Here

You're in the supermarket and someone drops a tin. Your whole body contracts before your brain catches up. Just beans hitting linoleum, but your shoulders are already up by your ears, your breath caught somewhere in your throat.

Three years out, and you're still checking the car park before you unlock your door. Still reading texts five times before hitting send, editing out anything that could be twisted. Still waking at 3 AM with your jaw clenched so tight your teeth ache.

You survived something designed to unmake you. No wonder your body still startles at dropped tins. It was trained to. You smiled through dinners where you were the entertainment. You remembered to buy their specific brand of milk but forgot you were allowed preferences too. You learned to read footsteps like weather forecasts—heavy means storm coming, light means temporary peace, silence means calculate your next move carefully.

And now you blame yourself for not being „further along." You scroll through recovery accounts where people post about their breakthroughs, their new relationships, their trust restored. Meanwhile, you're still asking to sit facing the door like it's a quirk, not a survival reflex. Still apologising for needing to know the plan in advance because your chest doesn't unclench until you do.

But that tightness in your chest when nothing's even happening? That's not weakness. That's your body remembering danger you couldn't acknowledge while you were in it.

You Thought You'd Be Healed by Now. That Means You're Healing

You're sitting with a friend who's telling you about their bad day. Your hand is on their shoulder, your voice is soothing, but inside you're calculating whether their mood is your fault. Three years out, and you're still performing emotional labour like it's oxygen.

The triggers are quieter now, but not gone. Last week, someone raised their voice in excitement and your stomach dropped. Yesterday, a door slammed in the wind and you lost an hour to the shaking. You still explain your feelings like you're presenting evidence in court. Still phrase your „no" like a question. Still brace for consequences that aren't coming.

And you hate that. Because you thought this part would be over by now. You thought there would be a clear line—before and after. Broken and healed. But instead, you're in this grey space where you're better but not better enough, where progress feels like standing still because the mountain is so high.

A woman told me she'd been in recovery for five years when she realised she was still asking permission to use the bathroom in her own home. "I lived alone," she said. "There was literally no one to ask. But I'd stand there in my hallway, waiting for… what? Permission from a ghost?"

But that frustration you feel about not being over it"? It means you know what peace should feel like now. It means you're no longer accepting chaos as normal. The anger at your own healing pace is actually evidence that you're healing.

Becoming Isn't Clean. It's Messy, Raw, and Quietly Brave

Tuesday afternoon, you're folding laundry and suddenly you're crying about something that happened four years ago. The grief hits fresh, like it just happened, even though you've processed this memory seventeen times already. Your stomach knots at nothing in particular. Your skin prickles when footsteps sound in the hallway, even though it's just your neighbour coming home.

Some days you ache for the version of you who didn't scan every conversation for hidden meanings. Who could accept a compliment without searching for the trap. Who didn't need to document everything just in case.

Some days you grieve who you were before you knew words like "gaslighting," "trauma bond" and "coercive control."Before, you hadn't had to become an expert in psychological warfare just to understand what happened to y

A survivor once told me, "I kept saying I wanted to be whole again. Then my therapist asked, 'When were you whole before?' And I realised—never. I was always bending myself into acceptable shapes. Now I'm not trying to get back to whole. I'm building it for the first time, piece by piece. Some days I add a piece. Some days I just hold what I've got. Both count."

The Ordinary Courage No One Sees

This week, notice one thing you do now that you couldn't do a year ago.

Maybe you disagree without apologising first.
Maybe you buy the coffee you actually like.
Maybe you take up space in conversations without shrinking.
Maybe you sleep through the night twice a week instead of never.

Write it down: "I still do this, but less than before." It might be whisper-small—"I still check my phone obsessively, but only twenty times instead of fifty." Or "I still rehearse conversations, but sometimes I just speak."

That's not nothing. That's everything.

Consider sharing one of these "still but less" wins with someone safe. Not for validation, but to hear your own progress spoken aloud.

Sometimes saying "I only checked the locks twice instead of five times" to another person makes the progress real in a way your brain can't dismiss. Progress doesn't look like pride. It looks like resistance. And resistance is its own kind of pride.

Like getting through another Tuesday without texting them back.
Like saying "I need a minute" instead of "I'm fine."
Like choosing the restaurant even though choice still feels dangerous.

If You Remember One Thing

You're not behind schedule.
There is no schedule.
You're not failing because you still jump when doors slam,
still doubt your own memories,
still feel safer alone than trusting someone new.

You're in the part of recovery they don't make films about.
The boring part.
The part where you do the same small, brave things over and over
until your nervous system starts to believe
that maybe, possibly, the danger has actually passed.

You're not weak for still struggling with things you thought you'd be past by now.
You're just deeper in the work than the people who post inspirational quotes about "letting go" and "moving on."

You're at the part where you know that healing isn't a destination you arrive at, but a practice you keep showing up for.

And becoming?
It doesn't feel like transformation.
It doesn't feel like butterflies emerging from cocoons.

It feels like making breakfast even though your appetite hasn't returned.
Like going to the gathering even though you'll need three days to recover.
Like setting the boundary even though your voice shakes.
Like walking back into the same storm, but this time you brought an umbrella.
This time you know it's weather, not truth.

Still startled.
Still becoming.
That's the point.

That stubborn, ordinary, unglamorous persistence?

That's not just recovery.

That's revolution.

One Tuesday at a time.

13.7
Recovery Isn't Pretty
But It Deserves a Celebration

Author's Note:

This one's for the survivor who survived what no one else saw. Who smiled when it hurt. Who shrank so no one would ask questions. If the world made you feel dramatic, broken, or invisible for trying to name it, this is where that ends. You're not crazy. You're not overreacting. You were surviving a kind of abuse most people aren't brave enough to see. And if no one else ever says it: I see you. Fully. Fiercely. You don't have to explain a single thing. And I'm so glad you're still here.

You Survived Hell That Nobody Could See

You're at dinner with friends, and they're complaining about their partners leaving dishes in the sink. You nod along, but inside you're remembering how you used to wash dishes with your hands shaking, knowing that the wrong plate in the wrong place would trigger three days of silent treatment. Your hands clench under the table, nails digging into palms, anchoring you to the present.

You held hands with someone who was dismantling you piece by piece. Posted anniversary photos while your soul was being systematically erased. No one saw the gaslighting because it happened in whispers, in the space between his public charm and private coldness. No one heard the blame-shifting, the calculated confusion, the emotional landmines buried in every conversation.

He didn't yell. Never raised his voice. He just sat there, calm as a therapist, and said: "You're too sensitive." "You always ruin everything." "Why do you make everything about you?" Each word delivered with the precision of a scalpel, designed to make you doubt your own pain.

When you finally tried to tell your best friend, she tilted her head and said, "But he seems so supportive of you." Your throat tightened. You opened your mouth to explain how support can be surveillance, how concern can be control, how love can be a slow assassination. But the words died in your throat. Because how do you explain psychological torture that happens in suburban kitchens and looks like normal life?

You Pretended You Were Fine
Because the Truth Was Too Complicated

"How are things?" your colleague asked at the coffee machine.

"Good," you said, stirring sugar you didn't want into coffee you couldn't taste. "Just tired."

You didn't lie. You just edited. Smoothed the edges. Said "We're going through a rough patch" when what you meant was "I'm disappearing in plain sight and no one notices because I've gotten so good at looking normal."

You posted the holiday photos where you're both smiling. You didn't post the part where he ignored you for the entire drive home because you laughed too loud at someone else's joke. You shared the birthday dinner. Not the itemised list of everything you'd done wrong that year, delivered between courses.

You didn't fake your life. You performed survival so others could stay comfortable.

You've Been Doing This Recovery Work Alone

Everyone says, "You're not alone." But you are.

You're alone at 3 AM when the panic hits and your chest feels like it's caving in. You're alone when you see his name pop up and have to talk yourself out of responding. You're alone when you practise saying no in the bathroom mirror before a phone call with your mother.

The friends who rallied around you in the first month have gone back to their lives. The "checking in" texts stopped after week six. Your family thinks you should be "over it by now." But the work didn't stop. The nightmares didn't stop. The body memories didn't stop.

And neither did you.

A woman told me she'd been rebuilding herself for two years when her sister said, "You seem so much better! It's like it never happened."

"I wanted to scream," she said. "Better? I'd learned to trust my own thoughts again. Stopped checking my phone fifty times before sending a text. Rebuilt my entire sense of reality from scratch. I'd done the hardest work of my life, and she thought it just... happened. Like healing was automatic."

She paused. "I realised I was the only witness to my own recovery. And somehow, that had to be enough."

Even the People Who Loved You Didn't Always Believe You

You sat across from your mother, trying to find words for something that defied language. "He makes me feel like I'm going insane," you said. Your breath went shallow, waiting for understanding.

"All couples have problems," she replied, buttering her toast. "Maybe you're both just stressed."

Your brother said, "That doesn't sound like him. He's always been so nice to me."

That kind of dismissal doesn't just sting. It erases you twice. Once by the person who hurt you. And again by the people you thought might understand.

Nobody Applauds the Daily Victories

Tuesday: You didn't check his social media. Wednesday: You ate lunch without your stomach churning. Thursday: You slept six hours straight without nightmares. Friday: You disagreed with someone and didn't apologise fourteen times. Saturday: You bought the coffee you actually like, not the one he approved of.

Small things. Invisible things. Things that would mean nothing to someone who's never had their preferences pathologised, their boundaries mocked, their reality rewritten.

While the world moved on and forgot what you survived, you kept showing up to reclaim what they stole. Every choice you made for yourself was a small revolution. Every boundary was a victory. Every moment of peace was earned through combat no one else could see.

This Sacred Work Deserves Recognition

You've been carrying yourself through this recovery like a medic carrying wounded through a war zone. Making hard choices nobody sees. Doing the uncomfortable work nobody applauds. Choosing recovery over everyone else's comfort.

Some days that looked like not answering when they called. Some days it looked like crying in your car after therapy. Some days it looked like saying "I need space" when what you really needed was to scream.

That's not small work.

That's sacred work.

That's the work of taking a shattered psyche and rebuilding it one decision at a time, with no manual, no witnesses, no applause.

Marking Your Own Survival

This week, do something to mark your survival. Buy a bottle of something that makes you feel fancy. Light candles you've been saving. Wear the dress that makes you feel powerful. Write yourself a letter. Get a tattoo that means something only you understand.

Do it alone if you need to. Do it with someone who gets it if you can. But do it. Or if resources are tight, simply sit quietly and write your name followed by the word "survivor" and let yourself see it in your own handwriting.

Because surviving coercive control without losing your mind deserves recognition. Because rebuilding yourself from psychological rubble deserves celebration. Because you've been doing the hardest work of your life, and if no one else marks it, you must mark it yourself.

Say it out loud, even if only to your reflection: "I survived what tried to kill me. I rebuilt what they destroyed. I did this work when no one was looking. And I deserve this celebration.

If You Remember One Thing

You walked through invisible hell with a smile painted on your face. You survived what most people will never understand, let alone believe. You've been rebuilding yourself one choice at a time, mostly without witnesses, definitely without applause.

Every time you chose silence over defending yourself to people who wouldn't understand. Every time you got out of bed when your body felt like concrete. Every time you trusted your own memory when the world told you to doubt it. Every time you said no without justifying it. Every time you chose your healing over their comfort.

That's not just recovery. That's resistance. That's revolution. That's the sacred work of reclaiming a self someone tried to steal.

So light the candle. Pour the drink. Buy the flowers. Mark this moment.

Because you survived what was designed to destroy you. You kept breathing when someone was stealing your air. You kept standing when someone was pulling the ground from under you.

You kept becoming when someone was trying to erase you.

You earned this.

Every invisible victory.

Every private breakthrough.

Every moment you chose yourself over their version of you.

And you're still here. Still fighting. Still becoming.

You didn't come back to who you were. You became who you are.

And that deserves everything.

13.8
They Said No One Else
Would Want You. They Were Wrong

Author's Note:

This chapter is for the part of you that still hears their voice when you try to picture a life beyond them. The part that wonders, "What if they were right?" They weren't. And they knew it. That's why they said it. Because someone who believes they are lovable is harder to control. You are not unlovable. You were just in a system that needed you to believe you were. Let's pull that lie out by the root.

It Wasn't a Warning. It Was a Weapon

You're standing in the bathroom, looking at your reflection after another fight. Their words still ringing: "Who else would put up with you?"

It started subtle. A comment while loading the dishwasher: "You're lucky I'm so patient." A sigh during dinner: "Most people wouldn't tolerate this." Then it got sharper. "No one else will ever want you." Said flatly, like stating the weather. Said during fights, when your defences were down. Said as a half-joke while folding laundry, so you couldn't call it cruel without being called oversensitive.

They said it after you spoke up about needing more affection. After you cried about feeling lonely in the relationship. After you dared to suggest counselling. Always aimed at maximum impact—when you were already doubting yourself, already vulnerable.

Your stomach dropped each time. Your throat tightened. You swallowed it like truth. You started to believe it. Started seeing yourself through their lens: too needy when you asked for a hug, too sensitive when their jokes hurt, too damaged when you couldn't just "get over" their cruelty. You'd lie awake calculating your flaws, wondering who could possibly want someone so difficult.

But they didn't say it because it was true. They said it because they could feel you slipping. Starting to see through their performance. Beginning to imagine a life without them. And nothing snaps a survivor back into place like the terror that there's nowhere else to go.

It Was Never the Truth. It Was Insurance

You're at your friend's wedding, watching the couple exchange vows. "You make me want to be better," the groom says, voice breaking. Your partner leans over and whispers, "Good thing I already accept you as you are. No one else would."

When someone repeats that line—"no one else would want you"—it's not insight. It's strategy.

They wanted you grateful. Grateful they hadn't left yet. Grateful they "put up with" your needs, your emotions, your humanity. They positioned themselves as the only person on Earth who could tolerate you, let alone love you. But that's not a relationship. That's a hostage situation dressed up as romance.

Love doesn't make you feel replaceable. It doesn't say, "You're lucky I haven't found someone better." It doesn't keep a running tally of your inadequacies. Real love makes you feel chosen, not settled for. Cherished, not tolerated.

A woman told me she stayed an extra two years because of one sentence: "Nobody else would love you the way I do."

"The way he said it," she explained, "like he was doing charity work. Like loving me was this noble sacrifice. I spent those two years trying to earn what should have been freely given."

She finally left when she realised something crucial: "He wasn't warning me. He was warning himself. Because he knew that once I saw my own worth, once I realised I deserved actual love, not this performance of tolerance, he'd lose his power. He wasn't right. He was terrified."

You Were Never the Problem. You Were the Mirror

They called you difficult because you had needs. You lowered your voice each time you asked. You shrank your appetite for affection. You still carried the blame. They called you too much because you felt things. They called you broken because you remembered their promises and expected them to matter.

But here's what was really happening: Every time you asked for more, you reflected back how little they were giving. Every boundary you set showed them their own violations. Every tear you cried revealed their cruelty.

They didn't say "no one else would want you" because you were unlovable. They said it because if someone else saw you clearly—really saw you—they'd give you the love you were begging for. And then you'd know. You'd know how little you'd been surviving on. You'd know what you'd been missing. You'd know you deserved more.

The Lie Is Still There, But Quieter Now

You're on a first date, two years after leaving. They ask about your last relationship. Your throat tightens. The old voice whispers: "Don't tell them. They'll run. You're too much baggage now."

You catch yourself apologising before you've even said anything. "Sorry, I know this is heavy for a first date." They smile and say, "Life is heavy sometimes. That doesn't make you heavy."

You realise you've been carrying their verdict like a life sentence. "Too damaged." "Too difficult." "Too much." But those weren't descriptions. They were prison bars, designed to keep you from trying to leave.

Practical Step

If you feel able this week, take a sheet of paper and write down the exact words they used to make you feel unloveable.

Every insult passed off as honesty.
Every joke that was really a cut.
Every prediction about how you would never be loved again.

Then rewrite them for what they really were.
"You're lucky I put up with you" becomes "You needed me to feel lucky so I wouldn't leave."
"No one else would understand you" becomes "You were terrified someone else would understand me better."
"You're too damaged for anyone else" becomes "You needed me to believe I was damaged so I would stay."

Read your versions out loud. Their fear, not your worth. Their control, not your destiny. Your voice saying their strategy instead of their verdict—that's when the spell starts to break.

Why It Matters

Because their words were never prophecy. They were tools of coercive control. When you rewrite them, you begin to hear what's been true all along—the shame was never yours.

If You Remember One Thing

They said no one else would want you. Said it like they were doing you a favour by staying. Like they were a saint for tolerating your existence.

But love isn't tolerance. It isn't endurance. It isn't a favour.

You are not too much. Your feelings aren't too big. Your needs aren't too many. You're a human being who wanted to be loved, not managed. Cherished, not contained. Seen, not surveilled.

The person who told you no one else would want you was telling you their deepest fear:

that someone else would. That someone would see what they saw—all of you, flaws and beauty alike—and choose to love you properly. Not as a project to fix or a burden to bear, but as a person worthy of genuine care.

You were never unloveable. You were just with someone who didn't know how to love.

And now? Now you get to learn what real love feels like. Starting with the revolutionary act of believing you deserve it. Because you do. You always have.

They said no one else would want you. But here you are—becoming someone who knows better.

Not someday. Not after you're "fixed." Not when you're "less difficult."

Now. Exactly as you are. Healing and messy and becoming.

That's not too much to love.

That's exactly enough.

13.9
It's Not the Rush. It's the Return

Author's Note:

This isn't a checklist. It's not a Pinterest board. It's a look into the kind of love that doesn't need to be loud to be life-changing. If no one ever showed you what real love looks like, if all you've known is intensity, silence, walking on eggshells, and trying to earn a sliver of warmth, this is what it looks like on the other side. No rainbows. Just something real enough to rest in.

Real Love Doesn't Blow Your Mind. It Grounds Your Body

The dots appear. Your stomach drops.

Disappear.

You count—one, two, three, four—

Appear again.

Your thumbs hover over the keyboard, already drafting apologies for things you haven't done. "Everything okay?" Too needy—he'll think you're checking up on him. Delete. "What time will you be home?" Too controlling. Delete. "Love you." Too manipulative—he said that's what you do, use love as a weapon. Delete, delete, delete.

The dots disappear. For good this time.

You put the phone face-down but flip it back over within seconds. Check the volume. Check the brightness. Check if maybe you missed it. Your shoulders are somewhere near your ears now, neck so tight it hurts to turn your head. This is what your body does now—braces for impact even when he's ten miles away.

A woman told me she once spent three hours—three actual hours—drafting a text asking if her partner could pick up milk on the way home. Wrote it seventeen different ways. Added emojis, removed them. Added "please," worried it sounded sarcastic. Removed "please," worried it sounded demanding. Three hours. Because the last time she asked for something, he didn't speak to her for four days. Just moved through the house like she was furniture. Four days of silence for asking him to stop at Woolies.

This is love as you know it. Your heart racing, but not from joy. From calculating whether "See you later" with a full stop means anger or just punctuation.

Then one day, someone else walks into your kitchen. You're standing at the sink, shoulders rigid, and they're just... chopping vegetables. Humming something off-key. They look up, clock your face.

"Hard day?"

Just that. No "What did you do?" No "What's wrong with you now?" Just "Hard day?" like hard days are normal, allowed, not evidence of your failure.

Your shoulders drop. Actually drop. Not because you're forcing them down, reminding yourself to relax. They just... fall. Like your body suddenly remembers it doesn't have to be a clenched fist.

They go back to chopping. The knife hits the board in steady rhythm. No aggressive chopping. No pointed silence. Just making dinner while you stand there, amazed that your breath has gotten deeper without trying.

No hundred texts demanding your location. But when the Thai food arrives, your pad thai has no coriander—they remembered without being reminded. When you go quiet at dinner, they don't interrogate. They make you tea, the real tea you hide in the back of the cupboard, and just... wait. When you finally crack and the tears come, they don't file it away to use against you next fight.

A survivor told me she knew it was different when they had their first disagreement. "I waited for the punishment. The silence. The look that meant I'd pay for this for weeks. Instead, he said, 'I need to think about this. Can we talk after dinner?' And then—get this—after dinner, we just talked. No jury. No prosecution. Just talking."

That's real love. Not the adrenaline rush that leaves you empty. The quiet return that lets you rest.

It Doesn't Punish You for Having a Bad Day

Your eyes open to grey. Not the walls—they're the same white they always are. The grey is inside. Heavy, like someone filled your bones with wet cement while you slept.

In your old life, you'd already be moving. Bathroom. Cold water on your face. Practising in the mirror: corners of mouth up, eyes bright, tilt your head like you're listening, interested, grateful. Ten minutes to transform into someone who deserves to take up space in this house.

But this morning, you just lie there. Staring at nothing. The words come out before you can stop them:

"I'm not okay today."

You wait. For the sigh that says you're exhausting. For the eye roll. For the mental cash register to start tallying—remember when I picked you up from work? Remember when I listened to you cry about your mother? Remember, remember, remember, all the times I was there, building a debt you'll never clear.

Instead: "Do you want company or space?"

That's it. Both options real. No wrong answer. No test.

"Space," you whisper.

They kiss your forehead—gentle, no performance required—and pad out to the kitchen. Twenty minutes later, the front door closes. Soft. Not pulled shut with that particular force that says you'll pay for this when I get home.

Later, there's a plate in the fridge. Sandwich made just how you like it. Crisps on the side—the good ones, not the healthy ones they prefer. A note: "For whenever you're hungry."

No "I hope you feel better soon" that means hurry up. No "Let me know if you need anything" that means don't. Just food, waiting, no strings attached.

A woman told me about the first time her new partner saw her at her absolute worst. "Three days without washing my hair. Same trackies I'd been sleeping in. Crying at a commercial about bloody insurance. And he just walked in, made me coffee—proper coffee, not instant—with exactly the right amount of milk. Handed it to me like I was dressed for a gala. No mention of the hair. The trackies. The fact I was sobbing over a cartoon gecko selling insurance."

You can exist in all your states. Bad days don't cost extra. Sadness doesn't require an explanation or an apology or a promise to try harder tomorrow.

It Shows Up in Small Things and Means Them

We were in Target, buying laundry baskets we didn't need and candles that smelled like "Calm Ocean Breeze." Nothing special about the day. Just Tuesday. Fluorescent lights making everyone look slightly ill. That particular Target smell—popcorn and plastic and possibility.

I saw Georgie stop at the clearance rack. Her fingers found this cardigan—soft, moss-coloured, the kind of green that makes you think of forests you've never walked through. She lifted it off the rack, held it up. The fabric caught the light. Her face changed—just for a second—like she was seeing herself wearing it somewhere beautiful.

Then, smooth as water, her hand flipped to the price tag. Thirty-five dollars. On special.

The cardigan was back on the rack before I could blink. No hesitation. No lingering. The motion so practised, so automatic. Like breathing. Like bleeding. Forty years of muscle memory: see, want, check price, replace. Don't need it. Don't deserve it. Don't ask.

She moved on to dish soap. Comparing prices on bottles she didn't care about.

I doubled back, grabbed the cardigan, buried it under the unnecessary laundry baskets.

At the register, she saw it emerge from our pile. Her whole body went still. Not frozen like fear—frozen like her brain couldn't process the data. We got to the car, her holding the bag like it might dissolve if she squeezed too tight.

She sat in the passenger seat. Silent. The cardigan in its bag on her lap.

Then her face crumpled. First tear escaped. Then another. Then she was sobbing— proper sobbing—in the Target car park, clutching this thirty-five dollar cardigan like I'd just handed her the moon.

"No one's ever done that before," she managed between gulps of air.

"Bought you clothes?" I was genuinely confused. Twenty-two years of marriage before this. Surely someone had—

"Just... noticed. Saw me want something and just... bought it. Without me having to hint. Or justify. Or earn it. Like I was worth thirty-five dollars without question. Without negotiation. Without proving I needed it more than wanted it."

She cried for twenty minutes. In the Target car park. Over a cardigan that was never about a cardigan. It was about being seen without performing for it. Being valued without proving it. Being loved without paying for it in pieces of herself—gratitude, service, silence, shrinking.

That's real love. Not grand gestures that come with hidden invoices. Just someone who sees you want something and doesn't make you hate yourself for wanting it.

You Don't Have to Earn It

A woman told me she knew her new partner actually loved her when he noticed she kept her shoes by every door. Running shoes by the front door. Sandals by the back. Even slippers by the bedroom door. Always pointed out, ready.

"Forty years of marriage and I never stopped planning my exits," she said.

He never mentioned it. Just one day, she came home to find a small shoe rack by the front door. Pretty thing. Wooden. Room for three pairs. Her running shoes already on it, still pointed toward the door.

"In case you need them," he said. That's all. No psychoanalysis. No "You don't need to run from me." Just understanding that safety meant knowing where the exits were, and making space for that.

You learned early that love was conditional. Not in words—never in words. In the sigh when you asked for something. In the silence after you said no. In the tally kept of every kindness, every gift, every gesture, building interest you'd never clear.

So you got smaller. Cheaper. Easier. Needed less, asked for nothing, shapeshifted into whatever was easiest to love that day. Believing if you cost nothing, you might be worth keeping.

But here's what real love looks like: You can need things. Say them out loud. "I need to sleep alone tonight." "I need you to not touch me right now." "I need to cry about this without you fixing it." And they just... acknowledge it. No negotiation. No hurt feelings you have to manage. No debt you've just increased.

Practical Step

This week, write down three things you need in love now—not what you think you deserve, just what you actually need. Maybe it's "text me when you're running late" or "don't raise your voice" or "let me keep my own bank account."

As you write each one, notice what your body does. Does your chest tighten? Does your breath catch? That's your nervous system telling you what matters for your safety.

Why It Matters

After abuse, we're trained to ignore our needs, to make them smaller, cheaper, easier.

Writing them down and noticing your body's response helps you recognise what real safety requires for you specifically. Not anyone else. You. These aren't signs you're damaged—they're your survival wisdom speaking. Listen to it.

If You Remember One Thing

You don't need the butterflies. You've had those—they were moths, and they ate holes in everything you wore, everything you were.

What you need is someone who makes your shoulders drop when they walk in. Someone who can sit with your bad days without making them about themselves. Someone who buys you a thirty-five dollar cardigan like it's nothing, because seeing you smile is worth more than keeping score.

Real love after abuse isn't a fairy tale. It's messier. Quieter. It's eating cereal for dinner because neither of you can cope with cooking. It's them doing the grocery shop when crowds make your skin crawl. It's laughing at something stupid while you're both crying about something real.

It's standing in a Target queue, them buying you something you didn't ask for, while your nervous system slowly, carefully, begins to believe that maybe—maybe—this time, you're safe enough to stay.

Real love doesn't resurrect who you were. It meets who you are now—with your shoes by the door and your exits mapped—and says, "This is enough. You're enough. Stay as long as you feel safe."

Everything ends. Everything begins. And somewhere in between, in the Target car park tears and the soft cardigans and the quiet Tuesday mornings, you discover what love was always supposed to feel like:

Like breathing without counting the breaths. Like safety without checking the exits. Like something you never have to earn.

Like finally, finally, coming home.

13.10
You Were the Proof All Along

Author's Note:

This part ends not because everything's resolved, but because something stronger has begun: self-trust. There was never going to be a perfect moment where everyone believed you. No apology good enough. No witness brave enough. But here you are. Still breathing. Still becoming. And that is the proof.

You Don't Need Another Confirmation. You Lived It

You're scrolling through old messages at 2 AM again, looking for evidence. Screenshots that prove you weren't imagining it. Texts that show the pattern. Emails that demonstrate the cruelty hidden in reasonable words.

But you already know.

The way your shoulders still rise when you hear footsteps that sound like theirs. The way you still check your phone with your breath held. The way certain phrases make your stomach drop, even now, even from other people's mouths.

They questioned you. Called you unstable when you finally spoke. Dramatic when you set boundaries. Too sensitive when their words cut deep. They rewrote history while you were still living it, edited your memories in real time, made you doubt the bruises you couldn't see.

But you got out. You're here. You started breathing again.

That is the evidence.

A woman told me she only cried watching films where abuse victims were believed. "It's not that I don't believe myself," she said, gripping her coffee cup like an anchor. "It's that the world spent so long telling me I wasn't allowed to trust my own experience."

One day, alone in her flat, she said it out loud to her reflection: "He hurt me. It happened. I'm not crazy." Her voice shook, but she said it again. Louder. "It happened."

She didn't wait for anyone's approval. She didn't need permission anymore. She just said it. And knew it. That was the moment she became free.

The Moment You Stop Seeking Permission

You're at a family dinner. Your aunt is telling everyone about your ex's new job, their new relationship, how well they're doing. "Such a shame it didn't work out," she says, looking at you with pity. "They tried so hard with you."

Three years ago, you would have defended yourself. Explained. Pulled out receipts. Begged them to see what really happened. But tonight, you just take another sip of wine and let them believe their fiction. Because you know the truth, and you no longer need them to validate it.

One of the hardest lessons for survivors is this: you don't need their permission to know what happened to you. You don't need a jury. You don't need witnesses. You don't need them to admit it.

A woman told me she spent years trying to get her family to acknowledge what her brother had done to her. Every holiday, she'd find quiet moments to try again. Hoping someone would finally say, "Yes, we see it too. We believe you."

They never did. They changed subjects. Made excuses. Suggested therapy for her "anger issues."

One day, sitting in her car after another failed Christmas dinner, tears streaming, she had a revelation: "I don't need them to believe me for it to be true. I lived it. Every instinct I have now, every boundary I set—that's my proof."

She stopped trying to convince them. Stopped bringing it up. Stopped needing their validation. "The strangest thing happened," she told me. "Once I stopped begging them to see my truth, I could finally rest in it myself."

You Are the Evidence

Not the story you perfected for therapists. Not the explanation you rehearsed for friends. Not the proof you gathered in folders, screenshots saved "just in case." Not the apology you'll never receive. Not the justice that never came.

You. Your survival itself.

The way you held yourself together with safety pins and determination while someone was systematically taking you apart. The way you kept your heart soft when cruelty tried to calcify it. The way you found humour in hell, even if it was gallows humour that kept you sane.

Every time you chose yourself when they made it dangerous to do so. Every boundary you set while your voice shook. Every "no" you said when "yes" would have been safer.

You don't need them to admit what they did. Your recovery is the admission. Your boundaries are the testimony. Your peace—hard-won, still fragile, but yours—is the verdict.

Practical Step

This week, write one sentence that captures your truth. Not the whole story. Not what happened. Not what they did. But what you know about yourself because you survived it. Maybe it's "I am more resilient than I ever needed to be" or "I deserve gentleness after so much war" or "My intuition was right all along."

Don't pad it with explanations. Don't soften it with maybes. Don't defend it with evidence. Just write your truth, clean and clear. Stick it somewhere you'll see it—your mirror, your wallet, your phone background. When you read it back, notice if your chest loosens, if your shoulders drop. That response is proof too.

Why It Matters

You've spent years living inside their story about who you are—difficult, too sensitive, never enough. Writing your own verdict isn't about revenge or proving them wrong. It's about claiming authorship of your own truth.

When you declare what you know about yourself, you become the authority on your own life. Their version stops being the loudest voice in the room. This single sentence becomes your North Star when the old doubts creep in—evidence that you know what you know, regardless of what they made you believe.

If You Remember One Thing

You were the proof all along.

Not in your ability to convince others. Not in your perfectly articulated explanation of psychological abuse. Not in the witnesses who were too scared to speak up. Not in the paper trail you kept just in case you needed evidence that you weren't crazy.

You. Your existence. Your persistence.

The way you stayed kind when it would have been easier to let bitterness eat you alive. The way you kept showing up to life when life felt like a threat. The way you learned to trust your own mind again after someone tried to colonise it.

Every morning you got up when your body felt like concrete. Every time you chose healing over revenge. Every moment you believed yourself when the world told you not to.

You were always enough evidence. You were never not enough.

Even when they gaslit you. Even when they convinced others you were the problem. Even when you half-believed them yourself on the dark days.

But here you are. Reading this. Still breathing. Still becoming. Still learning to trust the voice inside that whispers, "You know what happened. You know who you are. That's enough."

Knowing what happened doesn't resurrect who you were before them. It reveals who you are now—and that's enough.

And now? Now you get to be the author of what comes next.

Not them. Not their flying monkeys. Not the people who should have protected you and didn't.

You. Writing your own story. One true sentence at a time.

That's not just proof. That's power.

13.11
If You Remember One Last Thing

Let This Be the Beginning

You made it here. To the end of this part of the book. To this moment. To tomorrow. Still standing, even if you're swaying. Still breathing, even if it's shallow. Still yours, even if you're still learning what that means.

A little undone. Maybe a lot undone. But not erased. Never erased. And that matters more than you know. That counts for everything.

You get to want more now. Not just survival—though god knows you've earned the right to rest in that victory alone. But something softer. Something that doesn't require armour. Something real.

A morning where your first thought isn't damage control. A laugh that surprises you with its fullness. A Tuesday that's just a Tuesday. Moments that feel like they belong to you, not to your history.

Georgie once told me she never thought she'd see Paris. Twenty Two years in a cage built from someone else's voice saying she wasn't worth the ticket price. That no one would ever want to take her anywhere. That she was lucky to have a roof, let alone dreams.

And then, somehow, at forty six, she found herself there. With me. In a top-floor apartment with Eiffel Tower views, watching her discover she was allowed to want things. Beautiful things. Simple things. Everything.

For three years, maybe four, we went back. Every time, I watched this woman come alive a little more. At the markets, running her hands over fabric she would have walked past before. In cafés, ordering dessert without apology. On our balcony at sunset, tears streaming down her face, saying, "I'm so happy. I'm just so bloody happy."

"I'm learning to speak French," she announced one morning, laughing at herself. "At my age. Can you imagine?"

I could. I still can.

She sent me a photo from our favourite café that last trip, her hand wrapped around a coffee cup, wedding ring gone, replaced by a silver band she'd bought herself at the market. The message just said: "Who knew I was allowed to want this?"

So if the world ever told you your story was over—
If they said you'd never be anything more than what happened to you—
If you believed them, even for a moment—

They were wrong. You were wrong.

It wasn't over. It isn't. Not yet.

Not while you're still here, reading this, feeling that small flutter of "maybe" in your stomach. That's not false hope. That's your life, asking to be lived. Not survived. Lived.

And we hope—Georgie and I, that some part of your life surprises you too.

That you find yourself somewhere you never thought you'd be. Not necessarily Paris. Maybe just Tuesday morning in your own kitchen, realising you're humming. Maybe in someone's arms who sees you, really sees you, and stays. Maybe alone and discovering that alone isn't lonely anymore.

Maybe just here, right now, knowing that two people who never met you wanted you to know: You made it. You're making it. And that's not the end of anything.

That's where everything begins.

Part 14
Never Too Late

By Georgie Bailey

Introduction

Apparently life begins at 40, a truism I often reflect upon because as I entered my forties, I found myself standing on the edge of a new beginning, looking out at the vast and open expanse of possibility. For so long, I'd given everything I had to everyone else, neglecting my own needs and desires. But then, something unexpected happened - I was given a gift. I was cast aside and left to find my own way, but I didn't realisee it was a gift at first. It took some time, until eventually, I came to understand that this was my chance to start anew, to live the life I'd always dreamed of.

This book is a reflection of my journey, of the endings and beginnings that have shaped my life. It's a testament to the biggest lesson I've learned - that no matter what happens, my inner light can never be fully extinguished. It's up to me to let it shine, to embrace the things that make me feel alive and to celebrate every moment of this precious existence.

My story is one of courage, of taking risks and embracing the unknown. It's a love story, not just for others but for myself - for the person I am and the person I am becoming. I am a survivor, an artist, an adventurer, a writer, a mother, a cook, a lover. Above all, I am a woman who has learned to live life on my own terms, to embrace my innate creativity and to find joy in every moment.

Looking back on my childhood, I see now how it was a training ground for the abuse that would come later. My father's obsession with money and success, my mother's focus on physical appearance and pleasing men—these were the values I was taught, the standards to which I was held. But I have broken free of those chains, and I am proud of the person I have become.

This book is my tribute to the journey that has brought me here, to the person I am today. It's a reminder that no matter what life throws our way, we always have the power to choose our own path, to embrace our true selves and to live a life that's filled with purpose and meaning.

So Full of Beauty
So Full of Magic

by Georgie's Little Brother Murray Booker

To capture the essence of my big sister Georgie in a few simple lines is just not possible. What words could ever articulate such an amazing soul?

"Loving."
"Selfless."
"Passionate."
"Powerful."
"Artistic."
"Human."
Even "broken," sometimes.

There just aren't enough words.
And no single word could ever do her justice.

My big sister was the one who was always there for me, without judgment, without scorn, no matter the latest misadventure or chaos I'd brought into my life. When I was young, I struggled at school. Reading well for my age was a real challenge. It was Georgie who spent countless hours teaching me how to read and write in a way that made sense to me, something no other teacher had managed to do.

She encouraged all my passions, even the more misguided ones, and she gave me drawing lessons as her own talents began to bloom. But it wasn't all roses and tea-cake. We were siblings, after all. I knew exactly how to drive her crazy. You must remember, this is also the girl who once split my head open with a well-aimed stone at the bus stop. How we laughed about that later.

When I joined the Royal Australian Air Force at nineteen, it was Georgie who told me: "You can do anything, if you just have the courage to dream." She never stopped saying

that, in one form or another. She was always there, always giving, always supporting.
In 2010, when I found myself battling serious mental health challenges, Georgie was there again. She didn't try to fix it. She just listened. And somehow, she got me drawing again, a turning point in my recovery.

What I didn't know at the time was that her own world was falling apart. Her marriage was collapsing. Her life was in turmoil.
And yet, she gave to me, fully, selflessly, without concern for the cost.

After the freedom of emancipation, my sister began to live again.
It was incredible to witness. Her passion reignited. Her art was breathtaking. Her career was exploding. And she had found love, real love, the kind that enriched her soul.

It was as if the years had rolled off us. We were siblings again, like when we were kids — only better. Stronger. Closer.
But that's her story to tell. I won't give away all the spoilers.

So how do I sum up my big sister, Georgie, in just a few words?
She was a unicorn. The world will never again see a creature quite like her, so full of beauty, wildness, magic, and light.

The stories they tell about her might sound impossible.
But I promise you, they're all true.

I know. I was there.

14.1
The Answer Is Elusive
But It's Urgent

How do we raise our children to become strong and confident adults, unburdened by the toxic patterns that we have inherited from previous generations? It's a question that's been asked countless times, yet the answer is still elusive. As a survivor of domestic violence and abuse, I've spent a great deal of time reflecting on this issue, trying to understand how I fell into these destructive patterns, and how I can prevent others from following the same path.

When we think of abuse, we often think of physical violence, but there's another insidious form of abuse that's equally damaging: the abuse of control—coercive control. This type of abuse is less obvious, but no less destructive. It's the kind of abuse that erodes your self-worth, makes you doubt your instincts, and convinces you that you are powerless.

For a long time, I struggled to understand how someone could think it's okay to abuse me, and how I could have stayed in such a harmful situation for so long. I realised that I had been groomed to be the perfect victim, and that the grooming had started in childhood. I had been taught to be compliant, to disregard my own instincts, and to put the needs of others before my own.

The reality is that we are not born to live up to the expectations of others. We are born to be our own unique selves, to experience our own pleasure, and to be in charge of our own bodies and minds. We need to teach our children to trust their instincts, to celebrate their uniqueness, and to know that they are amazing beings with the right to be who they truly are.

It took me many years to unlearn the patterns that had been instilled in me from childhood. But writing has been a powerful tool in my healing journey. Through writing, I've been able to process my traumas, to think out loud, and to gain a deeper understanding of myself. I've learned to listen to my instincts, to trust myself, and to take charge of my own life.

As a society, we need to start having more open and honest conversations about domestic abuse, including the non-physical forms of abuse like coercive control. We need to teach our children that abuse is never okay, and that they deserve to be treated with respect and dignity.

And most importantly, we need to empower them to be their own true selves, so that they can go out into the world with confidence, strength, and resilience.

14.2
Good Girls Are Subservient

My dad's devotion to work was all-consuming, and my mother's reliance on alcohol consumed her. Their absence was palpable, leaving my siblings and me to navigate life without their guidance. My dad was tough and determined to instil in us a sense of that toughness. He held steadfast to his beliefs that men were superior and women were merely there to serve the needs of men and boys. My mother, on the other hand, seemed to accept and enable his views, further perpetuating his way of thinking.

From about eight years old, I was expected to care for my two little brothers (two and a half and six months old) so that both my parents could work in our country pub late into the night. At only eight years old I was often asked to take care of the customers' tiny babies too so that their parents could carry on drinking downstairs. My mind struggles to get around the idea of such a young child being given that sort of responsibility…I'm grateful that nothing went wrong.

I was also expected to work and I regularly looked after the drive through bottle-o at my Dad's pub, serving customers, lifting cartons of beer, and most importantly, handling cash transactions. I got paid a small amount but the golden rule was that I had to balance the till. Any shortfall would be deducted from my pay. At the time it all seemed perfectly normal, but it was really child labour and completely inappropriate for an eight-year old.

Mum was already a full-blown alcoholic by that stage. Why on earth Dad chose a country pub as his business, when he had the burden of an alcoholic wife, I really don't know. What I do know, however, is that both my grandparents followed us to that country town and did their best to stick around.

At that age my days consisted of going to school, caring for my baby brothers, completing my chores and fending for myself. Mum and Dad worked morning to midnight seven days a week and had very little time for us kids. Dad was the consummate gregarious host, and mum was the pretty young thing serving behind the bar. When not propping it up or charming the clientele, Mum was mostly passed out drunk.

One of my favourite tricks was asking Mum, while she was semi-conscious in an alcoholic stupor, if my mates from school could come round for a sleep-over. She'd say, "Yes, of course," only to come to hours later to find me, Peta and Donna, my besties, camped out for the night in my room. I tried to make the best of having parents who largely ignored my existence. My schoolmates were quite envious in that they thought it was cool that "after school snacks" at my place consisted of a bag of chips and raspberry cordial and lemonade from behind the bar.

The reality however was a little different, as the weight of my responsibilities bore down on me. My job as a mere girl was to serve, whether caring for my little brothers or fetching and carrying in the pub. I frequently ran up and down the main street fetching fish and chip orders from the takeaway for pub customers. It wasn't long until my education began to suffer as no one paid any attention to it.

By the time we left that country town, to move on to Dad's next entrepreneurial adventure, I found myself behind in school and needing to repeat a year. Mum and Dad moved on to the next pub and took my little brothers with them. But they didn't take me, and I didn't understand why. I was left with my grandparents and after getting over the sense of abandonment it turned out to be one of the best times of my young life. Those months living with my grandmother's dedicated love and care cemented my core sense of self that, despite many later attempts to squash it, stayed with me.

My mother was an enigma at the best of times. As I grew older, her way of relating to me slowly changed. No longer a little girl, she started to pay more attention to me, trying to shape me for womanhood. I think she was hoping to have a second chance, living vicariously through me, but I seemed to be a continual disappointment and frustration to her.

On reflection, I see that she pushed her lack of worthiness on to me. She reinforced the gender stereotype that I was just a girl; that despite my good marks and aspirations to be something, my aim should be to find a man. Although, as she often reminded me, I would probably have more difficulty than her on that front. She wanted me to be a model because she once had a brief stint working for June Dally Watkins. Mum was tall with long, shapely, beautiful legs. Her perfect proportions were 36", 24", 36"(bust, waist, hips). I was a disappointment having inherited my grandmother's pear-shaped bum and shorter stature. At fifteen, I was 56 kilos, size 10 and only 165 cm tall with small boobs. Mum kept hoping I'd grow taller, but I disappointed her there too.

Mum was a stickler for manners at the table. We all had to be seated on time and sit up straight, no elbows on the table. But Mum never sat down to eat with us. Instead, she'd be drinking wine and smoking in the kitchen while she prepped, cooked and cleared away. I helped serve the plates to the men first and was then allowed to sit to eat my own food. There was never a plate set for Mum. She'd hover, like a scary servant, fetching sauce or drinks or anything else that Dad requested. In between requests, she slowly circled the table watching us eat, ready to stab a sharp fork into your spine if you relaxed and let your shoulders slouch. It wasn't long before the hovering escalated into full-blown lectures about what knife went where, which side the bread plate went and where your hands should be when not actually putting food in your mouth.

Mum even insisted on me attending deportment classes where I was taught to walk, cross my legs correctly, go up and down a staircase properly, and get in and out of a car without flashing my knickers. However, even after all the polishing, my height and proportions meant I still wasn't picked up for modelling assignments like several of the other girls. Mum's aspirations were sadly dashed, and Dad decided I needed to start focusing on something slightly less glamorous like being a teacher or a nurse.

Mum's future-proofing plan was focused on where to find me a boy, but I didn't have any friends, let alone boyfriends. I wasn't allowed to go to the parties of girls in my class and it wasn't an appealing thought to invite anyone to my house … I didn't need the added complication. She tried to get me to go with my little brother to his football club social events where there would be lots of slightly older boys but I had zero interest in sports. A rugby league front-row forward was hardly my idea of a catch anyway.

My mother had developed a crush on one of my teachers and in hindsight, I realise that she indirectly flirted with him through me. Although she hadn't shown much interest before, she started showing up at school and checking my homework for his class to ensure it was flawless. It appeared that she had forgotten that I was already an 'A' student in various advanced classes and believed her involvement was necessary.

We watched To Sir With Love together while she drank, babbling about how it was just like Mr R, how handsome he was and that maybe I could marry him one day. She even arranged for a To Sir With Love T-shirt to be made as a gift for him from me when he announced he was leaving the school. Mum was devastated at the news … I just needed to adjust to a new commerce teacher.

I'd never experienced any sort of companionship with my mother before, so this new woman giggling and singing along with musicals with me was kind of nice. She even started to let me drink a little wine while we watched our movies. "Don't tell your father," she said. She was changing the dynamic between us from that of mother and daughter to one of confidant. She began confiding in me about her grievances with Dad, as if I were her closest friend. As far as I can remember, she didn't really have any friends at that time. There were acquaintances but they seemed to be more Dad's friends. For some reason they stopped visiting and the parties seemed to come to a halt.

Dad had been learning to fly and had purchased his own small plane. Mum complained that he was always at the Flying Club with the other local pilots. Meanwhile, she said that he wasn't giving her any money and she had to buy our clothes from second-hand stores. I wasn't aware at the time, but it turned out that Mum had developed a new addiction. She was feeding all the money Dad was giving her into poker machines. Her explanation for why she had to buy cheap second-hand clothes and school uniforms only added to the image that Dad had already created of himself as an aloof, misogynistic bully. It was entirely believable.

Many years later, we discovered the true extent of Mum's deceit. She manipulated mortgages, leased vehicles, and squandered it all, almost bankrupting Dad. In the midst of it, she spoke negatively about Dad to me, highlighting how he treated my brothers differently than me. She made it seem like there was a boys' club that neither she nor I could be a part of. By doing so, she sought an ally and someone to be on her side.

To keep me on her side, she ensured that I felt unwelcome elsewhere. She took every opportunity to reinforce that I was inferior. It wasn't overt, but I somehow sensed that I was the reason behind her miserable life and she created a cloud of worthlessness that hung over both of us. This cloud continued to overshadow me for the rest of my life.

Dad's way of motivating me towards greater success was to keep pushing me and nothing I did was ever good enough. I could never seem to satisfy him and I desperately wanted to be seen and recognised. He made time for the boys' sports but since I was just a girl and not particularly talented in sports or anything he could boast about, he didn't pay much attention to me. I was artistic but he didn't value that. However, I was a good student, so I tried my best. But no matter how well I did, he didn't seem to be pleased. "Dad, I scored 96% on my exam!" I once told him. "Hmph, imagine what you could have achieved if you had studied harder!" he replied."

Dad was a strict disciplinarian who demanded respect and ruled with an iron fist. Though he was rarely violent, occasionally he would belt us. He exuded an intense, powerful, commanding energy that made us all feel small. If we left a light on in our room, even if we were coming back shortly, he confiscated the light bulb. If we left music playing, he took away our tape deck. We were expected to be tidy and quiet, and all the housework had to be done. I saw my mother's nervous, frightened energy as she rushed to ensure everything was just so before he came home.

When she wasn't there (she was also expected to work long hours in whatever business we had at the time), I stepped up and filled her shoes. I protected my brothers, checked their rooms to make sure they would pass inspection, fixed loose bed covers, picked up forgotten toys and made sure their afternoon tea makings were tidied and washed up, that the washing was off the line folded and put away, that any toys the boys may have played with after school were packed up and homework was underway before Dad got home. Or Mum, for that matter.

Her fear of what Dad might say pushed her to push me. She was more physically abusive than Dad and often hit us with the wooden spoon. I recall one time when my brother decided he was not going to cry anymore no matter what, so he just held his hand out and held his breath, refusing to let a tear fall. She just kept going harder and harder, getting more and more frustrated. Finally, the spoon broke and she broke down herself, falling to her knees, bawling and screaming at him, "You're supposed to cry!"

Growing up with a workaholic father and an alcoholic mother, I learned that my creativity, which was the essence of my being, held no value in my father's eyes, as he worshipped the god of money. My mother, on the other hand, saw success as the ability to attract a man, and constantly told me not to cut my hair as it was my only asset. As a female, I was instantly categorised as an "also-ran" and was taught to be subservient. Looking back, I realise that my childhood was a training ground for becoming the perfect target for abuse.

When considering domestic abuse, most people immediately recognise physical violence but there is another form of abuse that's just as dangerous and soul-destroying, though less obvious: the abuse of control. I have personally experienced both forms of domestic violence and abuse and I'm heartened to see society rising up and publicly denouncing it. However, it's occurred to me that until recently, the majority of public discussion has been focused on physical abuse.

I've often wondered how someone could believe it's okay to abuse me and how I could have endured and remained in such harmful situations. I don't consider myself a complete victim. I acknowledge that I made choices that contributed to the way my life looked. I chose partners who turned out to be abusers, I stayed in those situations for longer than I should have and I accepted appalling behaviour. Why? Because that's what I thought I was worth and it's what I was taught to believe.

I realise that this learned sense of unworthiness was something I was taught from a very young age. I was groomed to be the perfect candidate for domestic abuse and I don't believe it was intentional. Rather, it was a form of parenting common in that era, with a few little twists, that moulded me into a shy, subservient, insecure girl and my brothers into chauvinistic boys.

The grooming was a marathon, with the baton unintentionally passed from parent to abuser. The intent was to make a child malleable enough to push them down a pathway of perceived success by teaching them compliance. The reality is that teaching a child to disregard their own instincts in favour of compliance is not a pathway to success. Rather, it robs them of the natural protective mechanism they are all born with and sets them up to be taken advantage of.

We need to teach our children to trust their instincts about what feels good and right to them. To celebrate their uniqueness and not belittle their differences from a perceived norm. We need to ensure that they understand they're amazing beings with the right to be in charge of their own body and mind. They are not born to live up to the expectations of their parents or to be like someone who is not them. They are born to experience their own pleasure and they are not responsible for pleasing others. It's only now, well past middle age, that I've finally learned to listen to my instincts and inner guidance.

14.3
Grumpy

My grandmother was named Wanda but only my grandfather called her that and I doubt many others knew it. To everyone else, she was known as Grumpy. When I was young, I had two grandmothers named Price— her and Great Granny Price. To simplify things, she told me, "You can just call me Granny Grump, love!" Eventually, the "granny" part was dropped and she became simply known as Grumpy. There were times when she cursed being stuck with that name, like when we kids got separated from her in the supermarket and ran through the aisles shouting "Grumpy" at the top of our lungs. But for the most part she loved not being just any ordinary Nan or Gran.

I had another grandmother who we seldom saw. She was so different from my Grumpy. The best way to describe the contrast between them is to compare them to dolls. Nanna was like a porcelain doll with immaculate hair and a silk dress that sat on the shelf and you were too afraid to touch her in case you dirtied or broke her. She looked lovely but she was aloof, which was actually quite intimidating and not at all enjoyable.

Grumpy, on the other hand, was like a Raggedy Ann doll that you could take with you anywhere. She was scuffed up, flawed, practical but always with a permanent smile. It didn't matter if you got her pinafore dirty while making mud pies or if her hair got mussed and tangled up with leaves and twigs while climbing trees together. You could just dust her off and she'd be ready to play again the next day. She was a friend for all seasons and loads of fun. She was the furthest thing from grumpy you would ever meet. It was she who taught me unconditional love. My grandmother was the one shining light throughout my life. She was a beacon that led me home… back to me.

At the age of eleven, I was sent to live with my grandmother in the small town she and my grandfather had moved to earlier. Besides helping me get my education back on track, the life lessons she taught me during this time equipped me to find a way to survive.

My grandmother and I had always been close. I was never frightened or made to feel inferior when I was with her. Staying with her was always like coming home, the one place in the world where it was okay to just be me.

She was a country girl, not full of airs and graces, but down-to-earth and practical. Most importantly, she was always positive and never saw a problem without a solution. She was known for being able to fix anything with a stick of chewing gum and a bobby pin and could miraculously make something out of nothing. My Grumpy had faced a life of challenges but she always managed to get by.

My grandfather, known as Pa, was a professional gambler and greyhound trainer, so feast and famine were the norm. His personality disorder meant he had no idea just how manic he could be. Most of the time, my grandmother struggled to keep food on the table because Pa had more losing streaks than wins. On the odd occasion he had a big win, he would come home dressed to the nines in a new hat and coat and bringing a fur, a silver tea service, or some other extravagance. Really, all Grumpy wanted was to know she could buy groceries or pay the rent, but Pa had blown the lot before he got home.

We loved Pa; to us kids, he was great fun. He was the candy master, handing out sweets from his big colourful jar of sugary treats that lived on the side table next to his big plum-coloured armchair. It was always surrounded by what seemed like magical swirls of smoke. We loved dipping one hand deep into this treasure trove or sneaking up and pressing the big button in the middle of his spinning ashtray, sucking in his burning cigarette and not just the ash, invoking his highly animated horror. It was all great fun.

Pa was a mischievous and charming man, and we children loved him for it. He would let us sit on his lap and steer the car down the highway, and we would give the greyhounds their "vitamin" shots before a race. He even gave us a few dollars to place bets on the dogs at the track and it always seemed that the dogs we gave the shots to won. Looking back, I realise that Pa would have been just another kid for Grumpy to take care of and probably the worst one at that. But she loved us all, even Pa.

Grumpy had a variety of survival tricks up her sleeve to keep food on the table. I loved conspiring with her; it felt like she was teaching me magic. She had an agreement with the local fruit and vegetable shop to collect scraps for her "chickens" (which she didn't actually have). We would return home with boxes filled with all sorts of goodies. We stuffed cabbage leaves with flavoured rice and a bit of minced meat, steamed them in a tomato-based broth, and passed them off as a meat dish. We turned bruised and imperfect fruits into fruit salad, stewed fruit, or jam. "They're the best because they're ripe and sweet," Grumpy said. "Other people who only take the perfect-looking produce are missing out!" It made me feel so special.

There was no waste in my grandmother's kitchen. A whole chicken was a rare indulgence and it would first be roasted to perfection. Then, every last scrap of meat would be carefully picked off and mixed with shredded lettuce and mayonnaise to stretch it for sandwiches the following day. Finally, the stripped carcass would be boiled with any leftover bits of vegetables to make soup. Fat dumplings were added at the end to make the meal even more satisfying. Despite the simple ingredients, every dish was infused with love.

To the best of my knowledge, Grumpy and Pa never owned a home because their finances were too uncertain. When I came to live with them, they were renting a small fibro cottage that was so small they had to convert the tiny front porch into a room for me. The front porch was mostly glass, but it had a metre of wall around the bottom for privacy. We managed to fit in a small bed, a bedside table with a lacy doily, and a little lamp powered by an extension cord that ran under the front door. Grumpy sewed white, soft, flowing curtains and when they were hung on the three glass walls, the tiny room was transformed into a fairy tale princess's secret hideaway. I loved sitting cross-legged on the chenille bedspread among the pile of pretty cushions, playing or reading at the end of each day.

Living with Grumpy, I also learned to sew. The rhythmic sound of the pedal Singer sewing machine was meditative and it was magical to watch a piece of fabric transform as the machine nibbled at it, spitting it out as something new. Since we couldn't afford to buy the same clothes as the other kids, Grumpy and I would go to the shop and I'd point out the skirt I liked. She'd examine it, turn it inside out and figure it out. We would then find fabric or, even better, an old garment at an op-shop that we could cut up and repurpose. Before long, I had a new skirt just like the other girls but better because no one had it in the same fabric as I did! I learned that anything was possible with imagination and that if I could conceive it, I could find a way to create it.

With Grumpy, the phrase, "I can't" didn't exist. She instilled in me the belief that there was nothing I couldn't do, only things I hadn't yet figured out. This attitude permeated every aspect of her life. When her husband was away at war and she needed to make ends meet, she saw a "seamstress wanted" sign in a suit store window. Surveying the jackets and trousers on display, she decided it couldn't be that difficult and approached the store owner. "Yes, she was a seamstress, and of course she could tailor to measure." She got the job, learned by observing the other seamstresses and pretending to know what she was doing.

Through Grumpy's influence, my creativity and problem-solving abilities grew. She never gave me direct instructions but instead asked for my thoughts and let me experiment, make errors, and most importantly, find solutions. At the time, I didn't understand it but on reflection, I now see that it was one of the few times in my life when my thoughts and ideas truly mattered.

When I first arrived at Grumpy's, I was very behind in my education and convinced that I was stupid. Through practical means, she showed me that I could figure anything out if I decided to. When it came to improving my education, she continued to take a practical approach. Spelling meant that items all around the house had large labels stuck to them. Each cupboard in the kitchen had a label stuck on it, indicating what it contained. At dinner time, Grumpy would jump in front of the cupboard containing the next item needed, point at the label "plates," and then cover it up. I had to spell it out, P L A T E S, before I was allowed to get them out. For maths, it was a matter of figuring out how many items we needed for dinner. We would require knives, forks, spoons, plates, bowls, glasses, salt, pepper, curry powder for Pa, a bread and butter plate, the butter box, and the tablecloth. "How many things do we need?" "Twenty-four!"

I was sent to a new school, where I repeated year five. All the kids in my class were younger and as a result, in a small country town, I was an outsider. After having spent my previous school years with the same kids, it was a shock to find myself lost and lonely with the other kids having known each other for years. It turned out to be a repeating story for the rest of my education, with several more schools yet to come.

Despite the difficulties, I have some good memories of that school. It was so small that it only had two classrooms, with each having multiple school years. Even though the kids in my grade saw me as an outsider, the younger kids were too young to care. So I played with the younger children and often helped the teacher of the younger ones.

There was no school canteen so most days I brought sandwich lunches from home. One of my favourite school memories was Friday fish day. As a treat you could bring a brown paper bag with your order written on the front and your money inside and one of the teachers would go to the local fish and chip shop. They brought back steaming brown paper bags filled with battered fish cocktails and my favourite, a potato scallop. Grumpy always made sure I had Friday Fish money.

Along with learning that my own mind was a cool place to explore, I also learned that living in my imagination could be more satisfying than needing other people. The lack of friends became inconsequential. My playmates were made of sticks tied together with string. School photos of that time show me standing between other children I don't remember, with my bowl hairstyle cut with sewing shears by Grumpy. I looked happy. It was a special time in my life that ended too soon.

14.4
Life Interrupted

My happy life with Grumpy was abruptly interrupted when my parents summoned me to join them and my two brothers at the pub they had bought and were renovating. I still don't understand why they brought me back. I suppose it's logical for parents to want their children to live with them but for me it was confusing. I was content with Grumpy; I was living in a world where I knew I mattered. Yet, I was abruptly taken out of that secure place and placed in a strange no man's land.

It was delightful to see my younger brothers again. However, moving from being valued and engaged with every day back into the "seen but not heard" category was challenging. Suddenly, all the adults were too preoccupied with working in the pub. My mother was still either inebriated or sleeping every day and my father had two personalities. He was both the jovial, charismatic friend to all the customers and the fierce, domineering figure who expected unquestioning obedience from his wife and children.

He did not tolerate questions and expected blind compliance. My joyful inquisitiveness and eagerness to learn, nurtured and encouraged by Grumpy and Pa, who were always willing to answer my "but why" questions, were quickly extinguished. Dad did not tolerate or entertain what he saw as disrespect. When I asked "Why" with genuine interest in understanding the motive and anticipated outcome of one of his demands, his obtuse response driven by control was always, "Because I said so."

School was another nightmare. For some reason I was sent to a strict Catholic school when my family were not even practicing Catholics. I expect the choice was based on the perception of a better education.

I was fitted for a dreadful, itchy, wool, navy tunic dress. Mum chose one large enough to fit me for the next five years… long, heavy and uncomfortable. The dark navy wool tunic was worn over a white button-up blouse and thick knee-high socks. The heaviness and oppressiveness of the uniform mirrored my feelings.

I arrived at my new school trussed up in the hideous uniform and immediately felt the familiar sense of being an outsider. It was yet another country town where the other kids had grown up together since childhood, forging strong bonds. The school was extremely strict and our class was ruled by an old nun who was absolutely terrifying. She barked commands and orders at us before patrolling up and down the aisles of the classroom, wielding a thick, doubled-over leather strap in her hand. She watched and waited, like a crazed, hungry beast, for someone to make the slightest mistake before pouncing on them. Perhaps a student would ask for further clarification on a task, but she would drag them by the scruff of their neck to the front of the class, bend them over her desk and bring the leather strap down with great force.
"Just as the fear of God will save you from a life of sin and an afterlife in hell, so too will a fear of disobedience in my classroom save you from a life of foolishness," she preached.

To me, it felt like going straight to the hell bit and that she'd missed the point of life altogether. Her classroom was like hell on earth. I can't recall actually learning anything, aside from the ability to keep quiet and keep my head down. The true essence of me, which had begun to blossom during my time with Grumpy, was squashed but not entirely killed. Grumpy taught me to look for the good things in life and I found moments of joy in the little things. She showed me how to make the best out of whatever life threw my way.

I remember discovering cicada shells clinging to the trees in the big park we walked through on the way to school. They fascinated me—full replicas of the big insect left behind when the creature had grown to the next stage. Imagine being able to step out of your old, weathered skin and walk away fresh and new, leaving old scars behind. When I showed my little brothers, they thought they were scary and creepy and chased me with them. Eventually, we hung them on our clothes, their crispy little feet sticking beautifully to our woolly uniforms.

Another cherished memory was when I took my little brothers to the local swimming pool on the weekend. Our parents were busy as usual so they trusted us to keep ourselves entertained. There was no adult supervision, just me responsible for my younger siblings. We were given enough coins to use the turnstile to gain access to the pool. As we swam we noticed other children accompanied by mothers who were neither working, nor drunk. These children were lucky enough to receive additional coins from their mothers' purses, allowing them to purchase sweet treats like icy poles, lollies, pies or milkshakes at the pool shop after swimming.

One day, while my brothers and I were strolling to the town wishing fountain, opportunity arose. We were amazed by the shiny blanket of coins at the fountain's bottom. "What are your wishes?" I asked. "I wish I had some of that money to buy a lolly at the pool," replied my youngest brother. As the idea grew in our heads, we looked at each other. "You're going to get wet at the pool anyway. How about an early swim now?" I said. My youngest brother's eyes grew wide as he promptly removed his shirt and scaled the guard rail. In he went, while my other brother and I stood guard. Up to his knees in the fountain, he scooped up a few handfuls of coins and off we went to the pool.

After spreading our towels on the grass to create a picnic blanket, the boys went to the pool shop to get some goodies while I watched over our things. They returned with a small stash of chewy raspberry pink sticks called Redskins, fizz wizzes, sachets of sweet-sour powder with a tiny spoon that fizzed and made your eyes water and raspberry icy poles. The quick stop at the fountain to get our picnic money became a tradition and we enjoyed pool days thoroughly. Mum and Dad were too busy and we were too invisible for them to notice when we returned home with bright red or green tongues and lips, or in the case of my littlest brother, a mouth covered in raspberry stains.

It was only a couple of school terms during which I had been back with the rest of the family when Dad sold up again, moving us all to a new town. The journey to our next house was another reminder of how far down the priority list we kids were. We were traveling in two cars, with Dad towing a caravan piled high with all our belongings and Mum with me and my two brothers in the other car.

As it got late at night, Dad's idea of finding a hotel along the way turned out to be not so great as everything was full. We ended up having to sleep on the side of the road.

Dad dug some of our stuff out of the caravan to find us a place to lie down while he slept in the car. The next morning, the three of us kids woke up thirsty and hungry. Mum opened the car boot to see what she could find to quench our thirst. Three small children on a road trip and no water, no juice, definitely no food but surprise, surprise—a big box of Moselle wine.

There we were, me about twelve and my brothers about five and seven, standing by the roadside while Mum poured sweet wine straight from the box into our mouths! This seemed perfectly normal as a kid, but looking back at it from an adult's perspective, it's definitely one of those things that slightly horrify you.

14.5
Accidental Friend

Our new house was situated in a small coastal town, with a swimming pool in the backyard. I was pleased to have my own room with a small walk-in wardrobe. Unlike our previous home, there was no pub nearby. This time, Dad had decided to try his hand at being a professional bookmaker, not as his religious mother had assumed, by binding books in a factory, but by taking bets on horses at the racetrack.

As usual, I became a valuable member of the team. At the age of twelve, I was taken to the racetrack and trained to swing the bag, which involved standing on the betting stand with a large leather bag hung across my shoulder containing the money. Dad focused on watching the race and adjusting the odds, while Pa, who was excellent at mental arithmetic, served as the penciller. He recorded the bets in the ledger as they came in and Dad wrote the ticket for the punter.

My job was simple and the training was straightforward. Dad placed the wide leather strap of the large bag over my shoulders and instructed me to, "Grab the bloody money, then ask 'em what they want." It was a fast-paced and intense job, with money being handed to me quickly and bets being called out. I counted as fast as I could to ensure that the punter handed over the amount they had said. As with any job under Dad's watch, a mistake could be costly. If the bag was short at the end of the day, it could be a disaster.

The taking and paying of bets was quite fun. Anticipatory energy building momentum and hands clutching wads of cash were shoved in my face up until the moment the race started. In that moment the tide of people that had been pressing hard against me suddenly evaporated, leaving me feeling frightened and exposed. When the race started, all the adults ran to watch the horses run and left me standing there alone with sometimes tens of thousands of dollars hanging around my neck. I held my breath until they got back and the post-race craziness of settling of bets commenced.

Our small coastal town did not have a high school, so I was sent to a tiny school with other kids who were already planning which high school in the bigger town twenty minutes away they would attend. Many had already made friends with kids from the bigger town through sports, dance and other after-school activities. As the new kid, a year older than the others, I felt left out and alone.

I just had to get through one term at this tiny school and then I would have a chance at high school. Surely, given that many small towns fed their student population to one of the big high schools, someone else would be new and I could possibly find a friend.

Finally, I made it to the end of the school year, hoping for a fresh start in the new year. The school holidays were a welcome relief. I thought it would be a few peaceful weeks but a freak accident turned all my hopes upside down. Dad was a water skier and had made me go along on boating days despite my lack of interest. During the holidays he borrowed a boat, and with a couple of mates organised a river skiing day. While he jetted around the river, towing skiers and kids who wanted to try a toboggan ride, I wandered along the edge of the river looking for pretty stones in the sand.

I was standing ankle-deep in the water when the accident occurred. Dad was circling the boat around, towing a young boy on a toboggan behind him. Suddenly, the rope snapped, sending the boy hurtling out of control across the water and into an outcrop of rocks on the river's edge. The toboggan skidded across the little sandy beach where another boy was sitting, slicing open both his legs, and then kept going. As it passed by me, the loose end of the rope wrapped itself around my big toe. Dad had seen the first boy go and quickly spun the boat around to get back to the other end of the beach. All the other people on the beach were running to help the injured children. No one noticed as I was swiftly and silently dragged into the water.

It all happened so fast that I don't remember feeling any fear, just a strange sense of peace as I looked up through the surreal green water rushing past me. It was quiet and calm until suddenly, I was being dragged to the surface and spluttering back into the world. Fortunately, another group of people down the river bank had seen me go and swam out after me. The boat had dragged me out quite a way, unbeknownst to anyone in my group. The boys who saved me told me to look away as they unwrapped the rope from my almost-severed toe. They swam me back to shore, wrapping my foot in an old T-shirt to prevent losing the toe.

The rest of the afternoon continued to play out like some weird slapstick comedy sketch. Dad bundled three injured kids into the car and drove to the nearest phone box where he tracked down a local doctor. The closest hospital was too far away. Off we went to the doctor's home, where his poor wife played nurse while he triaged us and set about patching us back together. The head injury won first place, with the kid who hit the rocks stitched up, followed by the kid with both shins sliced open. Then me, the most complicated with twenty-two stitches in my toe.

That freakish few seconds that tried to steal my toe ended up stealing my hopes of finally not being the new kid with no friends at high school. I started the school year several weeks late and missed my moment. I arrived to find all the friendship groups pretty well established. There was one girl who seemed just as awkwardly out of place, so she and I ended up hanging out together by default even though we were very different.

Catherine was often naughty but my ingrained fear prevented me from joining in her mischievous antics. Instead, I buried myself in my studies and became a good student. During most lunch hours at school, I watched Catherine do pick-up rubbish duty as a punishment for her latest wrongdoing, whether it was smoking in the toilets, stealing, or back-talking a teacher. Catherine was fiery and outgoing, in stark contrast to my quiet and compliant nature. She dealt with bullies with a punch in the nose, while I tried to use the "pen is mightier than the sword" approach.

Despite our differences, we shared a common sense of unworthiness. Catherine had been adopted by much older parents and while her father was sweet, her mother was a dragon. Catherine often came to school with deep welts across the back of her legs where her mother had punished her with a thick, metal-edged ruler for failing academically. Looking back on our friendship, I realise that we were not good for each other. Although we were opposites in many ways, we thought we were helping each other get through high school.

I'm conscious that our friendship continued to normalise toxicity in relationships.

Neither of us had a friend with a family that set a different example. We both assumed that what went on in our homes was just how it was. Our lack of other friends also reinforced acceptance of bad behaviour in our friendship. She stuck with me even though she found me boring and unadventurous. She chose to test my loyalty by treating me badly while reminding me she was all I had. I chose to accept her poor treatment of me and condoned her misbehaviour rather than try to guide her more strongly for fear of losing her and being alone again.

14.6
Coming of Age

Thirteen was a year full of changes. My body started to change, my breasts began to bud, my hips widened, hair grew in all sorts of places, worst of all on my eyebrows and legs. Other girls were shaving and plucking but Dad wouldn't allow it, resulting in more fodder for the bullies, along with being called "nerd" and "geek" because I kept myself occupied with reading and learning. Boys made their disgust obvious and girls would speculate within my earshot whether my mother had been sleeping with a werewolf when I was conceived.

I begged Dad to let me shave like the other girls and pluck the middle of my mono brow. It made for such awful days at school that I started not wanting to go, claiming I was sick. In the end Mum caved in and we just did it anyway and then waited for Dad's wrath. It never came because he didn't even notice. So we secretly kept it up and it was one less thing for me to cope with at school. Dad not noticing was further confirmation of my irrelevance.

I was a pretty blonde girl and as my thirteen-year-old body started to change so did the way Dad and other men interacted with me. Dad called me in one day for "the talk". A talk with Dad was unheard of unless it was for a dressing down—which generally I was pretty good at avoiding. I learned to do as I was told, no questions. It was all very weird and I held my breath and tucked tightly scrunched fists under my knees as I sat on the sofa, trying to hide my anxiety about what it might all be about. He explained that boys might start talking to me and I should behave properly. "What do you mean? What do I do?" I asked. "Well don't ever put your hand on a boy's knee," he barked. "Why not?" I asked. "Just don't!" He left the room and I sat for a minute, bewildered.

Soon enough, I did feel a shift. Dad had parties at home, always the gregarious host, he had plenty of friends over for barbecues and drinking and what seemed like grown-up fun and laughter. Previously shooed away and made to feel like a nuisance at these events, I was now being asked to fetch drinks and snacks, followed by a pat on the bum in thanks.

At a public picnic at the local park once, Dad was laughing with his mates and pushing me to enter the wet T-shirt competition. I was horrified. Not too long afterward, at a pool party at home, I'd come out in a long white nightdress to say goodnight. I was feeling awful and wanted to go to bed because I had gotten my period that afternoon. Pissed and fooling around with his mates, Dad teased me about not wanting to enter the wet T-shirt competition. "Why are you such a bloody sook?" he asked. "Let's have one now."

He scooped me up in my thin white night dress and threw me in the pool, he and his mates laughing and wolf whistling, waiting for what the wet white fabric might reveal when I surfaced. All the blood drained from my face as I imagined a red streak following me as I swam to the edge of the pool. I frantically climbed out while trying to cover myself with my hands and ran indoors. I showered and changed and went to my room alone. My mother never came to see if I was OK: she was too busy being the perfect hostess. I was left alone with my humiliation.

Later that year, my cousin from New Zealand came to stay with us. He had come to Australia to study. His mother was my father's sister, although we'd never really had much contact with them before. We'd only met once before, during the previous Christmas holiday. During that time, we had a great deal of fun with his brother, my brothers and another cousin and his sister, all of us getting to know each other for the first time. When my cousin started university, Dad agreed that he could come and live with us for a while and my brothers and I were excited about his arrival. It would make a nice change.

I think Dad was trying to make a good impression on his nephew as a way of reconnecting with his sisters. Dad had become a bit of a black sheep in his family when he walked away from his strict Seventh Day Adventist upbringing. My mother believed that she was not liked by Dad's family and she often said that she thought they saw her as the reason why Dad had become a sinner—drinking, smoking and eating meat, running pubs and gambling, instead of doing something more suitable like becoming a minister. We had never even been to church.

Upon his arrival, my cousin was given the spare room. Although he was much older and about to start university, he was tolerant of his younger cousins who wanted to play with him all the time. Lots of family dinners were put on which were filled with laughter for his benefit. Mum even tried to make vegetarian food but it was unfortunately quite sad, consisting of tins of nutmeat cut into rounds with a slice of tomato on top. My brothers would gag at the table and exclaim disappointingly, "Oh no, not dog food again," which would bring much back-slapping laughter from my dad and cousin but caused great upset for my mum.

When Dad was around my cousin didn't pay much attention to me but other times he would strike up a conversation and we would chat. He seemed charming and nice. One afternoon only he and I were home. I was sitting in the lounge room reading a book. He came and sat next to me but much closer than he ever had before. I felt his hot breath on my ear. "What are you reading?" he asked.

I felt the hair on the back of my neck stand up as my heart started to pound. I snapped the book shut and tried to stand but he quickly grabbed my wrist with one hand and reached to brush my hair away from my face with the other. "You're really beautiful," he said. "I've got to go" I said, wrenching my wrist free.

I wasn't quick enough, in only two steps he had sprung, grabbing me with two powerful arms, pushing me against the wall and pressing his pelvis hard against me. He pulled me down to the floor. He was a big guy, muscle-bound and strong and several years older than me. Holding me down with one arm and the whole weight of his body, his free hand roamed under my top and up my skirt, trying to liberate my underwear and unzip himself. His thin lips were on my face as his tongue attempted to force my mouth open. My struggle and plea's for him to stop only seemed to excite him more. I finally wriggled to a position where I could swiftly lift my knee, taking his breath away for just enough time to break free. I ran to my room and locked myself inside. My walk in wardrobe also had a lock on the door, so I ran in there and locked that door as well.

Curled up under the hanging clothes with my knees tucked under my chin, held tight by white knuckled hands, I waited, wishing someone would help me. I listened as the others came home. I heard voices carrying on as normal, including his. "How was your day, what did you get up to?" All the usual meaningless chatter at the end of a day. It was a long time before anyone wondered where I was. When I hadn't made an appearance by dinner time, Mum finally came looking for me. She tried to open the bedroom door only to find it was locked. She called out, "It's dinner time, come on!"

Unsure what to say, I finally blurted "I'm sick, I don't want any dinner". What happened next helped to make it obvious where I stood and what would be expected from me as a woman. Mum demanded I open the door and stop being difficult. I opened the door and let her in, slamming it shut behind her and flicking the lock. She looked at my red face, puffy eyes and trembling hands with a mixture of confusion and annoyance. "What is wrong with you?" she demanded. "I can't go out there," I said. I showed her the emerging bruises on my hip and breast where my cousin had squeezed so hard, blurting out what had happened, between gasps for air. "Did he put "it" inside you?" "No," I said, "I got him with my knee." "That's OK then. Wait here," she said, pointing for me to stay on my bed.

She went out the bedroom door and then I heard her quickly return, whispering to my father as they went along the hall to their room. Through the adjoining wall I heard angry whispering but couldn't make out the words. Finally, their door opened, my dad leaving first. Mum called after him but only his final statement was loud enough to hear.   "I said that is the end of the matter!" he hissed. Then all went quiet.

I imagined he was about to go and punch my cousin on the nose and toss him out into the street. But it was only a minute later when I heard loud jovial belly laughs between them coming from downstairs.

It was a few minutes before mum reappeared, looking upset. "You must come to dinner, or we'll both be in strife," she said. She fetched a cold face washer and helped me cool down my face. "Just eat your dinner and then you can go straight to bed."

She led me to the dining room where my brothers, my Dad, and my cousin were all sitting, laughing and joking. I sat quietly in my seat, my eyes fixed on my hands, which were firmly clasped on my lap in an attempt to stop them from trembling. To say that I was confused does not even begin to describe the emotional turmoil I was experiencing. Sitting there, listening to the jovial banter between my dad and my cousin while trying to choke down whatever Mum had put on my plate so I could leave as soon as possible was inconceivable.

Dad knew what he had done to me, what he had tried to do to me, and it was me he stared daggers at, silently imploring me to behave. My cousin, who also knew what had happened, sat there looking smug and nonplussed, seemingly unaffected by the situation. He even winked at me, raising an eyebrow when no one was looking.

I choked down the last bite. "May I be excused?" I asked. My mouth was still half full, and my bum was already lifted off the seat. Without waiting for an answer, I hurried away from the table and up the hallway straight to the loo, where I promptly deposited the entire dinner.

I shut myself in my room, trying to process what had happened. Obviously, my cousin's nose was still intact and he wasn't being put out on the street, so where did that leave me? I didn't feel safe. What if he tried again? Clearly, my parents were not going to protect me. I made up my mind that I would have to leave. I packed a small bag of things and climbed out the window into the darkness.

I didn't get very far because I had nowhere else to go. From my hiding place in the bushes on the reserve across the road, I watched the house, half expecting a search party to set out at some point. All night, I cuddled up in the small rug I had brought, unable to rest. The house across the way, where I used to live, was just the same. Music and laughter carried on until late, then one by one the lights went out until all was dark.

No one came looking for me. Clearly, no one missed me. Slowly, the darkness ebbed as the morning light crept in and the realisation of a new day emerged. I watched from my cubbyhole as my brothers tore up and down the street on their bikes before being called to go to school. They hurried off up the street to the bus stop. I saw Dad and my cousin leave in one car and finally Mum left too. Not knowing what else to do, I crept out from my spot and back to my bedroom window and into the house. The pretend pillow me that I'd stuffed under the covers on the bed was still as I left her, undisturbed. How strange, I thought, wondering why I didn't matter. Was I invisible? Irrelevant? Unimportant? Was it my fault?

I decided that being invisible could be a good strategy. For some time after that, I spent most of my time in my own safe place, inside my walk-in wardrobe. I made a nest of blankets and pillows on the floor under the hanging clothes. I had a lamp and a thick pile of Trixie Belden mystery novels to read, as well as a few favourite toys. I emerged briefly for meals, making my excuses as quickly as I could. Finally, my cousin went off to university and the most anxious weeks, which had felt like months, came to an end.

However, I never felt safe in that house again. I could never trust my parents again, even after he left.

14.7
A Little Taste of Freedom

Dad was always talking about the importance of money, working hard, and saving it. He often preached, "Take care of the pennies and the pounds will take care of themselves." However, I was always confused to see him spend money on himself or my older brother but never for things that I wanted or needed. He would never part with a penny, claiming to be asset rich but cash poor. Whenever I tried to make a case for something I needed, he simply rebuffed me, saying, "What do you want me to do, rip a brick out of the wall?" I was expected to pay for things myself if I wanted them.

During one of his famous dinner table sermons on working hard and saving money, he looked each of us kids in the eye and made a promise that if we got a job as soon as we could and saved hard, he would go "dollar for dollar" when we wanted to buy our first car. I was thrilled and motivated. As the eldest, I would be the first one to benefit from this promise! I got not one, but two jobs. I worked at the counter at the Coles store back in the days when half the store was groceries and the other half clothing and household goods. I also got a job at a street-side fruit stall, where I selected, weighed, and bagged fruit and vegetables. A tiny notepad in my apron and a lead pencil were the only tools I had to calculate the cost by weight of each item and add up the total. I became a favourite at the stall for my swiftness and accuracy with numbers.

I saved every penny I could for my car and my freedom. Finally, as the time came to get my driver's licence I spotted a little car in my price range. I had my half of the money all saved up and went proudly to Dad to collect the other half. He reneged. No real explanation was offered. "Out of the question," he said. "You should be paying for these things yourself." He had absolutely no recollection of ever having promised to go halves. I'd already been paying for so much myself including my board and my own dental bills.

I was furious. The promise of freedom that that car had meant to me was what had kept me going and in one fell swoop he'd killed it. I stewed on it, the betrayal boiling in my belly until I had brewed a new idea. I was going to get a motor bike. It was all I could afford. Dad already said a motor bike was not an option… he wouldn't have his kids on one of those "death traps." I was determined, it was my money, I earned it and saved it for years. Serve him right if I fell off and killed myself. After so many years of anxious obedience, too frightened to put a foot wrong, I was bursting with angry rebellion.

Mum tried her best to console me behind Dad's back, reminding me that he was mean with his money and would never part with it, especially for a girl. I announced my decision with a "fuck you face". Dad, of course, thumped his fist on the table. "I will not allow it," he yelled. Mum promised to work on it and finally a compromise was arrived at. I could get a motor scooter, not a bike, and only if I could also afford all the appropriate safety gear.

And so begrudgingly I agreed to the less cool option, anything to be free to come and go as I pleased. I wanted a black one with a black leather jacket and black helmet. After several arguments about visibility on the road versus further humiliation and embarrassment at school, dark blue was agreed to but only if a bright yellow plastic rain coat was worn on every ride. That was never going to happen but none the less the small yellow parcel designed to be tucked into the scooter's glove box was added to the purchase. I wore it just until I got around the corner, where I stopped the scooter and tore it off to reveal the black vinyl jacket I wore underneath. It stayed stuffed in the glove box until I was at the same spot on the return journey. I felt naughty and rebellious but totally cool.

The best part of having the scooter was that I could go much further than I could on my push bike. This meant I was able to visit my grandparents whenever I liked. They were renting a small farm house a little way out of town. From the moment I got the bike, anytime things became too tense at home, or I'd had a bad day at school, I put a change of clothes in a back pack and called ahead to say I was coming. I offered to pay board for when I stayed but there was no way they would take my money. Each kilometre closer I got to Grumpy's house was another kilometre I put behind me. The air seemed to get sweeter and easier to breathe the further I was from home.

Visiting Grumpy and Pa's was always like returning home. The atmosphere in the house was so different from my own. Pa remained cheeky, naughty and needy, while Grumpy's calmness and gentleness meant she happily did everything for him without complaining. Pa still had his special chair in front of the television in a prime position for watching horse racing. He sat for hours, calling out for whatever he needed, even if it was just out of reach. Grumpy and I were out in the paddock, chopping wood for the fire, when we heard Pa calling, "Wanda...Waaanda." We rushed back in, to find that Pa just wanted a new packet of cigarettes from the cupboard only a metre away. "Bloody hell George, I was up the paddock getting the wood," Grumpy complained without much real conviction. Pa's cheeky grin appeared as he winked at us and I swear the little gold filling in his front tooth twinkled. While old king George perched in his chair, waiting to be tended to, Grumpy and I cut wood, serviced the cars and mended things that needed fixing.

My scooter gave me a little taste of freedom. The little trips out to Grumpy and Pa's house gave me a much needed break from the constant tension and the overwhelming sense of pointlessness I felt at home. Without that and without Grumpy I'm not sure I would have made it through to the end of high school.

14.8
Heartbreaker

I found my escape from everything and everyone in drama class. Something clicked within me when I explored my creativity in that class. I could pretend not to be myself, and in that pretence, I could be anything. I then decided that I wanted to be in the theatre. I somehow managed to convince my parents to let me attend a school holiday drama camp. However, when I returned full of enthusiasm, sharing stories of my fellow students getting roles on shows like Home and Away and my desire to go to NIDA, my parents shut it down quickly. Dad refused to pay for any education that was not for a "real job" like a school teacher or nurse. Mum reminded me that the tall, slim, and pretty girls would get the roles and it would be harder for someone short and curvy like me.

Despite their objections, I found the ability to step out of my own skin and become a character irresistible. When I wasn't myself, I felt good. I joined the local amateur theatre group and spent as much time as I could there.

On stage, dressed as an old lady and practicing my lines in the empty theatre, the only face in front of me was the lighting technician in the box at the back of the room. He led me perfectly across the stage with puddles of light that lifted and fell in unison with my performance. It was a dance that drew us together. He was a physically beautiful boy who seemed to spend as much time as I did at the theatre. We found any excuse to be there to help out.

The more time we spent together the more we wanted to spend together. David and I soon became inseparable, tortured by having to go to separate schools during the day, we couldn't wait till the bus home brought us back together.

David and his older brother lived with their single mum who seemed rarely to be at home. This suited us perfectly. Our afternoons were bliss and my responsibilities at home too easily forgotten. David was a talented musician; he played the saxophone and I loved to hear him play. It always felt raw like his soul was laid bare as his fingers danced along the keys. Dire Straits albums were the back drop to our days daydreaming about a creative life together.

I sketched him, gloriously bare chested and stretched out on his bed, his youthful body in complete contrast to his eyes of an old soul that I'd somehow known for a million years. For the first time it felt pretty damn good to be me. David was tender and gentle and our connection was one that didn't necessarily need words. Two creative souls that seemed to fit together so easily. Our physical connection was intense and palpable but I never for a moment felt pressured or unsafe. Everything evolved just as it was meant to, each of us feeling respected and safe.

We were happy and we were in love but our parents decided that they needed to get involved. They thought we were too young for such serious feelings and we were banned from seeing each other. They probably sensed that we were very close to exploring more than just touch. I was still deeply confused. Mum had been pushing me and coaching me to get a boyfriend as the key to my future, so why did she flip the moment I actually found my soulmate?

We were desperate to see each other. I sneaked out in the middle of the night and rode my bike the few blocks to his house. If his Mum was at home he crept out and we went down to the beach. The waves slowly sloshing up onto the sand was the only sound other than our deep, in-unison breaths. We held each other tightly, unable to figure out how we could survive the devastation our parents were wreaking upon us.

Inevitably we were caught and the seemingly malevolent power my father exerted proved too much for two young people to fight. There have been many times I wish we'd just run away then and there. I think both our lives may have been very different if we'd had the courage to do so. I have rarely been treated with such tenderness by men since. Indeed the day my heart broke seemed to be the start of a brokenness I couldn't seem to mend and an emptiness I couldn't fill.

I retreated even further into my own world. I ruminated on what could have possibly been so wrong about David that Dad could not accept him. He was not a bloke's bloke, he was a creative soul. Not someone Dad probably would have understood or appreciated. I decided to focus on proving to Dad that I was worthy. I thought if I worked hard and toed the line and showed that I could be trusted, Dad might relax and allow me to create a future I wanted. One that included David. I didn't know at the time that the next thirty years would continue to erode my soul until another deeply creative being would come into my life.

14.9
Time to Go

As the end of high school drew near and my peers discussed their plans for further education, I realised that I needed to leave home soon in order to preserve my mental health. My family would never fully support me for who I was and no matter how well I did academically, it was never enough. Despite excelling in my studies and receiving encouragement from my teachers to pursue medicine or law, I knew that I couldn't handle the pressure of continuing into years eleven and twelve. I needed to find a way out. While I enjoyed working with children and had done some work experience as a teacher's assistant, pursuing a career as a teacher would require more schooling and attempting that while still living at home would be too much for me to handle. So, I came up with the idea of pursuing early childhood care, which didn't require senior high school.

I discovered a course in Newcastle—fortunately, there was nothing similar in my local area—and applied, begging to start as soon as possible so that I could settle in before the course began. I argued that if I didn't make it into the first intake, I could work for a while and try again for the mid-year intake. My grandmother helped me make it happen. I think she knew I needed to leave. She found a family friend who would let me board with her and "keep an eye on me" and that sealed the deal.

Part of me was devastated to leave my grandmother. I could tell that her heart was breaking too. But we both knew it had to happen. A conversation we had before I left taught me a great deal about unconditional love. She told me that there was nothing I could do that would ever make her love me less.

"No matter what happens and whatever you have done no matter how bad, you can always tell me," she said. "Even if you've had to kill some bastard, you can tell me love!" We laughed but I do wonder if she had a premonition about the types of men I would end up involved with in my life.

And so as high school ended I had a plan. I just had to get through the embarrassment of the formal school graduation. Dad was generous with himself and his heir apparent but not with me. He wouldn't buy me a dress so I had to borrow a ghastly dated one from someone else's much older big sister. More fodder for the bullies as the weird, bookish girl turned up looking like a leftover 70's flower girl in pink frilly lace, complete with lace socks, white court shoes and home braided hair, while other girls wore elegant black, red or navy silk gowns with side splits, stockings and stilettos and sculpted updo's created by actual hairdressers. Naturally, there were no invitations to the after parties for me.

What was so very wrong with me that I didn't deserve any of that? It's not like we were poor and I could proudly say that was the best we could do. My Dad was a well-known businessman, who owned his own aircraft, sponsored local sports teams, invested tens of thousands in his oldest son's flying lessons but refused to throw a crumb my way. The only conclusion I could come up with was that somehow I wasn't good enough but I could never figure out why.

Just when I thought I had gotten through the final humiliation before I could leave town, I was faced with one more difficult situation…I was raped. I'd been babysitting for a family down the road for some time and gotten to know them well. I would often call in and see the kids and help out where I could.

One day when I called in, only the dad was home with the kids. "Their mum's away for a few days seeing her sick father. I'm struggling a bit with the kids to be honest," he said. Of course I offered to help. We made dinner for the kids, bathed them and put them to bed and as a thank you he offered pizza and a movie.

As we watched the film in the dark he moved closer to me and before I knew it he'd wrapped a big, strong, warm arm around me. It felt nice; he was a good looking man and had always been kind and caring. I got lost for a second in the feeling of getting a little attention. I was such an easy target for his seduction because most of the time no one seemed to know I even existed. At first his kisses were intoxicating and exciting but when his hands moved to other places, I knew it was wrong. "No, please stop," I cried but he was strong and swift, forcing himself on me. His kindness turned venomous.

"Nobody's gonna believe anything you say … you're just a girl only good for fucking," he said. "It's all your fault anyway. That skirt of yours is far too short; it's just an invitation and everyone knows it. How can any man resist? You tell a single soul and it will only shame your family. Who wants a whore for a daughter, anyway?"

Time stopped and what may have only been a few moments became a vast black hole in my soul. When he was done he told me to get out and that he looked forward to our next babysitting date. I already knew no one would listen. After all, I'd already tried to tell my parents that my cousin had tried to force himself on me when I was barely a teenager. No one listened then, so what chance would there be now? So I went home and I told no one—not even Grumpy. I knew I could but I just needed to get away and I didn't want anything to interfere with that. I knew that if she knew she'd just pull me closer to keep me safe.

So I made my plans to move away and I left. I moved to Newcastle to await news on whether I had gotten into my course. I also waited for my period that never arrived. I was 17 and away from home for the first time, living in a stranger's house and pregnant. Now what? Well I knew for sure I couldn't possibly have this baby. It would involve way too many conversations that I just didn't have the strength for.

Determined not to risk having to go home I just had to sort it out myself. I found an abortion clinic and made an appointment. My elderly landlady's daughter drove me to my appointment and picked me up again afterwards. "Pretend it didn't happen and get on with it," was her advice. She offered no comfort or other care and it was never spoken of again.

14.10
Violent Dancer

Life went on with no one else the wiser. I didn't get a place on the course so I started to look for work. I was adamant that I didn't want to go home. After a little while I met a boy. He was a street dancer, good looking and very cool. Strangely he'd also lived in my home town for a little while and I had seen him perform there. All the cool girls thought he was hot and now he was showing an interest in me. This was such a traumatic period in my life that I can't even recall how we met. After a while of dating he asked me to move in with him. I was still a little star struck and beginning to think that maybe I was OK after all. We got a small flat together, having no money to speak of. I got work at a takeaway and he drove taxis in between dance shows.

When my father heard I had moved in with a boy he cut me off. I had no problem with him opting out, it's not as though there was some kind of financial support tap or deeply rewarding emotional connection there. But he banned me from calling home to speak with my mother and my brothers; he didn't want me to infect them with my "sinful" ways. My grandmother was also on the banned list but we found a way to occasionally communicate.

My parents told me that the only way to fix the situation was to get married. When I told Lee he said, "Well, let's do it then." And so at 18 I announced my engagement and was begrudgingly welcomed back into the fold. A little wedding was planned, another dreadful second hand dress, this one blue—I didn't deserve a white one. Just my family and his at the registry office and one night at a 2 star motel.

I knew on my wedding night that I'd made a dreadful mistake. "You're mine now," my new husband whispered. I cringed, all I wanted to do was run, but I couldn't, I didn't think my father would let me come back. When I mentioned my uncertainty to him he said firmly, "You've made your bed, now you get to lie in it." And so I did.

Things turned so abruptly it made my head spin. Lee was suddenly angry with me about anything and everything. I didn't iron his clothes properly, I didn't have his outfit that he wanted ready for the show that I didn't even know he had on. I was no longer allowed to go to the shows because I was an embarrassment. We got evicted from our little flat because he hadn't paid the rent. He moved us to a very run down house, backing on to the rail line where the crockery would shake every time a train went by. He laughed as he hit me for fun…no one could hear me cry out above the noise of the rumbling trains.

Soon it became too difficult to go to work. I was bruised and sore and didn't want to be seen. My husband wanted me to be around in case he needed something and didn't want me wasting my time at work.

This only lasted a few months before we were again evicted. So we moved, this time to a house that had been split into upstairs and downstairs flats. Our upstairs flat had key lock windows and deadlocked doors.

It wasn't long before he started locking me in when he left—daytime on the taxi and night time to the dance clubs. He came home for dinner and a change of clothes in between. I wasn't given permission to go out anywhere. He brought the food he wanted me to cook, but only enough for him. Half the time the food I cooked for him wasn't to his satisfaction and ended up being hurled at my head. If I ducked or swerved and it ended up on the wall behind me, he grabbed me and slammed my head against the wall, rubbing my nose in it anyway. As long as it didn't include the plate, I learnt it was easier to cop the food bomb, after which he'd demand his marital rights as a man.

He only let me eat leftovers, if indeed there were any. He started to eat away from home, bringing food home less often. I became thinner and weaker but I'd figured out a survival plan. I could remove a louver from the laundry window and get outside. I'd wait till he was asleep and steal a few coins from his trousers but I had to be careful that it was not enough to be noticed, so I only took a few cents at a time. I hid the stolen coins carefully and once I had enough I sneaked out the skinny window to the corner store to buy a bag of flour. I was so frightened I'd get caught but I was hungry. I had to get back quickly to hide the flour. I surreptitiously made flour and water pancakes while my Lee was at work. There was no sugar, eggs or milk.

One night there was a knock on my back door. I'd been told never to answer the door. Outside were two girls, students who were renting the downstairs flat. They begged me to answer. "We know you're there, please talk to us, don't be afraid," they called.

We started talking through the door at first. "We know what's going on in there and you have to get out!" "But, I have nowhere else to go," I explained, "and anyway I'm afraid he'll find me and kill me." "Don't you realise that if you stay you'll probably end up dead anyway?" they said. I knew they were right, so they helped me and we planned my escape. I slithered out my secret window when my husband was at work and go down to their place where they fed me and we plotted. Turns out he had been flirting with them and telling them he was just waiting for his rich father-in-law to come good and he'd be a famous dancer. Boy, oh boy, he misread that one!

They talked me into it, solving every excuse I could come up with for why it wouldn't work. They convinced me it would be easy, all I had to do was get out that window one more time and they would sort the rest. I knew I wouldn't have courage for long and I was so frightened my husband would suspect something, so we had to be quick. We picked a time I knew was safest, the time he would be away longest, and they made me swear on it. They let me use their phone. I called home. "I'm coming home, Can you please pick me up at the train station?" I asked. I didn't say anything more.

As soon as the coast was clear I grabbed just a handful of things and popped them in a small plastic carry bag. I shoved it out the window and slid out after it, leaving every other possession behind. The girls were waiting, we jumped in their car and they sped to the train station. They bought my ticket and waited with me on the platform for the train to come. The anxiety of wondering if my husband had come home and realised I had run and would turn up at the train station was overwhelming.

When the train arrived, I climbed aboard, watching with a knot in my stomach for him to appear and willing the damn train to close its doors and get moving. Finally, it shuddered and pulled away from the platform. The two girls watching and hugging each other faded into the distance— and I was alone. The next few hours were surreal as the train rattled along and I travelled further and further away from a living death and closer to freedom.

When I arrived home I was 165cm tall, but only weighed 45kg. I was scrawny and frail and despite being "forgiven" for my sins, I still felt out of place and filled with shame. For a few months I tried to put my life back together. I found work and focused all my energy on just putting one step in front of the other. I still didn't have friends so it was work and home (sharing a bedroom with my little brother), home and work. I was pushed to attend a family friend's kid's 21st birthday and reluctantly agreed. Little did I know this would be a new door opening. Robbie, a boy I went to school with was also a guest and was a safe person for me to talk to. As we chatted and I asked about his life, not willing to share anything of mine, he shared that he was having a most wonderful time living in another city. In his gorgeously flamboyant style he opened his door to me. "Darling you simply have to come and visit, but there is something I need to tell you. Now, you might be shocked…. but I'm gay".

"Good lord man, how long have you known?" I laughed. "I could have told you that when you were 12 years old." We laughed and hugged and I felt a real human connection for the first time in so long. We spent the rest of the evening picking out good looking chaps together. It was the most fun I'd had in a long time. We vowed to keep in touch and I promised to think about a visit.

Weeks passed and life plodded on in no particular direction. Then a bunch of flowers were delivered to my work. The girls made a fuss about who the secret admirer might be. When I opened the card I literally fell to my knees. You are my wife, I know where you are, I am coming to bring you home. I went home and immediately rang Robbie. "Did you mean it when you said I could visit? Is tomorrow too soon?"

And so I ran again. When I arrived Robbie had a small one bed flat with no furniture and a mattress on the floor. It was nothing much but I had a lively and vibrant person to hang out with. Robbie took me out to my first gay bar. "Darling this will be the first time you've been out and I guarantee no man will hit on you," he said. I loved every minute of it.

I told Robbie I wanted to stay. I didn't share that I needed to. As we lay snuggled together on his mattress on the floor, we plotted our next steps. I would get work, then we would look for a furnished rental. I found a job, rang home and said I wasn't coming back. We found a cute little house all furnished with the best thing about it being a huge dining room and dining table. Weekends consisted of colourful dinner parties. Just me and a table full of queens. It was fabulous.

Sadly, it came time that Robbie wanted to move on. He had aspirations of a career as a flight steward and decided to go to Sydney. I found myself looking for new digs with absolutely no intention of going home again. I found a room in a share house with a lovely single mum and continued on.

One day her boyfriend said to me "I'm sick of looking at you every weekend, I've found you a date." It was the absolute last thing I was interested in but went along with a lunch time double date style meeting. And so the next chapter of my life began…

14:11
The Frog Pot Cook

My friend's boyfriend introduced me to the man who would become the father of my children and remain in my life for the next 23 years. I call this period of my life the "frog pot period". Like the frog in the boiling pot analogy, I found myself being slowly boiled alive.

The frog pot cook seemed kind and funny when we first met and we enjoyed each other's company. As we got to know each other, I recognised qualities that I thought might be a bridge to re-igniting my father's approval. He was money driven, focused on earning the next promotion at work and paying off the house that he had bought. He was not particularly adventurous. Work was his main focus. His family welcomed me with open arms and it felt strange but pleasant to instantly have a large extended family with lots of aunts, uncles and cousins, who all seemed to be quite close. His mother cooked a weekly family dinner and I loved to be a part of that.

I felt quite settled and moved into the frog's house. Life was pretty good. The first red flag that I ignored was being told I needed to up my game and find a better job. I'd been working in the beauty industry and although I really enjoyed it, the job was not well paid. My first attempt resulted in me getting a job at a higher end salon. I also got some part time work with a local modelling agency teaching manicures and nail care and styling nails for photoshoots. I painted tiny flowers and landscapes on fingernails. It was wonderful fun. I was so desperate to please and so anxious to earn my place in this big family. I scanned the jobs pages and soon found my thinking reverting to what job was considered a "proper" job for a young woman, a teacher or a nurse perhaps. I had no qualifications for either but when a job for a child care assistant appeared I thought it a good place to start.

Excitingly, Grumpy and Pa had chosen to move to my town to be closer to me. They rented a little townhouse only a couple of blocks down the road and I was able to walk down and see them all the time. It felt like life was finally coming together for me.

Back home my parents had split up. Dad had gone back to his first wife. This was the first I had heard of there even being a first wife and a hint that I was yet to discover more of the past I didn't know about. When he left, he sold one of the family motels and left one for mum to run. She also bought a small flat a few blocks from the motel. Mum's drinking and gambling was still a dominant feature and I was horrified to hear that my teenage brothers had been largely left to their own devices in the flat giving them ample opportunity to run amok. Over the years stories emerged of drinking, smoking and drugs, plus dangerous games of knife throwing into a mattress.

The youngest of the two boys, my dearest little buddy who I had been so protective of as a child, was the worst of the two. He, a little like me, was never Dad's favourite. Our middle brother was a handsome, strapping young man, a star footballer and a budding pilot and considered Dad's heir apparent. My dear goofy little brother was the little fat kid with crooked teeth and glasses who knew he couldn't compete for Dad's attention. To hear how badly he ran off the rails was deeply upsetting and the guilt I felt when I found out is something that weighs deeply on me still. He has battled with mental health issues and the "what if's" still bang about in my head whenever I see him struggling. I have found it incredibly difficult, if not impossible to forgive myself for letting him down.

What if I hadn't left? What if I could have found a way to take him with me? I should have protected him better. But the reality was, for my own sanity, I had to go. I left and didn't look back for some time. And when I did reconnect, everything had turned upside down. Things had gone so pear-shaped that our youngest brother had been shipped off to live with Dad and his first wife. Dad's discipline was supposed to sort him out but that didn't work too well.

It wasn't long before I found out that Mum and my brothers were also moving to my town. Our oldest brother and his girlfriend, a gorgeous human being that he'd been with since they were 14, were the first to arrive. With some of the money from the settlement of their house, Mum had bought him a milk run so he would have his own business. No job hunting required.

For more than twenty years, I was controlled by the frog pot cook. He didn't allow me to spend the money I earned or even collect the mail, which he locked in the mailbox to which he held the key. He scrutinised grocery receipts and set absurdly unreasonable budgets. My creative pursuits, such as cooking, painting, sewing, and writing, were seen as trivial and wasteful. It was confusing and torturous because the frog pot cook publicly supported my creativity, yet he would squash it behind closed doors. For example, he gave me a cookbook as a birthday gift in front of the family, only to berate me for buying ingredients to make a recipe from it later on. "What a waste of time. We don't need to eat dinner every night," he complained.

Whenever I tried to make time to paint, the frog pot cook would find another job that was supposedly more important. Nothing I did was ever good enough, fast enough, or cheap enough. Despite working full time, being solely responsible for all the needs of our two children (including homework and parent-teacher meetings), doing most of the housework and handyman work (since I was better at it) and renovating until the early hours of the morning (sometimes through the night), I was regularly subjected to bouts of fury and vitriol. According to the frog pot cook, I wasn't pulling my weight and was lazy and incompetent, especially as a mother.

As the children grew older, any signs of teenage rebellion or noncompliance were seen as a reflection of my failure as a mother by the frog pot cook. He made the rules, and I was the enforcer, foolishly trying to control what was ultimately uncontrollable. Every aspect of my life was scrutinised, criticised and micromanaged. Despite this, I was devastated when I was ultimately asked to leave this "domestic harmony." I'd already been told that nobody else would ever want me, so I was at a loss as to where to go and what to do. In my desperation to prove my worth, I foolishly agreed to continue renovating the house we'd been working on and sewing all the curtains for it, even though he'd made it clear that I wouldn't be getting a fair share. He deducted all of his financial contributions, including interest, after more than twenty years together.

So clear was he that everything financial was his, that the day I got my marching orders I found I'd been cut off from all bank accounts and credit cards. I had no cash because I was required to account for any spending and cards only made it easy to track my every move. After more than 20 years of faithful, unwavering service, I was simply cast aside.

14.12
Breaking the Spell of Control

Moving day was the catalyst that shook me to my boots and broke the spell of control. I'd fought to get access to a small share of a lifetimes accumulated assets. Settling for a fraction of what I should have. I had found my own place and the kids and I were moving. The truck arrived and twenty years of belongings got broken in two. At the new house I got on with the work of unloading the truck and trying to organise a new space.

My son was to ride his new motorbike over that afternoon after work. I got a call - the one all mothers whose teenage kid has bought a motorbike dreads. "Ah mum I've dropped the bike". He'd fallen off just at the start of our new road. At low speed thank goodness. When I got there it looked like a broken foot and the bike was a write-off. Very lucky he was not badly hurt.

With the moving truck still on the drive and not yet empty I called his dad to drive him to hospital, I'd meet them there as soon as I could. I arrived a hour or so later and my son had been left at hospital on his own - no father to be seen. I was furious. Later that night, after being treated and sporting a moon boot my son hobbled to my car in pain - he asked if we could go past the old house as he had left his backpack in his dads car.

I pulled into the driveway of my marital home. The one I hadn't even finished moving out of yet and there through the window, in the glow of the lights were two shadows not one. I knocked on the door and a quiet panic ensued, whispering and shushing before the door was opened a crack. I pushed the door open further. Seems I'd interrupted a celebration. 'A working bee' he said. A working bee with one person? 'How long?' I asked. Nothing. 'Well I hope she can fucking sew'.

That was it, truth, realisation, anger, hurt all at once. He'd been screwing his boss for how long I don't know and still driving me into the ground, flogging me night and day to complete his renovation. I didn't go back, I didn't do any more work on the property.

The next year was one of continual change. At first so broken I thought I might never be able to move again. Then a slow process of putting the pieces of my shattered soul back together. Gradually finding the courage to explore the freedom I now had.

I rebelled against all the restrictions I had been under for years. Daring to buy whatever groceries I needed to be able to explore my love for cooking. Recklessly purchasing new art materials. Getting great delight in leaving the heater on in the house to stay warm in the minus 8 winter.

I bought a thick comfortable orthopaedic mattress after sleeping on the same thin way too firm one for more than 20 years. My painful back was so relieved. I bought not one but two sets of sheets and pretty doona covers. No more "what do you need a second set of sheets for - we've got one". And on a frivolous whim I bought a cushion - just to make the bed look pretty.

My daughter and I searched garage sales and splashed out on second hand decor items to make the house feel more homely. This kind of extravagance unheard of and deplored was now a source of wicked enjoyment.

I scribbled arguments with myself down to help me process my emotions. Eventually I came to a place of peace. Of understanding that it was ok to have wants and desires, that I didn't need to hide these anymore. That it was ok to be me.

One day a poem just came through me, that for me encapsulated the entire experience in one. Of going down into the black hole of invisibility and of climbing back out to once again bask in the light.

Broken - a puzzle put back together - a year in the making......*Her Impenetrable Truth*.

14.13
Her Impenetrable Truth

All the parts of her broken into jagged piece.
Every day another fragment examined,
found flawed, damaged, deficient, inconsequential.

Crumpled on her knees at the end of another day
secretly gathering shattered shards from the floor,
desperately hoping to find them all.

Lovingly she wraps them up and kisses them goodbye.
Day after day, piece after piece after piece,
'till all that was her was gone.

She closed the box, wrapped it in chains
for safe keeping, carefully locking herself away
so she could hide while a lie lived for her.

Hollow, empty, she walked the earth but cast no shadow.
She left no footprints; she made no sound, no mark
And she was sure no one even knew she was there.

Look there I am, safe, she would tell herself
as she stole surreptitious glances at the box
looking for comfort in her waning illusion.

But at night clandestine whispers from the fragments of her soul
seeped from the box into her dreams.
Here I am, see me, hear me, feel me, love me...

Sparks of a primal energy began to flicker within

until the fire in her belly burned hot
screaming, "You're not safe, you are lost."

She had chosen to believe another's truth, not hers.
She had chosen to believe she was unworthy.
Realisation, sadness, anger, blame, owning choices, hope.

She crawled through the haze to her secret place,
dragged the chained box to her and held it tight,
willing that the pieces of her would still be there.

With tentative breath she slowly opened the box.
There inside the folds of love made long ago
the fragments of her soul still faintly glimmered.

She spread them before her and remembered.
And as she grieved time lost; she wept,
her tears falling upon broken pieces until they shone.

She lifted each glistening shard to her lips,
kissed it and loved it like a child,
then placed it back where it should have always been.

Now she stands magnificent before you,
her soul shining brightly for all to see.
Her loving truth impenetrable; now she is truly safe.

14.14
Teacher of Love

Then the next pivotal moment of my life appeared and I found myself, forty something, standing on the precipice of a new beginning.

Spending time just finding me, putting the pieces of my soul back together, I had very much learned what I didn't want in life and from there came clarity of what I did want. And with that clarity my soul called out and finally he came, the next powerful teacher of love.

Having the confidence to step forward wasn't easy. Funny thing though is when I did leap all I found was ease. I now understand that I am the creator of my life and that I call into my life everything that I am supposed to have and know.

Opening my heart to the possibility of new love was at first frightening. A little flood of poetry helped me to walk around the emotions of meeting a most wonderful and special human being.

Convinced by my beautiful daughter to take the risk of meeting new people online (a safe distance) I took my first ever foray into online dating. Inane conversations, obvious motives, second guessing myself that at this stage was a connection even possible.

Then one day something different, someone different. We talked and talked before meeting. Brief messages became long meaningful email conversations, then phone calls. Frightened - at a distance getting to know you, you getting to know me, you helping me get to know me. The night before we actually met I had a dream......

Awakening

Enveloped by a resonating light,
Warm radiance upon my skin

Breathing deeply arms open,
Face to the sky, basking in delight

The enchantment of possibility
Delicious daydreams dancing in my head
Relentlessly enticing me closer
Daring me to surrender to recklessness

Many layers of a complex soul
Tenderness and power dazzlingly juxtaposed
A grace, serenity and clarity
That finds in me my own

Beautiful words whisper to my spirit
So real I feel his breath upon my neck
I feel his rhythm deep within me
Yet I have not touched his face

Deeper and stronger he pushes
Opening me, feeling me, knowing me
I feel the crescendo as his words touch my soul
And I know I have never been in love before

Ancient Eyes

Hey you with ancient eyes
Do you feel me?
You fill me with lingering emotions
Infusing all my thoughts with you

Hey you with ancient eyes
Can you see me?
When you are near
My truth is laid bare

Hey you with ancient eyes
Do you hear me?
Your essence whispers endlessly
Enlivening my spirit

Hey you with ancient eyes
Can you taste me?
The exotic sweetness of you
Lingers on my tongue

Hey you with Ancient Eyes
Do you know me?
I feel a knowingness that
Wraps me in violet serenity

Hey you with ancient eyes
Do you remember me?
....No matter reminiscence
Our moment is now

Who Is She?

Over coming the fear of being open
is unrecognisable at first......

She kneels naked before him
Arms open, eyes open, heart open
Shamelessly baring her soul

She lifts her chin and tilts her head
Drinking in the delicious joy
Of simply knowing him

I am here watching and wondering
How can she be so open?

How can she give so freely?

She looks so beautiful exposed
Bathed in his exquisite light
I see her delicate vulnerability

I feel him touch her and I know
she is safe, she is loved
and I know now
....she is me

Knowing

In a moment it is clear....
There was a quickening
an inward breath
drawing of focus
down deep into the core

a strength of purpose
an understanding of self
a revelation, clarity
of what it means to be

Outwardly time slowed
With-in, a deep rush
the knowing of a life time

comes to pass in but a moment.

It Is Time
....Like no other

It is time to create a love like no other
A love that pushes the boundaries of sensibility

A love that celebrates every moment
A love of shared and powerful strength
Teaching me grace and choices

His Grace

Teaching me grace and choices

He stands strong in his knowing, personified self-control
He knows who he is, what he wants, where he has been and where he is going
The diffident onlookers wonder at his grace, at his peace, at his power

Don't they realise that he has built his tower on the deepest foundation
Love and loss, pain and fear, failure and success, more and less
Layers of learning built over a life of many lessons

Just like you he has fought and lost he has hurt and been hurt
Just like you he has been the maker of choices
His grace lies in the learning and the owning of those choices

Morning Song

Learning to listen to my soul….

I love the wonder of the morning's first tranquil hour
Wrapped securely in the serenity of my lovers embrace
Warm bodies and contented souls deeply connected
Together as darkness dissipates and dreams slowly fade

Consciousness moves through the delicious awakening of senses
Awareness of first sounds licking, teasing, at the edge of stillness
The emerging glow of morning light dancing at the window
The smell of the earth delightfully fresh after overnight rain

Slow deep drowsy breath gradually lightens and quickens
Bodies begin to move and lengthen, flushed with flowing blood

Invisible threads of connection whispering with no words
And skin on skin warmth evokes exquisite, mindful, touch.

No longer invisable.......I Am Real

I knew the taste of emptiness
Living locked in self denial
Watching from a distance
And felt the guilty sin of wanting more

I have grieved, mourned the loss
Of time, opportunity, experiences
I have come to own my choices
And to be thankful for the learning

I have found within myself all I need
My love my laughter my strength
My truth my honesty my joy
Now I know that I am real.

Together we now live a very centred, powerfully connected and passionate life.

Together we have travelled the world, exploring our mutual fascination with creativity, art, food, music, theatre, dance, everything that represents creative expression.

He gently yet firmly and confidently has taken my hand, encouraging me with his playfulness, creativity and carefree disregard for conformity. We live how we wish to live, do what we love to do with a refreshing frivolity that I have not experienced before.

Everything we do is imbued with the same core energy, whether we are cooking, eating or working on a project together.

14.15
Thoughts on Domestic Abuse

I wrote this short book initially to get all the emotional mess out of my head and heart and onto paper. It was a way for me to close a difficult chapter and express the evolution of a new one. Writing has become a peaceful place where I can be completely honest with myself. I was taken by surprise when poetry began to flow. I believe it was part of the healing process and a way for me to always remember the kaleidoscope of emotions I felt as I moved from being very disconnected from myself—standing on the outside looking in— to coming to realise that the joy I observed and wondered at actually belonged to me and it was okay to let myself feel it.

I decided to share my inner thoughts for a couple of reasons. Firstly, I touch lightly on the layers of abuse in my life, some of which clearly and obviously fall into the category of domestic abuse. I am grateful to see light being shone on domestic abuse these days, but much of the discussion seems to focus on the word "violence". I wanted to specifically touch on the fact that abuse is not just physical violence and that violence is to violate, which might not necessarily involve the laying on of hands.

Domestic violence also includes the following: exerting control, coercion, any form of bullying, humiliation, criticism and isolating the individual from their friends and family. Here are some examples of how these may manifest practically:

- controlling a person's finances money or credit cards.
- making a person account for every penny they spend.
- only allowing basic necessities (food, clothes, medications, shelter).
- limiting a person to an allowance.
- preventing a person from working or choosing their own career.
- sabotaging a person's job (making them miss work, calling constantly, bullying them into doing things other than their job so they are unable to meet work commitments)
- stealing from a person or taking their money.
- Judging or criticising everything a person does.

- Down playing a person's achievements.
- Gaslighting - make a person question or doubt themself.

All these things are indeed abuse, and all these things I experienced with the excuse being, "It's not abuse, I never touched you."

Now, however, I want to focus on the joy of possibility. The possibility of newness, of finding a peaceful space to know oneself.

It's never too late to start again and move through the confusion, confrontation and disbelief.

As the great English novelist, George Eliot said, "It's never too late to be what you might have been."

14.16
What Recovery Made Possible

When I first met Georgie, she carried her history in her body. Shoulders curved inward, apologising for stolen space. Eyes checking every face, calculating what they needed her to be. Between her words lived decades of silence.

Her life given away in the thousand ways survivors know: the hobby abandoned because he mocked it, the friend not called back because it would cause a fight, the promotion not taken because he needed her home, the opinion swallowed, the dream folded up and put away. Given away until she couldn't remember what she'd wanted to keep.

I wanted her to write. To find her voice buried under all that silence.

And I wanted us to travel. To discover who she was, once the walls came down.

She'd crossed borders before—Vietnam, the UK for his family—but always as a ghost, present but not there, serving but not experiencing. Trips planned around other people's needs, her own desires nowhere in sight.

Our travels were different. I handled the logistics—the secret of getting into the top booked-out restaurants, finding first-class seats for the price of standard, knowing which museum pass meant walking straight in. Not extravagance, just planning. It meant she could finally just experience rather than orchestrate. What I didn't know was that as we went, she was writing herself back into existence. Her journals weren't travelogues. They were maps back to herself.

"Here I am, forty-something, standing on the precipice of a new beginning. I am naturally a giver, and I had spent my life working hard and giving my everything to everyone but me. Then one day I was given a gift: I was cast aside. Given my freedom. I didn't immediately realise it was a gift, but now I know—starting a new chapter of my life was

starting my time."

She moved through life watching from somewhere near the ceiling—hands that poured coffee but couldn't feel the heat, a face that smiled but felt nothing, feet that walked but never felt the ground.

And yet here she was, claiming something new.

"Having the confidence to step forward wasn't easy. Funny thing though—when I did leap, all I found was ease. I now understand that I am the creator of my life, and that I call into my life everything I am meant to have and know. So I called. And then he came."

She meant me. But really, she was calling herself home.

That Woman Was Me

When I booked Paris, her hands flew to her mouth. Eyes darting—checking if this was real, allowed, if someone would take it back.

"I had always dreamt of travel, seeing the world and experiencing other places and cultures, but I always thought it was just that, a dream. I never imagined that I would ever really go to the places I dreamed of, I had been taught for years that those experiences were for others and not for me. When my love booked tickets to Paris I was so excited. Excited but nervous, lil ole me? Paris? Really?"

At the airport check-in, the passport trembled in her grip—stiff pages, barely creased. Not an entry document, but an unopened book of adventures waiting to be lived. *"I felt shaky as we handed over passports checking into our flight. I slipped into another level of consciousness and I watched from above as the young lady behind the counter handed a boarding pass that said Paris to that seemingly distant woman below. She looked closely at that pass and as she smiled I recognised the smile and the hand that held the boarding pass, I finally realised was mine."*

She held that boarding pass with both hands. Read her name three times like learning a spell.

The security scanner beeped. She lifted her arms, holding her breath like she used to when being searched for evidence of wanting too much.

"There was a flurry of cues and x rays and stamping of documents, shoes off, hats off, arms up, legs spread, bomb wand waved over bags until we finally emerged out the other end slightly more dishevelled than we were when we arrived at the airport."

The airline lounge reeked of reheated quiche and the peculiar sweat that money can't hide—executives downing their third whisky before take off, terrified of turbulence. The buffet gleamed with yesterday's sandwiches under heat lamps, congealed scrambled eggs, fruit salad turning brown at the edges. All of it free, none of it worth eating.

Around us, travelers in expensive suits sprawled across leather chairs, but Georgie perched on the edge of hers, handbag clutched in her lap, knees pressed together. She kept touching her boarding pass, running her thumb over the raised letters: PARIS CDG. Pressing it between her fingers to feel its thickness, its reality.

Finally Allowed to Want Things

Perfume hung thick as fog—vanilla, musk, something sharp and green that caught in her throat. She moved between counters, at first hugging her elbows close, then gradually unfolding. In the Chanel mirror, I watched her reflection change: shoulders dropping, chin lifting, a woman remembering she was allowed to want things.

The saleswoman sprayed her wrist. Georgie closed her eyes, breathing it in, then—for the first time I'd seen—she held her wrist to her neck, marking herself with sweetness.

"Chanel foundation. Clarins Beauty Flash Balm. MAC Lipglass. Victor & Rolf Flowerbomb. OPI polish. I felt spoiled and stunned. Part of me whispered, How the hell does he know all this girly shit?"

Each purchase swinging from her arm. The glossy bag bumped her hip with every step, and each time, her smile widened. Like a bell she was finally allowed to ring.

Hours later, somewhere over Germany, her head found my shoulder. In Dubai, we stumbled through neon and exhaustion. Then descent.

"I saw the Eiffel Tower in the distance. As the plane touched down, my stomach flipped. It was real. I was here. Me. In the city of light. And would you believe it? Our cab driver had a glass-roofed car. Paris had been waiting. And I had finally arrived."

Through that glass roof, April Paris poured light across her upturned face. A city so many had sung about, now singing to her.

My Body Is Not an Apology

The Louvre swallowed us whole. Marble rang cold under our feet, the sound echoing up to ceilings so high they made her crane her neck like a child seeing sky.

"We finally work out where the Rubens room is and oh my what a space. There are a couple of art students set up with easels, crafting amazing pieces based on the master's works. I could happily sit all day and watch them paint."

Standing before those canvases—celebrations of creativity—something shifted. Her hand moved unconsciously to her own hip, fingers pressing through fabric as if confirming she too was real, was allowed this shape. I watched her study how Rubens' brush had loved every fold, every dimple, like they were holy.

"Beautiful voluptuous women are celebrated. Rubens' brush sweeping around soft full breasts and wide generous hips and bottoms, to me caressing the sensuality of real women. Oh and where has the bush gone? Once the delight and mystery of the vulva was softly framed by lush generous cushions of curls, now women are desperately trying to preserve their prepubescent form. I would have thought having a less than innocent, confidently sensual being welcoming you to her bed should be enough for any man to want to investigate and celebrate the mystery of the real bush."

With each painting, her spine lengthened. By the third canvas, she stood with her weight evenly distributed—no longer ready to flee.

"As I move from painting to painting in the Rubens room I am so moved, it is incredible beautiful and emotional work. I leave the space, filled up and confident as a woman, proud of soft sensual breasts and fulsome bush and inspired and challenged as an artist."

Then the overwhelm hit. Room after room, beauty mounting.

"For a moment I am lost in a strange sensation of anxiety. I can't quite figure out if I am spinning or if I am standing still and the Louvre is spinning around me. Breathless for a moment I have to close my eyes and breathe deeply. As I try to regain my equilibrium holding tightly to the stair railing, I realise that the emotional wobble is because my soul is galloping full stretch like it never has before. Long full strides, eyes wide, mouth open sucking in the deep gasps of joy, tongue lolling happily, hair flying behind me as I come screaming in trying to catch up with the life I am supposed to live."

The marble railing was ice under her palms. Sweat bloomed between her shoulder blades. The paintings began to pulse with her heartbeat—Madonnas and martyrs breathing in rhythm with her lungs. She gripped tighter, knuckles white, feeling the stone's solidity while everything else spun. This was her body learning to hold joy it had never been allowed to carry—muscles burning like first use.

Our Table, Our Life

We stumbled out, pupils contracting in April brightness, into the orange awning of Le Petit Machon.

"Inside: pretty décor, a menu from Lyon, and a window table just for us. Soon came bread and a little pot of gooey white cheese—Cervelle de Canut. I had never tasted anything like it."

The bread arrived warm, its crust crackling under her fingers. She watched the butter melt into its holes, golden pools forming. When she bit down, I heard her make a sound—not performed for anyone, just pulled from her gut. The butter glossed her lips.

She didn't dab it away.

Her laugh came different here. In the past, she'd laughed from her throat—quick, bright, currency. Now it rolled up from her belly, rich and slow, making the couple at the next table smile. When she gestured, her arms swept wide, claiming air. Her knee found mine under the table and stayed.

"It quickly became our spot. Eric, our waiter, became 'our guy.' Our table, our table."

The Musée d'Orsay Awakening

"The beautiful Musée d'Orsay, once a Belle Epoque train station, now houses a staggering collection of Impressionist art… I am so excited about today."

Under that soaring glass ceiling, she moved from painting to painting like dancing with old friends.

"Oh wow what a space. The decorative glass ceiling arches upward, high above a wide central hall. Once a railway station the building is breathtaking, its vastness contrasting with incredible decorative architectural detail. Before we get to consider the artworks within, it is clear that the building itself is a work of art."

Her hand twitched at her side—the ghost of a brush. She leaned close to the Van Goghs, studying the violence of his joy, paint ridged like scars that had healed beautiful.

"I feel like every emotion has been evoked and I haven't seen a painting yet. This is definitely my favorite museum in Paris. We continue through an intoxicating journey. Soft pretty Manet works, misty and moody Monet, rich creamy Renoir, colourful dynamic Van Gogh, the unexpected frankness of Gustave Courbet's Origin of the World. So many works I can't possibly describe them all."

"Throughout the Musée, students are perched, sketchbooks on laps. I so wish I had paper and pencil in my bag—I close my eyes and imagine spending hours here letting these magic works inspire me. Wicked thoughts, like wouldn't it be amazing if I could hide

somewhere and stay here all night—just me, drawing and painting."

Her fingers moved in small strokes at her side, already drawing on air.

"This day has been so wonderful. As we emerge from the last salon, I am feeling so buoyant. I still feel like I am not ready to leave, to walk away from this incredible place. I find a beautiful book—paintings of the Musée d'Orsay, that we agree has to come home with us. The walk back to our apartment feels like I am walking on air. All daydreamy and fanciful, the creative energy of all the amazing artists I have just experienced seems to be pouring into me, filling me up.

Today has somehow taken little disparate pieces of me and pulled them together. There is a knowing, I know that my future is going to be one of creativity. I definitely know that I will come back to Musée d'Orsay one day to draw and paint here."

She held that book against her chest the whole walk home.

Naked, Whole, Mine

That night, Rue Saint-Honoré hummed below—heels striking cobblestones in rhythm, laughter spilling from doorways, the sharp scratch of lighters. We ate simply. She pulled books from shelves, running her fingers along French spines she couldn't read, studying images like maps to somewhere she was trying to go.

Then pulled out her iPad.

The white glow lit her face from below. Her fingers hesitated over the screen—that moment before the first mark when anything is still possible.

I pretended to read while my peripheral vision tracked her every movement. The stylus touched down. A curved line appeared—her hip. She drew it again, larger. Then again, taking up more space. She drew herself from memory, from the inside out, her free hand unconsciously confirming what she drew: fingertips grazing her own collarbone, palm pressed briefly against her ribs, measuring the truth of her own architecture.

The woman materialised on the screen slowly. Naked. Viewed from behind, seated on a chaise, but her head turned toward the tall sash windows. Not hiding. Not performing. Just existing in her skin while Paris glittered beyond the glass.

She studied what she'd created. Her finger hovered over the keyboard for a long moment. Then typed a single word beneath the drawing: *Voluptuous.*

The word sat there like a flag planted on conquered territory. She didn't delete it. Didn't add a question mark. Didn't soften it with explanation.

She set the iPad down and looked at me directly for the first time in an hour. Her eyes were wet but not sad. Like someone who'd just remembered their own name after years of amnesia.

"I paint a little picture on my iPad to celebrate this apartment and to capture the feeling of the naked truth of being in it. Here in this apartment, here in Paris I feel pretty, soft, elegant, real, grounded like I belong. In some ways it is a confusing feeling, I have never before felt like I have belonged anywhere. On the other hand there is simply a feeling of 'of course'—a knowing, a clarity of understanding after 40 odd years of not knowing."

I Will Never Be the Same

On our final evening, we returned to Le Petit Machon.

"Eric saw us and lit up. 'Again, sir!' he beamed. My love explained it was our last night in Paris. 'We will have a very good table for you,' he said, and made sure we did—clearing a four-top by the bar like we were royalty..."

Champagne appeared without being ordered. The steak came perfectly pink. When they discovered it was our last night, a hidden bottle of digestif appeared, and Eric performed an elaborate mime of seduction that left us gasping. We walked home through streets that had seen centuries of lovers. Her laughter rang off stone walls—not careful but wild and full. She walked in the middle of the narrow street, arms spread wide, head thrown back.

The next morning, she zipped her bag slowly. Then stopped, hands still.

"I thought I'd done a good job of putting the faintly glimmering fragments of my soul back together. But now I realise I'd kept them hidden. Safe in a little box in my heart. Paris ripped the lid off. I am open. The light inside is pouring out. It is dazzling me. And I will never be the same."

It's a Full-Body Yes to Being Alive

"I've always had the sense that life is something that happens around me, to other people—that I'm floating above it all, watching, but not in it. That feeling has begun to lift in the last couple of years. I've started listening to my inner guidance more. Trusting my instincts. Doing what feels good. Life at home is better now, more aligned. But I still often feel like I don't fit. Like I'm trying to translate a language I never fully learned. In Paris, my feet touch the ground."

"It's strange—here I don't speak the language. And yet, I feel more at home. I rather like not understanding French. The written words, the conversations around me—none of it makes sense, and that's okay. I'm not supposed to understand. So I stop trying to interpret. I start feeling instead."

"In Paris, I feel surrounded by birds of a feather—like-minded souls. Creativity and passion are in everything. Everything is not only done, but done beautifully, with love. At home, life is all 'get shit done, no fucking around.' But I love the fucking around. That's the good bit."

"Sliding into the centre of it all—feeling aligned with who I really am—is magical. And I'm so grateful that my travel companion, creative partner, best friend, and lover is wildly supportive of me drifting into fantasy. He gets it. He does it too. He loves the pleasure of it, the creativity, the moment. We are both artists. Both seekers. And in Paris, we are ourselves. Art, food, wine, travel, music, laughter, culture—it's all on the table. All of it is allowed. Pleasure in Paris isn't just a feeling. It's a full-body yes to being alive."

Walking Like I Belong Here

The second time we went to Paris, everything was different. Not the city—the woman.

Our apartment perched on the top floor in the 16th, windows framing the Eiffel Tower. Not a hotel where she was a guest, but a home where she could just be.

"Being honorary Parisians means shopping frequently. Most apartments have little storage space, small fridges, and many stairs, up which you have to haul the shopping. More importantly though, fresh produce is highly valued and respected."

The daily rituals became ceremony. The walk to Place Victor Hugo shops. She knew now to point with her whole hand, not her finger. The grocer began to nod, then smile, then ask "Ça va?"

In the basement grocery, she stopped breathing at the charcuterie counter. Wheels of cheese to the ceiling. Terrines like art. Truffles under lock and key.

"This is our local store, oh my goodness!"

She moved through those aisles completely present, fingers trailing over packages, choosing by colour and instinct and desire. We loaded our bags until our arms ached, squeezed into the tiny lift giggling.

"It is more and more clear to me that I am definitely French. Shopping like this, fresh, frequent, fabulous, supporting passionate producers feels more like honesty, more like me.

As I put the last tranche of pâté in the fridge my heart finally slows and I take a deep satisfying breath, I am home."

Keep the Feet

Dawn market. We walked through streets so quiet our footsteps echoed off shuttered shops. My breath clouded. Her fingers were pink with cold until she wrapped them around a paper cup of café, inhaling steam that smelled of morning.

The market exploded with life. Scallops arranged on ice like pearl necklaces. Chickens turning on spits, their skin crackling, fat dripping into the flames below. The air thick with competing scents—brine, smoke, blood, coffee, the earthy sweetness of winter vegetables.

She stood in the centre breathing through her nose, then her mouth, then her skin— trying to absorb it all.

The poultry man wore a stained apron, dark with years of honest work. He held up a bird by its feet, neck curled, a few copper feathers still clinging.

"You want me to prepare?" His finger drew across his throat. The gesture was matter-of-fact, but I saw her register it—the casual acknowledgment of death that makes life possible.

She laughed—not nervous but delighted. *"Oui, merci. But keep the feet."*

The sound of his knife through bone was precise, practiced. She watched him work, not flinching when blood spotted the wooden block. She chose by touch after that—oysters that smelled of storms, butter yellow as late afternoon light, cheese that gave under her thumb.

Each purchase wrapped in brown paper, the vendor's hands quick and sure, like they were wrapping gifts.

"In our meal that evening we taste love—the love of the farmers, the love of the market stall people and our love, the care and attention we put into preparing the food for each other."

"My palate has been teased and tantalised by incredible flavours and textures. The visual stimulation—from the enormity of elegantly, eclectically, colourfully designed spaces to the tiniest details on the plates before me—has been deeply inspirational. But more than

anything, the deepest pleasure has come from sharing experiences I never knew were possible with another truly beautiful soul."

"I feel more and more deeply connected as he gently peels away layers of practiced uncertainty, teaching me to embrace the simple truth of knowing who I am. I am a lover: a lover of life, of discovery, of sensuality and passion. This Paris adventure has been one of the most honest experiences of my life."

"Joie de vivre," she wrote. The joy of living.

Her Right to be Fully, Shamelessly Alive

Coercive control steals the ordinary things first.

Your voice. Your choices. Your body's ease.

It teaches you that joy is for other people. That beauty is something you serve, not something you get to taste. That you are only as worthy as your usefulness.

That is the lie survivors carry: a bone-deep unworthiness that feels immovable. You can leave, you can rebuild, you can even laugh again—but that sense that maybe life isn't "for you" lingers.

That's what made watching Georgie in Paris so extraordinary.

I saw her stand before Rubens' women and straighten her shoulders, no longer apologising for her curves. I saw her fingers twitch at the Musée d'Orsay, aching to draw, and then finally sketch herself naked and whole on an iPad screen. I saw her ask the butcher to keep the chicken feet, laughing at her own whimsy. I saw her press that museum book to her chest like she was carrying her own heart home.

For the first time in forty years, she wasn't hovering above her life. She was "in it."

"Paris ripped the lid off," she wrote. *"I am open. The light inside is pouring out. It is*

dazzling me. And I will never be the same."

She savoured it all. The butter without counting. The wine without permission. The colours, the laughter echoing through stone streets at midnight. She savoured her body uncurled, unhidden. She savoured being allowed to want, and to have. She savoured belonging.

"I am a survivor, an artist, an adventurer, a writer, a mother, a cook, a lover," she'd declared. "Above all, I am a woman who has learned to live life on my own terms."

This is what recovery makes possible. Not the absence of pain. Not a clean slate. Not a life untouched by memory. But the slow, unrelenting return of self. The discovery that joy is not for other people. It is for you. That beauty is not something you witness from the edges. It is something you inhabit. That worthiness is not earned through silence or shrinking. It was always yours—the birthright to a life both ordinary and astonishing, savoured in its fullness.

Paris didn't save Georgie. She was never broken. But Paris revealed what years of abuse could not kill: her light. Her creativity. Her right to be fully, shamelessly alive.

Discover Georgie's full travelogues at **sensoryfeasts.com**
Her maps back to herself, open to all.

14.17
Everyone Has a Chance to Live True

I have so much to appreciate and be grateful for. I am particularly grateful for my two amazing kids who have each found their own happiness. They have a loving extended family and have gone on to build a good relationship with their dad. Leaving that home was the opportunity for them to start a new way with him, one without him in position of daily oversight of their lives. Another great testament to the power of forgiveness— and I'm happy to say that we do still laugh about some things.

I'm grateful for finding a place of peace and love with my dad. His toughness has mellowed and I understand as an adult that his intentions as a father were good, just misguided. My relationship with my mother was probably more toxic than anything as a child. After a long and sad battle with alcoholism and ultimately disfiguring cancer, she finally passed away, finding her peace and giving her children theirs. Her burial plaque reads: Peace at last the restless soul.

I'm deeply grateful for my grandmother who is still with me in spirit every day. A teacher in so many ways.

I'm very grateful to my little brother—we have seen each other through tricky times. I know he's always there unconditionally for me.

I'm grateful to the frog pot cook's family. I realise that their generosity, particularly that of my parents-in-law, got me through many difficult times.

And in turning the corner to the future, I'm so grateful to have found the love of my life, my teacher, my best friend, my travel companion, my rock. He has gently taken my hand and dragged me into the 21st century, encouraging and seeking out the real essence of me. Loving me and challenging me as I have worked through the initial struggle of believing I count, that I deserve to live a fabulous life.

While the surrounding narrative in this story serves to highlight domestic abuse as a place I have lived, the aspirational true story is our love - the knowledge that everyone has a chance to live true, to really live life out loud.

I look forward to every next chapter in our wild and wonderful adventure together.

~ Georgie Bailey

14.18
Hope When I Had None

I have been a battler for most of my life — from a lonely, anxious childhood with an alcoholic mother and a workaholic father, to surviving domestic abuse. That battling became so automatic that I didn't notice when my body joined the fight against me. I'd been trained to ignore pain, to push through exhaustion, to never say 'I can't.'

In my forties, everything finally opened up. I met the most amazing person, and for the first time, I travelled the world, wrote about our adventures, and immersed myself in my lifelong dream of creating art. Whether painting a large-scale portrait or crafting the next chapter in our gourmet explorations, my creativity was finally free, and life was beginning to feel wonderful.

We had magical years together, travelling and discovering. One of our rituals was walking — from one side of a new city to the other, drinking it in. Early mornings in the half-light, watching a place stir awake. Wandering toward lunch through narrow lanes. Stopping at markets for fresh delicacies. Those walks became our way of knowing a place, and of knowing each other.

But just as this new life was beginning, something started to change. I couldn't keep up. I had to stop often. Exhaustion took over. Tasks I had always taken for granted — styling my hair, climbing stairs, rising from a chair — became difficult. Within two years, I went from walking across Paris to needing a cane to shuffle from one room to the next.

I knew something was terribly wrong. After months of searching, I was finally diagnosed with Myositis, a rare autoimmune disease. Only about 350 people in Australia are known to have Myositis, and my particular subtype affects only a small fraction of those.

Throughout this journey, writing became my way to process frustration and celebrate small wins. Reading the stories of others was equally vital. Those accounts gave me recognition, language for my symptoms, and most importantly — the knowledge that I wasn't alone.

As I was given knowledge, energy, and strength through the generosity of others, I decided to pay it forward. To share my own journey, in the hope that someone else — frightened, exhausted, searching — might find a lifeline in my words.

I learned the harsh realities of navigating a rare disease: the frustration of the diagnostic process, the disorientation of seeing doctors who had never encountered my condition, the obstacles of coordinating multiple providers across systems that seemed designed to keep my records from me. I learned to adapt to a body that no longer worked as it once had. I learned how to cope with constant pain, unpredictable rashes, and the loss of independence.

And yet, I was not alone. I was blessed with an extraordinary partner who carried me with kindness, humour, and love. Even in the midst of devastation, he found ways to make me laugh — giving everyone and everything a nickname, even my disease. One day, not long after my diagnosis, I heard him call out from the other room while on the phone with one of my children:

"Have you told her about your Mylie Cyrus?"

Confused, I gave him a look. He burst into song — off-key, as always — "I came in like a wre-e-ecking ball!"

It made perfect sense. My disease had crashed into our lives like a wrecking ball. But in that moment, laughter cut through fear.

I share this because stories matter. They anchor us when the system fails, when our bodies betray us, when the future terrifies us. The stories of others gave me hope when I had none.

This is mine, given back, in case you ever need it.

14.19
A Fight for My Life

One way we raise awareness is by having the courage to share our stories so others begin to understand the challenges we face, and why change is needed.

As someone diagnosed with two rare diseases, February 28 is an important day in my calendar. It's Rare Disease Day — a chance for members of the rare disease community to raise awareness with the broader public and decision-makers about rare diseases and their impact on our lives.

Acquiring two rare diseases has irrevocably changed my life. I had finally found my groove, starting again in midlife with an amazing partner, building a wonderful life filled with art, writing, and travel. But just as our new life was beginning, it began to unravel. Simple pleasures like our morning walks became difficult. Exhaustion and chronic pain became daily features, and suddenly I was unable to keep up with the life I had been leading.

Simple tasks like holding my arms up to style my hair, climbing stairs, or even rising from a chair became exhausting endeavours. Within a couple of years, my mobility declined from being able to walk across Paris to needing a cane to shuffle from one room to the next.

Throughout my journey, writing has been a way to process frustrations and celebrate small wins. Reading the experiences of others has also helped me immensely. Their stories gave me recognition, knowledge, energy, and strength. This Rare Disease Day I want to pay forward the gift that others have given me.

The Challenge of Being Rare

One of the biggest changes I would like to see is a more effective approach to the diagnostic journey.

The business that is the medical system — and make no mistake, it is a business, not a social service — is not structured in a way that supports rare disease patients. The system forces doctors to work fast, tick boxes, write a script, and get the patient out the door. This might be an acceptable method if the patient has a common condition, but for those of us with a rare disease it can become a nightmare.

There is also an insular approach to practice: doctors focus narrowly on the part of the body they specialise in. The maddeningly slow, sequential engagement of different specialties can cause devastating delays in diagnosis. Patients are left in a powerless limbo as their bodies deteriorate without treatment or access to support from the National Disability Insurance Scheme (NDIS). That limbo can last years.

I have spoken with many people, like myself, left frustrated, drained of resources, and fearful for their future.

There Has to Be a Better Way

According to Rare Voices Australia — and supported by the National Strategic Action Plan for Rare Diseases — a disease is considered rare if it affects fewer than five in 10,000 people. More than 7,000 different rare diseases have been identified worldwide. Globally, around 300 million people are living with one of these conditions. Here in Australia, about 8% of the population — roughly two million people — are affected by a rare disease.

By definition, these diseases are rarely encountered, even by the professionals tasked with treating them. Many doctors may never have seen a case first-hand until a patient walks through their door. Because rare conditions don't offer a profitable return, the pharmaceutical industry invests less in researching them than in more common diseases. This is why donations, philanthropy, and advocacy are so essential.

My Journey With Myositis

I have been diagnosed with two rare diseases: Myositis and Interstitial Lung Disease (ILD). Myo means muscle and sitis means inflammation.

Though classified as a muscle disease, Myositis is an incurable, systemic autoimmune condition that can also affect the heart, lungs, skin, gastrointestinal tract, and is often associated with cancer. It is essentially an overactive immune system launching an attack on the body's own tissue.

I experience everything except heart difficulties at this stage. My other condition, Interstitial Lung Disease, is also rare and often associated with Myositis. ILD causes scarring and inflammation in the lungs, which makes breathing increasingly difficult. Combined with Myositis, it means even small amounts of exertion leave me exhausted and breathless.

Myositis itself is a group of related diseases with overlapping but distinct features. Scientists have discovered that particular antibodies are linked to specific forms of Myositis. Testing for these antibodies helps categorise patients and may indicate severity and prognosis.

I tested positive for the Anti-SRP antibody, which is extremely rare and associated with more severe disease and poor prognosis.

SRP is a protein regulator found in all protein-processing cells. When the immune system attacks it, many parts of the body can be affected.

According to the Myositis Support and Understanding Association (MSU), around 75,000 people in the United States live with some form of Myositis. Recent studies suggest 8–13% of these patients are Anti-SRP positive, which equates to roughly 6,000–8,000 people in the U.S. with my subtype.

In Australia, where prevalence estimates suggest only 250–350 people nationally live with Myositis, applying the same proportion means just 20–28 people here are Anti-SRP positive. That's how rare this disease is — and the subtype I have is rarer still.

The Diagnosis Mystery Flight

In my old life, a "mystery flight" would have been an adventure. The diagnostic mystery flight is anything but.

The journey to a rare disease diagnosis is long, arduous, and filled with false trails, dead ends, and dashed hopes. Holding on to hope becomes exhausting: hope for a doctor who will listen, hope for treatment, hope — often unrealistic — for a cure. Each time hope is snatched away, it is soul-destroying.

The only solution I've found is to keep replenishing my hope: keep asking, keep researching, keep going. Self-education has given me the knowledge to ask the right questions and to keep my hope bank topped up.

I have been fighting for years for a diagnosis and I am still battling to access the treatment I need. I've learned a lot about both the challenges of rare disease and the impracticalities of managing multiple providers. Battling the disease is one thing; battling the diagnostic process is another — often the greater battle.

The most distressing part is the waiting. Like sand slipping through an hourglass, months and years are lost while the disease wreaks havoc.

Self-Advocacy

This left me no choice but to become my own detective. I listened to medical talks, researched symptoms, chased leads. I pushed for tests I believed were needed. Finally, a breakthrough came: I tested positive for Anti-SRP. With other supportive results and my clinical presentation, my neurologist made the diagnosis — but referred me on, believing he lacked sufficient expertise to treat me.

That meant limbo again. A new doctor, a new round of tests, and the exhausting process of educating yet another specialist who had never seen my presentation.

In my case, the SRP protein attacked by my immune system is present in every cell. Clinical presentations vary widely, making it almost impossible to tick all the "standard" diagnostic boxes.

While researching, I discovered the Netflix series Diagnosis, based on Dr. Lisa Sanders' column in The New York Times Magazine. The series showed the power of crowdsourcing medical mysteries — specialists working concurrently instead of sequentially. It made so much sense. Why not here?

That's when I found Best Doctors, an international "Expert Opinion" service. Skeptical but desperate, I reached out. Within weeks, a Harvard professor reviewed my case and produced a detailed report confirming my diagnosis, explaining my unusual presentation, and urging immediate, aggressive treatment.

For the first time in years, I felt relief. I had been heard. I allowed myself to hope.

But my local doctors refused to adopt his recommendations. When I asked why, he told me bluntly:

"Quite frankly, I am baffled by the approach taken."

And so I remain in limbo, deteriorating, while doctors argue or defer.

Imagining a Different Way

In just two years, I have lost most of my mobility. My axial muscles are weakened, making it hard to hold myself upright. Dysphagia puts me at risk of choking. ILD leaves me breathless after a few steps. I now need nighttime breathing support. I am never pain free.

My life has been devastated, while doctors continue to disagree. The longer nothing is done, the greater the damage, the slimmer the chance of recovery.

We must do better for rare disease patients. I dream of a National Centre for Diagnostics, where multidisciplinary teams could fast-track testing and differential diagnosis. Why not international partnerships with established centres overseas?

Until then, we must encourage multidisciplinary practice and enable telehealth so international experts can treat rare conditions here.

I hope my story encourages other patients to be their own advocates, and reminds doctors of the cost of complacency.

I am not afraid of mistakes. I am afraid of doing nothing.

As someone with a rare disease, I face a tough and challenging future. I only wish the battle for care did not have to be one of them.

~ Georgie Bailey

14.20
A Letter to Doctors

Dear Doctor,

I am a patient with a rare disease. Because rare diseases often have much yet to be understood about them, we are all still learning. This means it's likely that you may not have seen someone in your practice with exactly my constellation of symptoms. The rareness of my condition may also mean that my particular presentation has not been reported, documented or studied before. This does not mean it doesn't exist — just that you may not be able to fit me neatly into the academic boxes currently available in the textbooks.

Before we begin a doctor–patient relationship I want you to understand what I need and expect from your care, and to let you know what to expect from me as a patient. This disease means you and I might be in this for some time, so it has to work for both of us.

First and foremost I need someone who is willing to be part of my team — someone prepared to work with me and other team members, and to think outside the boxes to find an approach to help me manage the situation I find myself in. I don't have a choice about the condition I have. My choices are about how I choose to deal with it and who I choose to collaborate with.

From me you will get honesty and frankness. I will share with you everything I know to help you understand what I am experiencing.

I come to this problem-solving table with tonnes of knowledge. I have this disease; I live with it every day and know, intimately and relentlessly, its manifestations on my body. You should assume that I have done a lot of research about my symptoms to help me understand what is happening.

Please don't resent me for being informed — or possibly misinformed — in my pursuit to learn. Please don't resent me for challenging or questioning based on the knowledge I have acquired. I might have found many of the pieces but I cannot do this alone; I need your help to solve this puzzle.

I am coming to you as a skilled health practitioner, not expecting you to be fully informed about my particular condition, but as someone who can bring to the table the skills and training I don't have, as we work together to figure out this insidious beast that seeks to control my life.

Don't expect me to blindly do as I am told. I will ask and question and will want to understand why. I want us to have a healthy, two-sided relationship where both of us feel comfortable to have a voice, and where we can engage in an open and collaborative decision-making process about my body and my future. Just like a marriage certificate, your qualification is comforting — but it is not my reason to trust you with my body. Trust comes from knowing we can talk openly, that I can ask you anything and that I can feel safe to say "stop" whenever I am unsure.

I acknowledge that the medical profession is one where you will be under extreme time pressure and often working with limited resources. Please know that I am — and will be — grateful for any of your precious moments when you can turn your attention to my case.

Please understand my time is also precious. Give me the respect of considering all the knowledge I bring, any notes I have carefully prepared, test results and reports from other medical practitioners, before you start thinking about my case. Please don't just hit the reset button and make me start all over again.

I don't expect you to have personally seen my exact scenario, but I do expect that you will listen and hear me when I share what I am experiencing. Dismissing my symptoms or telling me they are not in your textbook does not mean they are not very much on my list. If I say I am in pain, I am in pain — whether as a direct or secondary result of my condition.

I don't expect you to know everything — no one does — particularly with rare diseases; we are all still learning. I do expect your honesty, however: if you haven't seen the presentation I exhibit, just say so. "I haven't seen this before in association with this diagnosis" is OK. Writing off an entire diagnosis because one symptom is unusual is a blunt instrument. How can you be so definitive in a space where so much is still unknown?

Please know that if you say "watch and wait" instead of "I don't know," that leaves me rudderless and lost — powerless as I slowly deteriorate until such time as a symptom becomes bad enough to tick your box. How about saying, "I don't know, but let's find someone who does, together"? Please don't just walk away.

I don't expect a simple cookie-cutter solution or quick fix to what is clearly a complex and nuanced situation. I know it's a mystery. I need someone on my team who is interested in collaborating with me and other health professionals to do the detective work on my particular situation and form a plan that is just as nuanced. I understand, given the unusual nature of my condition, that this may take time and may be a case of trial and error. I am not afraid of mistakes; I am afraid of doing nothing — of not trying to take back some control of my future.

As someone with a rare disease I am facing a tough and challenging future, with many battles ahead. I do not have the time or energy for battling to receive the care I need. I need a health professional who is prepared to walk alongside me on a path of discovery, even though neither of us may know what is waiting around the next bend in the road.

If that is not you, please be kind enough not to waste my precious and limited time. Tell me now.

Otherwise, please join me as we co-create my future.

With gratitude,
Your patient
Georgie Baily

14.21
The Part I Can't Rewrite

Georgie fought harder than most ever will
through years of abuse,
through misdiagnosis,
through pain no one could see.

It rewired her nervous system,
her immune system, her life.

Still, she showed up.
She created, loved, hoped.

When diagnosis finally came,
she agreed to the biopsy
the only way to confirm,
to access treatment.

She came home.
Three quiet weeks.
Then nausea.
She couldn't walk.
The ambulance came.
She never returned.

It wasn't the illness that took her
but a blood clot, a pulmonary embolism
the cost of being believed.
Georgie died on August 31st, 2022.
Far too soon.
But she died knowing she was loved.
Deeply. Unquestionably. Fully

My love,
you left the party early,
but not before making sure
everyone had a chair,
a moment of care,
something warm on their plate to share.

This book is the seat you saved.
This story is the door you left open.
Your kindness is what lingers
through every word,
across every page,
inside every reader who finds hope here.

You were right.
About love lasting.
About hope surviving.
About beginning again.

You showed us, my love
it's never too late.

With love,
Geoffrey

For Georgie Bailey (née Booker)
1968 - 2022

About the Author

Geoffrey Clow is a writer, advocate, and counsellor who has spent the past decade helping survivors of coercive control, trauma, and emotional abuse reclaim their voice. Trained in forward-facing trauma therapy, crisis support, and person-centred counselling, he brings both professional insight and lived experience to every page.

Raised in difficult circumstances, Geoffrey has spent much of his adult life unpicking inherited patterns — learning how trauma shapes choices, beliefs, and relationships. His exploration of coercive control began with trying to understand what kept his mother tethered to an abusive partner. That journey took him from judgment to compassion, from lived experience to formal study, and to a deep clarity about what holds survivors captive — and what sets them free.

His partner, the late Georgie Bailey, was the heart of this book. Fiercely creative and deeply loving, Georgie's story runs through these pages, from a childhood that trained her for abuse, through rape and a teenage marriage marked by starvation, imprisonment, and violence, to over twenty years of coercive control. In time, she discovered what real love looks like and recognised her own worth. Her voice grounds this book in survival, courage, and truth.

Geoffrey lives in Canberra, Australia. He is the founder of Twinkling of the Soul—a survivor-led social enterprise offering support, recovery tools, and training in the language of coercive control. Enough: What Coercive Control Steals. What Recovery Makes Possible is his first book.

Be Part of the Change

Survivors of coercive control deserve resources that validate their reality, make sense of what happened, and offer tools to help them return to themselves.

Not clinical jargon. Not toxic positivity. Not promises of quick fixes. But accessible insights, grounded in lived experience, that reconnect survivors with their bodies and instincts.

Twinkling of the Soul is a survivor-led social enterprise and the publisher of Enough: What Coercive Control Steals. What Recovery Makes Possible. It provides direct support to survivors and specialised training for the professionals who work with them.

For survivors, there are practical tools designed to support recovery without shame. For clinicians, educators, and frontline workers, there is training in the nuanced language of coercive control—helping them recognise what traditional systems miss and respond with clarity and care.

Their work is driven by a simple truth: survivors deserve recognition, resources, and respect—not judgment for what they endured or how they survived.

A discreet, secure companion app based on Enough is also in development. It will translate the book's insights into daily support tools, giving survivors greater autonomy in recovery.

Every resource honours survivors like Georgie Bailey, who broke her silence so others might find their way back to themselves. Before her death in August 2022, Georgie wrote the words that would shape this book and inspire the platform that now carries her voice forward.

If you are a survivor seeking support, a professional working alongside survivors, or a purpose-driven investor wanting to change how we respond to coercive control, visit **twinklingofthesoul.com** to learn more or get involved.

www.ingramcontent.com/pod-product-compliance
Lightning Source LLC
Chambersburg PA
CBHW061749260326
41914CB00006B/1045

9 781764 245142